ISBN 978-1-390-52063-7
PIBN 10128540

1 MONTH OF
FREE
READING

at

www.ForgottenBooks.com

By purchasing this book you are eligible for one month membership to ForgottenBooks.com, giving you unlimited access to our entire collection of over 1,000,000 titles via our web site and mobile apps.

To claim your free month visit: www.forgottenbooks.com/free128540

English
Français
Deutsche
Italiano
Español
Português

www.forgottenbooks.com

Mythology Photography **Fiction**
Fishing Christianity **Art** Cooking
Essays Buddhism Freemasonry
Medicine **Biology** Music **Ancient**
Egypt Evolution Carpentry Physics
Dance Geology **Mathematics** Fitness
Shakespeare **Folklore** Yoga Marketing
Confidence Immortality Biographies
Poetry **Psychology** Witchcraft
Electronics Chemistry History **Law**
Accounting **Philosophy** Anthropology
Alchemy Drama Quantum Mechanics
Atheism Sexual Health **Ancient History**
Entrepreneurship Languages Sport
Paleontology Needlework Islam
Metaphysics Investment Archaeology
Parenting Statistics Criminology
Motivational

AN

ORIGINAL AND AUTHENTIC

JOURNAL of OCCURRENCES

DURING THE LATE

AMERICAN WAR,

FROM

ITS COMMENCEMENT

TO THE

YEAR 1783.

━━•◦◦❸❶◗❶◗❶◦◦◦•━━

BY R. LAMB,

LATE SERJEANT IN THE ROYAL WELCH FUZILEERS.

O GOD the LORD the Strength of my Salvation: thou
hast covered my head in the day of battle!

PSAL. CXL. 7.

DUBLIN:

PRINTED BY WILKINSON & COURTNEY, 6, WOOD-STREET.

1809.

PREFACE.

FOR many years past I have felt a strong desire to give to the Public, a Summary and Impartial View of that momentous and interesting Subject—the Rise, Progress, and Consummation of the late American War.

From my own personal Knowledge of many of the Events that are herein related, and from a diligent research into many respectable Authorities, I entertain a good hope, that, my Journal of Occurrences will not be unacceptable to the judicious Reader.

There are few probably to whom this Work will be more interesting than to those who have borne a Part in the Events which are here recorded, and whose Recollection of the important Transactions noticed in this Volume, the Author has no doubt will bear full accordance to the truth of his testimony.

It may be thought rather strange, that a Work of this kind should be announced to the Public so long after the Occurrences took place. But I beg leave to mention, that I have not seen any impartial Detail of the more minute, but no less important Occurrences of the War, which, as secret springs, actuated the public movements, and which were never any further disclosed to the world, but as comprised in the general result. The only attempt of the kind which I have seen, was a Work published in America, and written by a Member of Congress, but which I found to be exceedingly partial, both in its Statement of Facts, and Views of the Merits of the Question to be decided.

The present Work being edited at so late a period, will have this advantage, that all Party Views having now subsided, the Author has no Motive to influence his Publication, but that of being an Impartial Annalist, relating Facts which have come within his own Knowledge, and which will remain as a faithful Record of those Transactions, unbiassed by prejudice, for the information of the future Historian.

The impartial eye of posterity, will read the Work, and form their Opinion, unmoved by any political considerations, and having no other sensations than those arising from the Feeling of Regret.

R. LAMB.

OCTOBER, 1809.

CONTENTS.

CHAP. I.

a

CONTENTS.

CHAP. III.

CHAP. IV.

CHAP. V.

CHAP. VI.

CHAP. VII.

CHAP. VIII.

CHAP. IX.

CONTENTS.

CHAP. XIV.

CHAP. XV.

CHAP. XVI.

CHAP. XX.

SUBSCRIBERS NAMES.

LIEUTENANT GENERAL Sir CHARLES ASGILL, Bart, commanding the Eastern District.
Major Ashe, late of the Royal Welch Fusileers.
Colonel Arabin, Ranelagh
Counsellor J. Arthure, Mountjoy-sq.
John Adamson, Esq. Aungier-street
Japhet Alley, Esq. Abbey-street
Richmond Allen, Esq. Eccles-street
R. Andrews, Esq. Buckingham-st.
Surgeon Allen, Gardiner-street
Samuel Alleyne, Esq. Rehoboth
B. Arthure, Esq. Statford-street
R. Anthony, Esq. King's Inn-quay
Rev. Adam Averill, Tentower
Mrs. Adam, S. Cumberland-street
— Alteridge, North-strand
Mr. F. Alder, Arran-quay
.T. Arthure, New-street
John Anderson, Hardwicke-st.
A. Ashley, Henry-street
C. Armstrong, Bank of Ireland,
Edward Archer, do.
A. Armstrong, Abbey-street
J. Anderson, Britain-street
T. Anderson, College-green
W. Anderson, do.
Powell Allen, Bride-street
W. Atkinson, Ordnance Office
R. Atkinson, Coombe
J. Aylesbury, do.

Mr. W. Andrews, Castle-street
T. Atkinson, Crampton-court
A. Anderson, Church-street
— Anderson, Cork-street
H. Armstrong, Dolphin's-barn
D. Archer, Drumcondra
G. Allen, Fishamble-streeet
W. Ayckbowm, Grafton-st.
R. Allen, Mary-street
D. Atkinson, Marlborough-st.
S. Ashworth, Meath-street
W. Allen, New-street
P. Anderson, Ormond-market.
R. Armstrong, Ormondquay
J. Anderson, Sackville-street
R. Atkinson, Spitalfields
J. Auden, New-street

B

Sir Jonah Barrington, Bart. LL.D. Merrion-square.
Col. Benson, North-strand
Colonel Browne, Park-street
Captain Bray, Portland-row
Robert Blake, M. D. William-st.
Benjamin Biggs, M. D. Mount-st.
Henry Blennerhassett, M. D. Sackville-street.
James Browne, M. D. Jervis-street.

Lady Cecilia Brabazon, Merrion-sq.
Hon. Mrs. Butler, Great Charles-st.
James Butler, Esq. Buckingham-st.
John Bowden, Esq. Aston's-quay
Lieut. Burton, Assistant Deputy
   Adjuant Gen.
William Betty, Esq. Granby-Row
Counsellor Baldwin, Harolds Cross
Counsellor Bessonnet, Leeson-street
Counsellor Ball, Temple-street
Alexander Boyle, Esq. Gt.Charles-st.
George Booker, Esq. Buckingham-st.
R. D. Brady, Esq. Lower Rutland-
   street
Thomas Beasley, Esq. Dawson-st.
Mrs. Baker, North Great Georges-
   street
Mrs. Bury, Granby-row
Michael Blood, Esq. Gardiner-place
Rev. A. Bailie, Foundling Hospital
Richard Burton, Esq. Dominick-st.
John Breen, M. D. Abbey-street
Brabazon Browne, Esq. Baggot-st.
John Browne, Esq. Stephen's-green
J. Blacker, Esq. College-green
Rev. Francis Baker, N.Gt.Georges-st.
E. Buckly, Esq. Cavendish-row
E. Breham, Esq. Dorset-street
Robert Barnes, Esq. do.
Rev. W. Barber, Wintworth-place
Mrs. Burnett, Abbey-street
J. Bryan, Esq. Ushers Island
E. Burroughs, Esq. do.
Peter Bardin, Esq. Synnot-place.
R. Bride, Esq. Stephens-green
John Browne, Esq. do.
Miss Birkett, Sackville-street
T. Browne, Esq. Portland-row
Arthur Battersby, Esq. Peter-street
Mrs. S. Bourke, Molesworth-street
J. Burnet, Esq. Mecklenburgh-street
Captain T. Berry, Killishandra.
Captain Bevill, Royal-Hospital
G. Brooke, Esq. Hardwicke-street.
A. Browne, Esq. Gardiner-place
T Babington, Esq. N. Frederick-st.
Miss Bevan, Golden-lane
— Blake, Esq. Gardiner-place.
Mr. P. Byrne, S. King-street.

Mr. G. Barry, Coombe
T. M. Bates, do.
N. Barrington, Castle-street
John Boyle, Celbridge
Lot Brooke, Church-lane
J. Brown, do.
G. Beamish, Capel-street
Wm. Baird, Charlemont-street
J. Burgess, Cornwall, 4 copies
G. Beere, jun. Camden-street
J. Bentley, sen,Clanbrassil-place
James Bamber, Chapel-izod
Wm. Belton, Dawson-street
John Bentley, jun. Dame-street
W. Bull,   do.
E. Berney,   do.
— Byrne,   do.
— Bernard,   do.
T. Burton, Island-bridge
W. Bigger, Wood-street
J. Bryuan, Ushers Island
— Blake, Wood-street.
J. Barton, Bolton-street
Joshua Ball, do.
Simon Brigley, Clarendon-st.
W. Bell, Ordnance Office
— Butler, Temple-street
J. Byrne, Temple-bar.
William Browne, Bridge-street
— Binks,   do.
— Butler, Bishop-street
T. Buttle, do.
G. Bergen, Shaws Bank
G. Beckett, Stafford-street
R. Bailey,   do.
— Barr, Merchants-quay
— Boucher, Mecklenburgh-st.
H. Brown, Brabazon-row
— Baxter, Golden-lane
C Bonham, Grafton-street
— Bamber, Gardiner-street.
— Byrne, do.
Daniel Burrows, Edenderry, 6
   copies
J. Bowdler, Abbey-street
Wm. Buckley, Church-street
— Birch, do.
W. Barnet, Castle Yard.
— Byrne, Cork-street
H. Browne, Gloucester-street.

Mr. John Boyd, Cootehill
W Blair, Mount-pleasant
P. Burke, Stephen-street
W. Bruer, do.
J. Barnier, do.
— Bourne, Dorset-street
R. Ballantine, do.
J. Bermingham, Ord. Office
— Boursiquot, Essex-bridge
E. Bates, Anne-street
— Billing, Arran-quay
E. Bruen, do.
R. Boardman, Ardee-row
— Boardman, Ardee-street
H. Brady, Britain-street
O. Baskin, do.
— Balfe, do.
A. Bell, Bachelor's-walk
P. Brigley, Bank of Ireland
T. Blythe, do.
— Browning, New-row
James Brady, do.
P. Bourke, Leinster-street.
W. Babington, Mary's abbey
I. Brennan, Moore-street
W. Beddy, Kings-Inns-quay
W. Buckton, Greek-street.
A. Boyd, Henry-street
J. Brann, Francis-street

C

Major General W. H. Clinton, M.P.
Quarter-master Gen. of Ireland
Sir Charles Coote, Bart. Baggot-st.
Lady Chinnery, Mountjoy-square
Mrs. Clare, Britain-street
— Courtney, Mespil.
— Clements, do.
Alderman Carleton, Mt. joy-square
Surgeon Colles, Stephen's-green
Lieutenant Crummer, 28th Regiment
of Foot.
Captain Carden, Tipperary Militia.
Captain J. Christopherson, Bishop-st.
Captain Compton, Rutland-street
Major Campbell, Grenville-street

Counsellor Comerford, N. Cumber-
land-street
Counsellor Cox, S. Gt. George's-st.
I. Crampton, M. D. Gardiner-place
J. Cleghorn, M. D. Palace-Row
J. Cowen, M. D. Lower Gardiner-st.
J. Cuthbert, Esq. Surveyor General
of Custom.
R. Clarke, Esq. Stephen's green
James Cathrew, Esq. Harcourt-st.
Henry Connor, Esq. War-office.
George E. Clarke, Esq. Queen-st.
James Clarke, Esq. Granby-row
J. Clements, Esq. Custom-house
G. Cowell, Esq. Mabbot-street
Samuel Crummer, Esq. Birr
William Carroll, Esq. Granby-Row
A. Coffey, Esq. Pembroke-quay
J. Campbell, Esq. Bachelors-walk
A. Carroll, Esq. Mecklenburgh-st.
George Chamley, Esq. Gardiner-st.
David Courtney, Esq. Mespil.
D. Clancy, Esq. Carolina-row
R. Codd, Esq. Bank of Ireland.
Rev. J. A. Coghlan, Gloucester-
Place
Rev. H. Crofton, Royal Hospital
Rev. H. Crofton, Foundling do.
Mr. J. & J. Carrick, Bachelor's-walk
— Cornwall, Longford-street
R. Connell, Aungier-street
J. Carr, Britain-street
B. Clayton, Ryders-row
W. Clemenger, Kilmore
Wm. Connell, Barrack-street
E. Calvert, do.
C. Clinton, Bank of Ireland.
R. Connor, do.
J. Clement, do.
D. Corker, do.
E. Cuddy, Bridge-street
W. Craig, Brunswick-street
J. Carey, Black-rock
— E. Clemenson, Bishop-street
J. Coulson, Bolton-street
P. Cantrell, Bride-street
— Clark, do.
R. Connor, Back-lane
S. Cox, Ordnance Office
Wm. Clarke, Capel-street
J. Charraier, do.

Major Cane, Dawson-street
Lieutenant Colonel Colvill
Counsellor R. Colles, Stephen's-gr.
Mrs. Corbett, Montpelier-hill
--- Carter, Black-rock
Jane Cooke, Tuckers-row
J. Clarke, M. D. Granby-row
Rev. H. Campbell, Prussia-street
Captain Clements, Rogerson's Quay
Captain Chamberlyne, R. A. Island-bridge
Wm. Courtney, Esq. Suffolk-street
J. Campbell, Esq. James's street
John Chambers, Esq. Gardiner-st.
T. Clark, Esq. S. King-street
George Carroll, Esq. do.
Shawe Cartland, Esq. Harcourt-st.
------ Casson, Esq.   do.
A. Campbell, Esq. Gardiner-place
P. Caldwell, Esq. Henry-street
F. Crosbie, Esq. Dorset-street
T. Conrey, Esq.   do.
Wm. Carshore, Esq. do.
John Coyne, Esq. Molsworth-st.
R. Curtis, Esq. Mountjoy-place
M. Clarke, Esq. Camden-street
Mr. A. Calloway, Crampton-court
--- Carroll, Cavendish-row
T. Craig, Chancery-lane
T. Caffrey,   do.
A. Cooney, Cole-alley
--- Cox, Castle-street
J. Cooke, Kevin's-port
J. Cowan, Gordon's-lane
P. Crawford, Charlemount-st.
--- Cooper, Dawson-street
--- Cox, Dame-street
--- Crozier, do.
--- Crosbie, Dorset-street
--- Crawford, Exchange-street
C. Cotton, Essex-street
John Cooke, Fishamble-street
W. Cooper, N. Town Mt. Kenedy
R. Clifford, Georges-street
T. Crosbie. Golden-lane
--- Crosbie, North-wall
--- Crosbie, Collen
J. Corkran, Montague-st.
H. Clair, Grafton-street
F. Campbell, Henry-street
W. Curry, Docks
--- Coulter, James's-street

Mr. J. Courtney, Mary-street
D. Carney, James's-street
J. Crawford, Moore-street
G. Crawford, Bushey Park
E. Carolin, Mecklinburgh-st.
--- Coulter, Meath-street
J. Cockburn, Mark-street
Amb. Crane, Kevin-street
J. Crawford, New-street
T. Cantrell, New-row
--- Clarke, Ormond-quay.
D. Clarke, Portobello
Wm. Clarke, do.
Wm. Craig, Queen-street
--- Cornwall, Stephen-street
E. Cooke,   do.
W. Carmichael, do.
Wm. Cooke, Summer-hill
W. Courtney, Sackville-street
R. Cummings, L. Britain-street
James Collins, Stephen-reeng
J. Cornett, Townsend-street
G. Cunningham, do.
--- Cowdall, Whitefriar-street
N. Condon,   do.
H. Charles,   do.
O. Dougherty, Buckingham-st.

D

Captain Durnford, R. A. Island-bridge
Lieutenant Durnford, R. A. do.
Lieutenant Dawson, Charlemont-st.
Thomas Disney, Esq. Gardiner-st.
Whitmore Davis, Esq. North Strand
T. Christian, Esq. Ship-street
E. Conlan, Esq. New-row
Counsellor Driscoll, Harcourt-street
Counsellor Dixon, Gardiner-street
William Darley, Esq. York-street
Isaac D'Olier, Esq. Barrack Board
W. Davenport, Esq. Dorset-street
Arthur Dawson, Esq. Sackville-st.
Rev. Dean Digby, Mountjoy-square,
Alderman Darley, Abbey-street
James Digges Latouche, Esq.;
S. Draper, Esq. Baggot-street

R. Davis, Esq. Chancery-lane
J. Daly, Esq. M. P. Gt. Charles-st.
R. D'Olier, Esq. Charlemount-street
Edger Dickinson, Esq. Dawson-st.
Lewis Desmond, Esq. Gardier-street
L. N. Donevan, Esq. Mt. joy-square
J. Dumoulin, Esq. Stephen-street
W. Duncan, Esq. Portobellow
R. Drury, Esq. Stanhope-street
Miss Eliza Drury, Cathedral-lane
Miss A. Dodd, Camden-street
T. Dix, Esq. Mt. pleasant
J. Dance, Esq. Ship-street
M. Dillon, Esq. Mecklinburgh-street
Lady Harriet Daly, Henrietta-street
Mrs. Darley, Gardiner-street
Mrs. Dabzac, Gardiners-row
Mr. J. Davis, Arran-quay
J. Dunn, Cuff-street
— Doxey, Abbey-leix
R. Dickson, Brides-alley
J. J. Davis, Bachelors-walk
— Henry Doolittle, Bridge-st.
C. Dempsy, Black-rock
— Doyle, do.
— Doyle, junr. do.
R. Dawson, Bride-street
William Davis, Portland-row
W. Dempsy, Back-lane
— Dummikin, do.
P. Dickson, Cathedral-lane
J. Devitt, Crampton-court
J. Duncan, Church-street
R. Den, do.
J. Delamoure, Cuff-street
— Dwyre, Camden-street
B. Dugdale, Dame-street
J. Daly junr. do.
R. Dickson, Duke-street
J. Davis, do.
I. Dawson, Exchange-street
I. Donaldson, L. Temple-st.
T. Davis, Georges-street
I. Daly, Gt. Georges-street
I. Drake, Golden-lane
— Drew, Gloster place
C. Degroot, junr. Henry-street
— Daniell, S. King-street
R. Dockery, Ap. Royal Hospital
W. Dyett, Longford-stteet
J. A. Dubourdieu, Mabbot-st.
P. Dickson, Meckelnburgh-st.

Mr. S. Dowling, Hawkins-street
T. Delany, Mark-street
W. Dale, Maiden-lane
E. Delany, L. Ormond-quay
S. Dixon, do.
T. Dillon, Polebeg-street
— Dickinson, do.
P. Downes, Patrick-street
J. Dale, Wood-street
W. Delany Stephen-street
C. Dowling, do.
— Dillon, Ship-st. 2 Copies.
— Donaldson, Donny-brook
— Delander, Skinner-row
— Dumas, Temple-street
— Dycear, Wood-street
— Deane, do.
— Dunn, Black-rock
— Davis, do.

E

Captain Evans, Royal Hospital
Captain Everard, 14th Regt, Foot
William Evans, Esq. Rathangan
Henry Ellis, Esq. Eccles-street
W. Elliott, Esq. Mecklenburgh-st.
Henry Ensor, Esq. Mecklenburgh-s'.
W. Edington, Esq. College-green
W. Espinasse, Esq. Post Office
Mr. G. Enever, Abbey-street
- J. Eustace, Britain-street
— Eustace, Black-rock
D. Elliot, Beresford-street
W. Ellison, Bride-street
W. Eacches, Clonbrasil-place
P. Ennis, Purden-street
J. Elliott, Dorset-street
R. Ellis, Fishamble-street
G. Eagle, Grafton-street
— Eaton, Henry-street
W. Elsegood, Jervis-street
T. Earl, Cork-street
J. Evans, New-row
P. Elliott, Parliament-street
G. W. Eades, Stephen-street
W. Eacratt, Monasterevan

F

Captain Foss, Assistant Deputy Adjutant General to the recruiting service
Major Faviere, Holles-street.
Col. French, N. Frederic-street
Captain Frew, Royal S. Down Militia
Lieut. Forster, R. A. Island-bridge
G. W. Forster, Esq. North Strand
D. Fitzgerald, Esq. Stephen's-green
J. Erck, Esq. Rathmines
R. M. Fraser, Esq. Mountjoy-square
S. Fewtrell, Esq. Abbey-street
W. H. Fortescue, Esq. Fitzgibbon-st.
G. Gibbs, Esq. Blackhall-street
W. Fox, Esq. Charlemount street
— Ford, Esq. Palace-row
R. Freeman, Esq. Rathfarnham
P. Fullam, Esq. Summer-hill
J. Farrell, Esq. Merrion-square
John Fox Esq. Stafford-street
C. Forster, Esq. Dorset-street
A. Flattery, Esq. Ellis's-quay
James Freth, Esq. Earl-street
R. Faucett, Esq. Ormond-quay
L. L. Feuillaide, Esq. N. George's-st.
R. Freeman, Esq. Hendrick-street
Mrs. John Finlay, Jervis-street
— Fearis, Gardiner-place
— French, Peter-place
Miss Foley, Braithwaite-steet
— Fury, Swifts-alley
Rev. Roger Ford, Crumlin
Counsellor Fitzgerald, U. Mount-st.
Mr. J. Finn, Arran-street
Z. Foxall, Arran-quay
— Furlong, Rogers's-quay
R. Freeman, Aungier-street
— Foley, Abbey-street
J. Fitzsummons, do.
P. Field, Bank of Ireland
M. Fitzgerald, Clarendon-street
— Faulkner, Cathedral-lane
J. Freeman, Capel-street
— Fox, Coombe.
W. Fitzpatrick, Castle-street
J. Fenton, Clonbrazil-place
T. Fearon, Camden-street
— Franklin, do.
T. Farley, Dame-street
J. Finner, Dorset-street

Mr. J. Ferrar, Exchequer-street
G. Feake, Grafton-street
Amb. Folliott, Granard
John Franklin, Hardwicke-st.
— Flynn, Hendrick-street
— Fitzgibbon, S. King-street
J. Flanagan, Mary-street
T. Fannin, Bishop-street
Judge Fox, Merion-square
— Fowler, Mecklen-burgh-st.
— Fullton, Malpas-street
W. Figgis, Nassau-street
— Fitzgerald, Ormond-quay
J. Ford, Peter-street
P. French, Peter-place
— Ferrar, Exchequerstreet
— Francis, Ross-lone
R. Fell, Wood-street
S. Fisher, Westmoreland-st.

G

Colonel Gordon, Military Sec. to the Commander in Chief
Rev. T. Gamble, A. M. Paradise-row
Rev. —— Guinness, D. D.
Surgeon Gallagher, 74th Foot
J. Gahagan, M. D. Cumberland-st.
H. Giffard, LL.D. Fitzwilliam-street
Lieutenant T. Gledstanes,
A. Guinness, Esq. Cavendish-row
C. Gautiere, Esq. Earl-street
Colley Grattan, Esq. Athy
Mr. John Griffin, Aungier-st.
S. Graham, Bank of Ireland
T. H. Graves, Britain-street
Henry Grant, Bishop-street
— Graham, do.
F. Gainfort, Bride-street
Wm. Glynn, Clarendon-street
G. Gallagher, Cork-street
— Grey, Clare-street
A Gardiner, Chancery-lane
C. Gibbs, do.
J. Greenham, Cork-street
F. Graham, corporal, R. S. D. M.
— Grattan, Digges-street
— Giltrop, Faucett's Court
J. Geoghan, Francis-street
T. Gallagher, George's-street

Arthur Gardiner, Esq. Gardiner-st.
Wm. Goddard, Esq. do.
Captain R. Hinde, Whitehaven
Captain Grant, Charlemont-place
Mrs. Gore, N. Great George's-st.
Mrs. Guinness, Delgany.
C. Gibbons, Hendrick-street
Wm. Grimshaw, Linen Hall-st.
--- Green, Mary's Abbey
W. Glenton, Mary-street
James Greene, Myler's Alley
--- Geoghegan, mill-street
S. Grace, do.
T. Groves, New-street
W. Graham, do.
--- Gibbon, New-row
J. Goslin, Phibsborough
A. Gafney, Rathcool
T. Gentles, Rathangan
J. Gardiner, Sackville-street
M. Griffith, do.
--- Graham, Ship-street
T. Grattan, Shaw's Bank
James Grace, Townshend-st.
--- Graham, Thomas-street
J. Grant, Wood-street
G. Garty, William-street
W. Grey, Esq. York-street
W. Garty, George's-street
M. Groome, Golden-lane
J. Graham, Grafton-street

H

Right Hon. CHARLES EARL OF
HARRINGTON, Commander in
Chief of his Majesty's Forces in
Ireland.
Rt. Hon. S. Hamilton, Merrion-sq.
Col. Handfield, Commissary general
Colonel Hill, Russell-place
Dr. Hall, Provost. Trinity-college
Rev. J. Hutton, A. M. Summer-hill
Rev. T. Harding, Hardwicke-street
Rev. J. Horner, Dorset-street
J. Hamilton, Esq. Palace-row.
M. Handcock, Esq. Harcourt-street
T. Gill, Esq. Grange-lane
G. Howell, Esq. Ormond-quay
John Hagan, Esq. Abbey-street

Hon. Mrs. Cole Hamilton, Gardiner-street.
Mrs. Mary Ann Howard, Rutland-st.
Mrs. Huband, Charlemont-street
Edward Hill, M. D. Harcourt-street.
A. Humfrey, Esq. Gloucester-street
Captain Hemsworth, Kilkenny Militia
Captain Harpur, Russel-street.
George Hagan, M. D. Arran-quay
Major Hodson, Fitzgibbon-street
Hon. Rev. B. Howard, Gardiner-st.
Peter Hodgson, Esq. Buckingham-st.
Thomas Higgins, Esq. Hardwick-st.
James Hilles, Esq. do.
T. Humphreys. Esq. Blackhall-st.
Samuel Hood, Esq. Carolina-row
John Hill, Esq. Dorset-street
G. Hamilton, Esq. N. Frederick-st.
M. Hervey, Esq. Georges-street
--- Hone, Esq. Georges-street, N.
James Hamilton, Esq. Jervis-street
W. Holmes, Esq. Mabbot-street
James Hamilton, Esq. Meath-street
R. Hill, Esq. Mount-joy Place
J. H. Hyland, Esq. York-street
Abraham Y. Hill, Esq. William-st.
P. W. Hervey, Esq. Stephens-green
Captain Heron,
Miss Headey, Whitefriar-street
Serjeant W. Hill, R. S. D. militia.
T. Headen, Esq. Portobello
Alex. Hall, Esq. Synnot-place
G. Hamilton, Esq. Townsend-street
A. Hamilton, Esq. Dominick-street
Mr. Hyat, Black-rock
M. Hagarty, Prussia-street
J. Hosie, Portobello
J. Hutchinson, Vickers-street
J. Heally, Wormwood-gate
R. Harty, Westmoreland-street
R. Heaney, Whitefriar-street
A. Hamilton, do.
--- Holbrooke, do.
P. Hanlon, Ashmount
H. Holbrook, Bishop-street
W. Hetherington, Ross-lane
James Hethers, Dungannon
--- Hooper, Ranelagh
W. Hall, Pill-lane, 12 copies
H. Harrison, Queen-street
J. Howe, Skinner-row
--- Hendrick, Shaws Bank

Mr. W. Henry, Dominick-street
G. Hatton, Essex-street
W. Harvey, Exchequer-street
G. Harrison, Faucets-court.
R. Hunt, Francis-street
G. Hill, Georges-street
R. Hudson, Grafton-street
J. Heally,   do.
J. Hayes, Gardiner-place
M. Henley, Henry-street
I. Harrington,   do.
E. Hale, Hanover-street
--- Hughes, High-street
I. Hudson, Hibernia school
--- Hutchinson, Jervis-street
J. Hanlon, Johns-lane
C. Holmes, Longford-street
W. Humphreys, Leinster-street
--- Humphreys, Merrion-square
W. Hutchinson, Montague-pl.
D. Hall, Mill-street
--- Howard, Molesworth-street
M. Howard, Merrion-street
T. Herbert, Clonard, Co. Meath
--- Hall, Marrowbone-lane
J. Hamilton, Ormond-quay
R. Horton, Peter-street
W. Henderson, Cavendish-row
Robert Hill, Cork-street
W. Hodges, Camden-street
H. Hampton, Clontarf
--- Hemmins, Coal-quay
I. Hughes, Charlemont-street
G. W. Hulbert, do.
W. Heffernan, Cashill
S. Hanley, Dorset-street
R. Hill, Maryborough
--- Hunt, Braithwaite-street
--- Hart, King's Hospital
C. Hanlon, Ordnance office
I. Hart,   do.
--- Hunt,   do.
T. Hughes, Cathedral-lane.
--- Haughton, Charles-street
G. Harold, Arran-quay
— Hagan, M. D. do.
J. Hill, Aungier-street
J. Haden, do.
W. Hewson, do.
J. Halligan, do.
G. Harvey, Abbey-street
J. Hoffington, Bachelors-walk
W. Hebener, Bank of Ireland

Mr. J. Harding, N. Anne-street
--- Herdell, Britain-street
--- Henley, do.
--- Hays, Parnell-place
E. Hughes, Monastereven
W. Harding, Corn-market

J.

Major James, Mount. Pleasant
Major Irwine, R. Tyrone militia.
Lieutenant John Irwin, do.
Arthur Irwine, Esq. Granville-st.
Francis Johnston, Esq. Eccles-street
Surgeon Johnston, Temple-street
Mrs. Jackson, Gardener's-row
Jacaud, Park-street
S. Johnson, Esq. Carolina-row
W. Johnson, Esq. do.
John Jallett, A. B. do.
James Johnston, Esq. Mountjoy-sq.
Robert Johnston, Esq. do.
T. Johnson, Esq. Gardiner-street
R. Jones, Esq. Peter-street
G. Irwine, Esq. Bride-street
Mr John Jones, G. Georges-street S,
   Printer and Bookseller
Miss Ann Jones,   do.
Mr. Joyce, Bandon.
    W. Irwine, Barrack-street
    I. Jackson, Essex-street
    W. Jameson, Dorset-street
    W. Johnson, Exchequer-street
    T. Jones, Foundling Hospital
    I. Jones, Granard
    --- Iwing, Mabbot-street
    W. Jameson, Aungier-street
    W. Johnson, Molesworth-street
    W. Jackson, Mountrath
    J. Jones, Brabazon-row
    S. Jones, Black-rock
    --- Jones, sen. Dawson-street
    --- Jones, junior, do.
    P. Jordan, Bolton-street
    --- Jones, Back-lane
    --- Jones, Cork-hill
    W. Jones, Digges-street
    R. Jackson, Ryders-row
    --- Jackson, Patrick-street
    W. Jones, Summer-place
    --- Jones, sen. Stephen's-green
    --- Jones, junior, do.
    S. Jones, Westmoreland-st.
    R. Johnson, Ballywater

K

Richard Kirwan, Esq. LL.D. F. R. S.
P. R. I. A. Cavendish-row
Major King, Granby-row
Mrs. Kenn, N. Great George's-street
Mrs. Kearney, Delgany
P. Kilkelly, Esq. Gardiner's place
James Kearney, Esq. Mountjoy-sq.
J. V. Kildahl, Esq. Eustace-street
Alderman Kirkpatrick, North Great
    George's-street
Rev. H. Kearney, Delgany
Patrick Kelly, Esq. N. Frederic-st.
Alderman B. King, Merrion-square
S. Kearney, Esq. Mountjoy-square
Mark Kerr, Esq. Ormond-quay
Edward Kirby, Esq. Temple-street
I. Kerton, Esq. Richmond-place
Mrs. King, Marino
Hickman Kearney, Esq. Abbey-st.
B. Kearney, Esq. Stephen's-green
George Kidd, Esq. Rutland-street.
Mrs. Kelly, Castle-street
Miss Knox, Britain-street
Mrs. Mary Kiernan, Brunswick-st.
Richard Kellet, Esq. College
A. Keene, Esq. Charlemont-street
M. J. Kennedy, Esq. Gardiner-street
E. Kevill, Esq. Dunville-lane
Mr. Kerr, Whitefriar-st. 35 copies
    E. H. King, Anne-street
    I. Kavanagh, Abbey-street
    M. Kirwan, Brunswick-street
    J. Kennedy, Ordnance-office.
    Charles Knox, do.
    --- Kennedy, Cathedral-lane
    M. Keene, College-green
    W. Kirkpatrick, Custom-house
    --- King, Castle-street
    I. Keene, Charlemont-street
    R. Kyte, Cashill
    W. Keene, Dame-street
    --- Knaggs, Exchequer-street
    A. Kelly, Grafton-street
    G. Kiernan, Henry-street
    G. Kearney,   do.
    --- Kellett, N. King-street
    --- Keightly, Kings Inn-quay
    H. Kempston, Nassau-street
    W. Kertland, Ormond-quay

Mr. Wm. Kent, Stephen-street
E. Kinsley, 3 copies
Adam Keith, Liffey-street
I. Keating, Sackville-street
W. Kershaw, Smock-alley
C. Knaggs, Stafford-street
R. King, Stephen's-green
J. Kelly, Denmark-street

L

Sir John Lees, Bart. Black-rock
Rev. H. Lees, do.
John C. Lees, Esq. do.
Mrs. Lees, do.
E. S. Lees, Esq. Sec. Post Office
William Lees, Esq. Black-rock
Townsend Lees, Esq. do.
Thomas Orr Lees, Esq. do.
Rev. C. Littlehales, A. M.
William Larklin, Esq. North Strand
Mrs. P. Latouche, Belview
Thomas Lee, Esq. Aston's-quay
John Lalor, Esq. Gardiner-place
Nath. Low, Esq. Eccles-street
J. D. Latouche, Esq.
J. Digges Latouche, Esq.
Peter Latouche, Junior, Esq.
Rev. J. Lewis, A. M. York-street
Rev. T. Lanauze, Killishandra
Rev. A. Leney, Castle Dawson
    Academy.
William Ledwich, Esq. York-street
Patrick Long, Esq. Gardiner street
Thomas Lawrence, Esq. Rutland-st.
S. Lawrence, Esq. Marlborough-st.
G. Long, Esq. Braithewaite-street
Col. Linsey, Inspecting Field officer,
    Recruiting Service.
T. Lownde, Esq. Grenville-street
W. H. Lee, Esq. Gardiner-street
W. O'Brien Laidner, Esq. Jervis-st.
Mrs. Jane Lee, Merrion-square
Mrs. Leigh,   do.
Major Legge, Chapelizod
A. L. Lynn, Esq. Charlemont-street
A. Lowe, Esq. Ranelagh
Edward Leonard, Esq. Ushers-quay
A. Lackey, Esq. Richmond-place

J. Llewellyen, Esq. Rutland-street
E. Laughlin, Esq. Paradise-row
R. Litton, book-binder Chatham-st.
Mr. Ledsome, Anglesea-street
--- Lauree 　 do.
--- Lennon, Britain-street
--- Lynch, 　 do.
--- Lockyer, Brunswick-street
J. Litton, Bride-street
H. Levinge, Ordnance office
--- Lloyd, Harolds-cross
R. Lambert, Caple-street
--- Lawless, 　 do.
J. Lodge, Church-street
D. Leedom, Chancery-lane
--- Lapham, Chamber-street
T. Leech, Camden-street
--- Lewis, Gordons-lane
T. H. Lowther, Dame-court
--- Linfoot, Essex-street
R. Lynch, Exchequer-street
　 3 copies
--- Lloyd, Gloster-place
R. Lynes, Hoey's-court
B. Latty, Hibernia-school
--- Lodge, Jervis-street
H. Logan, 　 do.
--- Lyons, Johns-lane
G. Long, Mary-street
James Lever, North Strand
T. Locke, Nassau-street
P. Lynch, Ormond-quay
P. Lamb, Patrick-street
Cooke Lucas, Parliament-street
James Lowry, Pill-lane
A. Litton, Summer-Hill
--- Leech, Stafford-street
--- Lynett, 　 do.
--- Little, Ship-street
H. Laughlin, Townsend-street

M

Countess Dowager of Meath Merrion-square
Miss Mercer Dorset-street
Captain Morton, Rehoboth House
A. Montgomery, Esq. L. Dorset-st.
Mrs. Maffett, Capel-street

Richard Manders, Esq. James's-st.
Robert Manders, Esq. do.
Samuel Madder, Esq. James's-street.
Rev. H. Murray, 　 do.
Rev. M. Morgan, Lower Dorset-st.
Rev. B. W. Matthias, Dorset-street
Rev. E. Martin, York-street
Charles Meares, Esq. Dorset-street
F. L. Morgan, Esq. Hardwicke-st.
B. M'Kean, Esq. Hardwicke-place
R. Morrison, Esq. Mecklenburgh-st.
Lewis Morgan, Lower Rutland-st.
Daniel Mills, M. D. William-street
Thomas Mills, M. D. Dominick-st.
Robert M'Bride, Esq. Stephen's-gr.
Thomas M'Kenny, Esq. Stephen's-st.
Counsellor L. M'Nally, Harcourt-st.
Surgeon G. Macklin, Leinster-stre.
H. B. Molesworth, Esq. do.
Lieut. M'Manus, Assistant Sec to do.
Rev. A. Morgan, Blue Coat Hopital
Mr. R. E. Mercier, do.
　 R. Morrison, Aungier-street
James Malloy, do.
John Morris, Esq. Abbey-st.
A. M'Caul, 　 do.
J. M'Evoy, 　 do.
F. M'Dermott, 　 do.
Edward Mulligan, do.
James Madden, Aston's-quay
Wm Maffett, Britain-street
J. M'Gloin, 　 do.
Samuel Missett, 　 do.
William Maguire, Back-close
--- Moore, Bank of Ireland
C. Moore, 　 do.
Samuel M'Murray, Baggot-st.
J. M'Laine, Bishop-street
Robert Morgan, Bride-street
T. M'Glathry, Ordnance Office
A. Mason, Clarendon-street
R. Martin, College-green
D. Murray, Capel-street
A. M'Laughlin, 　 do.
--- Martin, 　 do.
J. Mills, do. 　 do.
J. Mahon, Church-street
B. J. M'Dermott, do.
--- M'Cormick, Chancery-lane
Thomas Magill, 　 do
--- Morris, Edenderry

A. Montgomery, Esq. Dorset-street
W. P. M'Alpin, Esq. Dominick-st.
P. Montgomery, Esq. Eccles-street
——Maziere, Esq.   do.
Captain M'Farland, Cowley-place
J Morgan, Esq. French-street
Adjutant Maxwell, Fowne's-street
Quarter Master M'Gleazy, Chapelizod.
Mrs. Molineaux, Mespil
W. M'Kay, Esq. Stephens-green
T. Murphy, Esq. Richmond
L. Morgan, Esq. Rutland-street
— Martin, Quarter Master, R. T.
I. G. Mulvany, Esq. Paradise-row
Wm. Mackenzie, Esq. Gardiner-st
H. I. Madden, Esq Mabbot-street
R. Mulhern, Esq. Marlborough-st.
Miss Eliza Mears, Mount-street
Capt. H. M'Clean, Royal Hospital
Lieut. M'Manus, Assistant Sec. do.
G. Musson, Esq.   do.
T. Meade, Esq. Jervis-street
A. Mazierre, Esq. James's-street
Wm M'Cannon, Exchequer-st.
--- H. Manning, Fade-street
. M'Comas, Fleet-street
Hugh Magee, Fordam's-ally
John Moses, George's-street
--- Merle,   do.
B. M'Dermott, Golden-lane
J. M'Dermott, do.
T. M'Adam, Grafton-street
A. B. Manifold,   do.
--- M'Dermott,   do.
--- M'Cornock,
R. M'Cann, Camden-street
I. Morton, Camden-street
Wm M'Cally, Donavan's-lane
C. Murphy,   do.
--- Morrison, Dawson-street, 3
copies
--- J. Montgomery, Dorset-st.
--- M'Kenny, Dame-counrt
--- Maxwell, Denmark-street
--- Molesworth, Gardiner-street
... Mooney, Glo'ster-street
... Magrath,   do.
T. M'Dermott, Granby-row
A. M'Mullen, Hoey's-court
P. M'Dermott, Jervis-street

I. Mills, Granard
L. Morgan, Henry-street
A. M'Minn, Strand-street
T. M'Minn,   do.
— Mullen,   do.
— M'Donald, Ship-street
C. Merchant,   do.
— Mullen, Summer Place
F. J. Mooney, Shaw's Bank
G. Matthews,   do.
W. Milner, Sycamore-alley
T. Matthews, Pool-street
T. M'Caskee, Ross-lane
L. Montgomery, Rogersons-quay
J. M'Crea, Stephen-street
W. Murphy,   do.
W. Magrath,   do.
— Miot,   do.
O. Mullanphy,   do.
M. Morton, Stephen-street
G. P. Mills, Peters-row
A. Madden, Peter-street
J. M'Cullogh, Paradise-row
B. Maxwell,   do.
W. Murray,   do.
W. M'Iutee, Meath-street
J. M'Kebbin, Merrion-street
P. Madden,   do.
J. M'Cauley, New-street
J. Mitchell,   do.
T. Matthews,   do.
J. Matthews,   do.
A. M'Gahy, N. King-street
— M'Keon, Kilkenny
J. M'Quig, Longford, 25 copies
J. M'Colly, Moore-street
A. M'Donald,
T. Magrane, Marlborough-st.
R. Magee, Montgomery-street
W. M'Comas, Malpas-street
W. Melven,   do.
— Murphy,   do.
A. Morgan,   do.
R. M'Cann, Hunts-alley
W. M'Clatchie,
R. Magee,   do.
— Molsworth, Island Bridge
G. Moulang, S. King-street
J. M'Allister. Townsend-street

Counsellor M'Gann, Ushers Island
S. Madder, Esq Ushers-quay
T. Millington, Esq. Temple-street
Mrs. Morton. Lower Mount-street
Mr. James M'Kee, Roscrea
    R. M'Donald, Whitefriar-street
    T. Murphy, Thomas-court
    S. H. Murphy, do.
    — M'Cabe, Ushers-quay
    T. M'Comas, Whitefriar-street
    J. Matthews, do.
    W. Matthews, do.
    — Martin, Dolphins-barn
    A. M'Connell, Henry-street
    T. M'Grath, Cannon-street

N

Hon. T. G. Newcomen, Bart.
Luke Norman, Esq Mt. joy-square
T. Norman, Esq. Gardiner-street
Wm. Newcomb, Esq. Jervis-street
A. B. Nevill, Esq. Camden-street
R. Nunn, Esq. N. Cumberland-st.
Samuel Neville, Esq. Stafford-st.
Mrs. Nicholson, Camden-street
Miss Napper, Capel-street
Mr. Newland, Aungier-street
    — Naylor, Britain-street
    T. Nelligan, Bank of Ireland
    — Napper, Cork-street
    W. Noble, C. Donegal
    — Nicholson, Golden-lane
    M. Nickson, Grafton-street
    — Nicholson, do.
    G. Nangle, Harolds-cross
    Wm. Newton, James's-street
    — Neile, New-market
    J. Noble, Parliament-street
    A. Nugent, Sackville-street
    — Nelson, Townsend-street
    J. Neill, Winetavern-street
    C. Nowlan, Wood-street
    — Nowlan, Black-rock

O

Mr. Orson, Denmark-street
T. H. Orpen, M. D. S. Frederick-st.
W. Oldham, Esq. Arran-quay

Myles O'Reilly, Esq. Margt.-place
T. Oxley, Esq. Merchant's-quay
John Oir, Esq. do.
Captain O'Reilly, Jervis-street
Mr. --- Oldham, Abbey-street
    --- O'Brien, Bank of Ireland
    D. O'Reilly, Bride-street
    W. O'Connor, Camden-street
    J. O'Brien, Eustace-street
    --- O'Flaherty, Exchequer-st.
    --- Osborne, Grafton-street
    J. A O'Reilly, Gardiner-place
    C. O'Neal, Capel-street

P

R. Percival, M. D. Kildare-Place
Jonathan Pim, Esq. William-street.
Matthew Pearson, Esq. Granby-row
J. Pollock, Esq. Mountjoy-square.
William Parks, Esq. Ushers-island
W. Powell, Esq. Sea fort Parade
Mrs. M. A. Pounden, Church-street
Captain John Peile, Bishop-street
Robert Purdy, Esq. Ormond-quay
    — Page, Esq. Leeson-street
J. Plunkett, Esq. Georges-street N.
Lieut. Power, R E Island-bridge
John Partington, Esq. York-street
W. Power, Esq. Pitt-street
R. Peter, Esq. French-street
    G. Parkinson, Anne-street
    G. Pierce, Aungier-street
    I. Perrin, Abbey-street
    — Percy, do.
    T. Price, do.
    — Perry, Britain-street
    W. Pountney, Bank of Ireland
    T. Parker, Brunswick-street
    — Page, Bull-alley
    H. Pexton, Ordnance-office
    I. Phair, Cathedral-lane
    T. Popplewell, Cork-street
    S. Page. Camden-street
    R. Patterson, Chatham-street
    R. Pegley, Royal S. D. militia
    --- Power, Trinity-place
    F. Philips, Temple-bar
    --- Prince, Shaw's Bank
    I. Phair, Skinner-row
    ---Preston, Temple-street
    R. Parke, Thomas-street

Mr. M. Paul, Portadown, 6 copies
— Peppard, New-street
T. Palmer, Peters-row
W. Pritchard, Polebeg-street
T. Pujolas, Parliament-street
— Philips, Pembroke-quay
G. Peck, Poddle
I. Petre, Dame-street
I. Paisley, Dorset-street
I. Paintard, Mount Pleasant
— Pujolas, Four Courts
— Power, Georges-street
T. Parsons, Golden-lane
I. Philips, do.
— Patterson, Gloster-place
— Perry, James's-street
— Purcell, Mount-street
I. Pemberton, Moore-street
James Parr, Montague-street
T. Price, Stephen-street

Q

Miss C. Quin, Belfast, 2 copies
R. Quintou, Esq. Ormond-quay

R

Colonel Raymond, Deputy Adj. Gen.
Henry Roe, M D. Aungier-street
Rev. P. Roe, Kilkenny
Mrs. Lucy Ray, Cavendish-row
John Rutherford, Esq Cavendish-row
P. Russell, Esq. Belvedere-place
Rev. I. Roberts, Capel-street
Lady Roche, Eccles-street
I. Reid, Esq. Clare-street
R. Ross, R. S. D. militia.
I. Reed, Esq. Gloster-street
C. Richardson, Esq. do.
Col. W. Reynall, N. Frederick-st.
John Renshaw, Esq. Ormond-quay
Lieut. Richardson, Mecklenburgh-st.
T. Reed Esq. Mountjoy-sq. 2 copies
A. Rooke, Esq. do.
J. Ryan, Esq. Marlborough-street
Major R. Ridge, Grenville-street
A. Richardson, Esq. Summer-hill
R. Roe, Esq. do.

Surgeon Redmond, Astons-quay
W. Roche, Esq. James's-street
D. Redmond, Esq. Rathmines
Mrs. Russell, Santry
Colonel Rogers, Ship-street
W. Richardson, Esq. Stephen's-green
Surgeon Rivers, Queen-street
Mrs. Rea, Peters-row
R. Roth, Esq. Georges-street, N.
Counsellor Ridgeway, Harcourt-st.
Rev. W. Russell, Hendrick-street
P. Reilly, Esq. Eccles-street
W. Roberts, Adjt. R. A.
Mr. — Richardson, Abbey-street
C. Rigney, Britain-street
H. Rolston, Barrack-street
I. Rutherford, do.
N. Russel, Bridge-street
— Robinson, Baggot-street
T. Robinson, Bishop-street
— Ryan, Blackhall-street
— Rathborne, Belvedere-place
G. Reed, Bride-street, 3 copies
I. Rounds, Bride-street
G. Rounds, Braithewaite-street
— Reed, do.
W. Radcliffe, Ordnance-office
H. Rooke, Crampton-court
— Ryan, Church-street
H. Ribton, Dame-street
— Robinson, Rogersons-quay
J. Rafter, Thomas-street
F. Russell, Shaws Bank
— Ridley, Skinners-alley
I. Reed, Ship-street
W. Robinson, Stephen-street
J. Roche, do.
P. Reynolds, Pill-lane
W. Robinson, Ormond-quay
A. Roberts, Fishers-lane
J. Robinson, Golden-lane
W. Roe, Grafton-street
G. Rooke, Exchange-street
— Reeves, do.
E. Robins, Mark-street
A. Rosborough, N. Strand
T. Ring, Mecklenburgh-street
— Rogers, Montgomery-street
Robinson, James's-street
T. Reilly, do.
J. Robinson, Darby-square

S

R. Shaw, Esq. M. P. Merion-square
Mrs. Shaw, do.
Sir Richard Steele, Fitzwilliam-place
　　2 copies
Major Shortall, R. A. Island-bridge
Captain T. O'Sherrard, Dorset-street
Captain Saurin, Summer-hill
Captain John Scott, Gardiner-street
Sejeant Sinclair
L. Slade, R. I. Island-bridge
Dr. Sheridan, Usher's-quay
Dr. Sharkey, York-street
James Singer, Esq. Annadale
Robert Smith, Esq. Abbey-street
James Stephens, Esq. Bachelors-walk
John Saunders, Esq.　　do.
S. Shaw, Esq. Bank of Ireland
J. Somerville, Esq. Belvedere-place
——— Standish, Esq. Castle
R. Stringer, Esq. Chancery-lane
H. F. Stock, Esq. Temple-street
Robert Smith, Esq. Thomas-street
R. Star, Esq. Cole-alley
S. Sparks, Esq. Charlemount-st.
F. Sharkey, Esq. Rathmines
S. Speer, Esq. Dorset-street
T. Swift, Esq. Dorset-street
W. A. Shaw, Esq. Gt. Denmark-st.
J. Straker, Esq. French-street
J. Smith, Esq. N. Frederick street
T. Sillery, Esq. Hardwicke-street
J. Scott, Esq Harcourt-street
R. Smith, Esq.　　do.
J. Simple, Esq. Marlborough-street
C. Sweeny, Esq. Mabdot-street
W. Steel, Esq.　　do.
T. Smart, Esq. Mecklinburgh-street
G. Stapleton, Esq. Mountjoy-place
J. Sullivan, Esq. Ormond-quay
Mrs. Stafford, Crampton-court
Miss Singleton, Cork-hill
Rev. Abraham Augustus Stewart,
　　Hibernia-school
Rev. F. Shultze, Polebeg-street
Rev. P. Sands, Sackville-street
Rev. A. Staunton, Clarendon-street
Rev. F. Sadlier, Mount-street
Mr. M. Smyth. Andrew-street
　　D. St. Leger, Aungier-street
　　W. Stockham,　do.

Mr. — Shaw, Ardee-street
J. Smith, Britain-street
J. Stokes, Barrack-street
P. Sharkey, Bachelors-walk
W. Smith, Brunswick-street
— Sterling, Bishop-street
R. Simpson, Clarendon-street
S. Saxmyth, Maiden-lane
E. Stretch, Church-street
J. Smith, Coombe
— Smith,　　do.
A. Samuels, Chancery-lane
— Smallman, Chatham-row
— Shaw, Castle-street
E. Singleton, Cork-street
— Sheil, Kevin-street
J. Sharman, Dawson-street
W. Scott, Charlemount-street
— Shaw, Dame-street
M. Singleton, Dolphin's-barn
R. Smith, Exchange-street
H. Sibthorp, do.
W. Stubbs, Eustace-street
Solomon Sproule, Earl-street
J. Sheridan, Francis-street
R. Sullivan, Fowns's-street
Val. Simnett, George's-street
Brent Smith,　do.
J. Stopford, Gregs-lane
— Sheilds, Henry-street
J. Sheilds, Hardwicke-street
　　20 copies
— Stewart, Hibernia-school
— Sandys, S. King-street
A. Savage, N. King-street
— Story, Longford street
W. Southerland, Mount-street
— Swan, Montgomery-street
A. C. Seymour, Baggot-street
J. Saxmyth, Maiden-lane
T. Shidow, Rathmolion C. M.
G. Sykes, New-row Thomas-st.
— Sharp, Nicholas-street
— Spilman, Patrick-street
L. Sipthorp, Palace-street
— Sweeney, Park-street
— Synnott, Pool-street
— Smyth, Rutland-street
— Smith, Ryders-row
E. Smith, Rainsford-street
C. Shaw, Stephen-street
J. Sturgeon, Grafton-street

Mr. S. Steele, Whitefriar-street
— Sherlock, Abbey-street
— Simpson, Sackville-street
— Smith, do.
M. Smart, Spitalfields
— Scott, Stafford-street
— Stokes, Ship-street
J. Sullivan, Stephens-green
E. Supple, Shaw's Bank
E. Shea, Townsend-street
W. Stoker, Wood-street
J. Sullivan, do.
S. Smallman, do.
— Stewart, Westmoreland-st.
W. Smith, Bandon
— Senior, Rathcoole
E. Spear, do.

Mr. W. Taaffe, Kevin-st. Book-Binder
W. Tims, Dame-street
J. Tobin, Delgany, 20 Copies
S. Taylor, Grafton-street
— Tysson, do.
J. Tully, Glasnevin
J. Taylor, Ormond-quay 4 Copies
G. Townsend, Poolbeg-street
W. Tassie, Paradise-row
E. Teap, Ranelagh
W. Tomes, Skinner-alley
W. Toole, Ship-street
T. Turner, Shaw's-bank
J. Teare, skinner-row 2 Copies
J. W. Talbot, Rathmines

T

Alderman Thorp, Mountjoy-square
Brig. General Trotter, Stephen-st.
Dr. John Toole, Gardiner-street
Surgeon T. Tuke, stephens-green
John Taafe, Esq. Blackall-street
G. Tottenham, Esq. Harald's cross
U. Thomson, Esq. Mecklenburgh-st.
W. Turner, junr. Esq. Chapilizod
H. Tandy, Esq. Custom-house
W. Tisdall, Esq. Marlborough-st.
P. Thomson, Esq. do.
Counsellor Torrens, Gardiner-street
J. Thompson, Esq. Gardiner-street
E. Tennant, Esq. Gloster-place
A. Todd, Esq. Gardiner-place
A. Torrens, Esq. Granby-row
Ralph Tornton, Esq. Dorset-street
J. Taaffe, Esq. Florinda-place
Mrs. Taylor, Digges-street
Mrs. Teeling, Thomas-street
Serjeant D. Taylor, Church-street
Mr. J. Taylor, Abbey-street
R. Tyndall, Bride-street
Isaac Tyndall, do.
— Tydd, Baggot-street
A. Torrington, Bolton-street
J. Tobin, College-green
J. Taylor, Castle-street
R. Turbett, do.
G. Taylor, Digges-street
A. Torrington, sen. Wood-st.
A. Torrington, jun. do.

U

Rev. Dr. Henry Usher, Clare-street

V

Col. Vesey, County Dublin Militia
Mr. T. Vero, Bride-street
— Vann, Coombe
G. Vaughan, Dorset-street
J. Vickers, Shaw's Bank
T. Vaughan, Dame-street
Rev. — Vigors, George's-street
Rev. Dr, Vesey, Royal Hospital
—— Villiers, Esq. Stephens-green
T. Vickers, Esq. Wicklow
E. Verdon, Esq. Golden-lane

W

Rev. J. Whitelaw, Clanbrassil-place
J. Wiere, Esq. Capel-street
C. Wiber, Esq. Ordnance office
R. Wrightson. Esq. do.
Vere Webb, Esq. Bedford-street
J. Wilson, Esq. Abbey-street
Mrs. Whitmore, Black-rock,
Counsellor Waller, Black-rock
Counsellor Williams, Baggot-street
P. Worthington, Esq. Cumberland-st.
H. A. Woodward, Esq Ellis's-quay
W. Wolfinden, Esq. Dorset-street
E. Wolfinden, Esq. do.
Serjt. Watterson, R. S. D. militia

Lieut. Col. Wulffe, Island Bridge
T. Walsh, Esq. James-street
H. White, Esq.   do.
Peter Warren, Esq. Henrietta-street
Counsellor Whitestone, do.
J. Whealy, Esq. Stephen's-green
W. L. Walker, Esq. Stafford-street
T. Waring, M. D.   do.
W. Walsh, Esq. Russell-street
M. Williamson, Esq. Paradise-row
J. Williamson, Esq.   do.
A. Williamson, Esq. . do.
J H. Walker, Esq. Ormond-quay
E. Wilson, Esq. New-street
Coun. R. Walker, Mecklenburgh-st.
T. Whealon, Esq. Liffey-street
C. Weekes, Esq. Stephen's-green
Rev. G. Whistler, S. Frederick-st.
B. Worthington, Esq. Fitzgibbon-st.
W. A. Walker, Esq. Chatham-st.
Mrs. Warren, Henrietta-street
J. H. Weldon, Esq. Gardiner-street
Mr. Samuel Wood, Whitefriar-street
R. Wade, Esq. Gardiner-st.
J. R. Worthington, Esq. do.
   C. Walton, Aungier-street
   G. Watson, Abbey-street
   S. Winter, Britain-street
   J. Wicksted, Bank of Ireland
   A. Wilson, Belfast 12 Copies
   G. Wood, Beaver-street
   J. Walsh, Belturbet ·
   T. Wilson, Bride-street
   A. Wheatly, Capel-street
   Z. D. Williams, do.
   G. Williams, Crampton-court
   J Walker, Church-street
   T. Webb,   do.
   — Walsh, Cuffe-street
   N. Williams, Cole-alley
   T. Whitehead, Cork-street
   — Whitam, Corn-market
   — Wilton,   · do.
   T. Watts, Cashel
   H. Wheeler, Dame-street
   J. Wheeler, Denmark-street
   T. West, Whitefriar-street
   J. Wright, Essex-street
   G. Ward,   do.
   J. Wright,   do.

Mr. J. Ward, French-street
P. Weire, Fishamble-street
W. Whitestone, Grafton-street
Messrs. Whyte,   do.
R. White,   do.
R. Williams,   do.
— Wilson, Mary-street
R. Westenra, Granby-row
— Warren, High-street
H. Willard,   do.
— Wadden, Park-street
— Wybrants, Peter-street
J. Wyon, Ormond-quay
R. Wright, Monaghan
— Walsh, Marrowbone-lane
T. Ward, New-street
P. Walsh, Marlborough-street
R. White, Montgomery-street |
W. Wallace, Mecklenburgh-st.
— Wright, Royal Hospital
— Waugh, James's-street
H. White, Jervis-street
J. Ward, Whitefriar-street
A. Whitesides,   do. |
— Winters, Winetavern-street
T. Wallace, Church-street
R. Walker, Athlone
— Ward, Mount Pleasant
R. Wornall, Portobello
G. Ward, Thomas-street
R. Wright, Westmoreland-st.
C. Walton, Ship-street
R. Webb, Earl-street
D. Weyman, Stephen-street
   Commissary
W. Watts, Sackville-street

Y

Hon. W. A. Yelverton, Gloster-st.
G. Yeates, Esq. Mecklenburgh-st.
Mr. C. Young, Bank of Ireland
   W. Yoakley, Mt. pleasant 3 Cop.
   H. Young, Belview, 20 Copies
   H. Young, Prussia-street,
   — Youdell, Monastereven
   — Young, Summer-hill
   J. Young, ship-street
   G. Young, do.
   W. Young, Shaw's Bank

ORIGINAL AND AUTHENTIC

JOURNAL OF OCCURRENCES

DURING THE LATE

AMERICAN WAR,

&c. &c. &c.

CHAP. I.

Mutual Regard between Great Britain and her Colonies. Character of the Colonies at the End of the Year 1763. Taxes laid on Goods imported into the Colonies: Opposed by the Americans. The Stamp Act framed. Disturbances in different Colonies. First Congress held in New York. Disturbances still continued. Stamp Act repealed. A Bill for New Taxes passed in Britain, and sent to America. Occasions new Discontents. Tea destroyed at Boston. Boston Port Bill. Received with extravagant Tokens of Resentment by the Bostonians. Congress meets at

Philadelphia. General Gage fortifies Boston Neck.
A great Army assembles before Boston, and pre-
pares for War.

As the rise and establisment of the American Republic,
has given a new face to the western world, a summary
view of the occurrences that led to the independence
of that country, (before I enter upon my Journal,) will
no doubt be pleasing to the Re-der.

The mother country, in planting her colonies in North
America, had endowed them with every privilege enjoyed
by her subjects at home. She left them at full liberty
to govern themselves by whatever laws the wisdom of
their own provincial assemblies might think expedient,
and empowered them to pursue their respective interests,
but claimed the exclusive benefit of their trade, and
their allegiance to the same sovereign.

The Americans, on the other hand, cherished the most
tender veneration for the mother country. The name
of an Englishman gave them an idea of every thing that
was great and estimable in human nature, and they considered the rest of mankind as barbarians, compared
with the people from whom they were descended. The
Colonists had often experienced the protection of Britons,
and witnessed their valor : as the contest* with France
had been begun on their account, they considered themselves bound to assist their protectors with zeal and
fidelity.

By a succession of the most brilliant victories by sea
and land, Great Britain effectually subdued the united
powers of France and Spain, and acquired possession of
a vast extent of territory in both the Indies. The peace
of Paris, in 1763, terminated a war which exalted her
to the zenith of military glory. By this treaty she

---

* *Viz.* the war of 1757, 1758, and 1759.

remained sole mistress of North America, and her Colonies were relieved from the fear of their ambitious French neighbours.

Such was the state of the British Colonies at the conclusion of a war, in which they had been more than conquerors. Indeed the cession of Canada had placed them in a state of perfect security from the French, and the Indians were too contemptible an enemy to excite much apprehension.

The colonies had for ages been accustomed to look to the mother country for aid against the French, from a consciousness of their inability to contend alone against that powerful nation. Protection on the one side, naturally implied obedience on the other; and her Colonies continued to view Great Britain with an eye of filial reverence, while the menaces of an ambitious neighbour kept them in awe. But when the cession of the French territory in America to the British crown removed a formidable and ambitious rival from the western hemisphere, the colonists began to view their situation in another light, and to cherish ideas of their future greatness.

Their flourishing condition at this period was remarkable. Their trade had prospered in the midst of all the difficulties and distresses of a war in which they were so immediately concerned. Their population continued on the increase, notwithstanding the ravages and depredations that had been so fiercely carried on by the French, and the native Indians in their alliance. They had many spirited and active individuals of all denominations. They were flushed with the uncommon prosperity that attended them in their commercial affairs and military transactions. Hence they were ready for all kind of undertakings, and saw no limits to their hopes and expectations.

As they entertained the highest opinion of their valor and importance, and of the immense benefit that Great Britain derived from its connexion with them, their notions were adequately high in their own favour. They deemed themselves entitled to every kindness and indulgence which the mother country could bestow.

Although their pretensions did not amount to a perfect equality of advantages and privileges in matters of commerce, yet in those of government they thought themselves fully competent to the task of conducting their domestic concerns with little or no interference from abroad. Though willing to admit the supremacy of Great Britain, they viewed it with a suspicious eye, and with a marked desire and intent speedily to give it limitations.

The French, who have for many ages been the professed and natural enemies of Britain, had long viewed, with equal envy and apprehension, the flourishing state of the colonies in North America. No doubt at present subsists, that they began immediately after the peace of Paris to carry into execution the scheme they had formed for the separation of the British colonies from the mother country, conscious that, whilst a good understanding subsisted between Great Britain and her colonies the superiority must henceforth remain for ever on the side of Britain. It was only by their disunion that France could hope to regain the station and consequence she had formerly possessed in Europe.

The first step taken by France to secure this object was to employ her secret emissaries in spreading dissatisfaction among the British colonists; and the effects produced by her machinations were precisely such as she had intended and expected. The disposition of the inhabitants of North America began gradually to alter from that warmth of attachment to the mother country which had so particularly characterised them,

They began to view her rather in the light of a sovereign than that of a parent, and to examine with a scrupulous nicety, the nature of those ties that rendered them parts of her empire.

The national debt of Great Britain had been much increased by the late war; a multitude of new taxes were levied at home, and as the quarrel originated on account of the colonies, and as they derived the principal advantages from the peace of 1763, it was thought equitable that they should contribute to the common exigencies.

In March 1764, a bill was passed in the British Parliament, laying heavy duties on all articles imported into the colonies from the French and other islands of the West Indies, and ordering those duties to be paid in specie into the exchequer of Great Britain.ª In the same session another bill was passed, to restrain the currency of paper money in the Colonies.

These acts of the English legislature excited the surprise and displeasure of the North Americans. They sent warm and energetic remonstrances to the mother country, and laid every argument before the ministry that ingenuity could suggest, but in vain. As they had hitherto furnished their contingent in men and money, by the authority of their representatives in the colonial assemblies, they asserted, that not being represented in the British parliament, it could have no right to tax them. Finding, however, that all their arguments were ineffectual to remove their grievances, they formed associations to prevent the use of British manufactures, till they should obtain redress.

The animosity of the colonists was further increased by the advice which they received in 1765, that an act was passed in the British parliament, to establish stamp duties in America, similar to those in Great Britain.

The General Assembly of Virginia was the first that openly declared against the right of Britain to lay taxes

B

on America. Of this assembly Washington was a member. He most zealously opposed what he considered an encroachment on the liberties of his countrymen. Upon reading the resolutions which were then passed in that assembly, the boldness and novelty affected one of the members to such a degree, that he cried out, " Treason !" " Treason !"

These Resolutions were nevertheless well received by the people, and immediately forwarded to the other provinces. They circulated extensively, and gave a spring to all the discontented. Till they appeared, most were of opinion, that the act would be quietly adopted. Murmurs indeed were common, but they seemed to be such as would die away. The countenance of so respectable a colony as Virginia, confirmed the wavering, and emboldened the timid. Opposition to the stamp act, from that period, assumed a bolder face, and the flame spread from breast to breast, till the conflagration became general. In the mean time, the minds of the Americans underwent a total transformation. Instead of their late peaceable and steady attachment to the British nation, they were daily advancing to the opposite extreme. A new mode of displaying resentment against the friends of the stamp act began in Massachusetts, and was followed by other colonies. About this time a few gentlemen hung out on the limb of a large tree towards the entrance of Boston, two effigies, one designed for the stamp master and the other for a jack boot, with an head and horns peeping out at the top. Great numbers both from town and country came to see them. A spirit of enthusiasm was diffused among the spectators. In the evening the whole was cut down and carried in procession, shouting " Liberty and property for ever : no stamps.". They next pulled down a new building lately erected by Mr. Oliver, chief justice of the province ; they then went to his house, before which they beheaded his effigy, and at the same time broke his windows. Eleven days after similar violence was repeated. The mob attacked the house of Mr. William Story, deputy register of the court of admiralty, broke his windows, forced into his dwelling house, destroyed the books and files belonging to the said court, and ruined a great part of his furniture. They next proceeded to the house of Benjamin Hallowel, comptroller of the customs, where they repeated similar excesses, and drank and destroyed his liquors. They afterwards proceeded to the house of the governor, Mr. Hutchinson, and soon demolished it. They carried off his plate, furniture, and apparel, scattered or destroyed letters and other curious and useful papers, which for thirty years he had been collecting.

Similar disturbances broke out in the adjacent colonies nearly about the same time. On the 27th August, 1765, the people of Newport, in Rhode Island, exhibited three effigies, intended for Messieurs Howard, Moffat, and Johnson, in a cart, with halters about their necks, and after hanging them on a gallows for some time, cut them down, and burnt them amidst the acclamations of thousands. On the day following, the people collected at the house of Mr. Martin Howard, a lawyer, who had written in defence of the right of parliament to tax the Americans, and demolished every thing that belonged to it. They proceeded to Dr. Moffat's, who in conversation had supported the same right, and made a similar devastation of his property.

In Connecticut they exhibited effigies in sundry places, and afterwards committed them to the flames.

In New York, the stamp master having resigned, the stamp papers were taken into Fort George, by lieutenant governor Colden. The people disliking his political sentiments, broke open his stable, took out his coach, and carried it in triumph through the principal streets to the gallows. On one end of this they suspended the effigy of the lieutenant governor, having in his right hand a stamped bill of lading, and in the other a figure of the devil. After some time they carried the apparatus to the gate of the fort, and from thence to the bowling green, under the muzzles of the guns and burned the whole amid the acclamations of many thousands. They went thence to Major James's house, stripped it of every article, and consumed the whole, because he was a friend to the stamp act.

The next evening the mob re-assembled, and insisted on the lieutenant governor delivering the stamped papers into their hands, and threatened in case of a refusal to take them by force. After some negociation, it was agreed that they should be delivered to the corporation, and they were deposited in the city hall. Ten boxes of the same, which came by another conveyance, were burned.

When the ship which brought the stamp papers to Philadelphia, first appeared round Gloucester Point, all the vessels in the harbour hoisted their colours half mast high; the bells were rung muffled till evening, and every countenance added to the appearance of sincere mourning.

About two months before this, the expediency of calling a continental congress, to be composed of deputies from each of the provinces, had occurred to the people of Massachusetts. The assembly of that province passed a resolution in favour of that measure, and fixed on New York as the place, and the second Tuesday of October as the time for holding the same. Soon after they sent circular letters to the speakers of the several assemblies, requesting their concurrence. This was the first Congress held in North America.

While a variety of methods were adopted to oppose the stamp act, the first of November on which it was to commence its operation approached. This in Boston was ushered in by a funeral tolling of bells. Many shops and stores were shut. The effigies of several persons were carried about the streets in public derision, and then torn in pieces by the enraged populace.

On the same day at Portsmouth, in New Hampshire, the morning was ushered in with tolling all the bells in the town. In the course of the day, notice was given to the people to attend a funeral. A coffin neatly ornamented, and inscribed with the word "Liberty," in large letters, was carried to the grave. The funeral procession began from the state house, attended with two unbraced drums, while the inhabitants who followed the coffin were in motion, minute guns were fired and continued till the coffin arrived ät the place of interment: an oration in favour of the deceased was then pronounced. It was scarcely ended before the coffin was taken up, it having been perceived that some remains of life were left, at which the inscription was immediately altered to "Liberty revived." The bells immediately exchanged their melancholy for a joyful sound, and satisfaction appeared in every countenance.

In Maryland the effigy of the stamp master, on one side of which was written, "Tyranny," on the other "Oppression," and across the breast, "D—n my country, I'll get money," was carried through the streets, from the goal to the whipping post, and from thence to the pillory. After suffering many indignities, it was first hanged and then burned.

In consequence of a petition from the new formed congress to the king and both houses of parliament, the stamp act was repealed ;* to the universal joy of the

* In the course of the debate, Lord Chatham rose and with an animation which no art or study can imitate, spontaneously flowing from the consciousness of great talents, delivered his opinion on the present situation of affairs in America ; concluding

colonists, and the general satisfaction of the English, whose manufactures had suffered a considerable depression in consequence of the American associations against their importation.

But the parliament by repealing the stamp act, did not relinquish the ideas of their right to tax the colonies, and the bill for laying a duty on tea, paper, painters' colours and glass, was passed, and sent to America in 1768. This act occasioned new discontents in the colonies, especially at Boston; and though parliament thought proper in 1770 to take off those duties, except three pence a pound on tea, yet even this trifling impost, kept alive the jealousy of the colonists, who denied the supremacy of the British legislature. The troops quartered in Boston were another cause of offence to the inhabitants, and on all occasions they manifested an inclination to quarrel with men whom they considered inimical to their liberties.

Reciprocal insults soured the tempers, and mutual injuries embittered the minds of the opposite parties; besides some fiery spirits who thought it an indignity to have troops quartered among them, were constantly exciting the town's people to quarrel with the soldiers.*

with these words, " Let affection be the only bond of coercion. The system of policy I would earnestly exhort Great Britain to adopt, in relation to America, is happily expressed in the words of a favourite poet :

Be to her faults a little blind,
Be to her virtues very kind ;
Let all her ways be unconfin'd,
And clap your padlock on her mind.—PRIOR.

Upon the whole, I will beg leave to tell the house in a few words, what is really my opinion. It is, That the stamp act be repealed, *absolutely, totally,* and *immediately*."

* Lord Chatham's state of health during the two preceding sessions, had precluded him from making any considerable parliamentary exertions, and he had rarely attended the house on any occasion, but, finding himself at this period somewhat relieved from the pressure of his complaint, he took the opportunity

In the beginning of March 1770, a quarrel between the military and the townsmen of Boston took place, more serious than any of those which had preceded it. A private of the 29th regiment, passing early on a Saturday morning along a public rope walk, was provoked by insulting words to engage a party of his comrades to attack the rope makers. The battle being indecisive, it was determined to fight it out on the Monday following. The populace being in the interim fully apprised of the intended

on the third reading of the bill, for quartering soldiers in America, to lay before the house and the public, his thoughts on it, and on American affairs in general, in a speech worthy of his distinguished talents and illustrious reputation. "If," said he, "my lords, we take a transient view of those motives which induced the ancestors of our fellow subjects in America, to leave their native country, to encounter the innumerable difficulties of the unexplored regions of the western world, our astonishment at the present conduct of their descendants will naturally subside. There was no corner of the globe to which they would not have fled, rather than to submit to the slavish and tyrannical spirit which prevailed at that period in their native country; and viewing them in their originally forlorn, and now flourishing state, they may be cited as illustrious instances to shew what great exertions mankind will naturally make, when left to the free exercise of their own powers. Notwithstanding my intention to give my hearty negative to the question now before you, I condemn, my lords, in the severest manner, the turbulent and unwarrantable conduct of the Americans in some instances, particularly in the late riots of Boston." And in the conclusion of his speech, he said, "Pass then, my lords, instead of these harsh and severe edicts, an amnesty over their errors; by measures of lenity and affection allure them to their duty; act the part of a generous and forgiving parent. A period may arrive when this parent may stand in need of every assistance she can receive from a grateful and affectionate offspring. The welfare of this country, my lords, has ever been my greatest joy, and under all the vicissitudes of my life, has afforded me the most pleasing consolation. Should the all disposing hand of Providence prevent me from contributing my poor and feeble aid in the day of her distress, my prayers shall be ever for her prosperity :—" Length of days be in her right hand, and in her left hand, riches and honor! May her ways be ways of pleasantness, and all her paths be peace!"

encounter, assembled in great numbers, armed with clubs
and other weapons, at the time appointed; the bells also
ringing an alarum, and violent clamours of " town-
born, turn out," being heard in all parts of the city.
The mob directed its course to Murray's Barracks,
and dared the soldiery, by very offensive language, to
combat, at the same time pelting them with snow-balls,
covering stones: at length retiring from the barracks,
the populace were addressed in the street, by " a tall
large man, in a red cloak and a white wig;" and after
listening for some minutes to his harangue with great
attention, they exclaimed with shouts and huzzas " for
the main guard!" for which they immediately began
their route in different divisions. Captain Preston,
the officer on duty, on the appearance of the frantic
multitude, who with oaths and execrations pressed in,
upon the soldiers, advancing to the very points of
the bayonets, endeavoured by every effort to restrain
the soldiers from violence. But a party of the most furious
of the populace, in sailors habits, struck the guns down
with their clubs, and a blow was aimed by one of
them at Captain Preston. On which a confused noise
of " fire!" was heard, and seven pieces were discharged,
seven persons were killed and wounded. The town was
immediately in commotion and nothing but the timely
retreat of the troops, and the expostulation of the
Governor prevented the people from proceeding to
open hostilities. A few days after the whole province
of Massachusetts rose in arms, and the soldiers
were obliged to retire to Castle William for protection.
On the removal of the troops, the ferment began to
subside. Captain Preston, who commanded the main
guard, with the seven soldiers who fired, were committed
to Jail ; but after a full and fair trial, were, by a verdict
worthy of the highest praise, honorably acquitted : two
only excepted, who were found guilty of man slaughter.

Mr. Quincy and Mr. J. Adams,* counsel for the prisoners, who were themselves warm partisans of America, exerted their utmost ability in their defence. " We must," said one of these gentlemen, addressing the jury, " steel ourselves against prepossessions, which contaminate the fountain of justice. To your candor and impartiality I submit the prisoners and their cause. The LAW, in all vicissitudes of government, fluctuations of passion, or flights of enthusiasm, will preserve a steady undeviating course. ´ To use the words of a patriot, a hero, a martyr to liberty, ALGERNON SIDNEY, 'tis *mens sine affectu;* without regard to persons it commands that which is good, and it punishes that which is evil; it is deaf, inexorable, inflexible. On the one hand, it is exorable to the cries and lamentations of the prisoners; on the other, it is deaf, deaf as an adder, to the clamours of the populace."

During the session of the Massachusetts assembly, in the summer of 1773, a discovery was made which added fresh fuel to the flame long since kindled in that province. The celebrated Dr. Franklin, deputy post master general of America, and agent of the house of representatives in Boston, had by some unknown means when in London, acquired possession of certain letters, written in confidence, by governor Hutchinson, and lieutenant governor Oliver, to some of their friends and correspondents´ in England, in which they expressed themselves very freely on the situation of affairs in America, and their sentiments were such as might reasonably be expected from their local situation: they saw that eloquent orators, were successfully employed to preserve the remembrance of every· disagreeable occurrence which had happened between the soldiers and the inhabitants. In those in

* Afterwards member of the American Congress.

C·

flammatory addresses, the blessings of liberty; the horrors of slavery; the dangers of a standing army; the rights of the colonies; and a variety of such topics were presented to the public view, under the most pleasing and alarming forms: these addresses administered fuel to the fire already kindled, and kept it burning with an incessant flame.* The governor and lieutenant governor were men very respectable in their private character, and viewing these transactions passing before them, in their zeal for the re-establishment of order and tranquillity, they recommended that government should adopt more vigorous measures in support of its authority, which they beheld every day more and more disregarded.

Those letters were, by a licence which cannot be justified, even though prompted by motives the most patriotic, transmitted by Dr. Franklin to his friends at Boston, upon whom they made an impression much easier to conceive than to describe.

The assembly of Boston, thrown into a violent flame by the reading of those letters, unanimously resolved to petition the king to remove general Hutchinson and the lieutenant governor Oliver, for ever from the government of the province.

The petition being transmitted to the agent of the assembly, Dr. Franklin, was by him delivered to lord Dartmouth: and on its being presented to the king, his majesty signified his pleasure that it should be laid before him in council. Dr. Franklin was summoned in his official capacity as agent of the province

---

* These extravagant and exaggerated addresses are a most striking evidence of that diseased and dangerous state of the public mind, which could prompt these effusions of enthusiastic zeal, by which a resentment, scarcely short of phrenzy, was excited throughout America. All seemed to feel the influence of " the madding hour."

in support of the petition, Mr. Wedderburn, afterwards lord Loughborough, and chancellor of Great Britain, appearing as council for the defendants. "Dr. Franklin," said Mr. Wedderburn, "stands in the light of the *first mover* and *prime conductor* of this whole contrivance against his majesty's two governors: and having by the help of his own special confidents and party leaders, first made the assembly *his* agent, in carrying on his own secret designs, he now appears before your lordships to give the finishing stroke to the work of his own hands. How these letters came into the possession of any one but the right owners, is a mystery for Dr. Franklin to explain. Your lordships know the train of mischiefs which followed the concealment.*

After they had been left for five months to have their full operation, at length comes out a letter, which it is impossible to read without horror, expressive of the coolest and most deliberate malevolence. My lords, what poetic fiction only had penned for the breast of a cruel African, Dr. Franklin has realized and transcribed from his own—His, too, is the language of a *Zanga.*

——Know then 'twas I,
I forged the letter, I disposed the picture :
I hated, I despised, and I destroy.

And he now appears before your lordships, wrapped up in impenetrable secrecy, to support a charge against his majesty's governor and lieutenant governor, and expects that your lordships should advise punishing them on account of certain letters which he will not

* In consequence of the transmission of these letters, a duel was fought between Mr. Wheatly, brother to the correspondent of the two governors, and his friend Mr. Temple, who mutually suspected each other of being accessary to the communication of them, and in this rencounter Mr. Wheatly was dangerously wounded.

produce, and which he dares not tell how he obtained. These are the lessons taught in Dr. Franklin's school of politics.* With regard to his constituents, the factious leaders at Boston, who make this complaint against their governors, if the relating of their evil doings be criminal, and tending to alienate his majesty's affections, must not the doing of them be more so? Yet now they ask that his majesty will gratify and reward them for doing these things, and that he will punish the governors for relating them, because they are so very bad, that it cannot but offend his majesty to hear of them."

The disputes between Great Britain and her colonies had now existed above ten years, with intervals of tranquillity. The reservation of the duty on tea, the stationing a standing army in Massachusetts, the continuance of a board of commissioners in Boston, and the appointing the governors and judges of the province independent of the people, were the causes of that irritation which pervaded all ranks of the community.

The American controversy was now recommenced, in consequence of tea being sent to the colonies by the East India company. The Americans took measures to prevent the landing of the tea. An universal spirit of opposition animated the colonists from New Hampshire to Georgia; and the province of Massachusetts distinguished itself by the most violent and

* Dr. Franklin was one of the first who employed his pen in the cause of America. Two pieces of his had about this time attracted a large share of public attention, and had an extensive influence in America. The one purported to be an edict from the King of Prussia, for taxing the inhabitants of Great Britain, as descendants of emigrants from his dominions. The other was entitled "Rules for reducing a great empire to a small one." In both of these he endeavoured to expose the claims of Great Britain, and the proceedings of the British ministry with the severity of pungent satire. These publications had a tendency of inflaming the Americans more and more against the mother country.

decisive proceedings. Three ships from England, freighted with tea; lay in the harbour of Boston; and the townsmen resolved to destroy it rather than suffer it to be landed. For this purpose a number of men disguised like Mohawk Indians, on the 18th December 1773, entered the ships, and threw overboard three hundred and forty-two chests of tea, being the whole of their cargoes.

The British government finding themselves every where insulted and despised, resolved to enforce their authority, and as Boston had been the principal scene of outrage, it was determined to punish that town in an exemplary manner. On the 25th of March, 1774, an act was passed, called the Boston Port Bill, " to discontinue the landing and discharging, lading and shipping, of goods, wares, and merchandizes, at the town of Boston or within the harbour."

The news of the bill was received by the Bostonians with the most extravagant tokens of resentment, and during the ferment the new Governor, General Gage, arrived from England. This gentleman had been appointed on account of his being an officer of reputation, and a man esteemed by the Americans, among whom he had resided many years.

The first official act of his government was the removal of the assembly to Salem, a town seventeen miles distant from Boston.

Virginia again took the lead in a public avowal of its sentiments, and recommended to the colonies to appoint a congress of delegates, to deliberate on the critical state of their affairs.

Mean while the Bostonians were not inactive. They framed an agreement, which they called a solemn *league* and *covenant*, by which the subscribers engaged in the most sacred manner, " to discontinue all commercial intercourse with Great Britain till the late obnoxious acts were repealed, and the colony of Massachusetts restored to its chartered rights. Resolutions of a similar nature were entered into by the other provinces, and when general Gage attempted to counteract the covenant by a proclamation, the Americans retorted by insisting that the law allowed subjects to associate, in order to obtain redress of their grievances.

Within little more than a month after the news of the Boston Port Bill reached America, it was communicated from state to sate ; and a flame of discontent was kindled in almost every breast, through the widely extended provinces.

His majesty's armed schooner, the Gaspee, having been stationed in Rhode Island to prevent the smuggling, for which that place was notorious, the vigilance of the officer who commanded that vessel, so enraged the people, that they boarded her at midnight, to the number of two hundred armed men, and after wounding him; and forcing him and his people to go on shore, concluded this daring exploit by burning the schooner. Though a reward of five hundred pounds, together with a pardon, if claimed by an accomplice, was offered by a proclamation for the discovering and apprehending any of the persons concerned in the atrocious act, no effectual discovery could be made.

- In the month of September 1774, the general congress of all the colonies met at Philadelphia. That body consisted of fifty-one delegates, chosen by the representatives of each province.

On the meeting of this congress, they chose Peyton Randolph their president, and Charles Thompson their secretary. The first act of congress was their approbation of the conduct of the Bostonians, and an exhortation to them to persevere in their opposition to government till the restoration of their charter. They avowed their allegiance to his Majesty; and drew up a petition in which they entreated him to grant them peace, liberty, and safety. After several resolutions tending to recommend unanimity to the provinces, and after having resolved that another congress should meet in Philadelphia, on the 10th of May following, if their grievances should not be redressed, they recommended to the people the speedy nomination of new delegates, and then separated.

To relieve the distresses of the people of Boston, liberal collections were made throughout the colonies, and forwarded for the supply of their immediate distresses. Domestic manufactures were encouraged, that the wants of the inhabitants from the non importation act might be diminished, and the greatest zeal was discovered by a large majority of the people, to comply with the determinations of the new made congress.

The terms Whigs and Tories, for want of a better, were now introduced in America, as the distinguishing names of parties. By the former were meant those who were for making a common cause with Boston, and supporting the colonies in their oppositions to the claims of the British government. By the latter, those who condemned the turbulent and unwarrantable conduct of their countrymen, particularly in the late riots of Boston.

Mean while reinforcements of British troops arrived in Boston, which increased the general disaffection to such a degree, that the people were ready to rise at a moment's warning. From inconsiderable causes love was changed into suspicion, that gradually ripened into ill will, and soon ended in hostility. The Americans now began seriously to prepare for war, embodied and trained their militia. The sound of drums and fifes every where saluted the ear. Parents and children, husbands and lovers, the young and the old, were possessed of the same martial spirit. Nothing was to be seen or heard of, but the purchasing of arms and ammunition, casting of balls, and the making of all those preparations, which testify the most immediate danger and determined re-, sistance ; and to render themselves independent of, foreigners for the supply of military stores, they erected mills and manufactures for gunpowder, both in Philadelphia and Virginia.

These hostile preparations which were daily made through the province, induced General Gage to fortify that neck of land which joins Boston to the main land at Roxbury.

He also seized upon the powder which was lodged in the arsenals at Cambridge and Charlestown. This excited a most violent and universal ferment ; several thousands of people assembled at Cambridge, and it was with difficulty they were restrained from marching directly to Boston, to demand a delivery of the powder, with a resolution in case of a refusal to attack the British troops.

The people thus assembled, proceeded to lieutenant governor Oliver's house, and to the houses of several of the new counsellors, and obliged them to resign, and to declare that they would no more act under the laws lately enacted. In less than twenty-four hours there were upwards of thirty thousand men in arms, who marched towards Boston. Other risings of the people took place in different parts of the country, and their violence was such, that in a short time the new counsellors, the commissioners of the customs, and all who had taken an active part in favor of Great Britain, were obliged to screen themselves in Boston. Even in Boston itself the company of cadets, consisting wholly of gentlemen who used to attend the governor, disbanded themselves, and returned the standard he had, (as was the custom,) presented them with on his accession to the government. This was occasioned by his having deprived the celebrated John Hancock, afterwards president of the congress, of his commission as colonel of the cadets.

About this time a meeting was held of the principal inhabitants of the towns adjacent to Boston. The purport of this, was publickly to renounce all obedience to the late acts of parliament, and to form an engagement to indemnify such as should be prosecuted on that account. All ranks and degrees of men were exhorted to learn the use of arms, and the receivers of the public revenues were ordered not to deliver it into the treasury, but retain it in their own hands, till the constitution should be restored, or a provincial congress dispose of it otherwise.

The awful moment now approached which was to involve Great Britain and her colonies in all the horrors of a civil war. In February, 1775, the provincial congress of Massachusetts met at Cambridge, several military institutions for the protection of the province were established, among the most remarkable of which was that of the *minute* men. A number of the most active and expert of the New England militia were selected, who were to be under obligations to turn out at a minute's warning, from which perpetual vigilance they derived their title. Jedediah Pribble, Artemus Ward, and Seth Pomeroy, were elected general officers to command those minute men, in case they should be called out to action.

Matters had now proceeded so far, that every idea of reconciliation with Great Britain was lost. The Americans, therefore, without ceremony, began to seize on the military stores and ammunition belonging to government. They first commenced at New Port, in Rhode Island, where the inhabitants carried off forty pieces of cannon, appointed for the protection of that place; and on being asked the reason of this proceeding, they replied that the people had seized them lest they should be made use of against themselves. After this, the assembly met, and resolved that ammunition and warlike stores should be purchased with the public money.

D

CHAP. II.

Skirmish at Lexington. Battle of Bunker's Hill. Washington appointed Commander in Chief of the American Army. Sketch of his Life. His Birth and Education. Appointed Adjutant General of the Virginia Militia. Defeated by the French. Aid-de-Camp to General Braddock. Covers the Retreat of the British Army. Appointed Commander of the Provincial Troops in Virginia. Marries. Settles at Mount Vernon. Appointed a Magistrate, a Member of the Assembly, and a Judge of the Court of Virginia.

GENERAL Gage having been informed that a large quantity of military stores were collected at Concord, about twenty miles from Boston, sent a detachment to that piace, under the command of colonel Smith and major Pitcairn ; the general wished to prevent hostilities by depriving the Americans of the means necessary for carrying on war. With this view he determined to destroy the stores, which he knew were collected for the support of a provincial army. Wishing to accomplish this without bloodshed, he took every precaution to effect it by surprise, and, without alarming the country. On the 18th of April, 1775, at eleven o'clock at night, the flank companies embarked at the common, landed at Phipps's farm, and proceeded with the utmost silence ; every person they met was secured, in order to prevent the country from being alarmed ; but notwithstanding these precautions, they soon found, by the continual firing of guns and ringing of bells, that they were discovered by the minute men. About five o'clock the next morning the British troops had reached Lexington, fifteen miles from Boston : here the militia and minute men were assembled on the green in order to oppose the British troops. Major Pitcairn, who commanded the advance guard, rode forward, and called out to them to disperse, but they still continued in a body.

At this moment some shots were fired at the British troops, from a house in that neighbourhood. The advance guard, finding they were fired upon, returned the fire, and three or four of the militia were killed on the green. The troops then proceeded to Concord, where they destroyed the stores, and engaged in a skirmish with the provincials, in which many were killed on both sides.

In the return of the British troops from Concord to Lexington, a space of six miles, they were pursued with the utmost fury by the Americans, who fired at them from behind stone walls, high enough to cover the assailants from the fire of men who were marching with the greatest expedition. At Lexington, the British troops were joined by a detachment under Lord Percy, with two field pieces. As the cannon were managed with the greatest skill and activity, they awed the Americans, and kept them at a greater distance, but they continued a constant, though irregular and scattered fire. The close firing from behind the walls, by good marksmen, galled the British troops, very much. A little after sun set the royal army reached Bunker's hill, worn down with excessive fatigue, having marched that day near forty miles. On the next day they crossed Charlestown ferry, and returned to Boston. The British had sixty five killed, and one hundred and eighty wounded. Among the latter were colonel

Smith and several other British officers.   The Americans had fifty killed and thirty-eight wounded.

By the nearest calculation that can be made, there were from one thousand eight hundred to two thousand troops on this service, being about half the force that was then stationed at Boston.   The event sufficiently showed how ill informed those were who had so often asserted at home, that a regiment or two could force their way, through any part of the continent, and that the very sight of a grenadier's cap, would be sufficient to put an American army to flight.

This affair at Lexington animated the courage of the Americans to the highest degree, insomuch that in a few days their army amounted to twenty thousand men. This formidable body of troops were joined by a corps from Connecticut, under general Putman, a veteran officer. ...The Americans now completely blockaded the town of Boston, which however was so strongly fortified by general Gage, that they did not venture to attack it. Meanwhile congress met at Philadelphia, on the 10th of May, 1775, and John Hancock was unanimously elected president.*

About the latter end of May, reinforcements of British troops from England arrived at Boston, under the command of generals Howe, Burgoyne, and Clinton, whose services in the preceding war had gained them great reputation. The town of Boston stands on a peninsula,

---

* This gentleman was born in the province of Massachusetts Bay, in which he enjoyed a very considerable fortune. From the first disturbance in America about the Stamp Act, he took a very active part in defence of what he considered to be the rights and liberties of his native country. Most of the addresses sent from America to England, originated from his pen. He was then in his thirty-eighth year, and was married to one of the most beautiful and accomplished ladies in America, who brought him a very considerable addition to his paternal fortune.

divided from Charlestown, by a river about the breadth
of the Thames, at London bridge. Eastward of Charlestown, there is an eminence called Bunker's Hill, which
commands the whole town of Boston. In the night
of the 16th of June, the Americans took possession of
this place, and worked with such diligence and silence, that before the dawn they had nearly com-
pleated a redoubt and strong entrenchment, which extended half a mile. When they were discovered by the
British troops, they were plied with an incessant cannonade from the ships and floating batteries, besides
the cannon that could reach the place from Boston.
The Americans however continued their work, which
they completed about noon, when a considerable body
of infantry, consisting of one battalion of marines, ten
companies of grenadiers, as many of light infantry,
and the 5th, 38th, 43d, 47th, and 52d battalions, with
proper artillery, amounting in the whole to two thousand men, were landed at the foot of Bunker's hill,
under the command of major general Howe, and brigadier
general Pigot, the former being appointed to attack
the lines, and the latter the redoubt. The British
troops ascended the hill with the greatest intrepidity,
but on their approach to the entrenchments, they were
received with a discharge of cannon and musquetry,
that poured down a full half hour upon them like a
torrent. The execution it did was terrible, insomuch,
that some of the oldest officers and soldiers, declared
it was the hottest service they had ever seen. General
Howe, whose fortitude was remarkable on this trying
occasion, stood for a few moments almost alone, the
greatest part of the officers and soldiers, who stood
near his person, being either killed or wounded. His
coolness, firmness, and presence of mind, on this occasion cannot be too much applauded. It fully answered
all the ideas, so generally entertained of the courage

of his family.* While these operations were going on at the breast work and redoubt, the British light infantry, commanded by general Pigot, was engaged with the Americans on the left, in order that they might take their line in flank.

Though they exhibited the most undaunted courage, they met with an opposition which called for its greatest exertions. The Americans here reserved their

---

* About seventeen years before this, general Howe's brother was killed before the French lines at Ticonderago. This gallant officer, colonel Howe, from the moment he landed in America, had conformed, and made his regiment conform to the kind of service which the country required. He did not suffer any under his command to encumber themselves with superfluous baggage; he himself set the example and shared like a common soldier. The first to encounter danger, to endure hunger, to support fatigue. Rigid in his discipline, but easy in his manners, his officers and soldiers readily obeyed the commander, because they loved the man. General Abercrombie under whose command he acted, in writing his dispatches to government, says: " But this success cost us very dear, not as to the loss of numbers, for we had only two officers killed, but as to consequence, his lordship (colonel Howe) being the first man that fell; and as he was very deservedly, universally beloved and respected throughout the whole army, it is easy to conceive the grief and consternation his untimely fall occasioned; for my part, I cannot help owning that I feel it most heavily, and lament him as sincerely."

Soon after the news of Lord Howe's death arrived in England, the following advertisement appeared in the public papers:

" *To the Gentlemen, Clergy, Freeholders, &c. of the Town and County of Nottingham.*

" As Lord Howe is now absent upon the public service, and lieutenant-colonel Howe is with his regiment at Louisbourg, it rests upon me to beg the favour of your votes and interest, that lieutenant-colonel Howe may supply the place of his late brother, as your representative in parliament.

Permit me, therefore, to implore the protection of every one of you, as the mother of him whose life has been lost in the service of his country.

Albemarle-street,
September 14, 1758.   " CHARLOTTE HOWE."

An application worthy of a Roman matron.

fire till the British troops were near, and then poured it upon the light infantry, with such an incessant stream, and in so true a direction, as mowed down their ranks, and threw our troops into disorder. At this critical moment general Clinton, who arrived from Boston during the engagement, by a happy manœuvre rallied the troops almost instantaneously, and brought them again to the charge: the works were now attacked with such fury, that the Americans were driven beyond the Neck that leads to Charlestown. The British troops having been annoyed by the enemy from the houses of that town, set it on fire, and in a short time the whole, consisting of about five hundred buildings, chiefly of wood, was in one great blaze. The lofty steeple of the meeting-house formed a pyramid of fire, above the rest, and struck the astonished eyes of numerous beholders with a magnificent but dreadful spectacle; thousands both within and without Boston were anxious spectators of this awful scene. In the town of Boston the heights of every kind were covered with citizens, and such of the British troops as were not on duty.

It was greatly dreaded by the Americans that the British troops would push the advantage they had gained, and march immediately to their head-quarters at Cambridge. The immediate advance of the king's troops into Cambridge, would, undoubtedly, at this critical period, have been productive of various and important advantages. The appearance of the royal forces, after such a contest would have animated their friends, discouraged their enemies, and continued the confusion, and dispersion of the American army. But they advanced no farther than Bunker's Hill. There they threw up works for their own security. The provincials did the same, on Prospect Hill, in front of them. Both were guarding against an attack, and both were in a bad condition to receive one.

In this short engagement the carnage was very great, in proportion to the number of troops. The loss of the British army amounted, in killed and wounded to one thousand and fifty-four, including eighty-nine officers. The battle of Quebec, in 1759, which gave Great Britain the province of Canada, was not so destructive to British officers as the battle of Bunker's Hill. That the officers suffered so much, must be imputed to their being aimed at. The generality of the Americans were good marksmen; the whole of their previous military knowledge had been derived from hunting, and the ordinary amusements of sportsmen. The dexterity which by long habit they had acquired in hitting beasts, birds, and marks, was fatally applied to the destruction of our officers. From their fall much confusion was expected; they were, therefore, particularly singled out.

Among those who were more generally regretted upon this occasion were lieutenant colonel Abercrombie, and major Pitcairn of the marines, majors Williams and Spendlove, the last of whom died of his wounds some time after the action. These brave officers sealed their lives with such distinguished honour as to render their loss the more sensibly felt. There was scarcely a single officer who had not some opportunity of signalizing himself; the generals and field officers used the most extraordinary exertions.

According to the American account their loss did not exceed five hundred men, beside all their cannon.

This disparity of numbers may be accounted for, by their having fought behind intrenchments, which sheltered them from the fire of the British troops, and whence their marksmen could take aim with precision.

Our troops justly claimed this dear bought victory. The spirited conduct of the British officers merited and obtained great applause. On the American side, they particularly regretted the death of General Warren. Considering, however, that this was the first time they had been in actual service, it must be owned that they behaved with great resolution and bravery, and by no means merited the appellation of *cowards*, with which they were so often branded in England.*

---

* The following letter was written by a British soldier to his wife in England, the day after this memorable battle.

" Yesterday we had a bloody and obsinate fight, in which many were killed, and numbers wounded. 1 have received two balls, one in my groin, and the other near the breast. I am now so weak with the loss of blood, that I can hardly dictate these few lines, as the last tribute of my unchangeable love to you. The surgeons inform me, that three hours will be the utmost I can survive. Alas, too true was the dire presage that brooded in my mind, that we should never meet again on this side an awful eternity.

" During our passage from England to America I gave myself up to read the bible, as it was the only book I was possessed of. The Almighty Parent of mankind was pleased to draw my heart to him, by the sweet attraction of his grace; and at the same time to enlighten my mind. There was in our regiment a corporal, whose name was Pierce; a pious man; I inquired after him, and we soon contracted a strong friendship: He was pleased to explain to me the amazing love of God, in giving his son Jesus Christ to bleed and die for mankind. He condescended to unfold to me the mystery of salvation by faith, the nature of the new birth, and the great necessity of holiness of heart and life. In short, he became my spiritual father; and, under God, to him I owe all the good I am acquainted with.

" Soon after we landed, God was pleased to speak peace to my soul. Oh the bliss, the unutterable joy that I then felt through the blood of the Lamb! How did I long to tell all the world what Jesus had done for me! But how did I long, yea, burn, to have you to taste and know the love of God in Christ Jesus! I would have given all the world to have been with you, to have informed you of the pearl of great price. As we shall never meet more in this vale of tears, let me impose this last, this dying obligation upon you; and if ever I was dear to you, let me beg of you not to neglect the last advice of your departing husband. It is, that you give yourself up to God, read the Bible, and good books, and be often found among them who inquire after salvation,

E

During these transactions at Boston, congress continued to act with all the vigour which its constituents had expected. They resolved on the establishment

And the Lord shall guide you in his ways. O endeavour to bring up the dear little ones in the fear of God. Never fix your heart upon the vain and unsubstantial things of the world. Heaven and the love of God are the only things that demand our hearts, or at least are worthy of engrossing them.

"And you, my dear infants, though you have not the perfect knowledge of your worthless father, I beg of you to meet me in the realms of bliss. The God that blessed Jacob and Joseph shall bless you. Seek him and he will be found of you; call upon him, and he will hear and bless you. What has the world but sin and sorrow. The rich are oppressed with wealth; and the poor are groaning for the want of that which the others are burdened with. The men in power are afflicted with holding the reins, and guiding the helm; and the governed are oppressed with imaginary evils. The life of a soldier is blood and cruelty, and that of a sailor, is filled with dangers and deaths. A city life is full of confusion and strife; and that of the country is loaded with toil and labour. But the evil of all evils, flows from our own sinful nature. Wherever we are, we may be happy; we have the key to bliss in our own breasts. The world itself never yet made any one happy. God is the bliss and solace of a reasonable soul; and God is every where, and we have every where access to him. Learn then, my dear children, when you grow up, to seek your permanent happiness in God, through a crucified Redeemer.

"My dear wife, should the spirits of the departed have any knowledge of things here below, and at the same time, any intercourse with them, (though unseen,) how shall I rejoice to be thy guardian angel, to attend you, and smile to see you combat sin, conquer the world, and subdue the flesh. How shall I smile to meet you on the bright frontiers of heaven. These hands shall weave for you, the wreath triumphant! I first shall hail you welcome to your native mansions! I first shall guide you to the celestial city, and introduce you among the jubilant throng, who tread the streets of the New Jerusalem. I first will lead you to the sacred throne of our God, where we will together bow, transported at the feet of the ever adorable Jesus. Then, then, will we strike our melodious harps of gold, in the most exalted of an army, and a large paper currency for its support; and they nominated a general to the supreme command of their forces. Washington was by their unanimous vote appointed commander in chief.

I hope it will not be esteemed an unnecessary digression, to give some account of the life of this celebrated man.

In the year 1657, his grandfather together with several relatives, emigrated from England to America, and settled in the colony of Virginia, where by unremitting industry, they became opulent and respectable, and gave their name to the parish of Washington, in Westmoreland county. George Washington was born in Chotank, in the above mentioned county, on the 11th Feb. 1732. He received a private education, was initiated in the elements of religion, morality, and science, by a private tutor. In the tenth year of his age he lost his father, who died in 1742, and the patrimonial estate devolved to an elder brother. This young gentleman had been an officer in the colonial troops, sent on the expedition against Carthagena. On his return he called the family mansion, Mount Vernon, in honor of the British admiral of

strains of harmony and love. Then shall our love be consummated, refined and eternalized!

> "The world recedes, it disappears
> Heaven opens on my eyes, my ears
> With sounds seraphic ring:
> Lend, lend your wings, I mount, I fly!
> Oh! Grave where is thy victory?
> Oh Death! where is thy sting?"

More would I say, but life ebbs out apace, my tongue ceases to perform its office; bright angels stand round the gorey turf on which I lie, ready to escort me to the arms of my Jesus; bending saints reveal my shining crown, and beckon me away: yea, methinks, my Jesus bids me come. Adieu! Adieu! Dear Love.

" JOHN RANDON."

E 2

that name, and destined his brother George to serve in the navy.

Accordingly, in his fifteenth year, young Washington was entered as midshipman on board a British frigate, stationed on the coast of Virginia; he prepared to embark with all the alacrity of youth, but his nautical career was stopped by the interposition of maternal love. Ever obedient to an affectionate mother, young Washington relinquished his desire of going to sea; the energies of his mind were to be exerted on a more stable element.

He remained at home during four subsequent years, employed in useful and elegant studies with a pleasing alternation of business; and in the delightful fields and groves of Mount Vernon, he gradually attained a knowledge of agriculture. Rural avocations appear to have been his delight, at this early period of life; yet he afterwards convinced the world, that martial ardour animates the breast of the husbandman.

In the year 1751, he was appointed adjutant general of the Virginia militia; and in consequence of the death of his brother, the family mansion of Mount Vernon, together with a large estate, came into his possession. At this time the extensive boundaries and increasing population of the colony, made it expedient to form the militia corps into three divisions, and Washington in his twentieth year was appointed Major. He attended to his duty as an officer, with exemplary propriety and vigilance; was indefatigable in the discipline of the troops; and generally beloved, both by the officers and privates, for his mildness and generosity.

In the year 1753, the encroachments of the French upon the western boundaries of the British colonies, excited a general alarm in Virginia, insomuch that governor Dinwiddie deputed Washington to ascertain the truth of those rumours; he was also empowered to enter into a treaty with the Indians, and to remonstrate with the French, on the injustice of their proceedings. The distance to the French settlement was more than four hundred miles, and one half of the rout led through a wilderness, inhabited only by Indians. He, nevertheless, set out in an uncommonly severe season, attended only by one companion. From Winchester he proceeded on foot, with his provisions on his back. When he arrived and delivered his message, the French commandant refused to comply, and claimed the country as belonging to the king, his master, and declared that he should continue to seize, and send as prisoners to Canada, every Englishman that should attempt to trade on the Ohio, or any of its branches. Before major Washington returned, the Virginians had sent out workmen and materials to erect a fort at the conflux of the Ohio, and Monongahela. While they were engaged in this work, the French came upon them, drove them out of the country, and erected a regular fortification on the same spot. These spirited proceedings overset the schemes of the Ohio company, but its members both in England and America were too powerful to brook the disappointment. It was therefore resolved to instruct the colonies to oppose with arms the encroachments of the French, on the frontiers of Virginia. It was now necessary to increase the military establishment; and early in the spring 1754, a new regiment was raised, of which Professor Fry, of the college, was appointed colonel, and Washington, lieutenant colonel. Mr. Fry died soon after the regiment was embodied, and was succeeded by Washington, who paid unremitting attention to the discipline of this new corps. He established magazines of provisions and ammunition, and opened the roads to the frontiers in order to pre-occupy that important

post, at the confluence of the Monongahela and
Allegany rivers. His regiment was to have been reinforced by a detachment of regulars, from the southern
colonies, and a corps of provincials from North
Carolina and Maryland; but impelled by the urgency
of the occasion, he proceeded without the expected
succours in the month of May. When he ascended
the Laurel Hills, fifty miles distant from the place of
destination, his scouts brought him intelligence that
the enemy were in possession of the posts, and soon
afterwards his troops were attacked by a detachment of
the French, and after a severe conflict defeated, and
compelled to lay down their arms.

The conduct of Washington on this occasion was
censurable.; he ought to have waited for the necessary
reinforcements, a junction with whom would probably have
crowned his enterprise with success. His inexperience,
and the active ardour of a youthful mind, may afford
some palliation of his imprudence; but his rashness in
this instance was so different from his subsequent prudence, that probably this inauspicious commencement
of his military career was the origin of the circumspection which afterwards marked his conduct in a
successful defensive war.

In the summer of 1754, the French having built
several forts within the boundaries of the British settlements, an army of veterans was sent from France
to support those unjustifiable encroachments. In the
following year, general Braddock was sent to America,
at the head of two veteran regiments from Ireland,
to reduce the forts on the Ohio. On his arrival, he
was joined by the independent and provincial corps of
America; but when the army was ready to march, the
want of waggons for the conveyance of stores, had almost
proved an insurmountable obstacle to the expedition.
In this emergency, an active American stepped forward,

and removed the difficulty ; this was the celebrated
Benjamin Franklin, he exerted his influence so effectually with his countrymen, that in a short time he
collected one hundred and fifty waggons, which proved
an ample supply for the army.

As in consequence of a military regulation, " no
officer, who did not derive his commision from the king,
could command one who did," Washington resigned ;
but emulous to defend his country with distinguished
zeal, he voluntarily served under general Braddock, as
an extra aid de-camp. That general marched against
Fort du Quesne ; but soon after he crossed the river
Monongahela, the van division of his army was attacked by an ambuscade of French and Indians, and
totally defeated. The thickness of the woods prevented
both the European and provincial troops from being
able to defend themselves with effect ; they could neither keep their ranks, nor charge the enemy with the
bayonet, while the Indians, who were expert at bush
fighting, and were widely scattered, fired on them from
behind the trees, where they were concealed, and took
a fatal aim. Washington had cautioned general Braddock in vain ; his violent desire of conquest had made
him deaf to the voice of prudence ; he saw his error
when too late, and bravely perished in his endeavours
to save the division from destruction. The gallant,
but unfortunate general, had four horses shot under
him before he fell, and almost every officer whom
duty obliged to be on horseback, was either killed
or wounded, except Washington. Amid this carnage,
Washington, with great presence of mind, rallied the
troops, and at the head of a corps of grenadiers, covered the retreat of the division, and secured their
passage over the ford of Monongahela.

Anxious for the preservation of the army, and unmindful of the fatigues he had undergone, during a

sultry day in July, in which he had scarcely a moment óf rest, he hastened to concert measures with colonel Dunbar, who commanded the rear division which had not been engaged; Neither the wilderness, through which he was obliged to pass, the innumerable dangers that surrounded him in his progress, nor his exhausted state, could prevent him from pursuing the line of his duty. He travelled during the night acompanied by two guides, and reached the British camp in safety. Thus his perseverance and wisdom saved the residue of his troops. Colonel Dunbar now assumed the chief command, and with considerable difficulty effected a retreat, but was obliged to destroy his baggage, to prevent it from falling into the hands of the enemy.

Soon after this transaction, the regulation of rank which had been considered as a grievance by the colonial officers, was changed in consequence of a spirited remonstrance from Washington; and the governor of Virginia, rewarded the services of this brave officer by appointing him to the command of all the troops of the colony.

The natural energy of his mind was now called into action; and his thoughts were continually employed in forming new plans for the protection of the frontiers. In the year 1737, Washington was in Fort Edward, under the command of General Webb, when Monsieur Montcalm, the French general, advanced to take Fort William Henry, on Lake George. Washington having heard of the intended attack, and being apprehensive that lieutenant colonel Monro, who commanded at Fort William Henry, would not be strong enough to resist the French, eagerly interceded with his general to be sent with his regiment to the assistance of Monro, but his services were rejected, and the unfortunate commander forced to make the best terms he could with the French general, who afterwards in violation of the treaty that had been made, permitted the Indian savages to fall upon them, and strip them of every thing of value. The following detail of the massacre of the English troops at fort William Henry is thus related by Mr. Carver, then a captain in one of the provincial regiments.

" General Webb, who commanded the English army in North America, which was then encamped at Fort Edward, having intelligence that the French troops under M. Montcalm were making some movements towards Fort William Henry, he detached a corps of about fifteen hundred men, consisting of English and provincials, to strengthen the garrison." In this party the relator went as a volunteer among the latter.

" The apprehensions of the English general were not without foundation; for the day after their arrival they saw Lake George, to which it lies contiguous, covered with an immense number of boats; and in a few hours they found their lines attacked by the French general, who had just landed with eleven thousand regulars and Canadians, and two thousand Indians. Colonel Monro, a brave officer, commanded in the Fort, and had no more than two thousand three hundred men. With these he made a gallant defence, and probably would have been able at last to preserve the Fort, had he been properly supported, and permitted to continue his efforts. On every summons to surrender sent by the French general, who offered the most reasonable terms, his answer repeatedly was, that he yet found himself in a condition to repel the most vigorous attacks his besiegers were able to make; and if he thought his present force insufficient, he could soon be supplied with a greater number from the adjacent army.

" But the Colonel having acquainted General Webb with his situation, and desired he would send him some

F

fresh troops, the general dispatched a messenger to him with a letter, wherein he informed him that it was not in his power to assist him, and therefore gave him orders to surrender up the fort on the best terms he could procure. This packet fell into the hands of the French general, who immediately sent a flag of truce, desiring a conference with the governor.

" They accordingly met, attended only by a small guard, in the centre between the lines. When Montcalm told the colonel that he was come in person to demand possession of the fort, as it belonged to the king his master, the colonel replied, that he knew not how that could be ; nor should he surrender it up whilst it was in his power to defend it. The French general rejoined, at the same time delivering the packet into the colonel's hand, " By this authority do I make the requisition." The governor had no sooner read the contents of it, and was convinced that such were the orders of the Commander in Chief, and not to be disobeyed, than he hung his head in silence, and reluctantly entered into a negociation.

", In consideration of the gallant defence the garrison had made, they were to be permitted to march out with all the honours of war, to be allowed covered waggons to transport their baggage to Fort Edward, and 'a guard to protect them from the fury of the savages.

" The morning after the capitulation was signed, as soon as day broke, the whole garrison, now consisting of about two thousand men, besides women and children, were drawn up within the lines, and on the 'point of marching off, when a great number of the 'Indians gathered about, and began to plunder. The British troops at first were in hopes that this was their only view, and suffered them to proceed without 'opposition. Indeed it was not in their power to make 'any, had they been so inclined, for though they were permitted to carry off their arms, yet they were not allowed a single round of ammunition. In these hopes, however, they were disappointed, for presently some of them began to attack the sick and wounded, when such as were not able to crawl into the ranks, notwithstanding they endeavoured to avert the fury of their enemies, by their shrieks and groans, were soon dispatched.

" Here the English were fully in expectation that the disturbance would have concluded, and their little army began to move, but in a short time they saw the front division driven back, and discovered that they were entirely incircled by the savages; they expected every moment that the guard, which the French, by the articles of capitulation had agreed to allow them, would have arrived, and put an end to their apprehensions, but none appeared. The Indians now began to strip every one, without exception, of their arms and cloaths, and those who made the least resistance felt the weight of their tomahawks.

" Captain Carver happened to be in the rear division, but it was not long before he shared the fate of his companions. Three or four of the savages laid hold of him, and whilst some held their weapons over his head, the others soon disrobed him of his coat, waistcoat, hat, and buckles, omitting not to take from him what money he had in his pocket. As this was transacted close by the passage that led from the lines on to the plain, near which a French centinel was posted, he ran to him and claimed his protection; but he only called him an English dog, and thrust him with violence back again into the midst of the Indians.

" He now endeavoured to join a body of his own troops that were crowded together at some distance; but innumerable were the blows that were made at him,

with different weapons as he passed on; luckily, however, the savages were so close together, that they
could not strike at him without endangering each
other; notwithstanding which, one of them found means
to make a thrust at him with a spear, which grazed
his side, and from-another he received a wound, with
the same kind of weapon, in' his ankle. At length
he gained the spot where his countrymen stood, and
forced himself into the midst of them. But before he
got thus far out of the hands of the Indians, the collar and wristbands of his shirt were all that remained
of it, and his flesh was torn and scratched in many
places by their savage gripes.

" By this time the war hoop was given, and the Indians
began to murder those that were nearest to them without
distinction. It is not in the power of words to give any
tolerable idea of the horrid scene that now ensued; men,
women, and children, were dispatched in the most wanton
and cruel manner, and immediately scalped. Many of
these savages drank the blood of their victims, as it
flowed warm from the fatal wound.

" The English now perceived, though too late to avail
them, that they were to expect no relief from the French;
and that, contrary to the agreement they had so lately
signed, to allow a sufficient force to protect them from
these insults, they tacitly permitted them; for captain
Carver could plainly perceive the French officers walking
about at some distance, discoursing together with apparent
unconcern. An unprejudiced observer would be apt to
conclude, that a body of ten thousand christian troops,
most christian troops! had it in their power to prevent
the massacre from becoming so general. But whatever was
the-cause from which it proceeded the consequences of it
were dreadful, and not to be paralleled in modern history.

" As the circle in which captain Carver stood inclosed,
by this time was much thinned, and death seemed to be

approaching with hasty strides, it was proposed by some of the most resolute to make one vigorous effort, and endeavour to force their way through the savages, the only probable method of preserving their lives that now remained. This, however desperate, was resolved on, and about twenty of them sprung at once into the midst of them.

" In a moment they were all separated, and what was the fate of captain Carver's companions he could not learn till some months after, when he found that only six or seven of them effected their design. Intent only on his own hazardous situation, he endeavoured to make his way through his savage enemies, in the best manner possible. And he has often been since astonished, when he has recollected with what composure he took, as he did, every necessary step for his preservation. Some he over-turned, being at that time young and athletic, and others he passed by, dexterously avoiding their weapons ; till at last two very stout chiefs, as he could distinguish by their dress, whose strength he could not resist, laid hold of him by each arm, and began to force him through the croud.

" He now resigned himself to his fate, not doubting but that they intended to dispatch him, and then to satiate their vengeance with his blood, as he found they were hurrying him towards a retired swamp, that lay at some distance. But before they had got many yards, an English gentleman of some distinction, as he could discover by his breeches, the only covering he had on, which were of fine scarlet velvet, rushed close by them. One of the Indians instantly relin-quished his hold, and springing on this new object, endeavoured to seize him as his prey ; but the gentle-man being strong, threw him on the ground, and would probably have got away, had not he who held captain Carver's other arm, quitted him to assist his brother.

Captain Carver seized the opportunity, and hastened away to join another party of English troops, that were yet unbroken, and stood in a body at some distance. But before he had taken many steps, he hastily cast his eye towards the gentleman, and saw the Indian's tomahawk gash into his back, and heard him utter his last groan; this added both to his speed and desperation.

" He had left this shocking scene but a few yards, when a fine boy about twelve years of age, that had hitherto escaped, came up to him, and begged that he would let him lay hold of him, so that he might stand some chance of getting out of the hands of the savages. Captain Carver told him that he would give him every assistance in his power, and to this purpose bid him lay hold ; but in a few moments he was torn from his side, and by his shrieks he judged was soon made an end of. He could not help forgetting his own cares for a minute, to lament the fate of so young a sufferer; but it was utterly impossible for him to take any methods to prevent it.

" He now got into the midst of his friends, but they were unable to afford each other any succour. As this was the division that had advanced the furthest from the fort, he thought there might be a possibility (though but a very bare one,) of his forcing a way through the outer ranks of the Indians, and getting to a neighbouring wood, which he perceived at some distance. He was still encouraged to hope by the almost miraculous preservation he had already experienced. Nor were his hopes in vain, or the efforts he made ineffectual. Suffice it to say, that he reached the wood, but by the time he had penetrated a little way into it, his breath was so exhausted that he threw himself into a brake, and lay for some minutes apparently at the last gasp. At length he recovered the power of respiration, but his apprehensions returned with all their former force, when he saw several savages pass by, probably in pursuit of him, at no very great distance. In this situation he knew not whether it was better to proceed, or endeavour to conceal himself where he lay, till night came on; fearing, however, that they would return the same way, he thought it most prudent to get farther from the dreadful scene of his past distresses. Accordingly, striking into another part of the wood, he hastened on as fast as the briars and the loss of one of his shoes would permit him; and after a slow progress of some hours, gained a hill that overlooked the plain which he had just left, from whence he could discern that the bloody storm still raged with unabated fury.

" After passing three days without sustenance, and enduring the severity of the cold dews for three nights, he at length reached Fort Edward, when with proper care his body soon recovered its wonted strength, and his mind as far as the recollection of the late melancholy events would permit, its usual composure. It was computed that fifteen hundred persons were killed, or made prisoners by these savages, during this fatal day. Many of the latter were carried off by them, and never returned. A few through favorable accidents found their way back to their native country, after having experienced a long and severe captivity.

" The brave colonel Monro had hastened away soon after the confusion began, to the French camp, to endeavour to procure the guard agreed by the stipulation; but his application proving ineffectual, he remained there till general Webb sent a party of troops to demand and protect him back to Fort Edward. But these unhappy occurrences, which would probably have been prevented, had the colonel been left to pursue his own plans, together with the loss of so many brave fellows, murdered in cold blood, to whose valour he had been so lately a witness, made such an impression on his mind that he did not long survive. He died in about three months, of a broken heart, and with truth it might be said, that he was an honour to his country.

"It is very remarkable, that very few of those different tribes of Indians that shared in this slaughter, ever lived to return home. The small pox, by means of their communication with the Europeans, found its way amongst them, and made an equal havoc, to what they themselves had done. The methods they pursued on the first attack of that malignant disorder, to abate the fever attending it, rendered it fatal. Whilst their blood was in a state of fermentation, and nature was striving to throw out the peccant matter, they checked her operations, by plunging into the water; the consequence was, that they died by hundreds. The few that survived were transformed by it into hideous objects, and bore to the grave deep indented marks of this much dreaded disease.

"Monsieur Montcalm fell soon after, on the plains of Quebec. That the unprovoked cruelties of this commander was not approved of by the generality of his countrymen, we have since been convinced of by many proofs. One only, however, which was received from a person who was witness to it, shall at present be given. A Canadian merchant of some consideration, having heard of the surrender of the English Fort, celebrated the fortunate event with great rejoicings and hospitality, according to the custom of that country; but no sooner did the news of the massacre which ensued reach his ears, than he put an immediate stop to his festivity, and exclaimed in the severest terms against their inhuman permission, declaring at the same time, that those who had connived at it, had thereby drawn down on that part of their king's dominions the vengeance of heaven. To this he added, that he much feared that the total loss of them, would deservedly be the consequence. How truly this prediction has been verified we all know."*

In the year 1758, Washington commanded the van brigade of the army, under general Forbes, and distinguished himself by the capture of Fort du Quesne. During this successful campaign, he acquired a perfect knowledge of tactics. His frequent skirmishes with the French and Indians, in the woody regions along the frontiers, taught him vigilance and circumspection, and roused that spirit of enterprize which is ever ready to seize the crisis that leads to victory. The troops under his command were gradually inured in that most difficult kind of warfare, bush fighting, while the activity of the French, and ferocity of the Indians were overcome by his superior valour. After the enemy had been defeated in several battles, and compelled to retreat far beyond the colonial boundaries, general Forbes left a sufficient garrison in the different forts which he had captured along the banks of the Ohio, and returned with the army into winter quarters.

In the course of this decisive campaign, which restored the tranquillity and security of the middle colonies, Washington had suffered many hardships, which impaired his health. He was afflicted with an inveterate pulmonary complaint, and extremely debilitated, insomuch that in the spring of 1759, he resigned his commission, and retired to Mount Vernon.

By a due attention to regimen, in the salubrious bowers of his family retreat, he gradually recovered from

* I was at this place in the year 1777, and many of the inhabitants recollected the dreadful circumstances which are here detailed; it is remarkable that the pond near to which the massacre was committed, is called the BLOODY POND to this day. R. L.

G

his indisposition. In the year 1761, love invaded his retirement. The object of his choice was an amiable young widow, whose maiden name was Dandridge. She was descended from a reputable family, and two of her brothers were officers in the British Navy. This lady was the widow of colonel Custis, who had left her sole executrix to his extensive possessions, and guardian to his two children. The union of Washington with this accomplished woman* was productive of their mutual felicity; and as he incessantly pursued agricultural improvements, his taste embellished and enriched the fertile fields of Mount Vernon. Meanwhile, he was appointed a magistrate, a member of the assembly of the state, and a judge of the court. These honorable avocations kept the powers of his mind in a state of activity; he attended to his civil duties with exemplary propriety; and gave a convincing proof, that the simplicity of the farmer is homogeneal with the more dig-nified views of the senator.

* Mrs. Washington was born, 1732. She died 1802.

CHAP. III.

*Congress appoints General Officers. British Troops closely
invested in Boston. General Gage sails for England.
General Howe succeeds to the command. Tremen-
dous cannonade on the Town of Boston, by the
Americans. British Troops evacuate the Town, and
sail for Halifax. The Motion for declaring the
Colonies free and independent first introduced into
Congress. They abjure all Allegiance to the British
Crown. Preparations made by England, to subdue
the Americans. Natural Strength of America. A
List of the Stations of British Regiments who were
ordered to act against the Colonies.*

THE moment now approached in which Washington
was to relinquish those honorable civil avocations, and
one of the most remarkable events recorded in history,
obliged him to act a conspicuous part on the great
theatre of the world.

Congress voted him as ample a salary as was in their
power to bestow, but he generously declined all pecuniary emoluments. His reply to the president of congress,
on his nomination to the supreme command of the
army, was in the following words :

" Mr. President, though I am truly sensible of the
high honor done me in this appointment, yet I feel
great distress from a consciousness that my abilities and
military experience may not be equal to the extensive

and important trust; however, as the congress desire it, I will enter upon the momentous duty, and exert every power I possess in their service, and in support of the glorious cause. I beg they will accept my most cordial thanks for this distinguished testimony of their approbation. " But least some unlucky event should happen, unfavourable to my reputation, I beg it may be remembered by every gentleman in the room, that I this day declare with the utmost sincerity, I do not think myself equal to the command I am honoured with.

" As to pay, sir, I beg leave to assure the congress, that as no pecuniary consideration could have tempted me to accept this arduous employment, at the expense of my domestic ease and happiness, I do not wish to make any profit from it. I will keep an exact account of my expenses; those I doubt not, they will discharge, and this is all I desire."

The appointment of Washington was attended with other promotions, namely, four major generals, one adjutant general, and eight brigadier generals.

1st.   Major General Artemus Ward.
2nd.   Charles Lee.
3rd.   Philip Schuyler.
4th.   Israel Putnam.*

Adjutant General Horatio Gates.

The eight brigadiers were,

1st.   Seth Pomeroy.
2d.   Richard Montgomery.
3d.   David Wooster.
4th.   William Heath.
5th.   Joseph Spencer.
6th.   John Thomas.
7th.   John Sullivan.
8th.   Nathaniel Green.

* General Putnam, who had served with reputation under lord Amherst, at the head of the Connecticut troops, during

On the following day a special commission was presented to Washington, by congress. At the same

the last war, had long since retired to a remote farm, which
he cultivated with his own hands; and when the intelligence of his appointment was notified to him, he was found
like another Cincinatus, in a leathern frock and apron, occupied amongst his labourers, in fencing in his land. Without
a moment's hesitation, within eighteen hours he repaired to the
head quarters at Cambridge, which was little short of one
hundred English miles distant.

The following anecdote is related from the life of the
general by colonel Humphries.

Soon after Mr. Putnam removed to Connecticut, the wolves,
then very numerous, broke into his sheep fold, and killed seventy
fine sheep and goats, besides wounding many lambs and
kids. This havoc was committed by a she wolf, which,
with her annual whelps, had for several years infested the
vicinity. The young were commonly destroyed by the vigilance of the hunters, but the old one was too sagacious to
come within reach of gun shot; upon being closely pursued,
she would generally fly to the western woods, and return the
next winter, with another litter of whelps. This wolf, at
length became such an intolerable nuisance, that Mr. Putnam
entered into a combination with five of his neighbours, to
hunt alternately until they could destroy her. Two, by rota-
tion, were to be constantly in pursuit. It was known, that
having lost the toes from one of her feet, by a steel trap, she
made one track shorter than another. By this vestage, the
pursuers recognized, in a light snow, the rout of this pernicious animal. Having followed her to Connecticut river, and
found she had turned back in a direct course towards
Pomfret, they immediately returned, and by ten the next
morning the blood hounds had driven her into a den, about
three miles distant from the house of Mr. Putnam; the
people soon collected with dogs, guns, straw, fire, and sulphur,
to attack the common enemy. With this apparatus several
unsuccessful efforts were made to force her from the den.
The hounds came back badly wounded, and refused to return.
The smoke of blazing straw had no effect. Nor did the
fumes of burnt brimsone, with which the cavern was filled,
compel her to quit the retirement. Wearied with such fruitless attempts, which had brought the time to ten o'clock at
night, Mr. Putnam tried once more to make his dog enter,
but in vain; he proposed to his negro man to go down
into the cavern, and shoot the wolf; the negro declined the
hazardous service. Then it was, that his master angry at
the disappointment, and declaring that he was ashamed

time, they resolved unanimously, "that they would maintain and assist him, and adhere to him with their

to have a coward in his family, resolved himself to destroy the ferocious beast, lest she should escape through some unknown fissure of the rock. His neighbours strongly remonstrated against the perilous enterprize: but he knowing that wild animals were intimidated by fire, and having provided several strips of birch bark, the only combustible material which he could obtain, that would afford light in this deep and darksome cave, he prepared for his descent. Having accordingly divested himself of his coat and waistcoat, and having a long rope fastened round his legs, by which he might be pulled back, at a concerted signal, he entered head foremost, with the blazing torch in his hand.

The aperture of the den, on the east side of a very high ledge of rocks, is about two feet square; from thence it descends obliquely fifteen feet, then running horizontally about ten more, it ascends gradually sixteen feet towards its termination. The sides of this subterraneous cavity are composed of smooth and solid rocks, which seem to have been divided from each other by an earthquake. The top and bottom are also of stone, and the entrance, in winter, being covered with ice, is exceedingly slippery. It is in no place high enough for a man to raise himself upright: nor in any part more than three feet in width.

Having groped his passage to the horizontal part of the den, the most terrifying darkness appeared in front of the dim circle of light afforded by his torch. It was silent as the house of death. None but monsters of the desert had ever before explored this solitary mansion of horror. He cautiously proceeding onward, came to the ascent, which he slowly mounted on his hands and knees, until he discovered the glaring eye-balls of the wolf, who was sitting at the extremity of the cavern. Startled at the sight of fire, she gnashed her teeth, and gave a sullen growl. As soon as he had made the necessary discovery, he kicked the rope as a signal for pulling him out. The people, at the mouth of the den, who had listened with painful anxiety, hearing the growling of the wolf, and supposing their friend to be in the most imminent danger, drew him forth with such celerity, that his shirt was stripped over his head, and his skin severely lacerated. After he had adjusted his clothes, and loaded his gun with nine buck-shot, holding a torch in one hand, and the musquet in the other, he descended a second time. When he drew nearer than before, the wolf, assuming a still more fierce and terrible appearance, howling, rolling her eyes, snapping her teeth, and dropping her head between her legs,

lives and fortunes, in the cause of American Liberty."
Instructions were also given him for his government,
by which, after reciting various particulars, he was
directed " to destroy or make prisoners all persons
who now are, or who hereafter shall appear in arms
against the good people of the colonies:" but the
whole was summed up by authorising him " to order
and dispose of the army under his command as might
be most advantageous for obtaining the end for which
it had been raised, making it his special care in discharge of the great trust committed to him, that the
liberties of America received no detriment." About the
same time twelve companies of riffle men were ordered
to be raised in Pennsylvania, Maryland, and Virginia.
The men to the amount of one thousand four hundred
and thirty, were raised and forwarded with great expedition, to the American head quarters at Cambridge.

In the beginning of July 1775, general Washington set out for the camp at Cambridge, in order
to assume the command of the army.

On his way thither he was treated with every demonstration of respect, escorted by detachments of gentlemen, who had formed volunteer associations, and was
honored with public addresses of congratulation, from
the provincial congress of New-York and Massachusetts.

was evidently in the attitude, and on the point of springing
at him. At the critical instant he levelled and fired at her
head. Stunned with the shock, and suffocated with the smoke,
he immediately found himself drawn out of the cave. But
having refreshed himself, and permitted the smoke to dissi-
pate, he went down the third time. Once more he came
within sight of the wolf, who appearing very passive, he
applied the torch to her nose; and perceiving her dead,
he took hold of her ears, and then kicking the rope (still
tied round his legs) the people above, with no small exultation, dragged them both out together.

Our troops at this time were entrenched on, Bunker's Hill, and defended by three floating batteries, in Mystic river and a twenty gun ship below the ferry, between Boston and Charlestown. The Americans were entrenched on Winter Hill, Prospect Hill, and Roxbury, with communications by small posts over an extent of ten miles; there were also parties in several towns along the sea coast. General Ward commanded the right wing at Roxbury, general Lee the left on Prospect Hill, and the centre was commanded by general Washington.

As the American soldiers had repaired to the camp in their ordinary clothing, the hunting shirt was adopted for the sake of uniformity. At the same time, the inhabitants were recommended not to fire a gun at beast, bird, or mark, in order that they might husband their stock of powder and ball for the purpose of destroying the british Troops.

The military spirit was now so high and general, that war and its preparations occupied the hands and the minds of all orders of people, throughout the provinces. Persons of fortune and family, who were not appointed officers, entered cheerfully as private men, and served with alacrity in the ranks.

The provinces of Georgia, Maryland and Pennsylvania, having now acceded to the confederacy, it from this time assumed the title of THE THIRTEEN UNITED COLONIES.

In September general Gage sailed for England, and the command of the British army devolved on general Howe. Meanwhile, the army under Washington continued the blockade of Boston so closely, as to prevent all intercourse between that town and the country.

The British troops at Boston, endured the tedious blockade, with their characteristic fortitude, and suffered many inconveniences from want of necessaries of every kind.

Washington exerted his skill and activity in order to compel the British army, either to surrender or evacuate Boston before any succours could arrive from England. On the 2d of March 1776, he opened a battery on the west side of the town, and bombarded it. This attack was supported by a tremendous cannonade, and on the 5th another battery was opened on the eastern shore. The garrison sustained this dreadful bombardment with the greatest fortitude; it lasted fourteen days without intermission; when general Howe finding the place no longer tenable, determined if possible, to drive the enemy from their works. Preparations were therefore made for a most vigorous attack, on an hill called Dorchester Neck, which the Americans had fortified in such a manner, as would in all probability have rendered the enterprize next to desperate. No difficulties, however, were sufficient to damp the spirit of the general; and every thing was in readiness, when a sudden storm prevented this intended exertion of British valor. Next day, upon a more close inspection of the works they were to attack, it was thought advisable to desist from the enterprise altogether. The fortifications were very strong, and extremely well provided with artillery, and besides other implements of destruction upwards of one hundred hogsheads of stones were provided to roll down upon our army as they came up; which, as the ascent was extremely steep, must have done prodigious execution.

On the 17th of March 1776, general Howe finding the town of Boston no longer tenable, resolved to embark for Halifax, and the voyage thither was both short and prosperous.

The evacuation of Boston was not interrupted by the Americans, lest our troops should set it on fire.

H

Thus was the long contested town of Boston at length given up, the colony of Massachusett's Bay, for the present freed from war, and left at liberty to adopt every measure which could tend to its future strength and security. The estates and effects of those loyalists, or tories, as they were then called, who accompanied general Howe, to Halifax, were ordered to be sold, and the produce applied to the public service. Some who ventured to stay behind, were brought to trial as public enemies, and betrayers of their country; and the estates of such as were found guilty, were confiscated in the same manner. But nothing occupied so much at present the minds of the people of Boston, or had so much attention paid to it, by the province in general, as the putting of that town into a formidable state of defence. Some French engineers were employed to superintend the works, and every inhabitant dedicated two days in the week to their construction,

As Washington was uncertain of the destination of the fleet and army, which had left Boston, and as New York lay exposed to any sudden attack, he detached several of his best regiments, under general Lee, for the defence of that city.

On the 7th of June, 1776, the motion for declaring the colonies free and independent, was now moved in congress, by Richard Henry Lee, of Virginia. When the time of taking the subject under consideration arrived, much ingenuity and eloquence were displayed on both sides of the question. The debates were continued for some time, and with great animation. In these, John Adams, and John Dickinson took leading and opposite parts. The former began one of his speeches, by an invocation of the god of eloquence, to assist him in defending the claims, and enforcing the duty of his countrymen. He strongly urged the immediate dissolution of the political connexion of the colonies with Great Britain : from the voice of the people ; from the necessity of the measure, in order to attain foreign assistance ; from a regard to consistency ; and from the prospects of glory and happiness, which opened beyond the war, to a free and independent people. Mr. Dickinson* replied to this speech. He began by observing that the member from Massachusetts (Mr. Adams,) had introduced his defence of the declaration of independence, by invoking an heathen god, but that he should begin his objections to it, by solemnly invoking the Governor of the universe, so to influence the minds of the members of congress, that if the proposed measure was for the benefit of America, nothing which he should say against it, might make the least impression. He then urged that the present time was improper for the declaration of independence ; that the war might be conducted with equal vigour without it ; that it would divide the Americans, and unite the people of Great Britain against them. He then proposed that some assurance should be obtained of assistance from a foreign power; before they renounced their connexion with Great Britain; and that the declaration of independence should be the condition to be offered for this assistance: He likewise stated the disputes that existed betweeen several of the colonies, and proposed that some measures for the settlement of them should be determined upon, before they lost sight of that tribunal, which had hitherto been the umpire of all their differences.

The fatal day at length arrived which must be deeply regretted by every true friend to the British empire,

---

*' Author of a series of letters signed a Pennsylvania Farmer.

when *thirteen English colonies in America, declared themselves Free and Independent States;* abjured all allegiance to the British crown, and renounced all political connexion with the mother country.

On this day, the 4th of July 1776, the congress published a manifesto stating a list of grievances, which, notwithstanding their repetitions, had remained unredressed ; for these reasons they determined on a final separation from the mother countr , and to hold the people of Great Britain as the rest of mankind, " enemies in war, in peace friends." Part of this declaration of independence was as follows :

" We hold these truths to be self evident, that all men are created equal; that they are endowed by the Creator, with certain unalienable rights; that among these are life, liberty, and the pursuit of happiness;* that to secure these rights, governments are instituted among men, deriving their just powers from the consent of the governed ; that whenever any form of government becomes destructive of these ends, it is the right of the people to alter or to abolish it, and to institute a new government, laying its foundation on such principles, and organizing its powers in such form, as to them shall seem most likely to effect their safety and happiness." It concluded in this manner, " We, the representatives of the United States of America, in general congress assembled, appealing to the Supreme Judge of the world for the rectitude of our intentions, do, in the name, and by the authority of the good people of these colonies, solemnly publish and declare, that the united colonies are, and of right ought to be, free and independent states, and that they are absolved from all allegiance to the British crown ; and that all the poli-

---

* At this time some of the members of congress were holding slaves. How specious, yet how palpably inconsistent these declarations from such a people !

cal connexion between them and the state of Great
Britain, is, and ought to be, totally dissolved; and that,
as free and independent states, they have full power
to levy war, conclude peace, contract alliances; establish commerce, and to do all other acts and things
which independent states may of right do. And for
the support of this declaration, with a firm reliance on
the protection of Divine Providence, we mutually pledge
to each other, our lives, our fortunes and our sacred
honor."

Many even of the friends of America were astonished at this bold act of congress, in breaking of all subordination to the parent state. "Great Britain," said
they, "has founded colonies at great expense, has incurred a load of debt by wars on their account, has
protected their commerce, and raised them to all the
consequence they possess, and now in the insolence
of adult years, rather than pay their proportion of the
common expenses of government, they ungratefully
renounce all connexion with the nurse of their youth,
and the protectress of their riper years!"

This solemn renunciation of allegiance to Great Britain was followed by the greatest preparations for war
throughout the United States.

Great Britain in the meantime was resolved to open
the campaign with such a powerful force, as would
look down all opposition, and effectuate submission,
without bloodshed; to the accomplishment of this end
three principal objects were to be carried into execution. The first was the relief of Quebec, and the recovery of Canada, which also included a subsequent
invasion of the north western frontiers of the adjacent
provinces. As the four provinces of New England had
originally begun the confederacy against Britain, and
were still considered the most active in the continuation of it: it was thought, that any impression

made upon, them would contribute in an effectual manner to the reduction of all the rest. For this purpose,
an army of four thousand, chosen British troops, and
three thousand Germans,* was ordered for Canada, to
accomplish the above purposes.

The second object was the making a strong impression on the southern colonies, which it was hoped, would
at least have succeeded so far as to the recovery of one
of them. The execution of this object was committed
to general Sir Henry Clinton, and admiral Sir Peter
parker. They had two thousand eight hundred land
forces, which they hoped, with the co-operation of the
shipping, would be fully sufficient.

The third and principal point of attack, and on which
the greatest hopes of success were founded, was
to take New York, with a force sufficient to keep
possession of Hudson's river, and form a line of communication with the royal army in Canada. The command
of this force, consisting of thirteen thousand Hessians
and Waldeckers, and seventeen thousand British troops,
was given to general Sir William Howe, and his brother,
admiral lord Howe. "America," said the congress, in
one of her public declarations, " is amazed to find the
name of Howe in the catalogue of her enemies——she
loved his brother;" referring to, the gallant nobleman, lord Howe, who so gloriously fell in the defence
of the colonies, in the former war at Ticonderoga.

The admiral and general, in addition to their military
powers, were appointed commissioners for restoring peace
to the colonies. This force was truly formidable, and

---

* Treaties had been lately entered into between his majesty,
the landgrave of Hesse Cassel, the duke of Brunswick, and the
hereditary prince of Hesse Cassel for the hiring of different bodies
of their troops for the American service, amounting in the
whole to seventeen thousand three hundred men. The conditions of these treaties were, that the troops were to enter into
pay before they began to march; and that the levy money was
to be paid at the rate of seven pounds ten shillings per man.

such as no part of the new world had ever seen before. Nor was it, perhaps, ever exceeded by any army in Europe, of an equal number, whether considered with respect to the excellency of the troops, the abundant provision of all manner of military stores and warlike materials, or the goodness and number of artillery of all sorts with which it was provided. It was besides supported by a very numerous fleet, particularly well adapted to the nature of the service.

In the mean time Washington took every precaution for defensive operations, by erecting forts, and stationing troops in different places, at the most vulnerable points. The nature of the country was peculiarly favourable to defence, and presented many natural barriers of hills and mountains, intersected by rivers, and interspersed with trees, rocks, and precipices; several defiles, skirted by impenetrable woods; and majestic rivers, flowing with impetuous currents, which seemed to bid defiance to the invader.

The following is a correct list of the stations of the British regiments, which were ordered to act against the Americans in the beginning of the year 1776.

STATIONED IN BOSTON.

17th Dragoons..Preston's.	43d Foot.....Cary's.
4th Foot.........Hodgson's.	44th do.......Abercrombie's.
5th do............Percy's.	45th do.......Haviland's.
10th do............Sandford's.	47th do.......Carleton's.
22d do............Gage's.	49th do.......Maitland's.
23d do............Howe's.	52d do.......Clavering's.
35th do............F. H. Campbell's	63d do......T. Grant's.
38th do............Pigot's.	64th do.......Pomeroy's.
40th do............Hamilton's.	65th do.......Urmston's at Boston and Halifax.

ROYAL ARTILLERY IN BSTON.

Five Companies, each

1 Captain,	1 First Lieutenant
1 Captain Lieutenant,	3 Second Lieutenants,

3 Serjeants,	12 Gunners,
3 Corporals,	1 Fife,
6 Bombardiers,	2 Drums,

48 Matrosses.*

IN QUEBEC, AND OTHER PARTS OF CANADA.

7th Foot.........Bertie's.   8th Foot.....Armstrong's, at the upper posts, Niagara, Detroit, &c.

26th do..........Lord W. Gordon's. M'Clean's, now raising in Canada.

ROYAL ARTILLERY.

1 Company at Quebec.   1 Company at Montreal.

IN NEWFOUNDLAND.

1 Invalid Company, do.

AT ST. AUGUSTINE.

1 Company do.

14th Foot........Cunningham's, partly at St. Augustine's, partly with lord Dunmore, in Virginia, and partly in Halifax.

ON THEIR PASSAGE FROM IRELAND TO BOSTON.

17th Foot.........Monckton's.	46th Foot....Vaughan's.
27th do............Massey's.	55th do........James Grant's.

READY TO SAIL FROM CORK TO AMERICA.

15th Foot...........Cavan's.	42d Foot.....Lord Murray's.
33d do.............Cornwallis's.	54th do........Frederick's.
37th do.............Coote's.	57th do........Irwin's.

ORDERED FOR BOSTON.

16th Dragoons......Burgoyne's.—One thousand of the king's guards to be drafted from the three regiments, and commanded by colonel Matthews. Marines intended to be made up two thousand.

29th Foot..........Evelyn's, destined for Quebec, and to sail so as to arrive there as early as the navigation of the river St. Lawrence will admit.

---

* When the British troops evacuated Boston on the 17th of March 1776, they did not exceed seven thousand effective men.

ORDERED TO BE IN READINESS FOR EMBARKATION AND TO
SAIL FROM IRELAND TO QUEBEC IN APRIL 1776.

9th Foot.........Ligonier's.	34th Foot......Lord Cavendish's.
20th do............Parker's.	53d do.........Elphinstone's.
24th do.............Taylor's.	62d do.........Jones's.

The Highland battalions, viz. lord John Murray's and
Fraser's, were to consist of one thousand each.

The marching regiments for the American service
were to consist of twelve companies, of fifty six
effective rank and file each company. Two companies of each battalion were to remain in Great Britain
and Ireland for the purpose of recruiting.

Sometime before this, orders were issued from the
war office that any person who should inlist as a soldier in any of his majesty's marching regiments of
foot should be entitled either to his discharge, at the
expiration of three years, or at the end of the war, at
the option of his majesty.

I

CHAP. IV.

The Author's Journal commences. Sails from the Cove of Cork. Remarkable Occurrences during the Voyage. Enters the Gulph of St. Lawrence. A particular Description of that River. Arrives at Quebec. Description of that City.

ON the 3d of April, 1776, I embarked with the 9th regiment of foot, in which I was then a non-commissioned officer, at the Cove of Cork, on board the Friendship, transport, and on the 8th sailed with the fleet for Quebec.

April 20th. Our ship sailing at the rate of five miles an hour, a soldier whose name was Brooks, leaped off the forecastle into the ocean; the vessel in a moment made her way over him, and he arose at her stern. He immediately with all his might, swam from the ship. The men who were upon the deck alarmed the captain and officers, who had just sat down to dinner; the ship was ordered to be put about, and the boat hoisted out, and manned, the unfortunate man was soon overtaken, and it was with difficulty that the sailors could force him into the boat. When he was brought back he was ordered between decks, and a centinel placed over him; the next morning he was in a high fever, and continued very bad the remainder of the voyage. The fear of punishment was the cause of this desperate action, as the day before he had stolen a shirt from one of his messmates knapsacks.

30th. The fleet sailing at the rate of six miles an hour: a serjeant had an altercation with his wife while they were sitting at breakfast, in consequence of which he got up in a rage, leaped overboard and was seen no more.

May 3d. The wind strong at N. W. and running at the rate of seven miles an hour, one of the recruits standing on the forecastle was so provoked by his comrades, that in a fit of rage he jumped over board, uttering at the same time dreadful curses upon them. He was swallowed up by the great deep in a moment!

14th. Sailing over the banks of Newfoundland, we passed by several islands of ice, which came floating down-from the river St. Lawrence.

18th. This morning we had a view of the mountains of Newfoundland, covered with snow; however, as we had been forty days at sea without seeing any land, this dreary island was very pleasant to our sight.

19th. This day we entered the noble bay of St. Lawrence, between Cape de Retz, on the island of Newfoundland and Cape Breton, (our fleet all in sight,) and after doubling Cape Rosieres, we entered the river, which is in this place about ninety miles in breadth; here the sea was very boisterous. On the south side lies the bay of - Gaspie. Below this bay is a steep rock, which is called the Bored Island, from an opening in its middle, through which a ship may pass with her sails up. At a league's distance from the Bored Island, lies the island Bonaventure; and at a league's distance from that, the Island Miscou, which has an excellent harbour, and is eight leagues in circumference. A spring of fresh water spouts up to a considerable height in the offing, not far from this island.

I 2

20th. Early this morning the Island Anticosti presented itself to our sight, the current setting strongly in upon it, rendered our navigation extremely dangerous, especially as the island is lined with breakers. This island is narrow, and lies in the middle of the river, it extends about forty leagues from N. E. to S. W. Our French pilot represented it as absolutely good for nothing; its coasts, however, are said to be well stored with fish.

21st. This evening after passing the island of Anticosti, our navigation became more tolerable, but still the fleet used great precaution.

22d. The weather remarkably cold this day; but the wind fair, which soon brought us in sight of the Mounts Notre Dame and Lewis; here we saw for the first time, a number of neat French plantations. In the evening we sailed by Trinity Point, which we endeavoured to avoid with great care, and before dark we had a view of the Paps of Montani, so called from the appearance of the mountain, situated about two leagues from the shore. The land in this neighbourhood was represented to be not only unprofitable, but frightful, being covered with rocks, sands, and impenetrable thickets. On the other side the river, lies the shoal of Maniconague, which is the most dangerous in this river.

23d. Our navigation was now very slow, the shores appeared uncomfortable, and uninhabited; in the evening we doubled a bay, called Tadoussac, on the south side of this bay lies Red Island, which is a dangerous rock of that colour, whose surface is equal with the water, and often proves fatal to shipping. Here the river St. Lawrence is not above three leagues wide; and the lands at each side lofty and thickly covered with trees.

26th. This day we sailed by the island of Caudres, which appeared to be very well inhabited and culti_ vated ; churches, crucifixes, and images, were now to be seen almost every where : here the passage of the river is dangerous without a fair wind, in particular there is a whirlpool, which we carefully guarded against. Next appeared in our view, the Bay of St. Paul, where the plantations on the north shore begin ; they consist of valuable woods of pine trees, among which are red pines, which are esteemed very beautiful. The village of St. Paul's is situated in a vale, and has a very romantic appearance from the river.

27th. Early this morning we had a view of a very high promontory, which we were informed terminates a chain of mountains, that reach near five hundred leagues to the westward. This promontory is called Cape Torment. A number of islands now presented themselves to our view, among which is that of Orleans, which forms a most beautiful prospect, a clear open country, with villages, and churches innumerable, and being all whitewashed on the outside, gave them a neat, elegant appearance, from our ships. This island is about fourteen leagues in circumference ; it produces excellent wheat and fine fruits, and forms two channels; of which the south is the most navigable. Here the water becomes fit to drink; for it is brackish at Cape Torment, though it is an hundred and ten leagues from the sea.

From the island of Orleans the river grows so narrow, that before Quebec it is not a mile over. The Point Levy, which juts out beyond the isle of Orleans, entirely hides the south channel of the river, as the Isle of Orleans does that on the north ; so that from thence to the port of Quebec appears like a large bason, or bay, land locked on all sides, and capable of containing one hundred ships of the line,

at four hundred and twenty miles distance from the
sea.

In the river St. Lawrence, are sea wolves, sea cows,
porpoises, the chaourasou, turtles, lobsters, sea plaise,
salmon, trouts, with a variety of other fish. The sea
wolf, so called from its howling, is an amphibious
creature ; his head resembles that of a dog ; he has
four very short legs, of which the fore ones have nails,
but the hind ones terminate in fins. The largest are
said to weigh two thousand pounds, and are of different colours. Their flesh is good eating, but the profit
of it. lies in its oil, which is proper for burning, and
currying leather. Their skins make excellent covering for trunks, and though not so fine as morocco
leather, they preserve their freshness better, and are
less liable to crack. The shoes and boots made of
these skins do not admit water, and when properly tanned
make excellent and lasting covers for seats. The sea
cow, is larger than the sea-wolf, but resembles it in
figure. It is as white as snow, and has two teeth of
the thickness and length of a man's arm, that, when
grown, look like horns, and are very fine ivory, as
well as its other teeth. It seldom happens that they
are caught in the water, but they are taken on shore
by the following stratagem. The inhabitants of Arca-
dia, tie a bull to a stake, fixt on the shore, in the
depth of about two feet water ; they then beat, and
otherwise torment him, by twisting his tail, until they
make him roar ; which as soon as these animals hear,
they make towards the shore, and when they get
into shallow water, they crawl to the bull, and are
taken with little difficulty. The Arcadians as well as
the Indians eat some parts of this animal, and what
they dislike they boil with its fat, to an oily or greasy
substance, with which they save or cure the skins of
other animals for leather.

Some of the porpoises of the river St. Lawrence, are said to yield a hogshead of oil, and of their skins are made waistcoats, which are exceeding strong, and musket proof.

The chaourasou is an armed fish, resembling a pike but is covered with scales, that are proof against a dagger; some of them are above five feet long, and about the thickness of a man's thigh: this fish is said even to catch and devour birds; in order to which, he conceals himself among the canes, or reeds, in such a manner, that nothing is to be seen besides his weapon, which he holds, raised perpendicularly above the surface of the water: the birds which come to take rest, imagining the weapon to be only a withered reed, make no scruple of perching upon it; but they are no sooner alighted, than the fish opens his throat, and so suddenly makes at his prey, that it rarely escapes.

29th. Our fleet now arrived at Quebec, which is the capital of the province of Canada, and an episcopal see. It is situated at the confluence of the rivers St. Lawrence and St. Charles, or the little river. It is built on a rock, partly of marble, and partly of slate. The haven which lies opposite the town, is safe and commodious, and about five fathom deep. Before the city was taken by our troops, in the year 1759, it is said to have made a very fine appearance. Among the principal edifices, were the episcopal palace; the cathedral; the fort or citadel, which was the residence of the Governor; the house and church of the Recollets; the church of the Ursuline nuns, in which is the tomb of Monsieur Montcalm, who commanded the French, and was killed at the battle of Quebec, in which also fell that young hero, Wolfe, who commanded the English; the sumptuous college of Jesuits; the intendant's house, the king's-magazines, &c. &c,

This city is divided into the upper and lower, and was well fortified, when Wolfe laid siege to it. The fort or citadel stands on the brink of the rock, and is a fine work : a pretty large esplenade, and a gentle declivity, the whole making a very fine platform, lies between the fort and the summit of Cape Diamond. About half a mile towards the county, lies the Hospital General,* which is the finest house in all Canada.

* To this house the French general, Marquis Montcalm was carried after he was wounded, at the taking of Quebec, in the year 1759. It is said that when his wound was dressed, and he settled in bed, the surgeons who attended him were desired to acquaint him ingeniously with their sentiments of him, and being told that his wound was mortal, he calmly replied, " I am glad of it." His excellency then demanded, " whether he could survive it long, and how long ?" He was told " about twelve hours, or perhaps less." " So much the better," rejoined the general ; " I am happy I shall not live to see the surrender of Quebec." He then ordered his secretary into the room, to settle his private affairs, which as soon as they were dispatched, he dismissed him. He was visited by Monsieur de Ramsey, the French king's lieutenant, and by other principal officers, who desired to receive his excellency's commands, with the farther measures to be pursued for the defence of Quebec. To this, the Marquis made the following answer ; " I'll neither give orders, nor interfere any farther : I have much business that must be attended to, of greater moment than your ruined garrison, and this wretched country : my time is very short, therefore pray leave me ; I wish you all comfort, and to be happily extricated from your present perplexities. He then called for his chaplain, who with the bishop of the colony, remained with him till he expired. Some time before this great man departed, he paid the British army this compliment. " Since it was my misfortune to be discomfited and mortally wounded, it is a great consolation to me to be vanquished by so brave and generous an army ; if I could survive this wound, I would engage to beat three times the number of such forces as I commanded this morning, with a third of their number of British troops."

CHAP. V.

*Ticonderoga and Crown Point taken by the Americans.
Congress endeavours to bring the Indians over to
their Side. Speech of the Commissioners from
Congress to the Indians. Montgomery attempts
the Conquest of Canada. Chamblee taken. General
Carleton repulsed. St. John's Fort and Montreal
taken. Attempt to . surprise Quebec. Montgomery
killed, and the Americans defeated. The humane
Conduct of General Carleton towards the American
Prisoners.*

OUR army was now informed of the military operations of the Americans in Canada last winter, with
a particular account of the siege of Quebec. It seems
that it had early occurred to the Americans, · that if
the sword · decided the controversy between Great Britain and them, the possession of Ticonderoga would
be essential to the security of their states ; this fort
situated on a promontory, formed at the junction of
the . waters of Lake George and Lake Champlain, is
the key of all communication between New York
and Canada.

A scheme was planned by the Americans, for obtaining possession of this valuable post. Having pro-
. vided a sufficient quantity of powder and ball, they
set off for Bennington, to obtain the co-operation of

K

colonel Allen of that place. Two hundred and seventy men, mostly of that hardy people, who are called green mountain boys, were speedily collected at Castleton, which was fixed on as the place of rendezvous. At this place colonel Arnold joined them. He had been early chosen a captain of a volunteer company, by the inhabitants of New Haven, among whom he resided. As soon as he received news of the Lexington skirmish, he marched off for the vicinity of Boston. Immediately after his arrival, he waited on the Massachusetts' committee of safety, and informed them, that there were at Ticonderoga many pieces of cannon, and a great quantity of military stores ; that the fort was in a ruinous condition, and garrisoned only by forty men. They appointed him colonel, and commissioned him to raise four hundred men, and attack Ticonderoga. On the 9th May, 1775, Allen and Arnold crossed over with their troops, and landed near the garrison. They contended for some time, who should lead on the attack, and it was at last agreed that they should both go in together, at the head of their troops. They advanced and entered the fort at the dawning of day. A British centinel fired his piece at them, and then retreated through the covered way to the parade. The Americans followed, and immediately drew up. The commander was called upon to surrender the fort. He asked by what authority ? Allen replied, " I demand it in the name of the Great Jehovah, and the continental congress." The fort, with its stores, and forty-eight prisoners, immediately fell into the hands of the Americans. A strong party was sent off to take possession of Crown Point, where a serjeant and twelve men performed garrison duty. This was also effected. The next object that drew the attention of the Americans, was to obtain the command of Lake Champlain ; but to accomplish this, it was necessary for them to get possession of a sloop of war, lying at St. John's, in the northern extremity of the lake. For the purpose of capturing this sloop, it was agreed to man and arm a schooner, lying at South Bay, that Arnold should command her, and that Allen should bring forward some batteaux on the same expedition. A favourable wind carried the schooner a-head of the batteaux, and Arnold got immediate possession of the sloop by surprise.

The wind again favoring him, he returned with his prize to Ticonderoga, and rejoined Allen. The latter soon went home, and the former with a number of men, agreed to stay there in garrison. In this rapid manner the possession of Ticonderoga, and the command of Lake Champlain was obtained. Intelligence of these events was in a few days communicated to congress, which met for the first time, at ten o'clock, on the same day, in the morning of which Ticonderoga was taken. They rejoiced in the spirit of enterprize displayed by their countrymen, and ordered the cannon and stores to be removed from Ticonderoga to Lake George.

At the same time, congress endeavoured to bring over the Indians to their side, for which purpose they resolved to appoint commissioners to explain to them the grounds of their dispute with Britain, and cultivate their friendship by treaties and presents ; to which end they determined to purchase and distribute among them a suitable assortment of goods, to the amount of forty thousand pounds sterling. They likewise sent the following speech to them :

" Brothers, Sachems, and Warriors ! We, the delegates from the twelve United Provinces, now sitting in general congress, at Philadelphia, send their talk to you, our brothers.

K 2

" Brothers and Friends, now attend! When our fathers crossed the great water, and came over to this land, the king of England gave them a talk, assuring them, that they and their children should be his children ; and that if they would leave their native country, and make settlements, and live here, and buy, and sell, and trade with their brethren beyond the water, they should still keep hold of the same covenant chain, and enjoy peace ; and it was covenanted, that the fields, houses, goods, and possessions, which our fathers should acquire, should remain to them, as their own, and be their children's for ever, and at their sole disposal.

" Brothers and Friends, open a kind ear! We will now tell you of the quarrel between the counsellors of king George, and the inhabitants ·of the colonies of America.

" Many of his counsellors. have persuaded him to break the covenant chain, and not. to send·us any more good talks. They have prevailed upon him to enter into a covenant against us ; and have torn asunder, and cast behind their back, the good old covenant, which their ancestors and ours entered into, and took strong hold of. They now tell us they will put their hands into our pockets without asking, as though it were their own ; and at their pleasure they will take from us our charters, or written civil constitution, which we love as our lives ; also our plantations, our houses and goods, whenever they please, without asking our leave. They will tell us that our vessels may go to that or this island in the sea, but to this or that particular island we shall not trade any more ; and in case of our non-compliance with these new orders, they shut up our harbours.

" Brothers, we live on the same ground with you ; the same island is our common birth place ; we desire

to sit down under the same tree of peace with you;
let us water its roots, and cherish its growth, till the
large leaves and branches shall extend to the setting
sun, and reach the skies. If any thing disagreeable
should ever fall out between us, the twelve United
Colonies, and you, the six Nations, to wound our
peace, let us immediately seek measures for healing
the breach. From the present situation of our
affairs, we judge it expedient to kindle up a small fire
at Albany, where we may hear each other's voice,
and disclose our minds fully to one another."

Arnold having begun his military career with a
series of successes, was urged by his natural impetuosity
to project more extensive operations. He wrote a
letter to congress, strongly urging an expedition into
Canada, in order to reduce the whole province.

Sir Guy Carleton, the king's governor, in Canada,
no sooner heard that the Americans had surprized
Ticonderoga and Crown Point, and obtained the command of Lake Champlain, than he planned a scheme
for their recovery. Having only a few regular troops
under his command, he ordered colonel Johnson* to
hold a conference with the Indians, and try to counteract the views of congress, by endeavouring to engage

---

* This gentleman was son to the famous Sir William
Johnson, who had so greatly distinguished himself in America,
in the war of 1755. The following anecdote is related of
Sir William : Soon after he had been appointed superinten-
dant of Indian affairs in America, he wrote to England for
some suits of cloaths, richly laced. When they arrived,
Hendrick, chief of the Mahawk nation was present, and particularly admired them. In a few days Hendrick called on
Sir William, and acquainted him that he had a dream. On
Sir William inquiring what it was, he told him he had
dreamed that he had given him one of those fine suits
which he had lately received. Sir William took the hint,
and immediately presented him with one of the richest suits.
Hendrick, highly pleased with the generosity of Sir William,

them to take up the hatchet. In order to gain their
co-operation, he invited them to feast on a Bostonian,
and to drink his blood. This, in the Indian style,
meant no more, than to partake of a roasted ox and
a pipe of wine, at a public entertainment, which was
given on design to influence them to co-operate
with the British troops. The American patriots,
affected to understand it in its literal sense. It furnished in their mode of explication, a convenient handle
for operating on the passions of the people, though
at the same time, it was well known that if we had
not employed them they would most certainly have
acted against us.

The Americans were now determined to make a
vigorous attack upon Canada. Their success at Ticonderoga and Crown Point, had already paved the way
for this bold enterprise, and had broken down the
fences which guarded the entrance into that province.
They were also sensible they had already gone such
lengths as could only be vindicated by arms; and
that if a certain degree of success did not attend
their resistance, they would be at the mercy of an
irritated government.

Montgomery, an enterprizing man, having been
appointed a brigadier general, flew to the new formed
congress. "Gentlemen," said he, " if you will give me
six thousand men, and proper provisions for the business,
I'll set off in the winter, march to Quebec, scale

---

retired. Sir William some time after this, happening to be in
company with Hendrick, told him also that he had a dream.
Hendrick being very solicitous to know what it was, Sir William
informed him, that he had dreamed that he, (Hendrick,) had
made him a present of a particular tract of land, (the most
valuable on the Mahawk River,) of about five thousand acres.
Hendrick presented him with the land immediately, with this
shrewd remark. "Now, Sir William, I will never dream with
you again, for you dream too hard for me."

the walls, take general Carleton by surprise, make his soldiers prisoners, take all Canada, and then we shall make better terms with the British parliament."

The congress agreed to his proposals. He crossed Lake Champlain, and made as much haste as the difficulty of the way would allow. His first step was to gain over the Indians whom general Carleton had employed, and this in a great measure he accomplished; after which, on receiving the full number of troops appointed for the expedition, he determined to lay siege to St. John's. In this he was facilitated by the reduction of Chamblee, a small fort in the neighbourhood, where he found a large supply of powder.

While Montgomery was prosecuting the siege, the governor general Carleton, collected a party of Canadians and Indians, intending to proceed to the garrison of fort St. John's, and to attack the besiegers; but colonel Warner, with a large party of green mountain boys, and a four pounder, prevented the execution of the design. The governor's party was suffered to come near the shore, but was then fired upon with such effect, as to make them retire, after sustaining some loss.

The failure of general Carleton to relieve the garrison, was a sufficient recompence to the Americans for that of colonel Allen, which had happened some time before. The success which had attended this gentleman against Crown Point and Ticonderoga, had emboldened him to make a similar attempt on Montreal; but being attacked by the militia of the place, supported by a detachment of regulars, he was entirely defeated, taken prisoner, and sent to England.

An account of general Carleton's repulse being communicated to the garrison of St. John's, major Preston, the commanding officer, seeing no hope of any relief, consented to surrender the fort. They received honorable terms of capitulation, and were treated with the greatest humanity by the Americans.

General Montgomery next took measures to prevent the British shipping from passing down the river from Montreal to Quebec. This he accomplished so effectually, that the whole were taken. The town itself was obliged to surrender at discretion, and it was with the utmost difficulty that general Carleton escaped in an open boat, under cover of a dark night.

Montreal stands on an island in the river St. Lawrence, which is ten leagues in length, and almost four in breadth, at the foot of a mountain which gives name to it, about half a league from the south shore. The whole island is a most delightful spot, and produces every thing that can administer to the convenience of life. The town is of an oblong form, well peopled, and surrounded by a wall. The streets are well laid out, and the houses built in a very handsome manner. It is divided into two parts, the upper and the lower; in the last the merchants and men of business generally reside. The upper town, however, contains the principal buildings, such as the palace of the governor, the houses of the chief officers, the convent of the Recollets, the Jesuits church and seminary, the free school, and the parish church. The governor's palace is a large fine building. Besides a general hospital, the neighbourhood of the city contains many elegant villas; and most of the vegetables of Europe grow in it. All the banks of the river from thence to Quebec, which is one hundred and eighty miles, is like one continued village, adorned with fine plantations, and gentlemen's seats at proper distances.

No further obstacle now remained in the way of the Americans to the capital, except what arose from the nature of the country, and these indeed were very considerable. Nothing, however, could damp the ardour of the provincials, notwithstanding it was now the middle of November, and the depth of winter was at hand.

About the same time Canada was invaded in the usual march from New York, a considerable detachment from the American army at Cambridge, was conducted into that province, by a new and unexpected passage. Arnold who conducted this bold undertaking, thereby acquired the name of the American Hannibal. He was detached with a thousand men from Cambridge to penetrate into Canada, by ascending the river Kennibec and descending by the Chaundiere to the river St. Lawrence. Great were the difficulties the Americans had to encounter so long, in marching three hundred miles through an uninhabited country. In ascending the Kennibec, they were constantly obliged to work upwards, against an impetuous current. They were often compelled by cataracts or other impediments, to land and haul their batteaux up rapid streams and over falls of rivers. Nor was their march by land more eligible than this passage by water. They had deep swamps, thick woods, difficult mountains, and craggy precipices alternately to encounter. At some places they had to cut their way for miles together, through forests so thick that their progress was only four or five miles a day. They, however, proceeded with unabated fortitude and constancy. Provisions grew at length so scarce, that some of the men eat their dogs, cartouch boxes, breeches, shoes, &c. At one time when they were an hundred miles from any habitation or prospect of a supply; their whole store was divided, which yielded four pints of flour for each man. On the last morning before their arrival, at their destination, after they had baked and eaten the remainder of their provisions, they had thirty miles to travel before they

L

could expect any further supply. The men bore up under these complicated distresses, with the greatest fortitude. They gloried in the hope of completing a march which would rival the fame of similar expeditions, undertaken by the heroes of antiquity. Having spent thirty-one days in traversing a hideous wilderness, without ever seeing any thing human, they at length reached the inhabited parts of Canada. The Canadians were struck with amazement, when they saw this armed force emerging from the wilderness, it had never entered their conception that it was possible for human beings to traverse such immense wilds. The most pointed instructions had been given to this corps to conciliate the affections of the Canadians. It was particularly enjoined upon them, if the son of lord Chatham,* then an officer in one of the British regiments in that province, should fall into their hands, to treat him with all possible attention, in return for the great exertions of his father, in behalf of American liberty.

The city of Quebec was at this time in a state of great weakness, but Sir Guy Carleton at this time arrived from Montreal ; his presence was itself a garrison, he was a man of ten thousand eyes, and was not to be taken unawares. The confidence reposed in his talents, inspired the garrison to make the most determined resistance. He issued a proclamation, in which he set forth, " that all persons liable to do military duty, and residing in Quebec, who refused to arm in conjunction with the royal army, should in four days quit Quebec, with their families, and withdraw themselves from the limits of the district, by the 1st of December, on pain of being treated afterwards as spies or rebels." All who were unwilling to co-operate with the British army, being thus disposed

---

* Now lord Chatham, and master of the ordnance.

of, the remaining inhabitants, though unused to arms, became in a little time so far acquainted with them, as to be very useful in defending the town. They supported fatigues, and submitted to command, with a patience and cheerfulness, that could not be exceeded by men familiarized to the hardships and subordinations of a military life.

On the 1st of December, general Montgomery joined Arnold upon the heights of Abraham before Quebec, and notwithstanding the extreme severity of the season in this inclement climate, he immediately began erecting his batteries, which by a perfect novelty in military science, being composed of snow and water, soon became solid ice. But finding his artillery make little impression, he determined on a general assault.* Early in the morning, on the 31st of December, 1775, during a snow storm the attack was made by two divisions, in two different quarters of the town. These divisions were commanded by colonel Arnold, and the general in person. Montgomery's division proceeded to make the attack, by the way of Cape Diamond, while Arnold's division attacked the suburbs of St. Rue. On the first onset, Montgomery led on his men with undaunted resolution ; he was attended with a number of carpenters with saws, in order to cut down the pickets, he even pulled some of them down with his own hands, and entered with his aid-de-camp, Mr. M'Pherson, and two more American officers at the

* During the siege, a woman from the American camp stole into Quebec, with letters addressed to the principal merchants, advising them to an immediate submission, and promising great indulgence in case of their compliance. Inclosed was a letter to general Carleton, with a summons to deliver up the town. The messenger was sent to prison for a few days, and then drummed out.

head of his division; here they were received with a
heavy fire of musketry Montgomery, with his officers
and a number of men were killed, and the remainder
of the division falling into immediate disorder, were
repulsed with much slaughter On the other side
colonel Arnold forced the first barrier, which consisted
of thirty men, but before he could attempt the second,
a reinforcement of the garrison, in consequence of the
defeat of Montgomery in the opposite quarter, was
collected against him ; here Arnold received a dangerous
wound in the leg, by a musquet ball, and was compelled to retire to the camp. To add to their embarrassment, they lost the help of one of their companies,
which was quartered on the north side of the river
St Charles, by their not having notice of the attack
in due time, which in endeavouring to join the main
body, were surprized by a party of our men, under
the command of . captain Laws, who made a sortie
through Palace Gate, and most of them were made
prisoners

The Americans near the second barrier took possession of some houses, but as our troops which sallied
out of Palace Gate, came upon their rear, and their
numbers being greatly lessened by being killed and
wounded, they were, obliged to retreat to the barrier
which they had but a little before taken, here they
maintained their ground until ten o'clock in the morning, when, after a brave resistance, they were obliged
to lay down their arms

The loss which the garrison sustained was but small
in comparison   One lieutenant of the navy, and six
rank and file killed, and thirteen rank and file wounded,
but the loss of the Americans was very considerable , seven officers were killed and six wounded, upwards of six hundred officers and men were taken prisoners Montgomery was shot through both his thighs

'and his head. When his body was taken up, his features were not in the least distorted, but his countenance appeared regular, placid, and serene; an elegant coffin was prepared, and he was interred with all military and funeral honors.* He was tall and slender, well limbed, of a genteel, easy, graceful and manly address; to the courage of the soldier he added the military skill of the general, and had the voluntary love, esteem, and confidence of the American troops, who greatly lamented him. In the afternoon, the American officers were confined in the seminary, and well accommodated with bedding, &c. they were treated with the greatest politeness and generosity by the British officers; the privates were confined in the Recollets, or Jesuits college, and well used.† Montgomery's knee

* In general Montgomery's memoirs written some time after his death, by Dr. Smith, of Philadelphia, a celebrated American partisan, speaking on this subject, he says, "O thou swift winged messenger of destruction, how didst thou triumph in that moment! the stroke that severed Montgomery from his army, deprived them of more than a member. It reached the vitals, and struck the whole body with a temporary death. As when the forked lightening, darting through the forest, . amidst the black tempests of night, rends some towering oak, and lays its honors in the dust, the inferior trees which it had long sheltered from the storm, stand mournful around. So stood the astonished bands, over their fallen, chieftain! nor over him alone, but over others, in their prime of glory, prostrate by his side.

Such examples of magnanimity filled even adversaries with veneration and esteem. Forgetting the foes in the heroes, they gathered up their breathless remains, and committed them to kindred dust; with pious hands, " and funeral honors meet;" so may your own remains, and particularly thine, O Carleton, be honored, should it ever be your fate to fall in hostile fields! or if, amid the various chances of war, your lot should be among the prisoners and the wounded, may you be distinguished with an ample return of that benevolence which you have shewn to others! such offices of humanity, softening the savage scenes of war, will entitle you to an honor which all the pride of conquest cannot bestow."

† Major Meig, who succeeded Arnold in the command after he was wounded, in writing upon this subject, says, " I dined

buckles, and his aid-de-camp's gold broach, with several other valuable articles found with the dead officers, were all restored to the Americans, which were highly gratifying to them. " British soldiers in the moment of victory, will have mercy on a prostrate foe, as the brave and generous cannot be cruel."

General Montgomery received a liberal education in Ireland, his native country. In the year 1758 he had obtained the rank of captain in the 17th regiment of foot, and stood full in the way of higher preferment; having borne a share in all our American wars, and the reduction of Canada, in the year 1759 ; as soon as peace was restored, he took leave of the army, and having soon connected himself by marriage with an antient and honorable family in the province of New York, he chose a delightful retirement upon the banks of Hudson's river, where he continued until appointed by the American congress a brigadier general.

Colonel Arnold with the shattered remains of his troops, retreated three miles from the city where he had the temerity to encamp. Early in the spring, the Isis, of fifty-four guns, accompanied by the Surprise frigate, and the Martin sloop, on board of which was part of the 29th foot, forced their passage through the ice, before the navigation of the river St. Lawrence was deemed practicable.

Governor Carleton was too great a proficient in the art of war, to delay seizing the advantages which the consternation of the besiegers and the arrival of this reinforcement afforded. He marched out at their head to attack the Americans. On his approach he found every thing in confusion : the late besiegers abandoning their artillery and military stores, had in great precipi-

this day with captain Law, whom in the morning I made prisoner; but in a few hours after I was in my turn made prisoner also. Captain Law treated me with the greatest politeness and generosity."

tation retreated. In this manner, at the expiration of five months, the mixed siege and blockade of Quebec was raised. The fortitude and perseverance of the garrison reflected honor on both officers and privates.

. The reputation acquired by general Carleton in his military character, for, bravely and judiciously defend-, ing the province committed to his care, was exceeded by the superior applause, merited from his exercise of the virtues of humanity and generosity. Among the numerous sick in the American hospitals, several incapable of being moved were left behind. The victorious general proved himself worthy of success by his treatment of these unfortunate men : he not only fed and cloathed them, but permitted them when recovered to return home. Apprehending that fear might make some conceal themselves in the woods, rather than by applying for a relief, make themselves known, he removed their doubts by the following proclamation : " Whereas I am informed; that many of his majesty's deluded subjects, of the neighbouring provinces, laboring under wounds and divers disorders, are dispersed in the adjacent woods and parishes, and in great danger of perishing for want of proper assistance, all captains and other officers of militia are hereby commanded to make diligent search for all such distressed persons, and afford them all necessary relief, and convey them to the general hospital, where proper care shall be taken of them : all reasonable expenses which may be incurred in complying with this order, shall be paid by the receiver-general.

" And lest a consciousness of past offences should deter such miserable wretches from receiving that assistance which their distressed situation may require ; I hereby make known to them, that as soon as their health is restored they shall have free liberty to return to their respective provinces."

A rich Frenchman, who commanded a regiment of Canadians under Montgomery, and who joined him in Montreal, was likewise taken prisoner. A few weeks after general Carleton ordered the Frenchman to make his appearance upon the parade of the castle. He was brought there under a file of soldiers; general Carleton was walking at the top of the parade. As soon as the man was brought in, he waved his hat for the soldiers to retire and shut the gates. An interview must now take place; let the reader imagine what the Frenchman felt: he expected to be hanged like a dog, or sent over to England to be tried by the English judges. Up to the general he must come, for he could not expect that the general would run towards him. He summoned his courage, and walked with a slow dignified step up to the parade towards the general. As soon as he came up he expected nothing but frowns and the most stinging reproaches, as he was one of the king's subjects in the governor's jurisdiction. The general stopped and looked at him with a mixture of dignity and condescension, and said, " Sir, when did you hear from your family ?" " General," replied the other, " I have not heard from them these three months." (The general knew that very well, for he had intercepted all his letters.) " Sir, said he, which way do you chuse to go home, by land or water ? If you chuse to go by water, you shall have my barge: if you chuse to go by land you shall ride in my coach." The man was struck with amazement, fell down at his feet, and clasping the governor's knees, burst into a violent exclamation; " O general, you are too good ! you are too good !" The general raised him from the ground, sent him home with honor and joy to his family, with such gratitude in his heart as never forsook him. He continued a faithful subject as long as he lived.

After this gentleman was gone home to Montreal, general Carleton sent for the American prisoners, in small companies, and addressed them with such sweetness and good humour, as was sufficient to melt every heart. "My lads," said he, "why did you come to disturb an honest man in his government, that never did any harm to you in his life? I never invaded your property, nor sent a single soldier to distress you. Come, my boys, you are in a very distressing situation, and not able to go home with any comfort; I must provide you with with shoes, stockings, and good warm waistcoats. I must give you some good victuals to carry you home. Take care, my lads, that you do not come here again, lest I should not treat you so kindly."

This humane line of conduct was more injurious to the views of the leaders in the American councils, than any severity that could be used against them.

In general Carleton's dispatches to government, particular mention is made of lieutenant colonel M'Clean, and his newly raised regiment of Scotch emigrants, for their indefatigable zeal in the king's service, during the siege. Also captain Hamilton of his Majesty's ship, the Lizard, with the officers and seamen, who were formed into a battalion on shore, discharged their duty with alacrity and spirit. Major Caldwell who commanded the militia likewise, proved himself an active and diligent officer.

M

CHAP. VI.

*Disturbances in Virginia. Major Connolly taken
Prisoner by the Americans. Lord Dunmore's
Letter to an Indian Chief. Logan's Speech to Lord
Dunmore. Norfolk destroyed by Fire. Lord Dun-
more sails with the Fleet. Charlestown attacked by
Sir Peter Parker and repulsed. Captain Morris's
gallant Behaviour and Death. Account of General
Lee.*

QUEBEC being thus freed from danger, it is now
necessary to take a transient view of the state of
affairs, at this period in some of the southern provinces. Lord Dunmore, the governor of Virginia, was
involved in disputes similar to those which had taken
place in other colonies; these disputes arose to such
violence, that his lordship was obliged to take refuge
on board the Fowey ship of war, into which he attempted to transfer the sittings of the assembly; a
requisition which the legislative body absolutely
refused to comply with. His lordship being thus
divested of his authority, carried on a sort of predatory
war against the province.

In order to protect the loyalists who now began to
flock to the royal standard, his lordship constructed
a fort near Norfolk, a maritime town of some conse-

quence : this fort he furnished with artillery. The Americans also fortified themselves within cannon shot of the same place, with a narrow causeway in their front. In this state both parties continued quiet for some days. Lord Dunmore now formed a design of surprizing the enemy in their entrenchments; this was undertaken before day-light, on the 9th of December, 1775. Captain Fordyce, at the head of the grenadiers of the 14th regiment of foot, amounting to sixty men, passed the causeway, and boldly marched up to the American entrenchments, with fixed bayonets, and with a coolness and entrepidity which first excited the astonishment, and afterwards the praise of their enemies. They were exposed without cover to the fire of the provincials in front, and enfiladed by another part of their works. The brave captain Fordyce with several of his men fell, the lieutenant and others were taken, and all the survivors of this valiant grenadier company, whether prisoners or not, were wounded. Captain Fordyce was interred with every military honor, by the victors; the English prisoners treated with kindness, but the Americans who had joined the king's standard experienced the greatest cruelties.

A short time before this, a scheme of importance was formed by major Connolly, a Pennsylvanian of an intrepid and aspiring disposition, and attached to the cause of Britain. The first step of his plan was to enter into a league with the Ohio Indians. This he communicated to lord Dunmore, and it received his approbation. Upon which, Connolly set out, and actually succeeded in his design. On his return he was dispatched to general Gage at Boston, from whom he received a colonel's commission, and set out in order to accomplish the remainder of his scheme. The plan in general was to proceed to Fort Detroit, where captain Lord of the Royal Irish was to meet him with two companies, and a field piece. Connolly was to raise a regiment, with as many Indians and partizans as he could; to enable him to do this, he had power to promise every person that entered into the service, three hundred acres of land, when the troubles were over, and what other pecuniary rewards he might think proper; was to appoint and commission all the officers under him, which commissions were to be confirmed by lord Dunmore. With this force he was to penetrate through the country, in order to cut off the communication between the southern and northern colonies, destroy Fort Pit, and Fort Fincastle, and meet lord Dunmore on the 10th of April following, at Alexandria. Connolly's companions were lieutenant Cameron and Dr. Smith. On their road through Maryland, they were all three taken, cast into prison, and closely confined. On searching their portmanteaus, a copy of Connolly's plan was found. The congress immediately published the following speech, from lord Dunmore to White Eyes, a famous Indian warrior, which they said was found in the colonel's custody:

" Brother, captain White Eyes, I am glad to hear your good speeches, sent to me by major Connolly, and you may be assured I shall put the one end of the belt which you have sent me, into the hands of our great king, who will be glad to hear from his brothers, the Delawares, and will take a strong hold of it. You may rest satisfied, that our foolish young men shall never be permitted to take your lands, but on the contrary, the great king will protect you, and preserve you in the possession of them. Our young people in the country have been very foolish, and done many impudent things, for which they must soon be sorry, and of which I make no doubt, they have acquainted you; but I must desire you not to listen to them, as they would be willing that you should act equally foolish with themselves. But rather let what you hear, pass in at one ear, and out at the other, so that it may make no impression on your heart, until you hear from me fully, which shall be as soon as I can give farther information, who am your friend and brother.

" Captain White Eyes will please to acquaint the Corn Stalk with these my sentiments also, as well as the chiefs of the Mingors, and the other six nations. Your sincere friend, and elder brother, Dunmore."

The Americans never lost an opportunity of magnifying every circumstance which would in anywise tend to the promotion of their own cause, while at the same time, they covered in obscurity the very motives and views with which they themselves used to accomplish their ends. Some months before this, the inhabitants of Virginia had endeavoured to gain the Indians over to their side, in order to assist them against the loyalists in that state.* This well known narrative is given by an American partizan. It begins as follows:

" We may challenge the whole orations of Demosthenes and Cicero, and of any more eminent orator, if Europe has furnished more eminent, to produce a single passage superior to the speech of Logan, a Mingo chief, to lord Dunmore, when governor of the state of Virginia. The story is as follows; of which and of the speech, the authenticity is unquestionable. In the spring of the year 1774, a robbery and murder were committed on an inhabitant† of the frontiers of Virgi-

* See page 76.
† One of the loyalists. Undoubtedly these Indians were instigated to take up the hatchet by the Americans against their brethren, and for what cause? Why, because they adhered to the British government.

nia, by two Indians of the Shawanee tribe; the neighbouring whites, according to their custom,* undertook
to punish this outrage in a summary way. Colonel
Cresap, infamous for the many murders he had committed on this much injured people, collected a party,
and proceeded down the Kanhaway in quest of vengeance. Unfortunately a canoe of women and children
with one man only, was seen coming from the opposite shore, unarmed and unsuspecting any hostile attack
from the whites. Cresap and his party concealed themselves on the bank of the river, and the moment the
canoe reached the shore, singled out their objects,
and at one fire killed every person in it. This
happened to be the family of Logan, who had long
been distinguished as a friend of the whites. This
unworthy return provoked his vengeance. He accordingly signalized himself in the war which ensued.
In the autumn of the same year, a decisive battle
was fought at the mouth of the great Kanhaway, between the collected forces of the Shawanees, Mingoes,
and Delawares, and a detachment of the Virginia
militia.† The Indians were defeated, and sued for
peace. Logan, however, disdained to be seen among
the suppliants, but lest the sincerity of a treaty
should be distrusted, from which, so distinguished a
chief absented himself, he sent by a messenger the
following speech, to be delivered to lord Dunmore:
" I appeal to any white man to say if ever he entered Logan's cabin hungry, and he gave him not meat;
if he ever came cold and naked, and he cloathed him
not. During the course of the last long and bloody
war, Logan remained idle in his cabin, an advocate
for peace. Such was my love for the whites, that my

---

* They were under the necessity in their defence to resist
force by force.
† Under the command of lord Dunmore.

countrymen pointed as they passed, and said, *Logan is the friend of white men.* I had even thought to have lived with you, but for the injuries of one man. Colonel Cresap, the last spring, in cold blood, and unprovoked, murdered all the relations of Logan, not sparing even my women and children. There runs not a drop of my blood in the veins of any living creature. This called on me for revenge. I have sought it ; I have killed many ; I have fully glutted my vengeance. For my country, I rejoice at the beams of peace ; but I do not harbour a thought that mine is the joy of fear. Logan never felt fear. He will not turn on his heel to save his life. Who is there to mourn for Logan ? Not one."

Lord Dunmore retreated from Norfolk, and that place was taken possession of by the provincials, who treated the loyalists that had remained there, with great severity, at the same time that they greatly distressed those on board lord Dunmore's fleet, by refusing to supply them with any necessaries. Nor was this all ; the vicinity of the shipping was so near, as to afford the riflemen an opportunity of aiming at the people on board, and exercising the cruel occupation of killing them, in which they did not fail every day to employ themselves. These proceedings at last drew a remonstrance from his lordship ; in which he insisted that the fleet should be furnished with necessaries, and that the soldiers should desist from the cruel treatment above mentioned ; but both these requests being denied, a resolution was taken to set fire to the town. After giving the inhabitants proper warning, a party landed, under cover of a ship of war, and set fire to that part which lay nearest to the shore ; but the flames were observed at the same time to break forth in every other quarter, and the whole town was reduced to ashes. This universal destruction, by which a loss of more than three hundred thousand pounds was incurred, is said to have been occasioned by order of the congress itself, that the loyalists might find no refuge there for the future. The Americans after this transaction, burned and destroyed the houses and plantations within reach of the guns of the ships of war, and obliged the inhabitants to remove with their cattle, provisions, and portable effects, further into the country.

The heat of the season, and the numbers crowded together in lord Dunmore's fleet, produced a pestilential fever, which made great havoc, especially among the negroes. At last finding themselves in the utmost hazard of perishing, by famine as well as disease, they set fire to the least valuable of their vessels, reserving only about fifty for themselves, in which they bid a final adieu to Virginia, some sailing to Florida, some to Bermuda, and the rest to the West Indies.

In South Carolina, the provincials had a more formidable enemy to contend with. A squadron whose object was the reduction of Charlestown, had been fitted out in December, 1775, but by reason of unfavourable weather, did not reach Cape Fear, in North Carolina, till the month of May, 1776; and here it met with further obstacles till the end of the month. Thus, the Americans, always noted for their alertness in raising fortifications, had time to strengthen those of Charlestown, in such a manner as rendered it exceedingly difficult to be attacked. The British squadron consisted of two fifty-gun ships, four of thirty guns, two of twenty; an armed schooner, and a bomb-ketch, all under the command of Sir Peter Parker; the land forces were commanded by general Clinton, lord Cornwallis, and brigadier general Vaughan. It was now determined to try the event of an attack on the city of Charlestown, the capital of South Carolina. The Americans had erected works on Sullivan's Island, mounted with thirty pieces of cannon, in a very advantageous situation, for annoying ships in their approach to the town. The militia of the province were also collected in great numbers for the defence of the metropolis, aided by several continental regiments, and the whole commanded by general Lee.

On the 23th of June, the Bristol and Experiment, each of fifty guns, supported by several smaller vessels, had with some difficulty crossed the bar, and advanced to the attack of the fort on Sullivan's Island, constructed entirely of palmetto, a soft and spungy wood, in which a ball entering is buried, and makes no extended fracture. Though an attack on this fort was practical from the sea, it was very difficult to obtain a co-operation of the land forces. This was attempted by landing them on an island adjacent to Sullivan's island, on the east, from which it is separated by a narrow creek. Opposite to this creek the Americans had posted a strong body of troops, with cannon and entrenchments, while general Lee was posted on the main land, with a bridge of boats between that and Sullivan's Island ; so that he could at pleasure send reinforcements to the troops in the fort on Sullivan's Island.

The attack commenced early in the morning by a bomb-ketch, which began to throw shells into the fort, and about mid-day the two fifty-gun ships came up and began a severe fire. Three other frigates were ordered to take their station, between Charlestown and the fort, in order to enfilade the batteries, and cut off the communication with the main land ; but, through the ignorance of the pilots, they all stuck fast ; and though two of them were disentangled, they

N

were found to be totally unfit for service : the third
was burnt, that she might not fall into the hands of
the enemy.

The attack was therefore confined to five armed
ships and a bomb-ketch, between whom and the fort a
dreadful fire ensued. The Bristol suffered exceedingly. The springs on her cable being shot away, she
was for some time exposed to the enemy's fire. As
the Americans poured in great quantities of red hot
balls, she was twice in flames. The brave captain
Morris after receiving five wounds, was obliged to
go between decks, to have his arm amputated. After
undergoing this operation, he insisted to be carried
on the quarter deck to resume his command ; here
he received another wound, but still refused to quit
his station ; at last he received a red hot ball in his
belly, which put an end to his life. A few moments
before he died, one of the officers asked him if he
had any directions to give with respect to his family,
to which he heroically answered, " None, I leave
them to the providence of God, and the generosity
of my country." His majesty on receiving an account
of this affair, sent the captain's widow an handsome
present, and settled a pension on her and her
children.

Of all the officers and seamen who stood on the
quatrer deck of the Bristol, not one escaped without
a wound, excepting Sir Peter Parker alone, though
he received several contusions during the action, yet
he modestly says in his dispatches they were not
worth mentioning. Indeed his intrepidity and presence
of mind during the action was very remarkable. The
engagement lasted till darkness put an end to it.
During the height of the attack, the provincial
batteries remained for some time silent, so that it
was concluded that they had been abandoned, but

this was found to proceed only from want of powder, for as soon as a supply of this article was obtained, the firing was resumed as brisk as before. During the whole of this desperate engagement, it was found impossible for the land forces to give any assistance to the fleet. The enemy's works were found to be much stronger than they had been imagined, and the depth of water effectually prevented them from making any attempt. Captain Scott of the Experiment, and lord William Campbell, late governor of the colony, who now with great gallantry served as a volunteer on board the fleet, were also dangerously wounded, with more than two hundred of as brave men as ever the British Navy produced, of the crews of these two ships only. Particular mention was made of the bravery of lieutenants Caulfield, Molloy, and Nugent, of the Bristol. Every man that was engaged did his duty. The Experiment and Bristol were so much damaged, that it was thought they could not be got over the bar; however, this was at last accomplished by a very great exertion of naval skill, to the surprise of the Americans, who had expected to make them both prizes. On the American side the loss was judged to be very considerable, as most of their guns were dismounted, and reinforcements had poured into the fort during the whole time of the action.

During this attack general Lee exposed himself to great danger; as the balls whistled about he observed one of his aid-de-camps shrink every now and then, and by the motion of his body seemed to evade the shot. " Death sir," cried Lee, " what do you mean, do you doge? Do you know that the king of Prussia lost above an hundred aid-de-camps in one campaign." " So I understand, sir," replied the officer, " but I did not think you could spare so many." A short memoir of this gentleman may not be unnecessary,

He was born in Chester, in the year 1726; his father, a man of considerable property in that county, was in the year 1745 appointed colonel of the 44th regiment of foot.

As Charles was an only son, his father bestowed upon him a very liberal education, and in the year 1745 he obtained a commission for him in his own regiment, in which he continued till the year 1760, passing through the ranks of ensign, lieutenant, and captain.

During this time Charles Lee was present at several actions, the first of which was at the defeat of general Braddock, at Monongahela; after this he was at the attack of the lines of Ticonderoga, in 1758, where he was shot through the body. The next year he was with general Prideaux at the reduction of Niagara, and in the year 1760 was at the conquest of Canada, with general Amherst.

The campaign being ended, captain Lee obtained leave to return to England, where, in the year 1761, he was appointed major in the 103d regiment, which, on the breaking out of the Spanish war, was sent to Portugal, under the command of lord Loudon. In Portugal, as well as in America, major Lee behaved with distinguished bravery; and general Burgoyne, under whose immediate direction he was, bore testimony of his firmness in executing the orders he received to surprise the Spanish camp, which he did with a bravery and intrepidy that settled his character as a distinguished officer.

At the peace of 1763, major Lee's corps was disbanded, and he, unwilling to remain inactive, obtained leave to enter into the service of the king of Poland, by whom he was greatly caressed; he afterwards went as a volunteer in the war between Russia and the Ottoman Porte.

In the year 1772, he returned to England, and in the month of May, in that year, he was honored with the rank of lieutenant colonel, after which he went to America, to visit a numerous set of friends he had in that country.

Whether he had at that time entertained any intention of intermeddling in the dispute between Great Britain and the colonies, we cannot pretend to decide: but as soon as the colonies began to raise forces, he immediately resigned his half pay, and with the greatest alacrity accepted the post of major general in their armies.

In person general Lee was five feet eight inches high, slender in his make, but able to endure the greatest hardships, little caring what he eat or drank, or on what he slept. His actions have shewn him to be brave, active, and determined; this may be seen by the following circumstance. At the time general Clinton sailed from Boston, Lee, at the head of a strong detachment from the American army before that place, immediately set out to secure New York from the attempt which it was supposed the British troops would have made upon that city. Having succeeded in that object, general Clinton could not but be surprised at his arrival in Virginia, to find Lee in possession, and in the same state of preparation in which he had left him at New York. Upon his departure for Cape Fear, Lee again traversed the continent with the utmost expedition to secure North Carolina: and at length upon the further progress of the fleet and army to the southward, Lee again proceeded with equal celerity to the defence of Charlestown.

General Lee was a studious man, and of intense application, not only in his profession as a soldier, but even that of a lawyer. As he visited most of the courts of Europe, he acquired a perfect knowledge of their languages. He spoke the Indian language as well as English, and as he passed great part of the former war among the Indians they had a particular friendship for him.

His resentment against the British government was very strong, but for what cause it is not conjectured; however, it is well known that he was of an ardent, fiery disposition, of which the following letter is a specimen; the reader will observe that this letter was written to a gentleman in Maryland,* in the beginning of the year 1776, some months before any reinforcements arrived from England to America.

" I know not," says this modern Achilles, ", in the whole course of my life, I ever read any thing which so much moved my pity and indignation as the late declaration of the convention of Maryland. They declare, they shall esteem separation from Great Britain as the last of misfortunes. What! when an attempt has been made to rob you and your posterity of your birthrights; when your fields have been laid waste, your towns have been burnt, and your citizens butchered;† when your property is seized and confiscated in all parts of the world; when an inexorable tyrant, an abandoned parliament, and a corrupt, pusillanimous people, have formed a hellish league to rob you of every

* Maryland was one of the last states which yielded to the declaration of independence to the British crown.

† When!—Where!——At this very time seven thousand British troops were shut up in Boston, surrounded by an innumerable host of Americans: Canada at the same time overrun by another army of Americans and Indians.

Surely one cannot help being astonished at the virulence with which Mr. Lee speaks, on the present occasion, against his country, which had loaded him and his family with honors.

" Describe Achilles, as Achilles was,
" Impatient—rash—inexorable—proud—
" Scorning all judges, and all law but arms."

thing men hold most dear ; is it possible there should be creatures, who march on two legs, and call themselves human, who can be so destitute of sentiment, courage, and feeling, as sobbingly to protest, they should con- sider separation from these butchers and robbers as the last of misfortunes ?

" Oh I could brain you with your ladies' fans.' "

Author's Journal continued. Further Description of the River St. Lawrence. Anecdote of an Algonquin Woman. An Attempt to surprise the British Troops at Three Rivers. Americans defeated. Retreat to St. John's. The British prepare a Fleet to cross Lake Champlain. Sails and engages the American Fleet, which is defeated. British Troops take possession of Crown Point. Retires to Winter Quarters.

IT is now high time to take notice of the military operations of the British forces to which I was attached in Canada. It has been already mentioned that colonel Arnold raised the siege of Quebec and retreated with the greatest precipitation towards Three Rivers.

On the 29th June, 1776, having accomplished our voyage to Quebec, general Carleton found himself at the head of twelve thousand regular troops, among whom were those of Brunswick. With this force we set out for Three Rivers, where we expected that Arnold would have made a stand, but he had fled to Sorel, a place one hundred and fifty miles distant from Quebec, where he was at last met by the reinforcements, ordered by congress, under the command of general Thomas ; who was appointed by that body, commander in chief in Canada, in the room of Montgomery. A few days after he arrived at the American encampment, he was seized with the small pox, and died, having forbidden his men to innoculate, he conformed to his own rule, and refused to avail himself of that precaution. On his death the command at first devolved on Arnold, and afterwards on general Sullivan.

In the mean time, our troops proceeded with all expedition from Quebec to Three Rivers, which place was appointed the general rendezvous of the army. In our passage up the river St. Lawrence, our eyes were entertained with beautiful landscapes, the banks being in many places very bold and steep, and shaded with lofty trees, and in others crowded with villages, the air became so mild and temperate, that we thought ourselves transported into another climate. June 5th our regiment was ordered to land, and to press forward with all expedition. 6th, Arrived at Three Rivers. This town lies half way between Quebec and Montreal, and about thirty leagues from each; it has its name from three rivers which join their current above a quarter of a mile below the village, and fall into the great one, St. Lawrence. It is much resorted to by the several tribes of Indians who come down those rivers, and trade with the inhabitants in various kind of furs. The country about it is fertile in corn, fruits, &c.

For the sake of many of my readers who perhaps have never read the following anecdote, which is related of an Algonquin woman, I shall take the liberty of relating it in this part of my journal.

That nation being at war with the Iroquois, she happened to be taken prisoner and was carried to one of the villages belonging to them. Here she was stripped naked, and her hands and feet bound with ropes, in one of their cabins. In this condition she remained ten days, the

O

savages sleeping round her every night. The eleventh
night, while they were asleep, she found means to dis-
engage one of her hands, after which she immediately
freed herself from the ropes, and went to the door.
Though she had now an opportunity of escaping unperceived, her revengeful temper could not let slip so
favorable an opportunity of killing one of her enemies.
The attempt was manifestly at the hazard of her own
life ; yet, snatching up a hatchet, she killed the savage
that lay next her ; and springing out of the cabin,
concealed herself in a hollow tree which she had
observed the day before. The groans of the dying
person soon alarmed the other savages, and the young
ones immediately set out in pursuit of her. Perceiving from her tree, that they all directed their course
one way, and that none of the savages were near her,
she left her sanctuary, and flying by an opposite direction, ran into a forest without being perceived. The
second day after this her footseps were discovered,
and they pursued her with such expedition that the
third day she discovered her enemies at her heels ; upon
this she threw herself into a pond of water, and diving
among some reeds and bulrushes, she could just breathe
above water without being perceived. Her pursuers
after making the most diligent search, were forced to
return. For thirty-five days this woman held on her
course, through woods and deserts, without any other
sustenance than roots and wild berries. When she came
to the river St. Lawrence, she made with her own hands
a kind of wicker raft on which she crossed. As she
went by the French for Three Rivers, without well
knowing where she was, she perceived a canoe full
of savages, and fearing they might be Iroquois, ran
again into the woods, where she remained till sun set.
Continuing her course, soon after she saw Three Rivers,
and was then discovered by a party whom she knew to

be Hurons, a nation in alliance with the Algonquins; she then squatted down behind a bush, calling out to them, that she was not in a condition to be seen, because she was naked. They immediately threw her a blanket, and then conducted her to the fort, where she recounted her story.

June 8th. At three o'clock this morning our drums beat to arms, and we soon marched out of the village to meet our foe.

This being the first skirmish I ever was engaged in, it really appeared to me to be a very serious matter, especially when the bullets came whistling by our ears. In order to encourage the young soldiers amongst us, some of the veterans who had been well used to this kind of work, said, " there is no danger if you hear the sound of the bullet, which is fired against you, you are safe, and after the first charge all your fears will be done away." These remarks I found to be perfectly true many a time afterwards. The cannon from the ships in the river, and the field pieces on land, began now to roar; many of the unfortunate Americans were killed and wounded.

" Present we heard the battle's loud alarm,
" The hideous cannon with continued roar,
" Proclaims approaching death and wide spread harm:
" Confusion echoes from the martial shore."

Surely war, whether offensive or defensive, is a picture of desolation !

This was a very bold enterprise indeed of the Americans to attack our troops. Two thousand of them crossed over from Sorel in fifty boats, landed at the Point du Lai, before day-light, with an intention to surprise us at Three Rivers. General Frazer, who commanded the British van, was not to be taken by surprise. The Americans soon found that they were greatly mistaken in their intelligence concerning our position:

when they discovered their mistake they were greatly
alarmed, particularly when they found that brigadier
general Nesbit, who had landed the troops from the
transports, had got behind them.   After some time
they gave up offensive measures, and retreated to the
woods   Our troops still pushed forward in hopes of
taking their boats and cutting off their retreat, two
boats only were taken, the rest escaped   The number of the Americans killed and wounded were considerable, about two hundred surrendered, or were taken
prisoners in the woods   Generals Thompson and Irwin,
who commanded this party, with several other American
officers were among the prisoners. few of the British
fell on this day

9th.   Ordered on board our transports with all expedition, the wind springing up fair, the fleet sailed
towards Sorel

11th.· Our ship grounded on a sand bank, just in
the middle of the river St Lawrence, here we remained fast near two hours, and then drifted, we
received no damage, and soon regained our station.

14th   Landed at Sorel, here we heard that the
Americans had retreated, only two hours before. All
the fires n their encampment were burning

15th   Our troops began to march n three columns,
under the command of general Burgoyne, who led the
pursuit

16th   Continued our march day and night, expecting every hour to come up with them   However,
n all their haste, they took care to set on fire their
batteaux, ships, military stores, &c   It must be confessed that their distresses at this time were very great
A British army close on their rear, and threatening
them with destruction, their men obliged to drag their
loaded batteaux up the rapids by mere strength, often
to their middle in water   They were likewise encum-

bered with great numbers labouring under that dreadful disease, the small pox, which is so fatal in America. It was said that two regiments at one time had not a single man in health, another had only six, and a fourth only forty, and two more were nearly in the same condition.

. While the Americans were retreating, they were daily annoyed by the remonstrances of the inahabitants of Canada, who had either joined or befriended them. Many of the Canadians had taken a decided part in their favor, rendered them essential ' services, and thereby incurred the heavy penalties annexed to the crime of supporting rebellion. These, though congress had assured them but a few months before, " that they would never abandon them to the fury of their common enemies," were, from the necessity of the case, left exposed to the resentment of their rulers. The retreating army recommended them to cast themselves on the mercy of that government, against which they had offended.*

18th. Took possession of the redoubts at St. John's, and found all the buildings in flames, all the craft and large boats the enemy could not drag up the rapids of Chamblee, with some provisions, were also burnt : twenty-two pieces of cannon were left behind, and several other marks appeared of great precipitation and fright, in the retreat of the enemy.

26th. We heard that the Americans had retreated across Lake Champlain to Crown Point. We could not for want of boats urge our pursuit any farther.

September 30th. We have been very busy these three months past in constructing a fleet, in order to face the

* They did indeed receive mercy, for I never saw any of them either imprisoned or otherwise punished by our government, for their joining the Americans at that time ; and I was in Canada for twelve months after this.

enemy on water. The spirit of our troops has risen in proportion to the difficulties which they had to encounter. A fleet is now prepared. The ship Inflexible, mounting eighteen twelve-pounders is ready to sail ; three weeks ago her keel was laid. Two schooners, one of fourteen and another of twelve six-pounders. A flat bottom radeau, carrying six twenty-four pounders, and six twelve-pounders, besides howitzers. A gondola, with seven nine-pounders. Twenty smaller vessels, with brass field pieces, from nine to twenty-four pounders. A number of long boats. A great number of batteaux, destined for the transportation of the army, have been in three months little less than created.

October 1st. Our little squadron was put under the command of Captain Pringle, and is now ready to sail.

Upon the 11th, our squadron came up with the American fleet, commanded by Arnold ; they were at anchor under the island Valicour, and seemed a strong line, extending from the island to the west side of the continent. The wind was so unfavorable, that the ship Inflexible, and some other vessels of force, could not be brought to action.

Orders were now given to anchor, in a line as near as possible to the American fleet, that their retreat might be cut off. This was frustrated by the extreme obscurity of the night, and in the morning the American fleet had got a considerable distance from our ships up the lake.

13th. Eleven sail of the Americans was seen making off to Crown Point, when after a chase of seven hours, captain Pringle, on board of the Maria, of fourteen six-pounders, having the armed vessels, Carleton and Inflexible, a small distance a-stern, came up with the enemy, the rest of the fleet almost out of sight. The action began at twelve o'clock, and lasted two hours. The

Washington galley struck during the action, and some time after, Arnold in the Congress galley, and five gondolas, ran on shore and blew up the vessels. In this perilous enterprize he paid attention to a point of honor. He did not quit his own galley till she was in flames, lest our sailors should board her, and strike her flag. The killed and wounded in our fleet did not amount to forty. General Carleton was on board the Maria during the action, and praised in the highest terms the conduct of the officers and men of the corps of artillery who served the gun boats, and who sustained for many hours the whole fire of the enemy's fleet,* the rest of the vessels not being able to work up near enough to join effectually in the engagement.

The Americans hearing of the defeat of their naval force, set fire to all the buildings and houses in and near Crown Point, and retired to Ticonderoga.

The result of this sea fight, though unfortunate for the Americans, raised the reputation of Arnold higher than ever; in addition to the fame of a brave soldier, he acquired that of an able naval officer. Waterburg, the second in command, and brigadier general in the American army, was taken. Out of fifteen American armed vessels which engaged our fleet in the morning, three only escaped; the rest were taken, burnt and destroyed.

General Carleton landed at Crown Point, and took possession of the ground from which the Americans had retreated, and was there joined by our army. He sent out several reconnoitering parties, and pushed forward a strong detachment on both sides of the lake, which approached near to Ticonderoga. Some of our vessels came within cannon shot of the American

* The matrosses who served in the gun-boats were drafts from the Irish Artillery in Chapelizod.

works at that place. But the strength of that garrison, and the season of the year restrained us from making any attempt, at that time, on Ticonderoga.

31st. Our army embarked on board of the batteaux, and on the 2d of November landed at St. John's, in Canada.

Such was the termination of the northern campaign in 1776. After the death of Montgomery, evacuations of posts, defeats, and retreats, had almost interruptedly been the portion of the Americans.

The Winter Quarters of the British army was in the following order :—

HEAD QUARTERS, QUEBEC.

Royal Artillery, commanded by General Phillips, } General Hospital, Montreal.

Van Brigade, commanded by gen. Frazer, grenadiers, light Infantry and 24th regiment, } At LePrairie, Longeuil, &c. extending on the south side of the river St. Lawrence to St. Curs.

First Brigade commanded by brigadier general Powel.

9th regiment.........................Isle Jesus.
47th do.†......................St. Luce, Recollet, St. Genevieze and St. Lawrent.
53d.....................................Chamblee.

Second Brigade, commanded by brigadier general Hamilton.

20th regiment........................Isle au Noix.
21st do...............................St. John's.
34th do...............................Quebec.
62d do...............................Point Levy, opposite to Quebec.

German troops commanded by generals Reidesel and Speicht, were quartered from Bertheier to Three Rivers, and forty miles below Three Rivers, on the road to Quebec.

Maclean's Royal Highlanders, emigrants, quartered at Chinage Bonne, and River du China.

Sir John Johnson's regiment, called the New Yorker's, quartered at Lachine, La Point Clare, and St. Ann.

8th regiment.........................Upper Posts, Niagara, Detroit, &c.

---

† Lieutenant colonel Nesbit died about this time, at Quebec; he was a brave, humane officer, and greatly beloved by the brigade which he commanded.

The Isle of Jesus where the 9th regiment was quartered, lies in the neighbourhood of Montreal, and is about eight leagues in length, and two in breadth; here as in other parts of Canada, the forests present a most beautiful appearance, and contain a great variety of trees, among which are pine, fir, cedar, oak, maple, ash, walnut, beech, elm, and poplar. The Indians hollow the red elm into canoes, some of which, made out of one piece, will contain twenty persons. About November, the bears and wild cats take up their habitations in the hollow elms, and remain there till April. Here are also found cherry trees, plumb trees, the vinegar tree, the fruit of which, being infused in water, produces vinegar; and an aquatic plant, called atoca, the fruit of which may be made into a confection; the white thorn, the cotton tree, on the top of which grow several tufts of flowers, which when shaken in the morning, before the dew falls off, produces honey that may be boiled up into sugar, the seed being a pod, containing a very fine kind of cotton: the sun plant, which resembles a marigold, and grows to the height of seven or eight feet; Turkey corn, French beans, gourds, melons, capillaire, and the hop plant.

Canada is said to be inhabited by two hundred thousand French, who live in affluence. They have full liberty to hunt, fish, fell timber for fuel, or building, and to sow and plant as much land as they can cultivate. Their greatest hardship is the winter cold, which is here so excessive from December to April, that the greatest rivers are frozen over, and the snow lies commonly two or three feet deep on the ground, though it extends no farther north than 48° of latitude.

The forests of Canada are also well stocked with birds. They contain two kinds of eagles, the largest

P

-of which have a white head and neck, and prey upon hares and rabbits, which they carry up to their nests: but the others are grey, and prey on birds and fishes. The patridges are grey, red, and black, with long tails, which they spread out as a fan, like a turkey cock, and make a very beautiful appearance. The chief Canadian bird of melody, is the white bird, which is very handsome, and remarkable for announcing the return of spring. The fly bird is thought to be the most beautiful of any in nature; with all his plumage, he is no larger than a cock chaffer, and he makes a noise with his wings, like the humming of a large fly: his legs are like two needles, and from his bill, which is of the same thickness, a small sting proceeds, with which he pierces the flowers, and thereby nourishes himself with the sap. The female has nothing striking in its appearance; but the male is a perfect beauty, having on its head a small tuft of the most beautiful black, his breast red, his belly white, his back, wings and tail green, like that of a rose bush: specks of gold scattered all over the plumage, add greatly to its beauty; and an imperceptible down produces the most delightful shadings that can be imagined. Rattle snakes are found here, some of them as thick as a man's leg: when he moves his body, which is covered with rows of scales, his tail rattles, whence he has his name: his bite is mortal, but an herb grows wherever this reptile is found in this country, called the rattle snake's plant, which is an infallible antidote to the poison of his bite, by chewing it and applying it in the nature of a plaister to the wound. The rattle snake seldom bite passengers, unless he is provoked or trod upon: the Indians, however, pursue them and greatly prize their flesh, which they eat. There is a carnivorous animal here called the carcajou, of the cat kind, having a very long tail; its body is about two feet in length. It is said that this animal, winding himself about à tree, will dart from thence upon the elk, twist his strong tail round his body, and cut his throat in a moment. Wolves are scarce in Canada, but they afford the finest furs in all the country; their flesh is white and good to eat, and they pursue their prey to the tops of the largest trees. There are three sort of squirrels here; that called the flying squirrel will leap forty paces and more, from one tree to another. This little animal is easily tamed, and is very lively. The Canadian porcupine is less than a middling dog; when roasted, he eats full as well as a sucking pig. There are two sort of bears here, one a reddish and the other of a black colour, but the former is the most dangerous. Some of the rivers breed a kind of crocodile, that differs but little from those of the Nile. The meadow grounds, in Canada, which are well watered, yield excellent grass, and breed vast numbers of great and small cattle; their horses are small, but very active; where the arable land is well manured, it produces rich crops, tobacco in particular, thrives exceedingly.

The lakes are both large and numerous, Lake Superior, or the Upper Lake, which is situated the farthest north, is reckoned one hundred leagues in length, and seventy where broadest. Indeed the whole country abounds with large lakes and rivers; so that here a man may wander one thousand miles on the banks of the finest lakes and rivers in the world, without meeting with a human creature.

CHAP. VIII.

Admiral Lord Howe and General Sir William Howe appointed Commissioners for restoring Peace to the Colonies. Arrives at Staten Island. Conversation between Colonel Paterson and General Washington. Hostilities commence. Americans defeated with great Slaughter. New York taken by the British. General Assault against Fort Washington, garrisoned by the Americans. Surrender Prisoners of War. Fort Lee and Rhode Island taken by the British. General Lee taken. Hessians defeated.

IT has been already observed, that the command of the force which was designed to act against New York was given to admiral lord Howe, and his brother Sir William; officers, who as well for their personal character, as their known bravery, stood high in the confidence of the British nation.

The admiral and general in addition to their military powers, were appointed commissioners for restoring peace to the colonies, and so desirous was the general to effect his favorite purpose of pacification, that he lay a considerable time before New York, without attempting to commence hostilities, until he should be joined by his brother, whom he expected daily from England, with an enlargement of their powers as commissioners for restoring peace to the colonies. On the 12th July, 1776, lord Howe reached Staten

Island, the head quarters of the general, and immediately sent on shore by a flag to Amboy, a circular letter, addressed to the governors of the different
colonies, acquainting them with his appointment as
commissioner in conjunction with the general, together
with a declaration to the inhabitants. Copies of these
papers were sent by general Washington to congress, who
immediately published them in all the newspapers, that
every one, as they said, might see the insidiousness
of the British ministry, and that they had nothing
to trust to besides the exertion of their own valor.

The admiral and general unwilling to proceed to
coercive measures, and anxious to effect their favorite
purpose of pacification, deputed colonel Paterson, the
adjutant-general, with a message to general-Washing-
ton, stating that the commissioners were invested with
powers of reconciliation, and that they would derive the
greatest pleasure from effecting an accommodation, and
wished this visit to be considered as the first advance towards that desirable object.

The following conversation passed at the interview
between general Washington and colonel Paterson :*

After usual compliments, in which, as well as through
the whole conversation, colonel Paterson addressed
general Washington by the title of excellency, colonel
Paterson entered upon the business by saying, that
general Howe much regretted the difficulties which
had arisen, respecting the address of the letters to
general Washington,† that the address was deemed con-

---

* This conversation was published by order of congress.

† A few days before this interview general Howe sent a
letter, directed " To George Washington, esquire," which he
refused to receive, as not being addressed to him in his
official capacity. In his letter to congress on the subject, he
wrote as follows: " I would not on any occasion sacrifice
essentials to punctilio, but in this instance I deemed it a duty

sistent with propriety, and founded upon precedents of the like nature, by ambassadors and plenipotentiaries, where disputes of difficulties of rank had arisen; that general Washington might recollect he had last summer addressed a letter to general Howe, " To the honorable William Howe, esquire ;" that lord Howe and general Howe did not mean to derogate from the respect or rank of general Washington; for they held his person and character in the highest esteem ; that the direction, with the addition of &c. &c. &c. implied every thing that ought to follow. He then produced a letter, which he did not directly offer to general Washington, but observed that it was the same letter which had been sent, and laid it on the table, with the superscription, " To George Washington, &c. &c. &c." The general declined the letter, and said, that a letter directed to a person in a public character should have some description or indication of it, otherwise it would appear a mere private letter; that it was true, &c. &c. &c. implied every thing, and they also implied any thing ; that the letter to general Howe alluded to, was an answer to one received, under a like address from him, which the officer on duty having taken, he did not think proper to return, but answered it in the same mode of address ; that he should absolutely decline any letter directed to him as a private person, when it related to his public station. Colonel Paterson then said,

to my country and appointment, to insist on that respect, which in any other than a public view, I would willingly have waved." Congress applauded his conduct in a public resolution, and at the same time directed, that no letter or message should be received on any occasion whatever, from the enemy, by the commander in chief, or others, the commanders of the American army, but such as were directed to them in the character they severally sustained.

that general Howe would not urge his delicacy any
farther, and repeated his assertions, that no failure
of respect was intended. He then said he would
endeavour as well as he could to recollect general
Howe's sentiments on the letter, and the resolution of
congress sent him a few days before, respecting the
treatment of our prisoners in Canada ; and added
that the affairs of that province were in another department not subject to the control of general Howe,
but that he and general Howe utterly disapproved of
every infringement of the rights of humanity.

Colonel Paterson then took a paper out of his
pocket, and after looking it over, said he had expressed nearly the same words. General Washington
then said, that he had also forwarded a copy of the
resolves to general Burgoyne, to which colonel Paterson
replied, he did not doubt but a proper attention would
be paid to them, and that he (general Washington)
was sensible that cruelty was not the characteristic
of the British nation. Colonel Paterson then proceeded to say he had it in charge to mention the case
of general Prescot, who they were informed was treated
with such rigour, that under his age and infirmities
fatal consequences might be apprehended.

General Washington replied, that general Prescot's
treatment had not fallen under his notice, that he had
treated all persons under his particular direction with
kindness, and made their situation as easy and comfortable
as possible ; that he did not know where general Prescot
was, but believed his treatment was different from their
information. General Washington then mentioned the
case of colonel Allen, and the officers who had been
confined in Boston jail. As to the first, colonel Paterson answered, that general Howe had no knowledge
of it, but by information from general Washington,
and that the Canada company was not under his di-

rection or control; but as to the other prisoners, at Boston, whenever the state of the army at that place admitted it, they were treated with humanity, and even indulgence : he asserted this upon his honor, and should be happy in an opportunity to prove it. General Washington then observed, that the conduct of several of the officers would well have warranted a different treatment from what they had received; some having refused to give any parole, and others having broken it when given, by escaping or endeavouring so to do. Colonel Paterson answered, that as to the first, they misunderstood the matter very much, and seemed to have mistaken the line of propriety exceedingly ; and as to the latter, general Howe utterly disapproved, and condemned their conduct. That, if a remonstrance was made, such violations of good faith would be severely punished ; but that he hoped general Washington was too just to draw public inference from the misbehaviour of some private individuals; that bad men were to be found in every class and society. And such behaviour was considered as a dishonor to the British army. Colonel Paterson then proceeded to say, that the goodness and benevolence of the king had induced him to appoint lord Howe and general Howe his commissioners to accommodate this unhappy dispute ; that they had great powers, and would derive the greatest pleasure from effecting an accommodation, and that he, (colonel Paterson,) wished to have this visit considered, as making the first advances to this desirable object. General Washington replied, he was not invested with any powers on this subject, by those from whom he derived his authority. But from what had appeared or transpired on this head, lord Howe and general Howe were only to grant pardons ; that those who had committed no fault, wanted no pardon ; that the Americans were only defending what they deemed their indisputable right. Colonel Paterson said, that would open a very wide field for argument. He expressed his apprehensions, that an adherence to forms was likely to obstruct business of the greatest moment and concern. He then observed that a proposal had been made of exchanging governor Skene for Mr. Lovell ; that he now had authority to accede to that proposal. General Washington replied, that the proposition had been made by the direction of congress, and having been then rejected, he could not now renew the business, or give any answer, till he had previously communicated with them.

Colonel Paterson was treated with the greatest attention and politeness during the whole business, and expressed strong acknowledgements that the usual ceremony of blinding his eyes had been dispensed with. At the breaking up of the conference, general Washington strongly invited him to partake of a small collation provided for him, which he politely declined, alleging his late breakfast, and an impatience to return to general Howe, though he had not executed his commission so amply as he wished. Finding he did not purpose staying, he was introduced to the general officers, after which he took his leave, and was safely conducted to his own boat, which waited for him, about four miles distant from the city.

While the two royal commissioners, admiral and general Howe were endeavouring in their civil capacity, to effect a re-union between Great Britain and the colonies, in order to avert the calamities of war, congress seemed more determined in opposition, and ridiculed the power with which the commissioners were invested " of granting general and particular pardons to all those, who, though they had deviated from their allegiance, were willing to return to their duty." Their general answer

Q

to this was " that they who had committed no fault, wanted no pardon," and immediately entered into a resolution, " that the good people of the United States may be informed of the plan of the commissioners, and what the terms, with which the insidious court of Great Britain had endeavoured to amuse and disarm them, and that the few who still remained suspended by a hope, founded either in the justice or moderation of their late king, might now at length be convinced that the valour alone of their country was to save its liberties." This was immediately followed by another resolution in order to detach the Germans who had entered into the service of Britain ; it was penned in these words : " Resolved, that these states will receive all such foreigners who shall leave the armies of his Britannic majesty in America, and shall chuse to become members of any of these States, and they shall be protected in the free exercise of their respective religions, and be invested with the rights, privileges, and immunities of natives, as established by the laws of these States ; and moreover, that this congress will provide for every such person, fifty acres of unappropriated lands, in some of these States to be held by him and his heirs as absolute property."

An attack upon Long Island being determined on by our commanders, the fleet covered the descent of the army, which effected a landing with forty pieces of cannon, in two hours and a half, near a town called Utrecht, on the south-western extremity of the Island, without any opposition, on the twenty-second of August, 1776. General Putnam, with a large body of troops, lay encamped and strongly fortified at Brooklyn : a range of hills were between the armies, the principal pass of which was at a village called Flat Bush. Large detachments of the American army occupied the hills and passes. The right of the British army was commanded by general

Clinton, lord Percy and lord Cornwallis; the centre, composed of, Hessians, under general Heister, took post at Flat Bush, and the left, under general Grant, near the shore. About nine in the evening of the 26th, the van of the army, consisting of, the light infantry, grenadiers, and light-horse, marched to the right in, order to seize a pass near the village of Jamaica. General Clinton being arrived within half a mile of the pass about two hours before day-break, settled his disposition for the attack. One of his patroles falling in with a patrole composed of American officers, took them all. The way being thus open, the whole army descended into the level country which led, to the American lines at Brooklyn.

At half past eight o'clock on the morning of the 27th, the attack was commenced by the light infantry and light dragoons, upon large bodies of the Americans, who retreated towards their camp. Here they were met by the Hessians, and exposed to the fire of two parties; generals Heister and Grant in their front, and general Clinton in their rear; they were immediately thrown into the utmost confusion; and in their effort to retreat back to the lines at Brooklyn, great numbers were killed and taken prisoners, among the latter major-general Sullivan, brigadier-general, lord Sterling,* brigadier-general Udell, ten field officers, eighteen cap-

* The following account of lord Sterling was given about this time in the English publications:

" His father, Mr. Alexander, (for that was his real name) went to America many years ago, where he acquired a considerable estate.

" Upon the death of lord Sterling, a Scotch peer, whose name was Alexander, either the late or present Mr. Alexander came over to England and laid claim to the title. When the cause was tried by the house of lords, and the claim rejected, the lords forbade him to assume the title on pain of being led round Westminster-Hall labelled as an impostor; but ever since, by the courtesy of his countrymen, he has been distinguished by the

tains, forty-three lieutenants, eleven ensigns, one adjutant, three surgeons, two volunteers, and one thousand
and six rank and file.

Washington had crossed over from New York in the
height of the engagement : when he saw the disposition of the two armies, it is said that he wrung his
hands and cried out " Good God ! what brave fellows
I must this day lose :" but he came too late to retrieve
the fortune of the day. He had the mortification to see
some of his best troops killed or taken without being
able to afford them any assistance, but he used his utmost exertions to save those that remained by a well
conducted retreat.

The victory was complete; the Americans lost upwards of three thousand men, including near eleven
hundred taken prisoners, with thirty-two pieces of cannon. Among the Americans who fell, a regiment from
Maryland was particularly regretted. It consisted wholly
of young men of the best families in that province.
They behaved with the most admirable heroism, were
every man killed or wounded; and thus perished in
the bloom of youth.

A member of congress* in his account of this engagement, says, " the British troops displayed great
valour throughout the whole day ; the variety of the
ground occasioned a succession of engagements, pursuits and slaughter, which lasted for many hours ; British
discipline, in every instance, triumphed over the native
valour of raw troops, who had never been in action,
and whose officers were unacquainted with the stratagems
of war."

title of lord Sterling. The first lord Sterling obtained a grant
of Long Island, and was the first that settled it with British
inhabitants. He died in 1640."

* Dr. Ramsay.

· The British army-had to lament the following officers and men killed and wounded :

KILLED.

Lieut. Col. Grant.........10th regiment,
Captain Sir A. Murray, 17th do.
Captain Nelson...........52d do.
Captain Logan, 2d regiment marines,
Second Lieut. Lovell, Royal Artillery,
3 Serjeants,
53 Rank and File.

WOUNDED.

Lieut. Col. Monckton....45th regiment,
Captain Grove...............23d do.
Captain Brown.............44th do.
Captain Kennedy.........do.. do.
Lieut. Morgan.............17th do.
Lieut. Crammond.........42d do.
Lieut. Mair.................43d do.
Lieut. Wier.................do. do.
Lieut. Brown..............44th do.
Lieut. Addison............52d do.
Lieut. Nugent, 1st regiment marines,
11 Serjeants,
3 Drummers,
231 Rank and File.

After this defeat Washington did not think it expedient to risk another battle against the British army. Conformable to this opinion, dispositions were made for an immediate retreat. In the beginning of the night of the 29th of August, in the most profound silence, he conveyed his troops on board of boats, crossed the East River, more than a mile wide, and landed them in the city of New York, on the opposite shore.

Soon after this retreat the first division of the British army, commanded by general Clinton, being covered by a few ships of war, proceeded up the East river to Kepps' bay, about three miles north of New York, where they landed without opposition.

The Americans now abandoned the city of New York, and a brigade of the British troops took possession of it.

After the Americans had evacuated New York they took up a strong position on the north of that Island, which is near sixteen miles long, and in some parts not more than two miles in breadth. Here, they fortified the strong pass of Kingsbridge, by which their communication with the continent was kept open.

General Howe formed a plan of cutting off Washington's communication with the eastern country, and enclosing him so as to compel a general engagement on the Island. On the twelfth of October, the guards, light infantry, together with colonel Donop's corps of Hessian grenadiers and chasseurs, marched from the advanced posts on New York Island, and embarking in boats at Turtle Bay, passed up the East River through Hell-gate, entered the sound and landed on Frog's Neck in Westchester county. About this time general Lee arrived from South Carolina, and in a council of war which was held immediately after his arrival at the American encampment, strongly urged the American commanders to quit the Island of New York immediately. He also urged the expediency of evacuating Fort Washington at the same time. In this last motion he was opposed by general Green, who maintained that the possession of that important post would prevent a large body of the enemy from joining their main force, and in conjunction with Fort Lee, would be of essential service to the Americans in covering their transportation of provisions and stores up the North River. He likewise said, that at the very worst the garrison could be brought off at any time by boats from the Jersey side of the river. Green's plan was adopted, and Fort Washington was garrisoned with three thousand men for its defence.

In the mean time the British troops crossed at Frog's Neck, and found the bridge which joined it to the main land broken down by the Americans, who had thrown up some works on the opposite side. Our troops having now been reinforced, embarked again in boats and landed at Pelham's Manor, and advanced towards New Rochelle; on their march they were annoyed by a party of Americans, under the command of general Lee, who had posted themselves behind stone walls on the line of march.

Our troops now gained the road which leads from Connecticut to Kingsbridge. The Americans apprehending their communication to the eastward would be cut off, moved from their camp at Kingsbridge, and extended their left to the White Plains, a chain of stony hills so called. On the 21st of October, the British troops took possession of the heights of New Rochelle. On the 25th our army marched in two columns, and took a position with the Brunx River in front. The Americans at the same time assembled their main force at White Plains behind entrenchments; where they seemed determined to make a stand. A general action was hourly expected.

On the 28th in the morning our army advanced to attack the enemy, who seeing our troops in motion, a body of eight thousand came out of their lines and posted themselves on the top of a very steep hill above the ford. The second brigade, commanded by general Leslie, consisting of the 5th, 28th, 35th, and 49th regiments, with a battalion of Hessians, and a party of light dragoons, marched down and crossed the ford, though much annoyed by grape shot, ascended the hill with the greatest intrepidity, attacked and routed the body of the Americans that were posted there, driving them to their entrenchments. General Howe, on the morning of the 1st of November, prepared to attack them but general Washington in the mean time, quitted his entrenchments, crossed the North River, and took post in the neighbourhood of Fort Lee, having previously set fire to the huts and barracks which they had built for their winter quarters. .

The Americans having retreated, general Howe finding they avoided a general action, and that the nature of the country did not admit of their being forced to it, was determined on the reduction of Fort Washington. This was the only post the Americans held on New York Island, almost opposite Fort Lee from which it was separated by the North River. Every thing being prepared for attacking Fort Washington, a general assault was determined on. On the 16th of November four attacks were made at the same time in the following order: the first, on the north side, was led on by general Knyphausen, with two columns of Hessians. The second, on the east, led by brigadier general Mathews,* at the head of the light infantry, and a battalion of the king's guards; this column was supported by lord Cornwallis, with the British grenadiers and 33d regiment. The third was under the direction of lieutenant colonel Sterling, with the 42d regiment; and the fourth was com-

---

* The fate of this gallant officer some years after this was truly lamentable.

In the beginning of the year 1783, general Mathews landed with a small army under his command, on the coast of Malabar, in the East Indies, in order to relieve the Carnatic, which was at that time suffering under the ravages of Hyder Ally's formidable, victorious army. After general Mathews had taken several important fortresses, his little army was obliged to surrender prisoners to Tippoo Saib, who in direct breach of the capitulation, treated them with a degree of inhumanity, which chills the blood even to think of. Seventeen British officers were compelled to swallow poison by his order, and all miserably perished in prison. General Mathews himself did not expire by the poison, but horrid to relate, had his head wrung from his body, by order of that tiger-hearted monster Tippoo Saib.

manded by lord Percy: The columns under general
Knyphausen when advancing to the fort, had to
pass through a thick wood which was occupied by a
large body of riffle men, and suffered very much
from their well directed fire: In the mean time a
body of British light infantry advanced against a
party of the Americans, who were annoying them
from behind rocks and trees, and obliged them to
disperse. This made way for the landing of the rest
of the troops without opposition. Lord Percy carried
an advanced work on his side, and lieutenant colonel
Sterling forced his way up a steep height, and took
one hundred and seventy prisoners. Their out works
being carried, the Americans retreated from their
'ines and crowded into the fort ; colonel Rahl, who
led the right column of general Knyphausen's attack,
pushed forward and lodged his column within one
hundred yards of the fort,, where he was soon after
joined by the left column. Two thousand seven
hundred Americans who were in the fort surrendered.
Shortly after Fort Washington had thus fallen, lord
Cornwallis, with a considerable force, passed over
the North River in order to attack Fort Lee, and
make a further impression in the Jerseys. The garrison, consisting of two thousand men, were saved by
an immediate evacuation, at the expence of their
artillery and stores.

General Washington now retreated to New Ark,
having abundant reason from the posture of affairs,
to count on the necessity of a farther retreat. He
asked colonel Reed " Should we retreat to the back
parts of Pennsylvania, will the Pennsylvanians support
us ?" The colonel replied; " If the lower counties
are subdued and give up,, the back counties will do
the same." The general replied, we must retire to
Augusta county, in Virginia, numbers will be obliged

R

to repair to us for safety, and we must try what we can do in carrying on a predatory war, and if overpowered, we must cross the Allegany mountains."[*]

The reduction of Fort Washington, the evacuation of Fort Lee, and the dimunition of the American army, by the departure of those whose time of service had expired, encouraged the British forces, notwithstanding the severity of the winter, and the badness of the roads, to pursue the retreating American army.

Lord Cornwallis led the van of the British army, and was close in the rear of general Washington, as he retreated successively to New Ark, Brunswick, Princeton, Trenton, and the Pennsylvanian side of the Delaware. The pursuit was urged with so much rapidity, that the rear of the American army pulling down bridges, was often within sight and gun-shot of the van of the British building them up.

During the retreat of the Americans, general Lee was taken prisoner at Baskenridge. He had been ordered to join general Washington with his division, but those orders were not obeyed. He continued to hang upon the rear of the advancing army. Colonel Harcourt having received intelligence of his careless situation, being attended only by a small guard, and at a distance from his troops, immediately formed a plan of surprizing him, which he effected with great address, and he was safely carried prisoner to the British camp. The Americans had reposed extravagant confidence in his military talents. To have lost such an idol of the state at any time would have been distressing, but it was an aggravation of the misfortune to lose him under such circumstances, which favored an opinion, that despairing of the American cause, he suffered himself to be taken prisoner. Congress

---

[*] Dr. Ramsay's American Revolution.

soon after interceded for his enlargement, and offered to give six British field officers in exchange for him, but this was at that time refused, as it was said that general Lee being a deserter from the king's service, did not come under the denomination of a prisoner of war: retaliation was then threatened by the Americans. To stop the effusion of innocent blood, the British commander gave him up.

How different was the conduct of the American leaders, in respect of major Andre, which shall hereafter be related.

During these successes in the Jerseys, general Clinton, with two brigades of British, and two of Hessian troops, accompanied by a squadron of ships of war, under the command of Sir Peter Parker, were sent to make an attempt on Rhode Island, and became masters of it without losing a man: at the same time they blocked up commodore Hopkins' squadron, and a number of privateers at Providence.

Hitherto the British troops had succeeded in every object since their landing at Staten Island. The American soldiers being greatly dispirited by repeated defeats, claimed their discharge; twelve months was the time of their engagement, at the expiration of that period numbers of them returned home, in consequence of which general Washington found his army greatly decreased.

Congress exerted themselves to retrieve their losses, and to recruit their army. They altered their mode of enlisting men, and ordered a new army to be levied, of which the soldiers should be bound to serve three years, or during the continuance of the war. Twenty dollars were allowed to ever soldier, besides an allotment of lands at the end of the war to all that survived, and to the families of those who should lose their lives in the service of their country. These promises of congress were accompanied with vigorous exertions. Pennsylvania, in this crisis of danger, raised a powerful militia; the merchant, the farmer, the tradesman, and the labourer, flocked to general Washington's standard.

The British army now occupied a chain of towns and villages through the Jerseys, even to the vicinity of Philadelphia.

A strong detachment of Hessians lay at Trenton, another at Bordenton, and a third at Burlington; these towns are on the opposite bank of the Delaware, and the latter is within twenty miles of Philadelphia.

On the evening of the 25th of December, general Washington, by a masterly enterprize, re-crossed the Delaware, marched his troops in two divisions to Trenton, drove in the Hessian out posts, and attacked the main body, who were thrown into confusion, after colonel Rhal their commanding officer was mortally wounded.

Finding they were now surrounded by the Americans, twenty-three officers and eight hundred and eighty-eight men, laid down their arms and surrendered prisoners of war; between thirty and forty were killed and wounded.

After this enterprise, Washington crossed the Delaware, and returned with the prisoners to Philadelphia; he then re-passed that river, and took possession of Trenton.

Several detachments of our troops now assembled at Princeton, where they were joined by a strong detachment from Brunswick, commanded by lord Cornwallis; who immediately marched to Trenton, and attacked the Americans on the 2d of January, 1777. At four o'clock in the afternoon, the advanced guard of the Americans were compelled to retreat, but our troops were checked by some field pieces which were posted on the opposite bank. Thus two armies, on whom the success or failure of the American revolution depended, were crowded into the village of Trenton, and only separated by a creek in many places fordable. The British troops, lay on their arms that night in order to be in readiness to make another attack next morning. Meanwhile Washington silently withdrew his troops, leaving fires burning in his camp and the usual patroles for the purpose of deception; favoured by the obscurity of night, and after a circuitous march, he reached Princeton early in the morning.

On their approach to Princeton, the centre of the Americans were charged by the 17th, 40th, and 55th, regiments under the command of colonel Mawhood with such intrepidity, that they were compelled to give way in disorder. In this emergency, Washington rode forward; he placed himself between his flying troops and the British, with his horse's head fronting the latter. The Americans encouraged by his exhortations and example, rallied and attacked the British in turn, and although Washington was for some moments between two fires, he escaped without a wound.

During this contest, the British troops displayed the most invincible valour. One of the three regiments commanded by colonel Mawhood, undismayed by the superiority of the Americans, in point of numbers, charged with the bayonet, forced their way through a column of the enemy, and marched forward to Maidenhead. The other two regiments, though they suffered severely, retired in good order and retreated to Brunswick.

The British army now evacuated Trenton and Princeton, and retreated to New Brunswick. General Washington immediately stationed troops in all these important
places which he had thus regained.

The American head quarters were at Morristown and
general Putnam was directed to take post at Princeton.

This campaign was closed with few advantages to
the British arms, except the possession of New York.

. We shall now turn our attention to the affairs of the
northern army.

CHAP. IX.

Northern Army opens the Campaign. Crosses Lake
Champlain. Ticonderoga taken. Fort Ann evacuated
by the Americans. British Troops move forward
to Fort Edward and Fort Millar. Miss M'Crea
murdered by the Indians. Germans defeated at
Bennington. British Army crosses Hudson's River.
Desperate Attacks made on the British Army. Are
obliged to retreat. Surrenders at Saratoga.

IN the beginning of June, 1777, the northern army,
which consisted of four thousand British troops, and
three thousand Germans, marched from their winter
quarters, in the different parts of Canada, and encamped
on the western side of Lake Champlain. Here they were
joined by some Canadians, and the army was put
under the command of general Burgoyne. The soldiers
were in a high state of discipline, and had been kept
in their winter quarters with the greatest care, in order
to prepare them for this expedition.

The British army proceeded up Lake Champlain,
in batteaux, in the greatest order and regularity,
and landed at the river Boquet, near Crown Point.
Here a body of Indians joined it. A congress was
held; general Burgoyne opened the meeting with
a speech to the Indians, part of which was as follows:

" This war, to you, my friends, is new: upon
all former occasions in taking the field, you held
yourselves authorized to destroy wherever you came,

because every where you found an enemy. The case
is now very different.

" The king has many faithful subjects dispersed in
the provinces, consequently you have many brothers
there : and these people are the more to be pitied,
that they are persecuted, or imprisoned, wherever
they are discovered or suspected ; and to dissemble,
is, to a generous mind, a yet more grievous punishment.

" Persuaded that your magnanimity of character,
joined to your principles of affection to the king,
will give me fuller controul over your minds than
the military rank with which I am invested, I enjoin
your most serious attention to the rules which I hereby proclaim for your invariable observation during
the campaign.

" I positively forbid bloodshed when you are not
opposed in arms.

" Aged men, women, children, and prisoners, must
be held sacred from the knife or hatchet, even in the
time of actual conflict.

" You shall receive compensation for the prisoners
you take; but you shall be called to account for
scalps.

" Base lurking assassins, incendiaries, ravagers and
plunderers of the country, to whatever army they
may belong, shall be treated with less reserve, but
the latitude must be given you by order, and I must
be the judge of the occasion."

After general Burgoyne had ended, an old chief of
the Iroquois stood up and made the following answer :

" I stand up, in the name of the nations present,
to assure our father that we have attentively listened
to his discourse. We receive you as your father, because when you speak, we hear the voice of your
great father beyond the great lake!

" With one common assent we promise a constant obedience to all you have ordered, and all you shall order ; and may the Father of days give you many and success !

" We rejoice in the approbation you have expressed of our behaviour.

" We have been tried and tempted by the Bostonians,* but we have loved our father, and our hatchets have been sharpened upon our affections.

" In proof of the sincerity of our affections, our whole villages,, able to go to war, are come forth. The old and infirm, our infants and our wives, alone remain at home."

In the mean time the attention of the Americans were exclusively fixed on plans of defence, in order to arrest the progress of the British troops. In the preceding summer, general Gates was ordered by congress with twelve thousand troops to Ticonderoga, in order to strengthen and fortify that important pass ; great was the confidence of the Americans in the strength of this post and the supposed superiority of the forces for its defence.

On the 30th of June, the British advanced to Crown Point, about twelve miles from Ticonderoga. In the evening the following orders were given : " The army embarks to-morrow, to approach the enemy. The services required on this expedition are critical and conspicuous. During our progress occasions may occur, in which, nor difficulty, nor labour, nor life, are to be regarded. This army must not retreat." From Crown Point they proceeded to invest Ticonderoga. On their approach to it they advanced on both sides of the lake, while the naval force kept in the centre. Within a few days they had surrounded three fourths

S

* See page 75.

of the American works at Ticonderoga, and Mount Independence, and had also advanced a work on Sugar Hill, the top of which overlooked and effectually commanded the whole works. The Americans vainly imagining that the difficulty of the ascent would be sufficient to prevent the British troops from taking possession of it. On the approach of the first division of the army, the Americans abandoned and set fire to their out works, and so expeditious were the advances, that by the 5th of July, every post was secured which was judged necessary for investing it compleatly. A road was soon after made to the summit of that eminence, which the Americans had with such confidence supposed could not be ascended; and so much were they disheartened, that they instantly abandoned the fort entirely, taking the road to Skeensborough, a place to the south of Lake George, while their baggage, with what artillery and military stores they could carry off, were sent to the same place by water. But the British generals were determined not to let them pass so easy; both were pursued and overtaken; their armed vessels consisted only of five galleys, two of which were taken and three blown up, on which they set fire to their boats and fortifications at Skeensborough. On this occasion the Americans lost two hundred boats, one hundred and thirty pieces of cannon, with all their provisions and baggage.

At the break of day, July the 6th, the American land forces, under colonel Francis, were eagerly pursued by brigadier general Frazer, at the head of his brigade, consisting of the grenadiers and light infantry; they were soon overtaken, and made (considering the opposition of raw and undisciplined troops to veteran soldiers) a brave defence. As they were greatly superior to the British in numbers, they had almost overpowered general Frazer, when general Reidesel, with a large body of Germans, came to his assistance ; the Americans were then overpowered in their turn, their commander and above two hundred men killed, and as many taken prisoners. The loss of the British was very inconsiderable ; major Grant of the 24th regiment, a brave officer, fell on that day.*

The fort abandoned by the Americans at Ticonderoga, was a place of great importance : the old French lines constructed in the late war, between England and France, which looked towards the encampment, had been repaired the year before, and were in good order. About the centre was a battery of six guns. This occupied about two thirds of the high ground directly opposite to the old Fort. The remaining third was open, but some great trees, with their branches outward, were spread about eighty yards for its security. The old Fort was in bad repair; but some guns were mounted on one of its ravalins, that looked toward Lake Champlain. There was also a battery of four guns in the old French lines, which had the same aspect. On the point above the bridge, was a battery of four guns, and on Mount Independence, another of six or eight. The fort on that side, was nearly a mile from the battery, and was formed of picquets. The defence of it might have employed four hundred men. From the battery at the point, a line of entrenchment ran round the mount, upwards of a mile and a half in length. There was a strong abbatis in front of this line. Towards the east of the mount was a block house. Another was on Ticonderoga side. New works were also begun on the mount. A bridge had been constructed, and thrown over the inlet, in order to secure their own

* Lord Balcarras, who commanded the British light infantry, distinguished himself in this engagement. The coat which he wore on that day was pierced through in several places with musquet-shot, yet he only received a slight wound.

vessels, and to obstruct the British fleet. This bridge was supported by twenty-two piers of timber, the spaces between these piers were filled with separate floats, fifty feet long, and thirteen feet wide, strongly fastened together with large iron chains. It was likewise defended, on the Lake Champlain side, by a boom composed of very large pieces of timber, fastened together by rivetted bolts, and double chains. This bridge, on which the Americans had bestowed so much labour for ten months, and which was deemed by them to be impregnable, was cut through in less time by the British seamen, than it would have cost them, to have described its structure.

The Americans were greatly grieved at the loss of Ticonderoga, and apprehensive of general distress, sought to cover the disgrace by throwing the blame on the general. A court martial was held by order of congress : cowardice, incapacity, and treachery were brought forward in court, against general St. Clair, who commanded at. Ticonderoga. In the course of the trial it was made to appear, that tho' thirteen thousand six hundred men had been early called for, as necessary to defend the northern posts; yet on the approach of general Burgoyne the whole force collected to oppose him, was not above half that number. St. Clair was honorably acquitted.

Such was the rapid torrent of success, which in this period of the campaign, swept away all opposition before the British army. The officers and men, were highly elated with their good fortune. They considered their toils to be nearly at an end; Albany to be within their grasp, and the adjacent provinces reduced to a certainty. The terror which the loss of Ticonderoga spread throughout the New England States was great; but nevertheless, no disposition to purchase safety by submission appeared in any quarter. The army after these successes continued some time in Skeensborough, waiting for their tents, baggage, and provisions. In the mean time, general Burgoyne detached the 9th regiment, commanded by lieutenant colonel Hill, to Fort Ann, a place of some strength, in order to intercept such of the enemy as should attempt to retreat towards that Fort. They had not proceeded many miles through the woods, before they overtook some boats laden with baggage, women, and invalids, belonging to the Americans rowing up Wood Creek, in order to escape to Fort Ann, these were immediately secured. They then proceeded on their march, till they came within a quarter of a mile of Fort Ann, which was at that time garrisoned by a strong party of the enemy; they halted and lay upon their arms all night.

Early next morning, 9th July, an American soldier came from the fort; he said that he had deserted, though it was afterwards discovered that he was a spy; he stated that there were one thousand men in the fort, and that they were in the greatest consternation, under an apprehension of the British attacking and storming them; upon this intelligence colonel Hill dispatched a message to general Burgoyne stating his situation, and how far he had advanced, which was eight or ten miles from the main army.

Not many minutes after this message was sent off, the pretended deserter disappeared; he had viewed the situation and seen the strength of the British, which did not amount to above one hundred and ninety men including officers. It was soon found that he made a faithful report to his friends, for in less than half an hour they came out of the fort with great fury. The British outline of centries received them with the greatest bravery and steadiness, and obliged them to retreat; they then formed again, and came on with redoubled violence. The officers could be heard encouraging them on to the

attack, though their numbers could not be seen, the
woods being so thick, but it was soon found that they not
only out flanked but were endeavoring to surround the
British, in order to prevent this they were obliged to
change their ground, and retire up a high hill, which was
in their rear, in performing this manœuvre several of the
men were killed and wounded. When the troops arrived
at the summit of the hill they formed in Indian file, and
kept up a well directed fire till all the ammunition
was expended, the enemy observing that the firing
ceased, was encouraged to press forward with redoubled
vigour, and endeavoured to surround them in order to
cut off all retreat. Just at this critical moment a war
hoop was heard, which resounded through the wood,
this sound, which was so obnoxious at that time to the
Americans, threw them into the utmost consternation.

The war hoop was sounded by captain Money, deputy
quarter master general, he had been detached by general
Burgoyne early in the morning from Skeensborough,
with a party of Indians, in order to join this detachment
when they came within four miles of Fort Ann, they heard
the firing, Captain Money ordered them to advance
as fast as possible to assist, but they refused to obey
him, and either stood still or advanced very slow.
Being anxious to join the party at all events, he ran
forward by himself with all his might, and came to
the bottom of the hill where, just as all the ammunition
was expended, he gave the war hoop.

In this affair the British had three officers and nineteen
men killed and wounded.

* " Captain Montgomery, son to Sir W Montgomery,
bart of Dublin, was wounded in the leg and taken
prisoner, with the surgeon who was dressing his wound,

---

* This passage being literally copied from the author's private
Journal, he hopes pardon for narrating it in the first person.

just before we retired up the hill. I very narrowly
escaped myself from being taken prisoner at that time,
as I was just in the act of assisting the surgeon in
dressing the captain's wound, when the enemy came
pouring down upon us like a mighty torrent, in consequence whereof I was the last man that ascended the
hill. I had not been there five minutes when lieutenant
Westrop, who was by my side was shot through the
heart; a few minutes after a man, a short distance upon
my left, received a ball in his forehead, which took
off the roof of his scull! he reeled round, turned up
his eyes, muttered some words, and fell dead at my feet!
After the Americans had retreated, we formed on the
hill. It was a distressing sight to see the wounded men
bleeding on the ground, and what made it more so the
rain came pouring down like a deluge upon us; and
still to add to the distress of the sufferers, there was
nothing to dress their wounds, as the small medicine
box which was filled with salve, was left behind with
surgeon Shelly and captain Montgomery at the time
of our movement up the hill. The poor fellows earnestly entreated me to tie up their wounds. Immediately I took off my shirt, tore it up, and with the help
of a soldier's wife, (the only woman that was with us,
and who kept close by her husband's side during the
engagement,) made some bandages, stopped the bleeding
of their wounds, and conveyed them in blankets to a
small hut about two miles in our rear. In the mean
time, general Burgoyne having heard of our critical
situation, moved forward at the head of a strong detachment, in order to support us; but the Americans had
set fire to Fort Ann, and fled with great precipitation,
before his arrival. Our regiment now marched back to
Skeensborough, leaving me behind to attend the wounded, with a small guard for our protection. I was
directed, that in case I should be either surrounded or

overpowered by the Americans, to deliver a letter, which general Burgoyne gave me, to their commanding officer. Here I remained seven days with the wounded men, expecting every moment to be taken prisoner; but, although we heard the enemy cutting down trees every night during our stay, in order to block up the passages of the road and river, yet we were never molested. Every necessary which we wanted was sent us from the camp at Skeensborough, and all the wounded men (except three who died) were nearly fit for duty when we arrived at head quarters."

. The British were now obliged to suspend all operations for some time, and wait at Skeensborough for the arrival, of provisions and tents; but they employed this interval clearing a passage for the troops, to proceed against the enemy. This was attended with incredible toil. The Americans, now under the direction of general Schuyler, were constantly employed in cutting down large trees on both sides of every road, which was in the line of march. The face of the country was likewise so broken with creeks and marshes, that there were no less than forty bridges to construct, one of which was over a morass two miles in extent. The difficulties of the march through this wilderness were encountered and overcome by the army with a spirit and alacrity which could not be exceeded; and on the 20th of July, it encamped at Fort Edward. General Schuyler now retreated to Saratoga, and immediately issued a proclamation warning the Americans that they would be dealt with as traitors, if they joined the British army, and requiring them, with their arms, to repair to the American standard. At the same time numerous parties were employed in desolating the country, felling trees, and throwing every obstruction in the way of the army. Indeed at first an universal panic intimidated the inhabitants, but they soon recovered from its operation.

The terror excited by the Indians, instead of disposing the inhabitants to court British protection, had a contrary effect. This was chiefly occasioned by the murder of Miss M'Crea, a young lady of the neighbourhood of Fort Edward. As this melancholy transaction made a great noise in Great Britain and America at this time, I shall take the liberty of relating it in the words of that great American partisan Dr. Ramsay.

" This, though true, was no premeditated barbarity. The circumstances were as follow: Mr. Jones,* her lover, from an anxiety for her safety, engaged some Indians to remove her from among the Americans, and promised to reward the person who should bring her safe to him, with a barrel of rum. Two of the Indians who had conveyed her some distance, on the way to her intended husband, disputed which of them should present her to Mr. Jones. Both were anxious for the reward. One of them killed her with his tomahawk, to prevent the other from receiving it. Burgoyne obliged the Indians to deliver up the murderer, and threatened to put him to death. His life was only spared, upon the Indians agreeing to terms, which the general thought would be more efficacious than an execution, to prevent similar mischiefs."

Had the execution taken place, there is every probability that the Indians would have retired from the army, massacring every body and destroying every thing before them; thus it would have caused the destruction of hundreds of the innocent inhabitants of the frontiers of Canada, if the assassin had been then put to death. When the murder of Miss M'Crea had reached the general's ears, he went to the Indian camp, and insisted in the most determined language that 'the culprit should be given up to justice, and had it not been for the re-

* An officer in a new raised American corps attached to our army.

T

monstrances of monsieur St Luc le Corne, a Frenchman who then presided over them, the murderer's execution would not have been deferred another day

St Luc informed the general that great discontent had
reigned among the Indians, at the restraint under which
they were kept   To which general Burgoyne replied,
" That he had rather lose every Indian in his army
than connive at their enormities "

The general afterwards said, " That he ever esteemed
the Indian alliances, at best a necessary evil, their
services to be overvalued, sometimes insignificant, often
barbarous, always capricious, and that the employment
of them was only justifiable, when by being united to a
regular army, they could be kept under controul "
Governed by these sentiments the general acted   In his
own expressive language, " he determined to be the
soldier, not the executioner of the state." Indeed it was
very remarkable, how he restrained their ferocity during
the short time they were with our army, and in order
to do this the more effectually, he took to his aid a
favorite priest of theirs, who had more control over
the passions of the Indians than all their chiefs put
together

By such assistance he was able to enforce obedience
to his commands n preventing them from barbarity.
The following instances are given as proofs of his
wisdom and humanity In a skirmish which happened
between the Americans and Indians, two of the American officers were wounded, the Indians, under a heavy
fire of the enemy, conveyed the wounded officers on
their backs to a place of safety. At another time, a
captain, with a detachment of Americans, were placed in
ambuscade, in order to cut off part of the British troops
on their march; these were discovered by the Indians,
who took them all prisoners without a man being hurt.
It is also worthy of remark, that no party of the Indians

was ever allowed to leave the camp without having a British officer at its head. Every possible exertion of humanity was used in order to restrain their ferocity.' The case of Miss M'Crea excepted, (which was not premeditated cruelty) no barbarity or murder was committed by the northern army. It is true, that charges of this nature, against that army, were fabricated by the Americans, and propagated in their news-papers, throughout the continent; but this was in order to accomplish the end which they had in view, which was to prevent the loyalists from joining the British standard. This might be pardonable in the Americans at that time, if it be allowed that " stratagems are justifiable in war." But what shall we say to a popular author, fostered in our own country, who, in writing on this campaign, says : " Such was the sanguine and savage spirit which breathed throughout this infamous proclamation,* unparalleled except in ONE very recent instance, that the following lines from Shakespeare's *Timon of Athens*, were not unhappily applied to it as a kind of comment or paraphrase :

———————— Let not thy sword skip one ;
Pity not honoured age for his white beard.
Strike me the matron—Let not the virgin's cheek
Make soft thy trunchant sword—Spare not the babe
Whose dimpled smiles from fools exhaust their mercy,
Mince it without remorse."

' Lord Harrington, the present commander in chief in Ireland, was at that time aid-de-camp to general Burgoyne, and general Freeman, the present barrack master general in Ireland, was also in that service, and both his lordship and the general well know the principle of humanity which dictated even this very proclamation. Its object was to terrify into allegiance, not to massacre to extermination, which the latter quotation of Mr. Belsham

* Alluding to general Burgoyne's proclamation, issued at the camp at Putnam Creek, June 29th, 1777.

more than insinuates it avows. General Burgoyne in his examination before the house of commons, fully and explicitly explained the motives which induced him to the proclamation " I have," said he,
    " Spoken daggers—but USED NONE !!!"

After all, it is not much to Mr Belsham's credit that he does not give the quotation as his own, nor even present the reader with the slightest intimation where, on what occasion, or by whom it was made   The application of such savage motives to one of the most humane and enlightened officers in the service, is more than ungenerous   One of these two facts appears pretty evident—either Mr Belsham was ashamed of the authority from whence he took the quotation, or too much convinced of its inapplicability to take it upon himself

The militia was now raised every where, and drafted to join the American army at Saratoga ; and that they might have a commander whose abilities could be relied on, general Arnold was appointed, who repaired to Saratoga with a suitable train of artillery ; but receiving intelligence that colonel St. Leger was proceeding with great rapidity in his expedition on the Mahawk River, he moved to Still Water, a place about half way between Saratoga and the junction of the Mahawk and Hudson Rivers

Before general Burgoyne had crossed Lake Champlain, colonel St. Leger was sent with a detachment, consisting of two hundred and fifty British troops, drawn from the 8th and 34th regiments, colonel Johnson's corps of New Yorkers, a few German chasseurs, a company of Canadians, and another of rangers. These troops were joined by a body of Indians This detachment, which consisted of near eight hundred men, ascended the River St. Lawrence, crossed Lake Ontario, and commenced the siege of Fort Stanwix, now named by the Americans Fort Schuyler.

A detachment of American militia, consisting of eight hundred men, was immediately ordered to relieve this important fortress. Colonel St. Leger having intelligence of the march of this reinforcement, and knowing the danger of being attacked in his trenches, judiciously detached colonel Johnson, with a party of regulars and Indians, in order to attack them on their march, either openly or covertly, as circumstances should offer. On the 6th of August, at five o'clock in the morning, Sir John Johnson met the American troops. The Indians, on the sight of the enemy, forgetting the judicious disposition formed by Sir John (which was to suffer the attack to begin with the troops in front, while they should be on both flank and rear) rushed in hatchet in hand, and thereby gave two hundred of the enemy's rear an opportunity to retreat. Almost all the American officers, with one hundred and sixty men, were slain. Numbers were wounded. Among the latter was general Harkimer, who expired soon after the engagement. Thirty of the Indians were killed and wounded, and the misfortune was doubly aggravated, as some of their favourite chiefs and confidential warriors fell in the carnage. The siege now continued with unabated labour of officers and men. Great was their toil, the smallness of their numbers never admitting the relief of three hours cessation for sleeping or cooking.

While the British troops were carrying on the siege with vigour, intelligence was brought in, by scouts, of a second corps of a thousand men being on their march. This brigade of continental troops was headed by general Arnold, who was detached from the American head-quarters at Still Water, for the purpose of relieving the fort. The following stratagem was practised by Arnold : On his march he took up a gentleman, who resided in that country, of the name of Schuyler, accused him of being a spy in the British service, and threatened him with immediate death. Mr. Schuyler was greatly alarmed, solemnly declared his innocence of the crime laid to his charge, and interceded with Arnold in the most impressive manner for his life. The American general then raising his voice, said, " Your life and estate shall be given you, on condition that you will repair immediately to the Indians in the British camp before Fort Stanwix, and represent to them that general Burgoyne's army is cut to pieces, and that Arnold is advancing upon them by rapid and forced marches ; and be sure to swell the number of my troops to three thousand men."

Mr. Schuyler performed this service very faithfully, for he immediately proceeded to the Indian camp, and being able to converse in their own language, he laid before them every syllable that Arnold told him, adding a great deal more on his own account. This intelligence spread from tent to tent among the Indians. The zeal that they formerly possessed no longer animated them ; they complained of the small number of British troops and their former losses. Colonel St. Leger was greatly alarmed at the change he perceived in them ; he immediately called a council of the chiefs, encouraged them by every argument he could suggest ; promised to lead them on himself, and bring into the field three hundred of the best troops. They listened to this with great attention ; promised to follow him, and agreed that he should reconnoitre the ground most proper for the field of battle next morning, accompanied by some of their chief warriors.

But Mr. Schuyler's tale had taken too great hold of their fears ; they kept not their word, and the colonel was higly mortified on being informed next-morning that two hundred of them were already decamped ; and to add to his mortification, those of them who remained on the ground insisted that he should retreat, or they

would abandon him. Hard, indeed, was the situation
of colonel St Leger at this crisis The king's troops
did not then exceed more than two hundred and fifty men;
he was therefore under the necessity of yielding to their
resolves, and retired from before the fort at night,
sending on his sick, wounded, artillery, &c

In the mean time the British army halted at Fort
Edward, while some were employed n bringing forward
provisions, stores, &c over the carrying place from Lake
George to Hudson's River This was found a work
of much difficulty, owing to the want of horses and
carriages To remedy this great inconvenience, which
retarded the movement of our troops, it was determined
to send out a detachment, in order to bring in horses
to mount the Brunswick dragoons, if a sufficient number
could be found

. Lieutenant colonel Baum, a German officer, was ordered on this service with the following troops :—

Brunswick dismounted dragoons ,	150
Captain Frazer's Rangers*	50
Peter's Provincial Corps .	150
Provincial and Canadian Volunteers	56
Iudians -	80
Total .	486

Governor Skeene was sent with this detachment, from
whose supposed knowledge of the country, and influence
among the inhabitants much was expected

Lieutenant colonel Baum was instructed by general
Burgoyne to march directly to Bennington, a place about
twenty miles east of Hudson's River, intelligence having
been received that the Americans had a considerable magazine there.

On the 11th of August, colonel Baum took post at
Batten Kill, and on the 14th he proceeded to Cambridge,

* This company was composed of picked men from different
regiments.

where his advance guard fell in with and defeated a party
of American troops, took eight prisoners, one thousand
bushels of wheat, and one hundred and fifty bullocks,
which he sent to the British camp. Here the colonel
was informed that near eighteen hundred of the enemy
were posted at Bennington, and that they had a very
considerable magazine there, besides two thousand bullocks and three hundred horses. Encouraged by the
success of his first attack, the colonel determined to
press forward and dislodge the enemy from that post.
He sent every day exact reports of his progress and
situation to general Burgoyne, with which the general
was perfectly satisfied, and approved his design of attacking Bennington so soon as the colonel could be fully
informed of the enemy's number and situation, that it
might be attempted with a prospect of success, and
without running any risque. Early in the morning of
the 14th of August, the colonel was attacked by a body
of seven hundred Americans, who, after having a few
shot fired at them, retired, and dispersed. By some
prisoners taken on this occasion, he was informed that
the enemy were strongly entrenched at Bennington, that
they expected a large reinforcement from the American
army, and intended to attack him as soon as the reinforcement had joined them. On receiving this information, the lieutenant colonel very properly deferred his
intention of pushing on to Bennington, and halted in
his post, sending off an express to inform general Burgoyne of his situation, and desiring that some troops
might be ordered to sustain him. His report was
written in such high spirits, that the general was induced to believe that he asked for a reinforcement
more to enable him to attack the enemy, than from
any apprehension of his corps being in danger of
an attack themselves. In consequence of the above
information, lieutenant colonel Breyman was ordered

to march with his corps, the battalion of German grenadiers, and that of Barnier's, (about five hundred men); with two pieces of cannon, to sustain lieutenant colonel Baum: an officer was sent off to inform the latter that lieutenant colonel Breyman had began his march early on the 15th. The distance between the two corps, rendered this reinforcement useless to lieutenant colonel Baum, as they could not get up time enough, to support him, owing to excessive bad roads, and a continued rain. August the 16th, in the morning, several bodies of men in arms were observed approaching his post. Lieutenant colonel Baum was assured they were loyalists; but their numbers increasing, he ordered out parties to reconnoitre, and soon perceived he was surrounded by the Americans, from Bennington. On a signal being made by the Americans, he was attacked on all sides by superior numbers; he maintained his post above two hours, and often repulsed the enemy; but finding that his men had expended all their ammunition, and lieutenant colonel Breyman's corps not yet appearing, he was obliged to think of a retreat, with the dragoons, (the Provincials, Canadians, and Indians being already cut off from him). He twice forced his way through the enemy; and was as often attacked by fresh troops. As a last resource, he ordered his men to draw their swords, and rush in upon the enemy, where, notwithstanding every effort of bravery, this valiant corps, overpowered by superior numbers, was entirely broken, and most of them were either killed or taken prisoners: among the latter was their wounded commander.

Colonel Breyman had not received the smallest information of this engagement; he arrived on the same ground, and on the same day, but not till the action was over. Instead of meeting his friends, as he ex-

U

pected, he found himself briskly attacked on all sides.
Notwithstanding the severe fatigue they had undergone, his troops behaved with great vigour and resolution, and drove the Americans from several hills, on
which they were posted   They were, however, at
length overpowered, and their ammunition being unfortunately expended, they were obliged with great reluctance to abandon two pieces of artillery they had brought
with them, and retreated with good order in the dusk
of the evening.

Accustomed to success as the royal troops had been
in the preceding part of the campaign, they felt unusual
mortification from this unexpected check. Though it
did not diminish their courage, it abated their confidence;
it deranged every plan for pursuing the advantages
which had been previously obtained. Among other em-
barrassments it reduced them to the alternative of halting
till the supplies were brought forward from Fort George,
or of advancing without them at the risque of being
starved   The former being adopted, the army was
detained till the 13th September before they crossed
Hudson's River. This unavoidable delay gave time
and opportunity to the Americans to assemble in great
numbers.

About this period congress appointed general Gates
to command their northern army, while the militia,
flushed with their recent success, collected in great
numbers to his standard

The affair of Bennington, though of great importance to the Americans, was of still more consequence
in a national sense to the British army, as it gave
occasion to a correspondence which tended to wipe off
the reproaches of inhumanity from them, which
had gone forth and astonished all Europe   Colonel
Baum, who commanded the detachment, being wounded
and a prisoner in the American camp, general Burgoyne

was desirous of sending not only to that officer, but all
those whom the fortune of war had put on that occasion,
into the enemy's hands, all the succour in his power,
and with that view wrote to general Gates to permit
the baggage and servants of the prisoners to pass to
them unmolested. In this letter, dated 30th of August,
after the formal requisition, he says :

" It is with great concern I find myself obliged to
add to this application, a complaint of the bad treatment the provincial soldiers in the king's service received after the affair of Bennington. I have reports,
upon oath, that some were refused quarter after having
asked it : I am willing to believe this was against the
order and inclination of your officers ; but it is my
part to require an explanation, and to warn you of
the horrors of retaliation, if such a practice is not in
the strongest terms discountenanced and reprehended."

To this complaint, general Gates expressed his
astonishment that general Burgoyne should mention inhumanity or threaten retaliation : " Nothing, says he,
happened in the action at Bennington but what is
common, when works are carried by assault. That the
savages of America should in their warfare mangle and
scalp the unhappy prisoners is neither new nor extraordinary ; but that the famous Lieutenant General
Burgoyne, in whom the fine gentleman is united with
the soldier and the scholar, should hire the savages of
America to scalp Europeans, and the descendants of
Europeans; nay more, that he should pay a price for
each scalp so barbarously taken, is more than will be
believed in Europe until authenticated facts shall in every
gazette, confirm the truth of the horrid tale. Miss
M'Crea, a young lady, lovely to the sight, of virtuous
character and amiable disposition, engaged to an officer
of your army, was, with other women and children,
taken out of a house near Fort Edward, carried into the

woods, and there scalped and mangled in a most shocking manner Two parents with their six children were
all treated with the same inhumanity, while quietly
residing in then once happy dwelling

" The miserable fate of Miss M'Crea, was particularly aggravated by her being dressed to receive her
promised husband , but she met her murderers employed
by you Upwards of one hundred men, women, and children have perished by the hands of the ruffians, to whom
it is asserted you have paid the price of blood "

To these specific charges general Burgoyne answered :

" I have hesitated, sir, upon answering the charges
in your letter I have disdained to justify myself against
rhapsodies of fiction and calumny, which from the first
of this contest it has been an unvaried American policy
to propagate, but which shall no longer impose upon the
world I am induced to deviate from this general rule,
in the present instance, lest my silence should be construed an acknowledgment of the truth of your allegations,
and a pretence be thence taken for exercising future
barbarities by the American troops

" By this motive, and upon this only, I condescend
to inform you, that I would not be conscious of the acts
you presume to impute to me, for the whole continent
of America, though the wealth of worlds were in its
bowels, and a paradise upon its surface.

" It has happened that all my transactions, with the
Indian nations last year and this, have been clearly
heard, distinctly understood, accurately minuted by
very numerous, and, in many parts, very unprejudiced
persons, So immediately opposite to truth is your
assertion that I have paid a price for scalps, that one of
the first regulations established by me at the great
council in May , and repeated, enforced, and, in-
variably adhered to since, was, that the Indians should

receive compensation for prisoners, because it would prevent cruelty, and that not only such compensation should be with-held, but a strict account would be demanded for scalps. These pledges of conquest, for such you well know they will ever esteem them, were solemnly and peremptorily prohibited to be taken from the wounded, and even the dying, and the persons of aged men, women, children, and prisoners, were pronounced sacred even in assaults.

" In regard to Miss M'Crea, her fall wanted not the tragic display you have laboured to give it, to make it as sincerely abhorred and lamented by me as it can be by the tenderest of her friends. The fact was no premeditated barbarity ; on the contrary, two chiefs who had brought her off for the purpose of security, not of violence to her person, disputed which should be her guard : in a fit of savage passion in one, from whose hands she was snatched, the unhappy woman became the victim. Upon the first intelligence of this event, I obliged the Indians to deliver the murderer into my hands; and though to have punished him by our laws, or principles of justice, would have been perhaps unprecedented, he certainly should have suffered an ignominous death, had I not been convinced, from many circumstances and observations, beyond the possibility of a doubt, that a pardon, under the terms which I prescribed and they accepted, would be more efficacious than an execution, to prevent similar mischiefs.

" The above instance excepted, your intelligence respecting the cruelties of the Indians is false.

" You seem to threaten me with European publications, which affect me as little as any other threats you could make ; but in regard to American publications, whether your charge against me, which I acquit you of believing, was penned from a gazette or for a gazette, I desire and demand of you as a man of honor, that, should it appear in print at all, this answer may follow it."

It cannot be matter of much surprize, that such reports were fabricated by the Americans to serve their own purposes; but that they should obtain circulation and credence at home is truly astonishing. Saunders's News-Letter of August 14, 1777, gravely asserts, " that seven hundred men, women, and children, were scalped on the sides of Lake Champlain ; that the light infantry and Indians scoured each bank, women, &c. flying in turns before them." Now the fact is, that from St. John's to Crown Point there were not more than ten human dwellings, the whole being upwards of eighty miles of woods and wilderness. Could inhabitants, *which never existed in a country,* be scalped, or fly before their enemies?—How necessary is it for those who fabricate such deeds, to acquaint themselves with the topography of a place in which they fix their scene of action !!!!

General Burgoyne being disappointed in his attempt on Bennington, a month's provision for the army was ordered to be brought-forward from Lake George. In the mean time he threw a bridge of boats over the river Hudson, which was crossed on the 13th and 14th of September, the army taking post on the heights and plains of Saratoga.

As the royal troops advanced towards the enemy along the side of Hudson's River, they found the country covered with thick woods, and the bridges broken down every quarter of a mile ; these they were obliged to repair. Every obstacle to impede their march was thrown in their way, and they soon discovered that the Americans were determined to dispute every inch of the ground with them.

September 19th. The royal army halted within two miles of the enemy's encampment, and formed for battle, in the following order:

(*See the annexed Plan.*)

ORDER

Of the BRITISH and GERMAN Troops at the Battle of Freeman's Farm, between and Still-Water, on the 19th of September, 1777.

Canadians, Provincials, and Indians, on their flanks and front;

RIGHT WING.	CENTRE.	LI
LED ON BY BRIG. GEN. FRAZER, MAJORS ACKLAND, AND LORD BALCARRES,* British Light Infantry and Grenadiers, and 24th Regiment, anchored by Colonel BREYMAN'S German Reserve.	LED ON BY BRIG. GEN. HAMILTON. AND LIEUT. GEN. BURGOYNE 9th Regiment.....Lieut. Col. Lynd. 21st do....Lieut. Col. Brig. Gen. Hamilton. 62d do..............Lieut. Col. Anstruther.	MAJOR GE
		British Artil
		MAJO Sepained
* These flank companies belonged to the 9th, 20th, 21st, 24th, 29th, 31st, 34th, 47th, 53d, and 62d regiments.	† Now Earl Harrington, the present Commander in Chief in Ireland.	† Two com were left on George.

Lord Petersham,† and Sir James Clarke, Aid-de-camps to Gen. Burgoyne.

9th Regiment....Lieut. Col. Hill, Reserve.

The signal guns; which had been previously settled to give notice that all was ready, now fired; and the troops advanced in the greatest order and regularity.

In the mean time the Americans came out of their entrenchments in great force, and moved forward to meet the British army. Their line extended upwards of two miles, while they were supported by several strong columns. The scouts and flankers of both armies were soon in contact, and the firing began a little after mid-day.

The Americans being incapable from the nature of the country, of perceiving the different combinations of the march,* advanced a strong column, with a view of turning the British line upon the right; here they met the grenadiers and light infantry, who gave them a tremendous fire. Finding that it was impossible to penetrate the line at this point, they immediately countermarched and directed their principal effort to the centre. Here the conflict was dreadful; for four hours a constant blaze of fire was kept up, and both armies seemed to be determined on death or victory.

> " Here mingling hands, but not with friendly gripe,
>   Join in the fight; and breasts in close embrace,
>   But mortal as the iron arms of death.
>   Here words austere, of perilous command,
>   And valour swift t' obey; bold feats of arms
>   Dreadful to see, and glorious to relate."

Men, and particularly officers, dropped every moment on each side. Several of the Americans placed themselves in high trees, and as often as they could distinguish a British officer's uniform, took him off by deliberately aiming at his person. Reinforcements successively arrived and strengthened the American line.

* As the country is thickly covered with woods, movements may be effected without a possibility of being discovered.

The 20th, 21st, and 62d regiments greatly distinguished themselves. The stress of the action lay chiefly on these regiments, which stood the repeated attacks of three times their number for four hours.

> " Not noise, nor number, nor the brawny limb,
> Nor high built size prevails : 'Tis courage fights,
> 'Tis courage conquers."

Most of the other corps of the army bore a good share in this desperate conflict. The 24th regiment, with the grenadiers, and part of the light infantry, were for some time brought into action, and charged with their usual spirit and bravery. Breyman's riflemen likewise did good service.

Major General Phillips, upon hearing the firing, made his way through a difficult part of the wood to the scene of action, and brought up with him major Williams and four pieces of artillery ; this reinforcement animated our troops in the centre, which at that moment were critically pressed by a great superiority of fire, and to which the major general led up the 20th regiment at the utmost personal hazard. Major general Reidesel then brought forward part of the left wing, and arrived in time to charge the enemy with regularity and bravery.

Few actions have been characterized by more obstinacy in attack or defence ; the British troops repeatedly tried their bayonet with their usual success. As the day closed, the Americans retreated on all sides, and left them masters of the field of battle.

It was supposed that during this engagement near fifteen hundred men were killed and wounded in both armies. The British had to lament more than three hundred brave officers and men, who were killed and wounded on that day !

General Burgoyne, in his dispatches to government, says : " The behaviour of the officers and men in general was exemplary, brigadier general Frazer took his position in the beginning of the day, with great judgment, and sustained the action with constant presence of mind and vigor. Brigadier general Hamilton was the whole time engaged, and acquitted himself with great honor, activity and good conduct. The artillery in general was distinguished, and the brigade under captain Jones, who was killed in the action, was conspicuously so." *

General Burgoyne during this conflict behaved with great personal bravery, he shunned no danger; his presence and conduct animated the troops, (for they greatly loved the general;) he delivered his orders with precision and coolness; and in the heat, fury, and danger of the fight maintained those true characteristics of the soldier—serenity, fortitude and undaunted intrepidity.

20th. The army moved forward, and took post nearly within cannon shot of the American's fortified camp. Here the English strengthened their camp by cutting down large trees, which served for breast works.

* The estimation in which these services of the artillery (especially the Irish drafts) were held at home can be best appreciated by the testimony of distinguished characters. Among many others, the following testimonial is deserving particular notice :

Extract of a letter from lord viscount Townshend, master general of the British Ordnance, to lieutenant-colonel Straten, commandant of the royal Irish regiment of artillery.

" Sir,

" By lieutenant Slack, who this evening arrived from Quebec, and who has related to me many transactions of the late unfortunate campaign in that part of America, I am informed that none among our gallant troops behaved more noble than the drafts from the royal Irish artillery, who being now exchanged are to return. I am sorry they suffered so much; but it is the lot of brave men, who, so situated, prefer a glorious discharge of their duty to an unavailing desertion of it. Be assured, sir, I have a sincere, a grateful pleasure, in doing this justice to part of that corps, whose zeal for his majesty's service, and ambition to distinguish themselves, I have never doubted would be equal to any whatever. I am, sir, &c.

" Townshend."

21st. This day a messenger arrived from Sir Henry
Clinton, informing general Burgoyne of his intention
to attack Fort Montgomery, in about ten days from the
date of his letter, which was the 20th of September;
this was the only messenger from him or Sir William
Howe which had reached our camp since the beginning
of August. This messenger was sent back the same
night to Sir Henry Clinton, and charged to deliver
him a silver bullet, and to give it into the general's
own hands. If he should happen to be suspected as
an enemy and taken prisoner by the American troops,
he was ordered to swallow the bullet which would prevent the message from being detected. Having reached
as far as Fort Montgomery, on the North River, he
made enquiry for general Clinton; and finding, on
being brought before him, that he was not the person
to whom he was sent, but that he was governor
Clinton of the state of New-York, and a general in
the American service, he turned aside and swallowed
the silver ball. Being observed by some of the attendants, he was immediately taken into custody; when
being interrogated as to what business he had with
general Clinton, and discovering some embarrassment in
his answers, it was proposed to administer an emetic,
to ascertain what he had swallowed with such precipitation. The idea was adopted, and the consequence was,
that he threw up the silver ball, which being unscrewed,
was found to contain a letter from general Burgoyne to
Sir Henry Clinton, the purport of which was, to explain
his situation and the necessity of a diversion up the
North River, in order to oblige general Gates to detach
troops from his army; and further, that general
Burgoyne would wait favourable events in his position
to the 12th October. The messenger was immediately
hung as a spy.

October 3d. This day the rations were diminished. The army saw the necessity of this measure. Not a complaint or murmur was heard throughout the British camp.

7th. A detachment of fifteen hundred men, led on by general Burgoyne in person, made a movement to the right in order to discover if there were any possible means of forcing a passage to Albany.

As they advanced they were checked by a very sudden and rapid attack of the enemy on the left; there major Ackland was posted with the British grenadiers, who sustained the attack with great resolution and firmness. The Americans extended their attack along the whole front of the German troops, who were posted on the right of the grenadiers, and they also marched a large body round their flanks, in order to cut off their retreat. To oppose this bold enterprize the British light infantry, with a part of the 24th regiment, were directed to form a second line, and to secure the return of the troops into camp. In the mean time, the Americans pushed forward a fresh and a strong reinforcement to renew the action upon the left; where the troops, overpowered by so great a superiority, gave way, but the light infantry and 24th regiment, by a rapid movement, came to give succour, and saved the line from being carried; in doing which, brigadier general Frazer received his mortal wound.

The action now became very serious, as the British lines lay exposed to the enemy's sudden attack. In this crisis of danger general Burgoyne appeared cool and intrepid. He directed generals Philips and Reidesel to cover the retreat, while such troops as were most ready were ordered for the defence of the camp. The British troops were hard pressed, but retreated in good order; they were obliged to leave six pieces of cannon behind, all the horses having been killed, and all the artillery men, who had, as usual, behaved with the utmost bravery, being either killed or wounded.

——————" Veteran bands
Here made their last campaign "

General Arnold, with a brigade of continental troops, pushed rapidly forward, for that part of the camp possessed by lord Balcarres, at the head of the British light infantry, and some of the line, here they were received by a heavy and well directed fire which mowed down their ranks, and compelled them to retreat in disorder. Arnold now left this brigade and put himself at the head of a fresh corps, which he ordered instantly to advance and attack the lines in their front, which were defended by lieutenant colonel Breyman, at the head of the German reserve. The Americans pressed on with rapidity, and carried the works. Arnold was one of the first who entered them, and was wounded. Lieutenant colonel Breyman was killed. The Germans retreated firing, until they had gained their tents in the rear of the entrenchments; but supposing that the assault was general, gave one discharge, after which some retreated to the British camp, but others surrendered prisoners. Night at length put an end to the engagement.

This day's battle added many brave officers and men to the melancholy list of killed and wounded.

Brigadier general Frazer, on account of his distinguished merit, was greatly lamented by the whole army. Sir James Clarke, general Burgoyne's aid-de-camp, was mortally wounded, majors Ackland and Williams were taken prisoners. The former was wounded. The general himself had some very narrow escapes, a shot passed through his hat and another through his waistcoat. It was with great truth said, that, in the service of this campaign, the British officers bled profusely and most honorably.

On the side of the Americans, the loss n killed and wounded was very great, and far exceeded ours.

The enemy now having made a lodgment on the right of the British, their rear of course was exposed. In order to avoid this, general Burgoyne, by a judicious manœuvre, took a position upon the heights above the general hospital ; this was executed in the night with the greatest order, regularity, and silence. By this entire change of front, the American army was under the necessity of forming a new disposition

October 8th The British remained under arms all this day, offering the enemy battle, but nothing more than skirmishes took place,' in one of which the American general Lincoln was dangerously wounded. ' ! • '

In the mean time, general Burgoyne discovered that the Americans were marching a strong column forward, in order to turn the British right, which, if effected would have enclosed them on every side ; nothing could prevent this but an immediate retreat to Saratoga.

The army began to march to this place at nine o'clock at night , major general Reidesel led the van, and major general Philips brought up the rear They were under the necessity of leaving the sick and wounded behind.

9th. This evening the van arrived at the heights of Saratoga, having endured much hardships on the march, from a heavy rain and bad road ; here it was discovered that a division of the Americans had already arrived, and were employed in throwing up entrenchments on the heights before the British, on whose approach they retired over the ford, and joined a large body there , who likewise were employed for the same purpose of preventing all retreat.

10th. The batteaux with what little provisions remained were constantly fired upon, from the opposite side of the river , many of them fell into the hands of the enemy, and several of the men who conducted them, were killed and wounded

11th. Several men were employed this day in landing the provisions from the boats, and conveying them up to the hill, under a very galling fire from the enemy.

Very great indeed were the distresses which the army had to encounter at this period, yet they were borne with fortitude. The greatest subordination was manifested throughout the British lines. The men were willing and ready to face any danger, when led on by officers whom they loved and respected, and who shared with them in every toil and hardship.

Numerous parties of the militia now joined the Americans and swarmed around the little adverse army like birds of prey. Roaring of cannon and whistling of bullets from their rifle pieces, were heard constantly by day and night.

12th. A council of war, composed of general officers was held, in which general Burgoyne stated the present situation of affairs to the following effect:

" Upwards of fourteen thousand of the enemy, with a considerable quantity of artillery almost surround us, threatening an attack every moment. Two large bodies with cannon at Fort Edward guard that passage. A brigade below Saratoga church, by which their two armies can have a free communication. Our batteaux destroyed, and the enemy in possession of the immediate passes over Hudson's River. The following routes are those which offer themselves for the retreat of the army :—

" 1st. To cross the river by the ford at Fort Edward.

" 2d. To take a passage over the mountains until we arrived at some place higher up the river, where it can be passed by rafts.

" 3d. To continue the march on the mountains until we arrive at a ford, reported to be passable, but the passage of which is acknowledged to be attended with much danger.

4th. To persevere in the march over the mountains, until we clear the head of Hudson's River, keeping on the westward of Lake George until the army shall arrive at Ticonderoga. The Indians, and some small bodies of stragglers only, have effected the latter passage.

At the same time, general Burgoyne submitted to the council his readiness to attack the enemy, and attempt forcing a passage through their ranks. The council, however, determined in favor of a retreat by night. It was also stated, that the provisions could not possibly hold out beyond the 20th, and that there were neither rum nor spruce beer.

It would be rendering an act of injustice to the memory of general Burgoyne not to copy distinctly the communications which he made to the council, and their answers on each head. This will clearly evince, that he then did nothing *of himself;* but, on the contrary, that he acted from the *collective wisdom* of the army. From the four different statements already given, the general deduced the following propositions, and to them the council gave the annexed replies :

" 1st. To wait in the present position an attack from the enemy, or the chance of favourable events.

" 2d. To attack the enemy.

" 3d. To retreat, repairing the bridges as the army moves for the artillery, in order to force the passage of the ford.

" 4th. To retreat by night, leaving the artillery and the baggage ; and should it be found impracticable to force the passage with musquetry, to attempt the upper ford, or the passage round Lake George.

" 5th. In case the enemy by extending to their left, leave their rear open, to march rapidly for Albany."

" Upon the first proposition resolved, that the situation would grow worse by delay ; that the provision now in store is not more than sufficient for the retreat, should

Y

impediments intervene, or a circuit of country became
necessary; and as the enemy did not attack when the
ground was unfortified, it is not probable they will do
it now, as they have a better game to play.

"The second unadvisable and desperate, there being no
possibility of reconnoitering the enemy's position, and
their great superiority of numbers known

" The third impracticable.

" The fifth thought worthy of consideration by the
lieutenant-general, major-general Phillips, and brigadier-
general Hamilton; but the position of the enemy yet
gives no open for it

" Resolved, that the fourth proposition is the only resource, and that to effect it, the utmost secrecy and
silence is to be observed; and the troops are to be put
in motion from the right in the still part of the night,
without any change in the disposition."*

The arrival of scouts prevented the execution of this
determination. They brought intelligence, that " the
enemy's position on the right was such, and they had
so many small parties out, that it would be impossible
to move without being immediately discovered Thus
circumstanced, general Burgoyne again assembled the
council This measure became indispensable, from the
situation of the British army and the character of their
general Rashly to have sacrificed the lives of those
over whom he had command, would have been temerity;
meanly to save their lives by compromise (unless no
other means existed) would have for ever tarnished his
own reputation. He summoned the officers for their

---

* It depended upon the delivery of six days provision in due
time, and upon the return of scouts who had been sent forward,
to examine by what route the army could probably move the first
four miles undiscovered, whether the plan should take place on
that day, or on the morrow.

opinion,* and, in this sad dilemma, acted on their resolves. But the minutes of this last proceeding, will best speak for themselves.

" Minutes and proceedings of a council of war, consisting of all the general officers, field officers, and captains commanding corps, on the heights of Saratoga, October the 13th, 1777 :

" The lieutenant-general having explained the situation of affairs as in the preceding council, with the additional intelligence, that the enemy was intrenched at the fords of Fort Edward, and likewise occupied the strong position on the pine plains between Fort George and Fort Edward, expressed his readiness to undertake at their head, any enterprize, of difficulty or hazard that should appear to them within the compass of their strength and spirit. He added, that he had reason to believe a capitulation had been in the contemplation of some, perhaps of all, who knew the real situation of things, that, upon a circumstance of such consequence to national and personal honor, he thought it a duty to his country, and to himself, to extend his council beyond the usual limits ; that the assembly present might justly be esteemed a full representation of the army , and that he should think himself unjustifiable in taking any step n so serious a matter, without such a concurrence of sentiments as should make a treaty the act of the army as well as that of the general. The first question, therefore, he desired them to decide was :

" Whether an army of three thousand five hundred fighting men, and well provided with artillery, were justifiable, upon the principles of national dignity and military honor, n capitulating in any possible situation ? Resolved, *nem con.* in the affirmative."

---

* The field officers and captains commanding corps were added to this council.

" Question 2. Is the present situation of that nature ?—
Resolved, *nem. con.* that the present situation justifies
a capitulation upon honorable terms."

General Burgoyne then drew up the following letter directed to general Gates, relative to the negociation, and laid it before the council. It was
unanimously approved, and upon that foundation the
treaty opened.

" After having fought you twice, lieutenant general
Burgoyne, has waited some days in his present position, determined to try a third conflict, against any
force you could bring to attack him.

" He is apprized of the superiority of your numbers,
and the disposition of your troops, to impede his
supplies, and render his retreat a scene of carnage
on both sides. In this situation he is compelled by
humanity, and thinks himself justified by established
principles, and precedents of state, and of war, to
spare the lives of brave men upon honorable terms.

" Should major general Gates, be inclined to treat
upon that idea, general Burgoyne would propose a
cessation of arms, during the time necessary to com-
municate the preliminary terms by which in any
extremity, he, and his army, mean to abide."

General Gates then transmitted the following proposals to general Burgoyne

"General Burgoyne's army being exceedingly reduced
by repeated defeats, by desertion, sickness, &c. their
provisions exhausted, their military horses, tents and
baggage taken or detroyed, their retreat cut off, and
their camp invested, they can only be allowed to
surrender prisoners of war.

" Answer. Lieutenant general Burgoyne's army however reduced, will never admit that their retreat is cut
off while they have arms in their hands.

" The troops under his excellency general Burgoyne's command, may be drawn up in their encampments, where they will be ordered to ground their arms, and may thereupon be marched to the river side to be passed over in their way towards Bennington.

" Answer. This article inadmissible in any extremity; sooner than this army will consent to ground their arms in their encampment, they will rush on the enemy determined to take no quarter. If general Gates does not mean to recede from this article the treaty ends at once. The army will to a man proceed to any act of desperation rather than submit to that article."

General Gates did recede from this article, and the following was substituted in its stead.

" The troops to march out of their camp with the honors of war, and the artillery of the entrenchments, to the verge of the river, where their arms and artillery must be left. The arms to be piled by word of command from their own officers.*

" A free passage to be granted to the army under lieutenant general Burgoyne to Great Britain, upon condition of not serving again in North America during the present contest ; and the port of Boston to be assigned for the entry of transports to receive the troops whenever general Howe shall so order."†

Such was the melancholy catastrophe of these brave men, after undergoing " a series of hard toil, incessant effort, stubborn action, till disabled in the collateral branches of the army, by the total defection of the Indians, the desertion or timidity of the Canadians

* While the British troops were marching from the heights of Saratoga to the verge of the river, the American drummers and fifers were ordered by General Gates to play the tune of " Yankey Doodle," while at the same time his troops were drawn up in a thick part of the wood out of sight of the British army. The arms were piled by order of the British officers.

† This article was never fulfilled.

and Provincials, some individuals excepted, disappointed n the last hope of any timely co-operation
from other armies, the regular troops reduced by
losses from the best parts to three thousand five hundred
fighting men, not two thousand of which were British ;
only three days provisions in store, upon short allowance, invested by an army of sixteen thousand men, and
no apparent means of retreat remaining "* The British
army, under these circumstances, were induced to open
the above treaty.

In the mean time Sir Henry Clinton had sailed up
the North River, attacked and carried Fort Montgomery,
and passed it in his attempt to favour the descent of
general Burgoyne, and in all probability a junction of
these two armies would have been effected, had the
expedition been earlier adopted, as meditated by Sir
Henry Clinton.

Fort Montgomery was erected by the Americans the
year before, there was laid a strong boom across the
river, guarded by two frigates, the Hudson being
navigable for ships of war of sixty guns much higher
than this fort, and at spring tides for frigates next
to Albany

After this fort was taken, the town of Esopus (now
called Kingston,) situated near the west bank of Hudson's
River, was destroyed by general Vaughan, it was here
that captain Rose and lieutenant Meddagh, two leaders
of the loyalists, were executed without a regular form
of trial, for their adherence to the British cause, this
circumstance, with others of a similar nature, had
rendered the place extremely odious to the loyal
followers of the British arms; and possibly might have
occasioned its conflagration. A large body of loyalists
were forming at this time on the eastern shore of the
river, to join the royal army, but the advanced state

* General Burgoyne's own words.

of the season prevented the continuance of Sir Henry Clinton's force in the rear, and they were obliged to return to New York.

It should have been mentioned, that, on the very day the royal forces crossed Hudson's River, the Americans in order to cut off the retreat of the British army, under general Burgoyne, in the most effectual manner, undertook an expedition against Ticonderoga. They conducted their operations with such secrecy and address, that on the 18th of September a sudden and general attack was made upon the carrying place of Lake George, Sugar Hill, Ticonderoga, and Mount Independence. The sea officer commanding the armed sloop stationed to defend the carrying place, as also some of the officers commanding at the ports at the Sugar Hill, and at the portage were surprized, and a considerable part of four companies of the 53d regiment were made prisoners. A blockhouse, commanded by lieutenant Lord of that regiment, was the only post on that side where they had time to make use of their arms, and they made a gallant defence, till cannon taken from the Surprize vessel was brought against them.

The enemy having twice summoned brigadier general Powell, and received such answers as became a gallant officer, entrusted with so important a post, and having tried during the course of four days several attacks, and being repulsed in all, retreated without doing any considerable damage.

Brigadier general Powell gave great commendation to the British and German troops stationed at Mount Independence. The brigadier mentioned with great applause the behaviour of captain Taylor of the 21st regiment, who was accidentally there on the road to the army, and lieutenant Beercroft of the 24th regiment, who, with the artificers in arms, defended an important battery.

On the 24th of September, the enemy enabled by the capture of the gun boats and batteaux, (which they had made after the surprize of the sloops,) to embark upon Lake George, attacked Diamond Island in two divisions Captain Aubrey, and two companies of the 47th regiment, had been posted at that island from the time the army passed the Hudson's River , the enemy were repulsed by captain Aubrey, with great loss, and pursued by the gun boats under his command to the east shore, where two of our principal vessels were re-taken, together with all the cannon , they had just time to set fire to the other batteaux, and retreated over the mountains

The sacrifice which, without obtaining its end, was made in the course of this campaign, will the more fully appear on perusal of the following list of those who suffered and those who fell :

July 2d   Lieutenant Haughton, 53d regiment, wounded near Ticonderoga

—— 6th. Second Lieutenant Clelland, Royal Artillery, killed at Hubberton

Volunteer Sutton, wounded at do

—— 7th   Major Grant,* 24th regiment, killed at do.

Lieutenant Douglas, 29th do   do   do

Haggart, marines,   do.   do

LIGHT INFANTRY

Major Lord Balcarres, 53d regiment, wounded at do

Captain Harris,	34th	do	do	do
—— Craig,	47th	do	do.	do
Lieutenant Cullen,	53d	do.	do	do
—— Jones,	62d	do	do	do

GRENADIERS

Captain Stappleton, 9th regiment, died of his wounds, at do

Major Ackland,	20th	do	wounded, at	do
Captain Ross,	34th	do	do	do
—— Shrimpton,	62d	do	do	do.
Lieutenant Rowe,	9th	do	do	do
—— Steele,	29th	do	do	do

* Major Grant was twice wounded at Ticonderoga, under general Amherst, in the former wars.

	Lieutenant Richardson, 34th regt.	wounded	Hubberton	
	Volunteer Lindsay,		do.	do.
July 9th,	Lieutenant Westrop, 9th regt.		killed	Fort Ann.
	Captain Montgomery, —	do.	wounded & taken prisoner,	do.
	Lieutenant Stavely, —	do.	wounded	do.
	———— Murray, —	do.	do.	do.
	Adjutant Fielding, —	do.	do.	do.
Aug. 16,	Lieutenant Wright, —	do.	killed	Bennington.
	Ensign Baron De Salons, —	do.	wounded,	do.
Sept. 19,	Captain Jones, Royal Artillery,		killed	Freeman's Farm.
	Lieutenant Cooke, 20th	do.	do.	do.
	———— Lucas, —	do.	do.	do.
	———— Currie, 21st	do.	do.	do.
	———— M'Kenzie, —	do.	do.	do.
	———— Robinson, —	do.	do.	do.
	———— Reynal, 24th	do.	do.	do.
	———— Hervey, 62d	do.	do.	do.
	Ensign Phillips, —	do.	do.	do.
	———— Taylor, —	do.	do.	do.
	———— Young, —	do.	do.	do.
	Lt. Col. Lynd, 20th	do.	wounded	do.
	*———— Anstruther, 62d	do.	do.	do.
	Major Forbes, 9th	do.	do.	do.
	———— Agnew, 24th	do.	do.	do.
	*——— Harnage, 62d	do.	do.	do.
	Captain Sweetenham, 9th	do.	do.	do.
	———— Dowling, 21st	do.	do.	do.
	———— Stanley, —	do.	do.	do.
	———— Farquire —	do.	do.	do.
	———— Weyms, —	do.	do.	do.
	———— Ramsay, —	do.	do.	do.
	———— Blake, 24th	do.	do.	do.
	Lieutenant Prince, 9th	do.	do.	do.
	————-Rutherford, 21st	do.	do.	do.
	Ensign Hervey, 62d	do.	do.	do.

Thus marked * were wounded in two different actions.

Z

Oct. 7th, Brig. general Frazer,   killed, { near Still Water.

SirJames Clarke, Aid deCamp to General Burgoyne, } { mortally wounded & taken prisoner, } do.

Captain Wight,	53d regiment,	killed	do.
Lieutenant Obin,	20th do.	do.	do.
———— Turnbull,	21st do.	do.	do.
———— Stewart,	62d do.	do.	do.
Lt. Col. Anstruther,	do.	wounded	do.
*Major Ackland,	20th do.	do.	do.
—— Harnage,	62d do.	do.	do.
Captain Strangways,	24th do.	do.	do.
———— Bunbury,	62d do.	do.	do.
————Green Aid de deCamp toGeneral Philips	31st do.	do.	do.
Captain Bloomfield, Major of Brigade	Royal Artillery,	do.	do.
Lieutenant Battersby,	29th light infantry,	do.	do.
———— Fisherton,	21st do.	do.	do.
———— *Richardson,	34th grenadiers,	do.	do.
———— Dowling,	29th regiment	do.	do.
———— Doyle,	24th do.	do.	do.
———— Williams,	29th do.	do.	do.
———— Richardson,	34th battalion,	do.	do.
———— Houghton,	53d regiment,	do.	do.
———— Smith,	Royal Artillery,	do.	do.
———— Howarth,	do.	do.	do.
Ensign Connel,	20th regiment,	do.	do.
———— Blake,	62d do.	do.	do.

Oct. 11th. Adjutant Fitzgerald, — do.   killed { at Saratoga.

—— 7th, Major Ackland, 20th do. } taken prisoner, { near Still Water

—— Williams, Royal Artillery, do. do.

July 9th. Captain Montgomery, 9th regiment, do. { Fort Ann.

Oct. 7th. ———— Money, Deputy Quarter Master General, } —— do. do. { near Still Water

Lieutenant Johnson, 29th do. do. do.

———— York, — do. do. do.

'Lieut. Howarth, Royal Artillery, } taken prisoner, { near Still Water

Ensign D'Antroch,   62d regiment, do. do.'

———— Naylor,   —   do.   do. do.

July 9th, Surgeon Shelly, 9th do.   do { at Fort Ann.

KILLED.	WOUNDED.
1 Brigadier General,	2 Lieutenant Colonels,
1 Major,	5 Majors,
1 Aid de Camp,	16 Captains,
3 Captains,	18 Lieutenants,
15 Lieutenants,	4 Ensigns,
4 Ensigns,	1 Adjutant,
12 Serjeants,	2 Volunteers,
5 Drummers,	38 Serjeants,
313 Rank & File.	4 Drummers,
	715 Rank & File.
355 Total killed.	805 Total wounded.

Killed.....................355
Wounded...................805

Total killed and wounded of the British army........1160

The following numbers surrendered prisoners at Sara-toga, on the 17th October, 1777 :—

British troops, including the sick and wounded, in camp..2240
German ditto,   do.   do.......1700
Canadians, Provincials, Batteaux-men, &c................. 480
Sick and wounded left behind in the British camp, } 460
when general Burgoyne retreated to Saratoga..... }

Total............4880

An account of brass ordnance taken :

2————24 pounders.
4————12 ditto.
18————6 ditto.
4———— 3 ditto.
5———— 5½ inch royal howitzers.
2———— 8 inch brass mortars.

Total.......35

Z 2

The loss of general Frazer was a severe shock to the army, and the sensation which it produced was felt by all ranks, from the commander in chief to the private. After he was wounded, he was supported by two officers, one on each side of his horse. When he arrived in camp, the officers all anxiously enquired as to his wound : the down cast look and melancholy that were visible to every one, too plainly spoke his situation, and all the answer he could make to the many inquiries, was a shake of his head, expressive that all was over with him. So much was he beloved that even the women flocked round, solicitous for his fate.

When he had reached his tent, and was recovered a little from the faintness occasioned by the loss of blood, he told those around him, that he saw the man who shot him ; he was a rifle man, and aimed from a tree. The ball entered a little below his breast, and penetrated just under the back bone. 'After the surgeon had dressed his wound, he said to him, very composedly, " Tell me, to the best of your skill and judgment, if you think my wound is mortal." When he replied, " I am sorry, sir, to inform you, that it is ; and that you cannot possibly live twenty-four hours." The general called for pen, ink, and paper, and after making his will, and distributing a few little tokens of regard to the officers of his suite, desired that he might be removed to the general hospital. Early the next morning, he breathed his last, and at his particular request was buried without any parade in the great redoubt, by the soldiers of his own corps.

About sun-set, the corpse was carried up the hill. The procession was in view of both armies. As it passed by, generals Burgoyne, Phillips, and Reidesel, with most of the officers of the army, joined the procession. The troops who fought immediately under general Frazer, not being acquainted with the privacy of burial that was enjoined by his will, construed it into neglect, and urged by a natural wish to pay the last honours to him in the eyes of the whole army, marched after the body in solemn procession to the grave.

The enemy, with an inhumanity deserving the con_demnation of every liberal mind, cannonaded the pro_cession as it passed, and during the service over the grave the aggression was repeated. Charity would in_cline us to hope, although probability is against the fact, that they were unacquainted with the nature of the awful ceremony. Sacred from interruption and hostility, even among the most barbarous of mankind, are the last sad offices which the living pay to the dead.

Nor should the heroism of lieutenant Hervey, of the 62d regiment, a youth of sixteen, and nephew to the adjutant general of the same name, be forgotten. It was characterized by all that is gallant in the military character.

In the battle of the 19th of September, he received several wounds, and was repeatedly ordered off the field by lieutenant colonel Anstruther, but his heroic ardor would not allow him to quit the battle while he could stand, and see his brave comrades fighting beside him. A ball striking one of his legs, his removal became absolutely necessary, and while they were conveying him away, another wounded him mortally. In this situation, the surgeon recommended him to take a powerful dose of opium, to avoid a seven or eight hours life of most exquisite torture. This he immediately consented to, and when the colonel entered the tent, with major Harnage, who were both wounded, they asked whether he had any affairs they could settle for him? His reply was, that being a minor, every thing was already adjusted; but he had one request, which he retained just life enough to utter: " Tell my uncle, I died like a soldier"——

Major Ackland when wounded, observed the British troops were retreating; he requested captain Simpson of the 31st regiment, who was an intimate friend, to help him into camp, upon which, being a stout man, he conveyed the major on his back a considerable way, when the enemy pursuing so rapidly, he was obliged to leave him behind to save himself. As the major lay, on the ground, he cried out to the men who were running by him, that he would give fifty guineas to any soldier who would convey him into camp. A stout grenadier instantly took him on his back, and was hastening into camp, when they were overtaken and both made prisoners.

Captain Bloomfield, of the artillery, received a wound which was very remarkable, a shot passing through both cheeks without hurting the inside of his mouth.

Lieutenant Howarth, of the same corps, was wounded in his knee. It was very singular, that he was so strongly prepossessed with an idea of being wounded, that when the orders came for the detachment's going out, being in company with lieutenant Anburey, after reading the orders, and that his brigade of guns were to go, he said to that officer, " God bless you, Anburey, farewell'; for I know not how it is, but I have a strange presentiment that I shall either be killed or wounded.

Some letters passed between the opposed generals. The first was from general Burgoyne, by lady Ackland, whose husband was dangerously wounded, and a prisoner, recommending her ladyship to the care and protection of general Gates. Gates's answer was pointed with the sharpest irony, in which he expresses his surprise that his excellency after considering his preceding conduct, should think that he could consider the greatest attention to lady Ackland, in the light of an obligation. These epistles, although mere communications between individuals, and frequently on private affairs, yet serve to pourtray the *disposition of the times,* and unveil the cause that gave rise to the unhappy contest.

" The cruelties," added he, " which mark the retreat of your army, in burning the gentlemen and -farmers houses as they went along, are almost, among civilized nations, without a precedent; they should not endeavour to ruin those they could not conquer; this conduct betrays more the vindictive malice of a monk, than the generosity of a soldier."

What gave rise to this charge, was the following circumstance: on the west bank of Hudson's River, near the height of Saratoga, where the British army halted after the retreat, stood general Schuyler's dwelling house, with a range of barracks and store-houses, &c. The evening the army arrived at these buildings, the weather being very wet and cold, the sick and wounded were directed to take possession of these barracks; while the troops took post on the height above it. In the course of the night, the barracks took fire by accident, and being built of wood, were soon consumed. It was with the greatest difficulty that the wounded soldiers were rescued from the flames.* Two days after this, the enemy had formed a plan of attack; a large column of troops was approaching to pass the river, preparatory to a general action: this column was entirely covered from the fire of the British artillery, by some of these buildings. General Burgoyne ordered them to be set on fire; but so far was the sufferer from putting an invidious construction upon that action, that one of the first persons general Burgoyne saw after the convention was signed was the owner, general Schuyler; who, instead of blaming the English general, owned he would have done the same

---

* The author was in the house when it took fire, and it was with the greatest difficulty he escaped.

upon the like occasion, or words to that effect. He
did more. He conducted him to his house; presented
him to Mrs. Schuyler; continued him in his family
during the whole time of his stay in Albany, with a table
of more than twenty covers for himself and friends, and
with every other possible demonstration of hospitality:
a situation painful at that time, but now pleasing, and
carrying undeniable testimony how little he deserved the
charges thrown out against him.

On this occasion, and at this distance of time, the
energetic language of general Burgoyne, when he demanded a trial, cannot be passed by. It speaks the
proud, dignified spirit of the soldier, alike conscious
of his humanity as his courage, and is a clearer
refutation of the calumnies advanced against him, than
the most laboured and artful defence, which wealth
could purchase, or ingenuity fabricate:

" As for myself, if I am guilty, I fear I am doubly
guilty: An army lost! The sanguine expectation of the
kingdom disappointed! A foreign war caused, or the
commencement of it accelerated! An effusion of as
brave blood as ever ran in British veins, and the
severest family distresses combined with public calamity!
If this mass of miseries be indeed the consequence of
my misconduct, vain will be the extenuation I can plead,
of my personal sufferings, fatigue, and hardships, la-
borious days and sleepless nights, ill health, and trying
situations; poor and insufficient would be such atone-
ment in the judgment of my country, or perhaps in the
eyes of God; yet with this dreadful alternative in view,
I provoke a trial. Give me inquiry. I put the interests
that hang most emphatically by the heart strings of the
man—my fortune—my honor—my head—I had almost
said my salvation upon the issue."

There were as many witnesses of the truth of this
statement of facts as there were men in the British

army. Indeed, the more these charges were sifted (and the general was very strictly examined in the house of commons) the more it tended to place the suffering officer in a very high point of view, whether considered as a man, a soldier, or the leader of an army, in the most trying and perilous service. It proved that he possessed the confidence and affection of his army in so extraordinary a degree, that no loss or misfortune could shake the one, or distress or affliction weaken the other. It established an instance, as far as it could be conclusive, (and a close examination was not able to weaken it), perhaps unequalled in the military history, that notwithstanding so long and continued a scene of unceasing fatigue, hardship and danger, finally ending in general ruin and captivity, not a single voice was heard through the army, to upbraid, to censure, or blame their general, and that at length, when all their courage and efforts were found ineffectual, and every hope totally cut off, they were still willing to perish along with him.

But perhaps the best testimonial of the rectitude of general Burgoyne's character, was what fell from the pen of his illustrious rival. A higher eulogium, and one more just, was never paid by the generous heart of one soldier to another. Near five months after the convention of Saratoga, general Burgoyne, finding his health declining, and hearing that his character had been much traduced in England, solicited congress to permit him to return, on his parole of honor, to England. He also applied to general Washington for his interference in the matter. The following is Washington's answer:

Head Quarters, Pennsylvania, March 11th, 1778.

" SIR,—I was, only two days since, honored with your very obliging letter of the 11th of February.

A a

" Your indulgent opinion of my character, and the polite terms in which you are pleased to express it, are peculiarly flattering , and I take pleasure in the opportunity you have afforded me of assuring you,' that, far from suffering the views of national opposition to be imbittered and debased by personal animosity,[1] I am ever ready to do justice to the merit of the gentleman and the soldier , and to esteem, where esteem is due, however the ideas of a public enemy may interpose You will not think it the language of unmeaning ceremony, if I add, that sentiments of personal respect, in the present instance, are reciprocal Viewing you in the light of an officer contending against what I conceive to be the rights of my country, the reverse of fortune you experienced in the field cannot be unacceptable to me , but, abstracted from considerations of national advantage, I can sincerely sympathize with your feelings, as a soldier, the unavoidable difficulties of whose situation forbid his success and as a man, whose lot combines the calamity of ill health, the anxieties of captivity, and the painful sensibility for a reputation, exposed, where he most values it, to the assaults of malice and detraction.

" As your aid-de-camp went directly on to congress, the business of your letter to me had been decided before it came to hand. I am happy that the cheerful acquiescence with your request prevented the necessity of my intervention. And, wishing you a safe and agreeable passage, with a perfect restoration of your health, I have the honor to be, &c. " GEORGE WASHINGTON "

The circumstances relative to Major Ackland and his lady are so very remarkable, and they have been so variously related, that it becomes necessary, on both accounts, to notice them. The accuracy of the following detail may be depended on. The communication comes directly from general Burgoyne. There is scarcely an instance, either in ancient or modern history, that more finely depicts the resolution, affection, and fortitude of woman toward the husband of her heart and vows than this. If war sometimes in bad men, calls forth all the viler passions of our nature, in woman it is otherwise; it rouzes into action an heroism otherwise unknown, an intrepidity almost incompatible with the sex, and awakens all the dormant susceptibilities of their mind.

" Besides the continuation of general fatigue, this day was, remarkable for a circumstance of private distress too affecting to be omitted. The circumstance to which I allude, is lady Harriet Ackland's passage through the enemy's army, to attend her wounded husband, then their prisoner.

" The progress of this lady with the army could hardly be thought abruptly or superfluously introduced, were it only for the purpose of authenticating a wonderful story. It would exhibit, if well delineated, an interesting picture of the spirit, the enterprise, and the distress of romance; realized and regulated upon the chaste and sober principles of rational love and connubial duty.

" Lady Harriet Ackland, sister to the earl of Ilchester, had accompanied her husband, major John Dyke Ackland, son of Sir Thomas Ackland, to Canada in the beginning of the year 1776. In the course of that campaign she had traversed a vast space of country, in different extremities of season, and with difficulties that an European traveller will not easily conceive, to attend him, in a poor hut at Chamblee, upon his sick bed.

" In the opening of the campaign of 1777, she was restrained from offering herself to a share of the fatigue and hazard expected before Ticonderoga, by the positive injunctions of her husband. The day after the conquest of that place, he was badly wounded, and she crossed the Lake Champlain to join him.

" As soon as he recovered, lady Harriet proceeded to follow his fortunes through the campaign, and at Fort

Edward, or at the next camp, she acquired a two-wheel tumbril, which had been constructed by the artificers of the artillery, something similar to the carriage used for the mail upon the great roads of England: Major Ackland commanded the British grenadiers, which were attached to general Fraser's corps; and consequently were always the most advanced post of the army. Their situations often called them to be so alert, that no person slept out of his clothes. In one of these posts of danger a tent, in which the major and lady Harriet were asleep, suddenly took fire. An orderly serjeant of grenadiers, with great hazard of suffocation, dragged out the first person he caught hold of. It proved to be the major. It happened that in the same instant she had, unknowing what she did, and perhaps not perfectly awake, providentially made her escape, by creeping under the walls of the back part of the tent. The first object she saw, upon the recovery of her senses, was the major on the other side; and in the same instant perceived him again in the fire, in the search of her. The serjeant again saved him, but not without the major being very severely burned in his face and different parts of the body. Every thing they had with them in the tent was consumed.*

" This accident happened a little time before the army passed Hudson's River. It neither altered the resolution, nor the cheerfulness of lady Harriet; and she continued her progress, a partaker of the fatigues of the advanced corps. The next call upon her fortitude was of a different nature, and more distressful, as of longer suspense. On the march of the 19th, the grenadiers being liable to action at every step,

---

* This accident was occasioned by a favourite Newfoundland dog, who, being restless, overset the table, on which a candle was burning, and which, rolling to the walls of the tent, instantly set them on fire.

she had been directed by the major to follow the route of the artillery and baggage, which was not exposed. At the time the action began, she found herself near a small uninhabited hut, where she alighted. When it was found the action was becoming general and bloody, the surgeons of the hospital took possession of the same place, as the most convenient for the care of the wounded. Thus was the lady in hearing of one continued fire of cannon and musketry, for four hours together, with the presumption, from the post of her husband at the head of the grenadiers, that he was in the most exposed part of the action. She had three female companions, the baroness of Reidesel, and the wives of two British officers, major Harnage, and lieutenant Reynal; but, in the event, their presence served little for comfort. Major Harnage was soon brought to the surgeons, very badly wounded; and a little time after came intelligence that lieutenant Reynal was shot dead. Imagination will want no helps to figure the state of the whole groupe.

"From the date of the action, the 7th of October, lady Harriet, with her usual serenity, stood prepared for new trials! and it was her lot that their severity increased with numbers. She was again exposed to the hearing of the whole action, and at last received the shock of her individual misfortune, mixed with the intelligence of the general calamity : the troops were defeated and major Ackland, desperately wounded, was a prisoner.

"The day of the 8th was passed by lady Harriet and her companions in common anxiety; not a tent nor a shed being standing, except what belonged to the hospital; their refuge was among the wounded and the dying.

"When the army was upon the point of moving, after the halt described, I received a message from lady Harriet, submitting to my decision, a proposal (and ex-

pressing an earnest solicitude to execute it, if not in.
terfering with my designs) of passing to the camp
of the enemy, and requesting general Gates's permission to attend her husband,

"Though I was ready to believe (for I had experience) that patience and fortitude, n a supreme degree,
were to be found, as well as every other virtue, under
the most tender forms, I was astonished at this proposal,
After so long an agitation of the spirits, exhausted not
only for want of rest, but absolutely for want of food,
drenched in rains for twelve hours together, that a
woman should be capable of such an undertaking, as
delivering herself to the enemy, probably in the night
and uncertain of what hands she might first fall into,
appeared an effort above human nature. The assistance
I was enabled to give was small indeed. I had not
even a cup of wine to offer her, but was told she
had found, from some kind and fortunate hand, a little
rum and dirty water. All I could furnish to her was
an open boat and a few lines, written upon dirty and
wet paper, to general Gates, recommending her to
his protection.

Mr Brudenell, the chaplain to the artillery, (the same
gentleman who had officiated so signally at general
Fraser's funeral) readily undertook to accompany her,
and with one female servant, and the major's valet-de-
chambre, (who had a ball which he had received in
the late action then in his shoulder,) she rowed down
the river to meet the enemy. But her distresses were
not yet to end The night was advanced before the
boat reached the enemy's out-posts, and the sentinel
would not let it pass, nor even come on shore. In
vain Mr. Brudenell offered the flag of truce, and represented the state of the extraordinary passenger The
guard was apprehensive of treachery, and therefore
threatened to fire into the boat if it stirred before day

light. Her anxiety and suffering were thus protracted through seven or eight dark and cold hours; and her reflections upon that first reception could not give her very encouraging ideas of the treatment she was afterwards to expect. But it is due to justice, at the close of this adventure, to say, that she was received and accommodated by general Gates, with all the humanity and respect that her rank, her merits, and her fortunes deserved.

" Let such as are affected by these circumstances of alarm, hardship, and danger, recollect, that the subject of them was a woman of the most tender and delicate frame; of the gentlest manners; habituated to all the soft elegancies, and refined enjoyments that attend high birth and fortune; and far advanced in. a state in which the tender cares, always due to the sex, become indispensably necessary. Her mind alone was formed for such trials."

A circumstance of as singular, but altogether of an opposite nature, happened in the desperate adventures of one Whitcomb, who undertook to steal a British officer for the Americans, and who, in executing his scheme, actually murdered brigadier general Gordon. Lieutenant Anburey, who was on the spot, thus relates the particulars:

" Whitcomb, a native of Connecticut, and a great partizan of the Americans, who, after the defeat upon the lakes, (in 1776, as already related in a former part of this work), offered his service to venture through the woods, and bring in prisoner an English officer, for which purpose he stationed himself among the thickest copses that are between La Praire and St. John's. The first officer who happened to pass him was brigadier general Gordon; he was mounted on a spirited horse, and Whitcomb thinking there was little probability of of seizing him, fired at, and wounded him in the shoulder.

The general. immediately rode as fast as he. could to the camp at St. John's, which he had but just reached, when with loss of blood and fatigue, he fell. from his horse ; some soldiers took, him up, and carried him to the hospital, where, after his wound was dressed, and he was a little at ease, he related the circumstance, which being immediately made known to general Carleton; a party of Indians were sent out to scour the woods, and search for Whitcomb ; but in vain, as he hastened back to Ticonderoga. General Carleton, however, imagining he might be lurking about the woods, or secreted in the house of some disaffected Canadian, issued out a proclamation among the inhabitants, offering a reward of fifty guineas to any one that would bring Whitcomb, alive or dead, to the camp.

"A few days after this general Gordon died of his wound, in whose death we sincerely lamented the loss of a brave and experienced officer.

"When Whitcomb returned to Ticonderoga, and informed the general who commanded there, that although he could not take an officer prisoner, he believed he had mortally wounded one, the general expressed his disapprobation in the strongest terms, and was so much displeased at the transaction, that Whitcomb, in order to effect a reconciliation, offered his service to go again, professing he would forfeit his life, if he did not return with a prisoner.

"He accordingly with two other men, proceeded down Lake Champlain, in a canoe, to a small creek, where they secreted it, and repaired to the woods, to the same spot where Whitcomb had stationed himself before ; the two men lay concealed a little way in the wood, whilst he skulked about the borders of it.

"The regiment of which our friend S—— is quarter-master, having occassion for some stores from Montreal, he was going from the camp at St. John's to procure them ; he was advised not to go this road, but by the way of Chamblee, on account of the late accident ; but you know him to be a man of great bravery and personal courage, joined with uncommon strength ; resolving not to go so many miles out of his road for any Whitcomb whatever, he jocosely added, that he should be very glad to meet with him, as he was sure he should get the reward ; in this, however, he was greatly mistaken, his reward being no other than that of being taken prisoner himself.

. " Previous to his setting out he took every precaution, having not only loaded his fusee, but charged a brace of pistols. When he came near to the woods I have already described, he was very cautious ; but, in an instant, Whitcomb, and the two men he had with him, sprung from behind a thick bush, and seized him before he could make the least resistance ; they then tied his arms behind him with ropes, and blind-folded him.

" It was three days before they reached the canoe that had been concealed, during which time they had but very scanty fare ; a few hard biscuits served to allay hunger, while the fruits of the wood was a luxury ! When Whitcomb had marched him to such a distance as he thought he could not make his escape, were he at liberty, through fear of losing himself ; for the greater ease on his own part, and to facilitate their march, they untied his hands, and took the cloth from his eyes. Only picture to yourself what must have been his feelings, at seeing himself in the midst of a thick wood, surrounded by three desperate fellows, and uncertain as to their intentions !

" At night, when they had partaken of their scanty pittance, two out of the three used to sleep, whilst the other kept watch. The first night he slept through fatigue ; on the second, as you may naturally suppose,

and from his great anxiety of mind, he could not close his
eyes. In the middle of the night an opportunity occurred
whereby he could have effected his escape, for the man
whose watch it was, fell fast asleep. He has since told
me how his mind wavered for a length of time, what
measures to pursue; he could not bear the idea of putting them to death, though justified by the rules of
war: if he escaped from them, they might in all probability retake and ill-treat him. The great hazard of
all, which determined him to abide by his fate was, that
by being so many miles in a tract of wood, where he
could not tell what direction to take (having been blind-
folded when he entered it) he might possibly wander
up and down till he perished with hunger. In this
restless state he remained till day-break, when they resumed their march, and in the evening came to the
creek where the canoe was concealed; they then secured
him again, put him in the canoe, and proceeded up the
lake to Ticonderoga, where they arrived early the
next morning. When they landed him he was again
blind-folded, that he might not see their works, and
thus conducted to the general, whose only motive for
endeavouring to get an officer was, either by threats or
intreaties, to gain information relative to our army. In
this, however, he was greatly disappointed, and as he
could not obtain the least intelligence from our friend,
he ordered him as prisoner of war upon his parole, to
some of the interior towns, from which place, as I informed you in my last, he is just returned as hearty and
as well as ever."

The same author also relates a circumstance, which
was well known to the whole British army, and which
the Author of this Journal can fully corroborate. It
happened after the battle of Freeman's Farm, on the
19th of September.

" We have within these few evenings, exclusive of other
alarms, been under arms most of the night, as there has
been a great noise, like the howling of dogs, upon the
right of our encampment; it was imagined the enemy
set it up to deceive us, while they were meditating some
attack. The two first nights this noise was heard, general Fraser thought it to have been the dogs belonging
to the officers, and an order was given for the dogs
to be confined within the tents; any that were seen
running about, the prevost had orders to hang them.
The next night the noise was much greater, when a
detachment of Canadians and Provincials were sent out
to reconnoitre, and it proved to have arisen from large
droves of wolves that came after the dead bodies; they
were similar to a pack of hounds, for one setting up
a cry, they all joined, and when they approached a
corpse, their noise was hideous till they had scratched
it up."

It is a remark which has been frequently made by
foreigners of most countries, that there is a feeling, a
sensibility observable in the Irish character, which, if
not absolutely peculiar to us, forms a most prominent
feature in our disposition. The following circumstance,
of which many then in the British as well as American
armies were witnesses, may not be altogether unappro-
priate, particularly to the native reader.

During the time of the cessation of arms, while the
articles of capitulation were preparing, the soldiers of the
two armies often saluted, and discoursed with each other
from the opposite banks of the river, (which at Saratoga
is about thirty yards wide, and not very deep,) a soldier
in the 9th regiment, named Maguire, came down to the
bank of the river, with a number of his companions, who
engaged in conversation with a party of Americans on the
opposite shore. In a short time something was observed
very forcibly to strike the mind of Maguire. He sud-

denly darted like lightning from his companions, and resolutely plunged into the stream. At the very same moment, one of the American soldiers, seized with a similar impulse, resolutely dashed into the water, from the opposite shore. The wondering soldiers on both sides, beheld them eagerly swim towards the middle of the river, where they met; they hung on each others necks and wept; and the loud cries of " My brother! my dear brother!!!" which accompanied the transaction, soon cleared up the mystery, to the asto_nished spectators. They were both brothers, the first had emigrated from this country, and the other had entered the army; one was in the British and the other in the American service, totally ignorant until that hour that they were engaged in hostile combat against each other's life.

CHAP. X.

Captured Troops march to the Vicinity of Boston. Their deplorable Situation. Congress refuses the Embarkation of the British Troops to England. Description of Boston. Of the Island of Nantucket. Of the Whale Fishery. Its Origin, and wonderful Improvement. Curious Method of Paying the Seamen. Account of Catching the Whales, &c. British Troops removed from Prospect-hill to Rutland County. Congress still refuses to ratify the Convention of Saratoga. Debates in the House of Lords on the Independence of America. Lord Chatham's Speech on that Subject. His Death.

IMMEDIATELY after their surrender, the British troops, were marched upwards of two hundred miles to the vicinity of Boston, where they were confined in boarded huts on Winter and Prospect Hills. It is true, the court of Massachusetts passed resolutions for procuring suitable accommodations for them, but from the general unwillingness of the people to administer the least civility, and from the feebleness of the authority which the American rulers had at that time over the property of their fellow citizens, their situation was rendered truly deplorable.

Such were the disagreeable and distressing circumstances, which on every side increased the miseries of confinement, that, at this time, the most faithful

recital must despair of credence. It was not infre-
quent for thirty, or forty persons, men, women and
children, to be indiscriminately crowded together in
one small, miserable, open hut ;* their provisions and
fire-wood on short allowance; and a scanty portion of
straw their bed, their own blankets their only covering. In the night time, those that could lie down,
and the many who sat up from the cold, were obliged frequently to rise and shake from them the snow which the
wind drifted in at the openings ; or, in case of rain, to
endure the " chill peltings of the merciless storm."

General Burgoyne, ever attentive to the welfare of
his army, remonstrated in a letter to general Gates,
and after making use of some strong expostulations,
he added, " the public faith is broken;" this letter
being laid before congress, gave an alarm. It corroborated, they said, an apprehension previously
entertained, that the captured troops, on their embarkation, would form a junction with the British garrisons
in America.

Some paltry resolutions which were passed, relative
to the British soldiers not having faithfully delivered
up all their accoutrements, were of so shameful a
nature, as to be highly disgraceful to the congress,
and seemed strongly to indicate that they were ready
to grasp at any pretence, however weak or futile,
by which they could evade the terms of the convention, without incurring the charge of a direct breach
of public faith.

Just at this time, a requisition was made by the
commander in chief at New-York, for the embarkation of the convention troops, either at the Sound
near New-York, or at Rhode Island, instead of Boston,
which was the place appointed for their departure to

---

* The officers (without any regard to rank), were frequently
crowded, six or eight together in one small hut.

Europe; and in consequence of the expectation entertained, that the proposals would have been complied
with, the transports for the conveyance of the troops
were assembled at Rhode Island. The congress, however, not only refused to comply with the requisition,
but made it a ground of a pretended suspicion that
the measure was proposed, merely to afford an opportunity to the convention troops to join their fellows,
with an intention of making some pretence to evade,
or break the terms of the capitulation, and continue
to act in America, to the great detriment and danger
of the common cause. To strengthen this colour of
suspicion, they pretended that twenty six transports,
which were provided at Rhode Island, were insufficient for the conveyance of above five thousand six
hundred men,* in a winter voyage to Europe; and
that, in the present state of things, with respect of
provisions, both in the British fleet and army, it was
scarcely possible they said, that they could have been
victualled for so long a voyage in so short a time.

General Burgoyne offered to pledge himself, that
notwithstanding the injurious suspicions entertained of
his own honor, and that of his officers, they would
still join with him in signing any writing, or instrument,
that might be thought necessary for strengthening,
confirming, or renewing the validity of the convention.
But the congress was inexorable. It was easily seen
that the measure which they had adopted, was not so
lightly taken as to be easily given up, and that ex-
planations and securities, could produce no effect on
their determination. They had passed a resolution,
from which they never receded, that the embarkation of
general Burgoyne's army, should be suspended.

* Here the congress magnified the numbers of the British,
even adding all the women and children belonging to the
captured troops.

When general Burgoyne found that congress was resolved that no ratification of the convention which was tendered, would be accepted, he applied for leave to return home, which was immediately granted; general Phillips therefore remained to command the captured troops, and general Burgoyne sailed for England.

The reader will here naturally expect some account of the town of Boston. The Author's own observation, when a prisoner on Prospect Hill, and which has been much assisted by a gentleman who a few years afterwards travelled through the country, enables him to offer the following. This part of America, (particularly the Island of Nantucket), has not been much benefited by the revolution. The proprietors of this island were in a much greater progress to wealth while under the British dominions, than they have been since.

Boston is the most populous, if not the largest city in North America, and stands upon a peninsula of four miles circumference, within forty-four miles of the bottom of Massachusetts Bay. It was greatly damaged by an earthquake in 1727, and by the bombardment of the Americans themselves in the year 1776. It is most advantageously situated for trade. On the north side are several small islands called Brewsters, one of which is called Noddle's Island. The only safe way for entrance into the harbour, is by a channel; so narrow, that three ships can scarce pass in abreast. But there are proper marks to guide them, and within the harbour there is room enough for five hundred ships to lie at anchor in a good depth of water, while they are covered by the cannon of a regular and very strong fortress. At the bottom of the bay is a very noble pier, near two thousand feet in length, along which, on the north side, extends a row of warehouses. The head of this pier joins the principal street in the town, which is like most of the others, spacious and

well built. The town has a fine and striking appearance at entering, as it lies at the very bottom of the
bay like an amphitheatre. It has a town-house, where
the courts meet, and the exchange is kept. Round the
exchange are a great number of shops. There are
several places of public worship. These buildings are
lofty and elegant, with towers and spires. It contains
upwards of nine thousand houses, and it is supposed
near sixty thousand inhabitants.

The trade of New England was very great, before
the unhappy contest with the parent country. They
were the coasters of all North America, the West Indies,
and many parts of Europe.

The activity and enterprize of the inhabitants of this
state are wonderful, particularly in the object of their
fisheries. Mr. Burke, in his speech in the house of
commons, in 1775, has thus characterized and immor-
talized them : " Behold !" says he, " the manner in
which the people of New England have carried on the
whale fishery. Whilst we follow them among the tumbling mountains of ice, and behold them penetrating
into the deepest recesses of Hudson's Bay and Davis's
Strats ! Whilst we are looking for them beneath the
arctic circle, we hear that they have pierced into the
opposite region of polar cold ! That they are at the
antipodes, and engaged under the frozen serpent of the
south ! Falkland's Island, which seemed so remote and
romantic an object for the grasp of national ambition,
is but a stage- and resting place in the progress of
their victorious industry ! Nor is the equinoctial heat
more discouraging to them than the accumulated winter
of both the poles. We know that whilst some of them
draw the line and strike the harpoon on the coast of
Africa, others run the longitude, and pursue their
gigantic game along the coast of the Brazils ! No sea

C c

but what is vexed with their fisheries ; no climate that
is not witness to their toils ! Neither the perseverance
of Holland, nor the activity of France, nor the dexterous
and firm sagacity of English enterprise, ever carried
this most perilous mode of hardy industry, to the extent to which it has been pushed by this recent people ;
a people, who are still, as it were, but in the grizzle,
and not yet hardened into the bone of manhood."

Nantucket, in the province of Massachusetts, is a
small island, about eighty miles from Boston, and one
hundred and twenty from Rhode Island ; it is the
great nursery for seamen, pilots and fishermen. This
island appears to be the summit of some huge sandy
sea-mount, affording some acres of dry land, for the
habitation of man.

The first proprietors of this island, began their career
of industry with a single whale-boat, with which they
went to fish for cod ; the small distance from their
shores, at which they caught it, enabled them soon to
encrease their business, and those early successes, first
led them to conceive that they might likewise catch
the whales, which hitherto sported undisturbed on
their banks ; after many trials, and several miscarriages
they succeeded. Thus they proceeded step by step.
The profits of one successful enterprise, helped them
to purchase and prepare better materials for a more
extensive one ; as these were attended with little costs,
their profits grew greater. The south sides of the
island from east to west, were divided into four equal
parts, and each part, was assigned to a company of
six, which though thus separated still carried on their
business in common. In the middle of this distance,
they erected a mast, provided with a sufficient number of rounds, and near it they built a temporary
hut, where five of the associates lived, whilst the sixth
from this high station, carefully looked toward the

sea, in order to observe the spouting of the whales.
Thus they went on, until the profits they made,
enabled them to purchase larger vessels, and to pursue them farther. When the whales quitted their
coasts, those who failed in their enterprises, returned
to the cod fisheries, which had been their first school,
and their first resource ; they even began to visit the
banks of Cape Breton, the Isle of Sable, and all the
other fishing places with which this coast abounds.
By degrees they went a whaling to Newfoundland, to
the Gulph of St. Laurence, to the Straits of Belleisle,
the coast of Labrador, Davis's Straits, even to Cape
Desolation in 70° of latitude; where the Danes carry
on some fisheries, in spite of the perpetual severities
of that inhospitable climate. In process of time they
visited the Western Islands, the latitude of 34° famous
for that fish, the Brazils, the coast of Guinea, Falkland's Islands, and the South Sea. Their confidence is
so great, and their knowledge of this branch of business so superior to that of any other people, that
they have acquired a monopoly of this commodity.
Such were their feeble beginnings, such the infancy
and progress of their maritime schemes; such is now
the degree of boldness and activity to which they are
arrived in their manhood. After their examples several
companies have been formed in many of the capitals,
where every necessary article of provisions, implements
and timber, are to be found. But the industry exerted by the people of Nantucket, has hitherto enabled
them to rival all their competitors; consequently this
is the greatest mart for oil, whale bone, and spermaceti, on the continent. They possess like the
generality of Americans, a large share of native penetration, activity and good sense, which leads them to
a variety of other secondary schemes, too tedious to
mention : they are well acquainted with the cheapest

method of procuring lumber from Kennebec river,
Penobscot,'¹&c. pitch and tar from North Carolina;
flour and biscuit from Philadelphia; and beef and pork
from Connecticut. They know how to exchange their
cod-fish and West Indian produce for those articles,'
which they are continually either bringing to their
island, or sending off to other places where they are
wanted. By means of all those commercial negocia-
tions, they have greatly cheapened the fitting out of
their whaling fleets, and therefore much improved
their fisheries.

The vessels most proper for whale fishing, are brigs
of about one hundred and fifty tons burthen, particularly when they are intended for distant latitudes.
They always man them with thirteen hands, in order
that they may row two boats; the crews of which
must necessarily consist of six, four at the oars, one
standing on the bows with the harpoon, and the
other at the helm. It is also necessary that there
should be two of these boats, that if one should be
destroyed in attacking the whale, the other, which is
never engaged at the same time, may be ready to
save the hands. Five of the thirteen are always Indians,
the last of the complement remains on board to steer
the vessel during the action. They have no wages,
each draws a certain established share, in partnership
with the proprietor of the vessel, by which œconomy
they are all proportionably concerned in the success
of the enterprise, and all equally alert and vigilant.
These whale-men seldom exceed the age of forty.

As soon as they arrive in those latitudes where
they expect to meet with whales, a man is sent up
to the mast head; if he sees one, he immediately
cries out " AWAITE PAWANA," " *Here is a whale ;*" they
then all remain still and silent until he repeats " PAWANA,"
" *A whale,*" when in less than six minutes, the boats are

launched, and filled with every implement necessary for the attack. They row toward the whale with astonishing velocity. There are various ways of approaching the whale, according to their peculiar species; and this previous knowledge is of the utmost consequence. When these boats are arrived at a reasonable distance, one of them rests on its oars, and stands off, as a witness of the approaching engagement; near the bows of the other the harpooner stands up, and on him principally depends the success of the enterprise. He wears a jacket closely buttoned, and round his head a handkerchief lightly bound: in his hands he holds the dreadful weapon, made of the best steel, marked sometimes with the name of their town, and sometimes with that of their vessel; to the shaft of which the end of a cord of due strength, coiled up with the utmost care in the middle of the boat, is firmly tied; the other end is fastened to the bottom of the boat. Thus prepared, they row in profound silence, leaving the whole conduct of the enterprise to the harpooner and to the steersman, attentively following their directions. When the former judges himself to be near enough to the whale, that is, at the distance of about fifteen feet, he bids them stop; perhaps she has a calf, whose safety attracts all the attention of a dam, which is a favourable circumstance; perhaps she is of a dangerous species, and it is the safest to retire, though their ardour will seldom permit them; perhaps she is asleep, in that case he balances high the harpoon, trying in this important moment to collect all the energy of which he is capable. He launches it forth—she is struck: from her first movement they judge of her temper, as well as of their future success. Sometimes, in the immediate impulse of rage, she will attack the boat and demolish it with one stroke of her tail; in an instant the frail vehicle disappears, and the assailants are immersed in the dreadful element. Were the whale armed with the jaws of the shark, and as voracious, they never would return home to amuse their listening wives with the interesting tale of the adventure. At other times she will dive and disappear from human sight, and every thing must then give way to her velocity, or else all is lost; sometimes she will swim away as if untouched, and draw the cord with such swiftness that it will set the edge of the boat on fire by the friction. If she rises before she has run out the whole length, she is looked upon as a sure prey. The blood she has lost in her flight, weakens her so much, that, if she sinks again, it is but for a short time; the boats follow her course with an almost equal speed. She soon reappears; tired at last with convulsing the element, which she tinges with her blood, she dies, and floats on the surface. At other times it may happen, that she is dangerously wounded, though she carries the harpoon fast in her body; when she will alternately dive and rise, and swim on with unabated vigour. She then soon reaches beyond the length of the cord, and carries the boat along with amazing velocity; this sudden impediment sometimes will retard her speed, at other times it only serves to rouse her anger, and to accelerate her progress. The harpooner, with the axe in his hands, stands ready. When he observes that the bows of the boat are greatly pulled down by the diving whale, and that it begins to sink deep and take much water, he brings the axe almost in contact with the cord; he pauses, still flattering himself that she will relax; but the moment grows critical, unavoidable danger approaches; sometimes men more intent on gain, than on the preservation of their lives, will run great risks; and it is wonderful how far these people have carried their daring

courage at this awful moment! But it is in vain to
hope; their lives must be saved, the cord is cut, the
boat rises again. If after thus getting loose, she reappears, they will attack and wound her a second
time. She soon dies, and when dead, she is towed
along side of their vessel, where she is fastened.

The next operation is to cut with axes and spades,
every part of her body which yields oil; the kettles
are set a boiling, they fill their barrels as fast as it
is made; but as this operation is much slower than
that of cutting up, they fill the hold of their ship
with those fragments, least a storm should arise and
oblige them to abandon their prize. They frequently
produce from one hundred and fifty, to two hundred
barrels of oil. After having once vanquished this
leviathan, there are two enemies to be dreaded, beside the wind; the first of which is the shark. That
fierce voracious fish, often comes alongside, and shares
with them on their prey. They are very mischievous;
but the second enemy is much more terrible and irre-
sistible; it is the killer, sometimes called the thrasher,
a species of whale about thirty feet long. They are
possessed of such a degree of agility and fierceness,
as often to attack the largest spermaceti whales; and
not seldom to rob the fishermen of their prey,' nor is
there any means of defence against so potent an adversary. When all their barrels are full, (for every
thing is done at sea,) or when their limited time is
expired, and their stores almost expended, they return
home, freighted with their valuable cargo.

The following are the names, and principal characteristics of the various species of whales, known to these
people.

The river St. Laurence whale.

The disko, or Greenland do.

The right whale, or seven feet bone, common on
the coasts of this country, about sixty feet long.

The spermaceti whale found all over the world, and of all sizes; the longest are sixty feet, and yield about one hundred barrels of oil.

The hump back, on the coast of Newfoundland, from forty to seventy feet in length.

The finn back, an American whale, never killed, as being too swift.

The sulphur bottom, river St. Laurence, ninety feet long; they are but seldom killed, being extremely swift.

The grampies, thirty feet long; never killed, on the same account.

The killer, or thrasher, about thirty feet; they often kill the other whales, with which they, are at perpetual war.

The black fish whale, twenty feet, yields from eight to ten barrels.

The porpoise, weighing about one hundred and sixty pounds weight.

In 1769, they fitted out one hundred and twenty five whalemen; the first fifty that returned brought with them eleven thousand and six barrels of oil. In 1770 they fitted out one hundred and thirty five vessels for the fisheries, at thirteen hands each; four West India men, twelve hands; twenty five wood vessels, four hands; eighteen coasters five hands; fifteen London traders, eleven hands. All these amount to two thousand one hundred and fifty-eight hands, employed in one hundred and ninety-seven vessels.*

---

* The Americans were undoubtedly injured in many valuable branches of trade, by the separation from the mother country. Their ship trade, in consequence of the revolution, received a great check. Their market for oil is not equal in France, to that which they formerly found for it in England. Shortly after the American war, the king of France offered the people of Nantucket a settlement at Dunkirk, with many immunities and privileges, such as building them a town, exempting them from taxes, and allowing them the free exercise of

" Marriage is so highly respected that all persons
marry here, and marry early, and the women are almost
universally the happy mothers of a numerous offspring.
Their children, born by the sea side, hear the roaring of
its waves as soon as they come into the world ; it is the
first noise with which they become acquainted, and by
early plunging into the water, they acquire that boldness,
that presence of mind and dexterity, which makes them
ever after such expert seamen. They often hear their
fathers recount the adventures of their youth, their
combats with the whales; and these recitals imprint on
their opening minds, an early curiosity and taste for
the same life. They often cross the sea to go to the main-
land, and learn even in those short voyages, how to
qualify themselves for longer and more dangerous ones ;
they are therefore deservedly conspicuous for their
maritime knowledge and experience, all over the continent. A man born here, is distinguishable by his
gait, from an hundred other men, so remarkable are
they for a pliability of sinews, and a peculiar agility
which attends them even to old age.

" In the name of honour, humanity, and justice, let
not one part of the quaker's conduct be forgotten!
there is not a slave on the whole island, at least,
among the Friends; whilst slavery prevails all around
them, this society alone, lamenting that shocking insult offered to humanity, has given the world a
singular example of moderation, disinterestedness, and
christian charity, in emancipating their negroes.

" Idleness is the most heinous crime that can be committed in Nantucket: an idle man would soon be

their own religion ; in consequence of which many went there.
But all, or at least the greater part of these privileges have been
lost by the changes in the French government; and they now
suffer a dimunition in their trade without any equivalent to
indemnify them for the loss.

D d

pointed out as an object of compassion; for idleness
is considered as another word for want and hunger.
This principle is so thoroughly well understood, and
is become so universal, so prevailing a prejudice, that
literally speaking, they are never idle. Even if they
go to the market place, which is, if I may be allowed
the expression, the coffee-house of the town, either to
transact business, or to converse with their friends;
they always have a piece of cedar in their hands,
and while they are talking, they will, as it were in-
tuitively, employ themselves in converting it into
something useful, either a bung or spoil for their oil
casks, or some other article"

In the summer of the year 1778, the captured army
was ordered to remove from Prospect-hill to Rutland
County, about fifty miles to the south of Boston
Here we were confined n a sort of penn or fence,
which was constructed in the following manner: A
great number of trees were ordered to be cut down
in the woods, these were sharpened at each end, and
drove firmly into the earth very close together, enclosing a space of about two or three acres American
sentinels were planted on the outside of this fence, at
convenient distances, in order to prevent our getting
out At one angle, a gate was erected, and on
the outside thereof stood the guard house, two sentinels
were constantly posted at this gate, and no one could get
out unless he had a pass from the officer of the guard;
but this was a privilege in which very few were indulged
Boards and nails were given the British in order to
make them temporary huts, to secure them from the
rain, and the heat of the sun. The provisions were
rice and salt pork, delivered with a scanty hand
The officers were allowed to lodge in-the farm houses,
which lay contiguous to the penn; they were permit-

ted likewise to come in amongst their men for the purpose of roll-call, and other matters of regularity.

While the captured troops remained here, Sir Henry
Clinton, the commander in chief in New York, applied again to congress, in behalf of general Burgoyne's
army. In a letter to Henry Laurence, Esq. president
of congress, dated New York, September 19th, 1778,
he acquaints the congress that his Majesty had given
him positive injunctions to repeat the demand, that
the convention of Saratoga be fulfilled according to
the conditions stipulated by lieutenant general Burgoyne,
in respect to the troops serving under his command,
and to require permission for their embarkation; to this
letter, congress sent the following answer:

" Sir,—Your letter of the 19th was laid before congress, and I am directed to inform you, that the congress
make no answer to insolent letters.　Signed,

" CHARLES THOMPSON, Sec."

Soon after the intelligence of the capture of general
Burgoyne's army reached Europe, the court of France
openly avowed a treaty of amnesty, commerce, and
alliance with the United States. France, from the beginning of the contest, had secretly encouraged the
Americans in their opposition, and supplied them liberally with the means of defence, while at the same time
they amused Great Britain with declarations of the most
pacific disposition.

" On the 7th of April, the duke of Richmond, in
the house of lords moved an address to the king on
the state of the nation. In his speech in support of
this address, his grace declared in strong terms, his
conviction of the necessity of an immediate recogni-
tion of American independence. " The mischief,"
he said, " whatever might be the magnitude of it,
was already done; America was already lost; her

independence was as firmly established as that of other
states   We had sufficient cause for regret, but our
lamentation on the subject was of no more avail than it
would be for the loss of Normandy and France " The
earl of Chatham in expectation that this point would
come under discussion that day, resolved, however en-
feebled and afflicted by his corporeal infirmities, to
make his appearance before the house, in order to
bear his decided testimony against it   The mind feels
interested in the minutest circumstances relating to the
last day of the public life of this renowned statesman
and patriot He was dressed in a rich suit of black velvet,
with a full wig, and covered up to the knees in flannel,
On his arrival in the house, he refreshed himself in the
lord chancellor's room, where he staid till prayers were
over, and till he was informed that business was going
to begin   He was then led into the house, by his son,
and son-in-law, Mr William Pitt, and lord viscount
Mahon, all the lords standing up out of respect,
and making a lane for him to pass to his own bench :
he bowed respectfully to them as he proceeded He
looked pale and emaciated, but his eye retained all its
native fire, which joined to his general deportment,
and, the attention of the house, formed a spectacle very
striking and impressive.

" When the duke of Richmond had sat down, lord
Chatham rose, and began by lamenting " that his bodily
infirmities had so long, and at so important a crisis prevented his attendance on the duties of parliament He
declared, that he had made an effort almost beyond the
powers of his constitution, to come down to the house
on this day, perhaps the LAST time he should ever enter
its walls, to express the indignation he felt at the idea
which he understood was gone forth, of yielding up
the sovereignty of America my lords," continued he,

" I rejoice that the grave has not closed upon me, that I am still alive to lift up my voice against the dismem-. berment of this ancient and noble monarchy. Pressed down as I am by a load of infirmity, I am little able to assist my country in this most perilous con-juncture ; but, my lords, while I have sense and memory, I never will consent to tarnish the lustre of this nation by an ignominious surrender of its rights and fairest possessions. Shall a people so lately the terror of the world, now fall prostrate before the house of Bourbon? It is impossible. I am not, I confess, well informed of the resources of this kingdom, but I trust it has still sufficient to maintain its just rights, though I know them not. Let us at least make one effort, and if we must fall, let us fall like men."

" The duke of Richmond, in reply, declared himself to be " totally ignorant of the means by which we were to resist with success the combination of America with the house of Bourbon. He urged the noble lord to point out any possible mode, if he were able to do it, of making the Americans renounce that indepen-dence of which they were in possession. His grace added, that if HE could not, no man could ; and that it was not in his power to. change his opinion on the noble lord's authority, unsupported by any reasons, but a recital of the calamities arising from things not in the power of this country to alter."

" Lord Chatham, who had appeared greatly moved during the reply, made an eager effort to rise at the conclusion of it, as if laboring with some great idea, and impatient to give full scope to his feelings ; but before he could utter a word, pressing his hand on his bosom, he fell down suddenly in a convulsive fit. The duke of Cumberland, lord Temple, and other lords near him, caught him in their arms. The house was immediately ·

cleared, and his lordship being carried into an adjoin-
ing apartment, the debate was adjourned. Medical
assistance being obtained, his lordship in some degree
recovered, and was conveyed to his favorite villa,
of Hayes, in Kent, where, after lingering some few
weeks, he expired, May 11, 1778, in the seventieth
year of his age."

IT is now time that we should return to general Howe's
army, which we left at the conclusion of Chap. VIII.
at New Brunswick. The reader will recollect that the
American head quarters were then at Morristown.

While the British troops lay at Brunswick and
Amboy, congress was indefatigable in recruiting their
army; at Morristown ninety-six battalions were ordered to
be raised for the service of the United States, and in some
of the colonies the enlisting of apprentices and of Irish
indented servants, was permitted; this army was distin-

guished by the name of continentals, and in addition
to their pay and bounty, they were promised one hundred a cres of land at the conclusion of the war.

Early n the spring of 1777, twenty-one thousand
stand of arms, and one thousand barrels of powder were
sent from France, and arrived in America, for the use
of the continental army

On the other side a considerable body of provincial
troops was formed under the auspices of general Sir
William Howe   They included not only Americans, but
British and Irish refugees, from the different parts of the
continent, and were officered by those gentlemen who
for their attachment to the royal cause, had been obliged
to abandon their respective provinces   Governor Tryon,
who already, in his civil capacity, commanded the militia,
and who had taken the utmost pains in its establishment, was now placed at the head of these new levies
under the title and rank of major general.

, Before the royal army took the field, n prosecution
of the main business of this campaign, two enterprises,
for the destruction of the American stores, were undertaken, the first was conducted by colonel Bird, who
in March landed with five hundred men, at Peck's
Kill, near fifty miles from New York.' The Americans
upon the approach of the British troops, set fire
to the barracks and principal store houses, and then retreated to a strong pass in the mountains.   The loss
of provisions and other valuable articles was considerable

In April, major general Tryon, brigadier general
Agnew, and Sir William Erskine, with a detachment
of two thousand men, embarked at New York, and
passing through the Sound landed between Fairfield
and Norfolk the next day   They now perceived that
the country was rising to intercept their return, and
as no carriages could be procured to bring off the stores,

they set fire to the magazine; in the execution of this service, eighteen houses, which were built near the magazine, were unavoidably burned.

The detachment returned by the way of Ridgefield, and was greatly harassed by the enemy under generals Wooster and Arnold. While Wooster hung upon the rear of the British, Arnold by crossing the country gained their front, and got possession of Ridgefield; here they found the American general covered by an intrenchment which he had hastily thrown up. The village was forced, and the Americans drove back on all sides. The action, while it lasted, was sharp. Arnold displayed his usual intrepidity. His horse having been shot under him, while he was extricating himself, a British soldier advanced to run him through with his bayonet, but he shot him dead with his pistol, and got off safe.*

General Tryon remained that night at Ridgefield, and renewed his march the next morning. The enemy, having been reinforced with troops and cannon, the British were exceedingly harrassed, during their march. Early in the evening the detachment gained the hill of Campo, within cannon shot of their ships, and formed. The Americans were now assembled in great numbers, and seemed determined on an attack. General Tryon ordered the British troops to advance and charge with their bayonets. This order was executed with such impetuosity, that the enemy was totally broken and dispersed.

The troops were now embarked without molestation. The loss of the British in killed, wounded, and missing, amounting to one hundred and seventy two, of whom

---

* Congress voted that a horse properly caparisoned should be presented to general Arnold, in their name, as a token of his gallant conduct on that day.

E e

more than two-thirds were wounded . No British officer
was killed It was supposed the Americans lost double
that number

. Several of the American officers were killed and
wounded , among the former doctor Atwater, a gentleman of respectable character and considerable influence   General Wooster, though seventy years old, behaved with the vigor of youth, and received a mortal wound
' The Americans were very industrous in calling forth
all the military talent of the country. Neither the extreme
of youth, or advanced age, formed any impediment to
their actual service. Brigadier general Wooster, (like
Putnam) was in the decline of life, when the troubles
began   He was born at Newhaven, in Connecticut,
a province of New England, in the year 1711. His
father was a man of great wealth and connexions ,
and this, his only son, received a liberal education.
High in blood, and fraught with youthful ardour,
the whole bent of his disposition seemed turned towards the pursuits of a soldier   For him the military
life appeared to possess every attraction. And his
father, it should appear, by no means wished or attempted to turn aside the current of his temper   He
entered the army when but twenty years of age , and
gained an high reputation from the many events in
which he signalized his courage and intrepidity. In
the war between France and England, when America
was the scene of action, he distinguished himself in a
manner much to his honor   He commanded a company n general Pepperall's regiment of foot, was present
at the taking of Cape Breton, to the reduction of which
place, the corps m which he served very much contributed, and during the whole war reaped those laurels in
America, which raised his name to no inconsiderable height
on both sides the Atlantic   After the peace, in 1749,
his regiment was reduced, and he returned home to .

the bosom of his relatives His father being dead,
he became the inheritor of his estate, and the greater
part of his wealth It was at this period, or shortly
after, that he married Miss Boroughs, a young
lady of Rehoboth, near Providence. This marriage
brought him a large accession of property, and thus
circumstanced, he resolved on retiring from the army,
and enjoying the charms of domestic ease and retirement He accordingly placed himself on the half-pay
list, in which he continued 'till the year 1776

When the troubles in America proved too violent
for any peaceable adjustment, and by repeated acts
of hostility, the parent country was at last roused to
arms, Clinton, Burgoyne, the Howes, and other distinguished officers were sent to America. The congress
thus opposed by experience and valour took on their
part, the wisest resolutions which human sagacity could
dictate, they determined likewise to call forth into
action the greatest military talents which America
could furnish * Agreeable to this resolve, it may be
naturally imagined that they could not easily pass by
such a character as captain Wooster. A most respectful invitation was sent desiring him " to assist
his native country in the hour of her calamity "
Embosomed in the affections of a beloved family, he
yet felt, and acknowledged the superior motive He
obeyed the mandate, and was appointed a brigadier
general in the service of congress. This, as might
have been expected, caused his name to be immediately struck off the half pay list. He was then
far advanced in years; but he entered a second time

* More than one third of the soldiers in the American
ranks had formerly been in the British service; and what
was still worse, these men were indefatigable in training the
raw recruits to the use of arms.

E e 2

on the military life with all the avidity of youth.
It was an unhappy circumstance for England, that
some of the bravest and most experienced officers in
her pay, then residing in America, turned against her
and supported the insurrection. To this, perhaps,
much more than to any other cause, was America
indebted for her ultimate success. This was precisely
the case with regard to general Wooster. In several
affairs of minor importance, but which, in the end
led to matters of the highest consequence, his knowledge of the art of war, rendered essential services to
the party to whom he attached himself, until at last,
when Montgomery was defeated before Quebec, general
Wooster, was ordered to march to the relief of the
besiegers. In this, however, his former success deserted
him, as the reader has already been informed.

On account of one circumstance which attaches itself to this country, it may be worth while to mention
general Wooster's issue, a son and daughter. The
former was finishing his education in England. When
the American troubles broke out, he came over to Ireland,
and the rupture between the two countries preventing
the regularity of his remittances from America, his
circumstances became, from youthful extravagance much
involved, until at last he was arrested, and thrown
into the Four Courts Marshalsea. All the letters and
remittances from his father being of course, intercepted by the British government, the young man remained
in confinement, until general Wooster, through another
channel, sent him money to pay his debts, the remainder of which enabled him, (though contrary to
his father's commands) to leave the country. The
general, fearful of the issue of the American struggle,
had positively enjoined young Wooster to remain in
England until the war was terminated. This injunc-
tion however he disobeyed, and as soon as he gained

the American shore, actually joined that part of the continental army which his father commanded.

The following is the inscription on a monument erected in honor of general Wooster, by order of congress:

In honor of
DAVID WOOSTER,
Brigadier general of the army of the
United States,
In defending the liberties of America
and bravely repelling the inroads of the British
Troops to Danbury, in Connecticut;
He received a Mortal Wound
on the 27th April, 1777,
and Died on the 2d May following.
The Congress of the United States, as an
acknowledgement of his merit and services, have
caused this Monument to be erected.

Four hundred dollars were allowed for erecting this monument.

On the 24th of May, colonel Meigs, an enterprising American officer, (who had attended Arnold in the expedition to Quebec, and had been taken prisoner in the attempt to storm that city, as before related) having passed his detachment, consisting of one hundred and seventy men in whale boats over the Sound, which separates Long Island from Connecticut, landed on the north branch of Long Island, within four miles of Sagg harbour, and notwithstanding the resistance they met with from the guard and crews of the vessels, they fully completed their design, having burned twelve, sloops and brigs which lay at the wharf, and entirely destroyed every thing on the shore, they brought off with them about ninety prisoners, consisting of the officer who commanded,

with his men, and most of the masters and crews
of the small vessels which they destroyed. A circumstance which renders this expedition particularly curious,
that the colonel and his party returned to Guilford in
Connecticut, in twenty-five hours from the time of
their departure, having in that short time, not only completed the object of their expedition, but traversed by land
and water a space not less than ninety miles. However this
may be, congress ordered an elegant sword to be presented to colonel Meigs for his good conduct in this
expedition.   About six weeks after the above transaction,
another daring enterprise was executed.   The circumstance was as follows.   The British troops on Rhode
Island, were divided into two large encampments, one
covering the town, the other subdivided into three parts,
and stationed towards the northern extremity of the
Island.   For the convenience of being as near as possible to all those encampments, general Prescot, who
commanded the troops, slept every night in the middle
between them, about five miles distance from each
extremity, and about half a mile from the western coast
of the Island; this place he thought secure, by its
great distance from the main land, and by means of some
ships of war which were stationed along that coast, at
no greater distance from it than two miles   However,
an American colonel of the name of Burton, accompanied by forty volunteers, passed from Warrick
Neck to Rhode Island, a distance of ten miles, by
water, eluded the guard ships, and landed about twelve
o'clock at night at the opening of a ravine, into which
they crept, and proceeded undiscovered to the general's
quarters, and carried off the general, his aid de camp,
and the sentinel   The enterprise was conducted with
so much silence and address, that no alarm was
given, though a guard was at 'a very little
distance from the house, until Burton and his party

had nearly reached the continent with their prize. Congress resolved that an elegant sword should be presented to colonel Burton, as a testimonial of his gallant behaviour.

Towards the latter end of May, general Washington quitted his winter encampment at Morristown, and took a strong position on the high lands round Middlebrook, in the vicinity of Brunswick. In this strong position he threw up works along the front of his lines, but his principle advantage was the difficulty to approach his camp, the ground being so judiciously occupied as to expose the British to every kind of danger in the attempt. On the one side he covered the Jerseys, and on the other, he observed the motions of the British army at Brunswick, of which he commanded a full prospect.

Many stratagems were employed by the British general, to draw Washington from this strong situation. On the 24th of June, general Howe, suddenly relinquished his position in front of the Americans, and retired to Amboy; at the same time preparations were made for passing the army to Staten Island, this feint had the desired effect, for as soon as the British army began to move, intelligence was received that Washington had moved down from the mountain, and taken post at Quibble Town, intending to attack the rear of the British army; general Howe lost no time in endeavouring to profit by this movement of the Americans: he immediately marched the army back, by different routes, in order to cut off some of the advanced parties of the enemy, and likewise, if possible, to bring Washington to a general engagement in the neighbourhood of Quibble Town; at the same time lord Cornwallis with his column, was directed to take a considerable circuit to the right, and by turning the enemy's left, take possession of some passes in the mountains, which had hitherto afforded them so advantageous a security. Soon after lord Cornwallis marched with his column, he fell in with a division of American troops, commanded by lord Sterling, whom he found advantageously posted in a country much covered with wood, and his artillery well disposed, the king's troops attacked them with the greatest impetuosity, and after a short conflict the Americans dispersed on all sides, leaving behind them three pieces of brass ordnance, three captains, sixty men killed, and upwards of two hundred officers and men, wounded and taken prisoners

The British troops had five men killed, and thirty wounded, captain Finch of the light company of the guards was the only officer who suffered, the wound he received proved mortal, and he died at Amboy on the 29th of June, greatly regretted by the British army. The troops engaged in this action were the 1st battalion of guards, queen's rangers, 1st battalion light infantry, 1st battalion of grenadiers, and 3d battalion of Hessian grenadiers. The enemy was pursued to Westfield, with little effect, for Washington seeing his error, immediately retook possession of his strong camp on the hills, and secured those strong passes on the mountains, the possession of which, by the British troops, would have exposed his whole army to certain ruin

General Howe, now found it necessary to make an attempt on Philadelphia by sea

About this time the following humane order was sent from the war office to general Howe.

" If a wound shall be received in action by any commissioned officer, which shall occasion the loss of an eye, or a limb, he shall receive a gratuity in money of one year's full pay, and be further allowed such expences relating to his care (if not performed at the king's charge,) as shall be certified to be reasonable by the surgeon general of the army, and inspector general of regimental infirmaries, upon examination of the vouchers which he shall lay before them.

" If the wounds received shall not amount to the loss of a limb, the charge of cure only shall be allowed, certified as above. When any commissioned officer shall lose an eye or a limb as aforesaid, the commanding officer of the corps in which he serves, shall deliver to him a certificate, specifying the time when, and the place where the said accident happened; a duplicate of which certificate, shall likewise be transmitted with the next monthly returns. When any commissioned officer shall be killed in action, his widow and orphan children (if he leave any) shall be allowed as follows:

" The widow, a full year's pay according to her husband's regimental commission; each child under age, and unmarried, one third of what is allowed to the widow; posthumous children to be included.

" All persons dying of their wounds, within six months after battle, shall be deemed slain in action.

" The commanding officers of corps, in which the slain officer served, shall, on demand, give a certificate of his being killed in action, to his surviving wife and orphans respectively, specifying the time when, and the place where, the said accident happened, a duplicate of which, shall likewise be transmitted with the next monthly returns."

It was about this time that colonel Maclean left New York, to join his new-raised troops in Halifax and Canada. He was a meritorious officer, and indefatigable in his exertions to obtain men for the service.

Lieutenant colonel Maclean's corps of emigrants, though partly raised in 1775, had not, from their

F f

dispersed situation, which compelled them to serve in different parts of America, an opportunity of being reviewed, or of receiving their colours in due form. The battalions however were reviewed in June last, 1777, by general Massey, at Halifax, when their appearance gave universal satisfaction to the general and the spectators. Previous to the review, their colours were consecrated, and their respective chaplains, preached a sermon suitable to the occasion. An oath was then solemnly administered to each individual; and the commanding officer delivered a charge to the men, which it is presumed may not be unacceptable to many readers, particularly to young officers and soldiers, who have never been present at any ceremony of the kind. The substance was as follows:

" Man is born under obligations of conforming to the rules of propriety and rectitude, and with a passion for the applause which is due to virtuous actions.

" While inferior professions hold out sordid views as a spur to emulation, the object of the military is of the most sublime nature, viz. to perform gallant actions, that shall gain the approbation of their sovereign and superior officers, the esteem even of the enemy, the gratitude of fellow subjects, and the admiration of posterity.

" Happy those who shall have arrived at this exalted summit! To gain it, the greatest men that ever existed did not think it too much to sacrifice interests, ease, and even life; nor is it inaccessible to private soldiers, whether as a collective body, or as individuals any more than to officers.

" In the histories of the most warlike nations of antient times, we find mention of the actions of private soldiers who are recorded by name, with the honors and reward that followed; and instances of the like merit are no less frequent in our modern armies.

" Who then does not feel the influence of that divine spark, which prompts us to rise above the common level? Who has not ambition to transmit his name with applause to posterity? Who does not wish and pant for the opportunity to signalize himself?

" It is in the strongest manner recommended to the soldiers, to cherish in their breasts this natural and laudable passion for true glory: it inspires a sentiment of dignity, which leads to cleanliness, and neatness in dress, to abstain from drunkenness and every other abject vice; it renders them attentive and diligent on duty, cool and brave in action; on all occasions they will be patient, obedient, disinterested, and generous. The approbation of their officers will follow, and from thence many indulgencies; nor will the esteem and rewards of their country be wanting, to enable such illustrious career, to spend the decline of life in tranquillity, ease and comfort. In these their honorable retreats, to recollect the memory of gallant actions, to relate and dwell on their circumstances, to meet now and then a companion of former dangers, will rekindle youthful ardor, and afford the most pure and exquisite pleasures, when the toil and pain that accompanied them are no more.

" Duty and prudence dictate to a soldier the greatest care of his arms and accoutrements; they are the instruments of his defence, and of acquiring the honor he contends for; his pride should consist in having them of the best quality possible, always neat and in good order, always fit for instant and certain execution. It is ever natural for a brave soldier to entertain for them the most ardent regard, and to wish that even in death they should not be separated. Thus it was a maxim with the Spartans, to return from battle with, or on their shields. Epaminondas, one of the best generals of antiquity, being mortally wounded, was only anxious lest his arms should fall into the enemy's hands. The arms of the Roman soldiers weighed sixty pounds, and it was death to throw away any part of them. But,

" The colours, are above all things the object of a soldier's particular regard, attention, and attachment; this was the case in warlike nations at all times. The Romans worshipped and swore by them, and to lose them was to incur certain death. We have many in-stances in antient history, of commanders, in a doubt-ful engagement, throwing the colours among the troops of the enemy, knowing that, therefrom the courage, ardour, and exertion, of the soldiery would instantly redouble, beat the enemy, and retake them.

" Though we do not worship the colours, yet the awful cermony of this day sufficiently evinces, that they are with us, as in antient times, the object of peculiar veneration; they hold forth to us the idea of the prince whose service we have undertaken, of our country's cause which we are never to forsake, and of our military honor which we are ever to preserve.

" The colours, in short, represent every thing that is dear to the soldier; at the sight of them all the pow-ers of his soul are to rouse, they are a post to which he must repair through fire and sword, and which he must defend while life remains; to this he is bound, besides every other consideration, by the acceptance of a most solemn oath: to desert them is the blackest perjury and eternal infamy: to lose them by such an accident, even as, one might otherwise judge una-voidable, is not to be excused, because to lose them, no matter how, is to lose every thing; and when they are in danger, or lost, officers and soldiers have nothing for it but to recover them or die.

" Penetrated therefore with innate eagerness for glory, mindful of the fame of their ancestors, emulous of the lustre of their countrymen, now on service in other parts of America, and incited by the example already exhibited, and the honor already acquired by officers and fellow soldiers of the regiment, the Royal Highland Emigrants, will, it is hoped, always act with a dignity becoming the military profession, acquit themselves on every occasion, of the oath emitted this day, and not only transmit their honor and colours unsullied to posterity, but let every individual think himself entitled, nay bound, to aim at something that may deservedly shine in the page of history."

The month of July was far advanced before the preparations for the expedition against Philadelphia were completed, and it was the 23d before the fleet was able to sail from Sandy Hook. The force employed on this occasion, consisted of thirty six battalions of British and Hessian infantry, a regiment of light dragoons, and a corps of loyalists, amounting in the whole to about sixteen thousand men. At the same time a strong detachment was left behind at New York, under Sir Henry Clinton, and seven battalions were stationed on Rhode Island.

After a tedious navigation, the fleet entered Chesapeak Bay, and was conducted as far up the river Elk as was practicable. Here the army landed without opposition, on the 25th of August. Part of the troops was left to guard the stores, while general Howe proceeded with the main body to the head of the Elk.

General Washington, on the news of the arrival of the British in the Chesapeak, left the Jerseys and hastened to the relief of Philadelphia, with fifteen thousand men. In the beginning of September, he met the royal army at Chad's-ford, on the Brandy-wine, a small stream which empties itself into Christiana Creek.

Here Washington, adhered to his former method of skirmishing, and harrassing the royal army on its march; but as this was insufficient to stop its progress, he retired to that side of the Creek next to Philadelphia, with an intent to defend the passage: This brought on a general action. On the 11th, our army advanced in two columns, that under general Knyphausen, to Chad's Ford, had arrived in front of the enemy about ten o'clock, while the other column under lord Cornwallis, having marched twelve miles round to the forks of the Brandywine, crossed both branches, taking from thence the road to Dilworth, in order to turn the enemy's right at Chad's Ford.

General Washington, having intelligence of this movement, detached general Sullivan to his right, with near 10,000 men, who took a strong position, with his left, near to the Brandywine, both flanks being covered by very thick woods, and his artillery advantageously disposed. About four o'clock the king's troops advanced, and lord Cornwallis having formed his line of battle, the light infantry and chasseurs began the attack; the guards and grenadiers instantly advanced from the right, the whole under a heavy fire of artillery and musquetry: but they pushed on with an impetuosity not to be sustained by the enemy, who falling back into the woods in the rear, the king's troops entered with them and pursued them closely for near two miles.

After this success, a part of the enemy's right took a second position in a wood, from whence the 1st light infantry and chasseurs soon dislodged them; from this time they did not rally again in force.

The 2d light infantry, 2d grenadiers, and 4th brigade moved forward a mile beyond Dilworth, where they attacked a corps of the enemy, strongly posted to cover the retreat of their army, which corps not being forced till it was dark, the enemy escaped a total overthrow.

A part of the Americans retired to Chester, and remained there that night, but the greater body did not stop until they reached Philadelphia. They had about three hundred men killed, six hundred wounded, and near four hundred made prisoners. In the list of their wounded, were two of their general officers, the marquis de la Fayette, and general Woodward. The former was a French nobleman of high rank, who had left his native country and offered his service to congress. While in France, and only nineteen years of age, he espoused the cause of the Americans; having determined to join them, he communicated his intentions to the American commissioners at Paris. They conceived that a person of so much importance would be of service to their cause, and encouraged his design. Before he left France, intelligence, arrived in Europe that the American insurgents, reduced to 2000 men, were flying through the Jerseys before a British force of 30,000. Under these circumstances, the American commissioners at Paris, thought it but honest to dissuade him from the present prosecution of his perilous enterprise, but their advice was in vain. Having embarked in a vessel, which he purchased for the purpose, he arrived in Charlestown early in 1777, and soon after joined the American army. Congress resolved that " in consideration of his zeal, illustrious family, and connections, he should have the rank of major general in their army." He was wounded in the leg while rallying the American troops.

The loss on the side of his majesty's troops, amounted to about three hundred killed, and four hundred and eighty-eight wounded. Eight pieces of cannon and a great quantity of military stores were taken from the enemy.

The British army lay during the night on the field of battle, and the next day, major general Grant, with the first and second brigade, marched to Concord; lord Cornwallis with the light infantry and British grenadiers, joined him within five miles of Chester.

At this period intelligence being received that the enemy were advancing on the Lancaster road, it was immediately determined to push forward and attack them; but a most violent fall of rain setting in, the intended attack became impracticable.

The enemy apprized of the approach of our army, marched the whole night and got to Yellow Springs, having all their small ammunition damaged by the rain. It being found that general Wayne was lying in the woods with a corps of fifteen hundred men, and four pieces of cannon, major general Grey, was detached on the 20th to surprize them; their out-post and pickets were forced without noise, with the bayonet, about four o'clock in the morning; the Americans had scarcely time to turn out, and when they did, they paraded in the light of their fires. This directed the British how and where to proceed; they rushed in upon them, killed and wounded not less than three hundred on the spot, taking between seventy and eighty prisoners, including officers, their arms, and eight waggons loaded with stores; on our side only one captain of light infantry, and three men were killed in the attack, and four wounded. The horrors of this conflict (although so few of the British army were lost) almost realized the terrific idea of one of our great poets:

" Uproar, revenge, and rage, and hate appear
　In all their murd'rous forms; and flame, and blood,
　And sweat, and dust, array the broad campaign
　In horror: Hasty feet and sparkling eyes,
　And all the savage passions of the soul
　Engage in the warm business of the day."

On the 22d of Sept. the British army crossed the Schuylkill at Fatland-ford without opposition, and on the
25th marched in two columns to German-town.* Lord
Cornwallis with the British grenadiers, and two battalions of Hessian grenadiers, took possession of Philadelphia the next morning.

The possession of one of the largest cities in the
United States, together with the dispersion of the congress which had hitherto conducted their public affairs,
were reckoned by the British as decisive of their fate.
One of their first objects after they had obtained possession, was to erect batteries to command the river,
and to protect the city against any insult from water.
The British shipping were prevented from ascending
the Delaware by thirteen gallies, two floating batteries,
two zebecs, one brig, one ship; besides a number
of armed boats, fire ships and rafts were constructed
or employed for the purpose. The Americans had
also built a fort on Mud Island, and erected thereon a considerable battery. This Island, or rather a
bank of mud and sand, which had been accumulated,
is admirably situated, for the erection of works to
annoy shipping on their way up the Delaware. It lies
near the middle of the river, about seven miles below
Philadelphia. No vessel of burden can come up, but
by the main ship channel, which passes close by
Mud Island, and is very narrow for more than a

---

* Germantown is now one of the most considerable towns
of Pennsylvania, and is principally inhabited by High
and Low Dutch, it contains near five hundred houses.
Peach trees are planted all along before the doors. It is
exceedingly pleasant, and situated at the distance of five miles
from Philadelphia; it has only one street, which however,
is two miles long. Many of the Philadelphians have their
country houses in its vicinity. The trade carried on here is at
present great; the place is particularly famous for coach-makers,
type founders, &c.

mile. On the opposite shore, on the Jersey side, is a height called Red-bank. This overlooks not only the river, but the neighbouring country. On this eminence, a respectable battery was erected. Between these two fortresses, which are half a mile distance from each other, the American navy for the defence of the river Delaware, made their harbour of retreat. Two ranges of chevaux de frise were also sunk into the channel; these consisted of large pieces of timber, strongly framed together in the manner usual for making the foundation of wharfs, in deep water. Several large points of bearded iron, projecting down the river, were annexed to the upper parts of these chevaux de frise, and the whole was sunk with stones, so as to be about four feet under the water at low tide. Their prodigious weight and strength, could not fail to effect the destructio n of any vessel which came upon them. Thirty of these machines were sunk about three hundred yards below Mud Island, so as to stretch in a diagonal line across the channel. The only open passage left, was between two piers lying close to the fort, and that was secured by a strong boom, and could not be approached but in a direct line to the battery. Another fortification was erected on a high bank on the Jersey shore, called Billings-port. And opposite to this, another range of chevaux de frise was deposited, leaving only a narrow and shoal channel on the one side. There was also a tempo-rary battery of two heavy cannon at the mouth of Mantua-creek, about half way from Red-bank to Billingsport.

In the evening of the 26th, three batteries were began by the British, in Philadelphia, to act against the enemy's shipping. These batteries were un finished when they were attacked by a number of gallies, gondolas and other armed vessels, and the largest frigate, the Dela-

ware, mounting thirty two guns, anchored within five
hundred yards of the town. About ten in the morn_
ing she began a heavy cannonade, but the tide fall_
ing, the Delaware grounded. In this condition she
was compelled to surrender. - The smaller frigates and
armed vessels were forced (except a schooner that was
driven on shore) to return under the protection of
the fort already described.

General Washington having received a reinforcement
of two thousand five hundred men, and presuming on
the British army being much weakened by the detachments to Philadelphia and Jersey, thought it a favorable
time for him to attack their post at Germantown, and
where the bulk of the royal army was posted in the
following order: their line of encampment crossed the
town at right angles near its centre: the left wing
extended to the Schuylkill, and was covered in front
by the mounted and dismounted chasseurs; the queen's
rangers, and a battalion of light infantry were in front
of the right: the 40th regiment, with another battalion of light infantry, were posted on the Chestnut-hill,
road, three quarters of a mile in advance. The
American commander recommended, that the attack
should be made in different places, to produce the
greater confusion, and to prevent the several parts of
the British force from affording support to each other.
From an apprehension, that the Americans from a
want of discipline, would not persevere in a long
attack, it was resolved that it should be sudden and vigorous, and if unsuccessful, they were to make an expeditious
retreat. The divisions of Sullivan, and Wayne, flanked
by Conway's brigade, were to enter the town, by the
way of Chestnut-hill, while general Armstrong with the
Pennsylvania militia, should fall down the Munatawny
road, and gain the left and rear of the British. The
division of Green and Stevens, flanked by M'Dougal's

brigade, were to enter by the Limekiln road; the militia of Maryland, and Jersey, under general Smallwood, and Furman, were to march by the old York road, and to fall upon the rear of their right; lord Sterling, with Nashe's and Maxwell's brigade, were to form a corps of reserve.

At three in the morning of the 4th of Oct. the British patroles discovered the enemy's approach, and the army was immediately ordered under arms. About break of day, the enemy began their attack with great impetuosity, the 40th regiment, and a battalion of light infantry, sustained this severe attack with great bravery, till they were nearly surrounded: they then retreated in good order to the town, where lieutenant colonel Musgrave, with six companies of the 40th regiment, took post in a large and strong stone house, which lay in front of the enemy. This party being so advantageously posted, kept one half of the American army in check; and from the windows of the house, did considerable execution. General Washington, says in his letter to congress, when speaking of this affair: " the party in Mr. Chew's house, who were in a situation not to be easily forced, had it in their power from the windows, to give us no small annoyance, and in a great measure to obstruct our advance." Major general Grant, now advanced with the right wing of the British, and attacked the enemy's left, which gave way and was pursued through a woody country, between four and five miles; but such was the expedition with which they fled, that it was not possible to overtake them. The whole American army now retired, near twenty miles to Penibacker Creek, and encamped. General Washington, in relating this action to congress, says: " The morning was extremely foggy, which prevented our improving the advantages we gained, so well as we otherwise should have done;

this circumstance by concealing from us the true situation of the enemy, obliged us to act with more caution, and less expedition than we could have wished; and gave the enemy time to recover from the effects of our first impression, and what was still more unfortunate, it served to keep our different parties in ignorance of each others movements, and hindered our acting in concert; it also occasioned us to mistake one another for the enemy, which I believe more than any thing else contributed to the misfortune which ensued. In the midst of the most promising appearances, when every thing gave the most flattering hopes of a victory, the troops began suddenly to retreat, and entirely left the field, in spite of every effort that could be made to rally them."

The loss of the royal army in this action, amounted to seventy killed, and four hundred and sixty five wounded; in the number of the former, were unhappily some very brave and distinguished officers, particularly brigadier general Agnew, of the 44th regiment, and lieutenant colonel Bird, of the 15th. The number of officers wounded was considerable. The American loss was esteemed between two and three hundred slain, six hundred wounded, and four hundred taken prisoners; among their slain was general Nash, and his aid de-camp, major Witherspoon. On the 19th, the British troops removed from Germantown to Philadelphia, as a more convenient situation, for the reduction of Mud Island, which at that time prevented the passage of the river, as the chevaux de frize could not be removed until possession of that post was obtained; the British army was well apprized that without the command of the Delaware, their possession of Philadelphia would be of no advantage; every exertion was therefore made to open the navigation of that river.

Colonel Donop, with a strong detachment of Hessians, crossed the Delaware on the 21st, with directions to proceed to the attack of Red Bank; the colonel led on the troops in the most gallant manner to the assault. They carried an extensive out-work, from which the enemy were drawn into an interior intrenchment, which could not be forced without ladders. The detachment in moving up, and returning from the attack, suffered much by the enemy's gallies and floating batteries; colonel Donop, being mortally wounded and taken prisoner, the command devolved upon lieutenant colonel Linsing, who, after collecting all the wounded that could be brought off, returned with the detachment to camp.

The ships of war designed for the attack of Mud Island, made their way with difficulty, and took the best possible disposition that the situation of the river would admit; they commenced their assault at the same time that colonel Donop was engaged at Redbank, but with as little success. The ships could not bring their fire to bear with any great effect upon the enemy's works. The Agusta ship of war, of 64 guns, commanded by captain Reynolds,* and the Merlin sloop of war, grounded. In this situation, though the skill and courage of the officers and crews of the several vessels, prevented the effect of four fire ships, which the enemy had sent to destroy the Augusta; she afterwards unfortunately took fire in the engagement, which obliged the other vessels to retire with the greatest expedition, in order to get beyond the effect of her explosion. It was at the same time found expedient to abandon the Merlin, and destroy her; the greater part of the officers and crew of the Augusta were saved, but the second lieutenant,

* Afterwards Lord Ducie.

chaplain, and gunner, with no inconsiderable number of the seamen, unhappily perished.

Though this first attempt for opening the navigation of the Delaware, was unsuccessful, it by no means damped the resolution of the naval commanders; new measures were immediately adopted, and on the 15th November, the attack was renewed with the greatest fury on both sides, till the works being nearly demolished, the garrison r etreated in the night, across the river in boats to Red Bank; three days after, Mud Island was evacuated. The Americans, upon the approach of lord Cornwallis, with a detachment of British troops, hastily withdrew from Red Bank, leaving their artillery and a considerable quantity of cannon and stores behind them. A few of the enemy's gallies and vessels escaped, by keeping close in with the Jersey shore, to places of security above Philadelphia; but seventeen of them were abandoned by their crews, and burned,

On the 30th and 31st of December, the British troops went into winter quarters in Philadelphia, and were well accomodated; while the American army, excepting a detachment of twelve hundred at Wilmington, were hutted in the woods, in a strong position at Valley Forge, sixteen miles from that city.

In May 1778, general Howe took his departure for England, and the chief command of the British army devolved on Sir Henry Clinton.

CHAP. XII.

*Arrival of the British Commissioners for restoring Peace.
Their bad Success. Correspondence between Lord
Carlisle, and the Marquis de la Fayette. Philadel-
phia evacuated. Battle near Monmouth. General
Lee, tried by a Court Martial, and suspended.
Monsieur Gerrard arrives Minister Plenipotentiary
from France. British Army arrives at New York.
French Fleet appears before Sandy Hook. Sails to
Rhode Island. Lord Howe sails to the Relief of
Rhode Island. British and French Fleets separated
at the Point of Engaging by a violent Storm.
French Fleet sails for Boston and is pursued by Lord
Howe. General Sullivan abandons Rhode Island.
French Fleet sails for the West Indies. Attacks St.
Lucia, but is repulsed. Province of Georgia reduced
by the British. The Author makes his Escape into
New York. His Narrative.*

IN the beginning of June, 1778, the earl of Carlisle,*
Mr. Eden,† and governor Johnston, arrived at New
York ; these gentlemen, with Sir Henry Clinton, were
appointed by the British government, to attempt a
reconciliation with the American colonies ; but in vain
were all their efforts, an implacable spirit of hostility

* His lordship, was lord lieutenant of Ireland from the
year 1780 to 1782.

† Now lord Auckland.

to the parent country had taken place in the breast of the Americans. They had thrown themselves into the arms of France, and no exertion of reason was able to unfetter the embrace. The following reflection, in the commissioners declaration, roused congress to such a degree of anger, that they declared, " Were it not under the idea of stopping the effusion of human blood, they would not have read a paper containing expressions so disrespectful to his most christian majesty, the good and great ally of these states, or to consider propositions so derogatory to the honor of an independent nation."

" In our anxiety," say the commissioners in part of their letter to congress, " for preserving those sacred and essential interests, we cannot help taking notice of the insidious interposition of a power, which has from the first settlement of these colonies been actuated with enmity to us both; for notwithstanding the pretended date, or present form, of the French offers to America, yet it is notorious, that these were made in consequence of the plans of accommodation previously concerted in Great Britain, and with a view to prevent our reconciliation, and to prolong this destructive war.

" But, we trust, that the inhabitants of North America, connected with us by the nearest ties of consanguinity, speaking the same language, interested in the preservation of similar institutions, remembering the former happy intercourse of good offices, and forgetting recent animosities, will shrink from the thought of becoming an accession of force to our late mutual enemy, and will prefer a firm, a free, and perpetual coalition with the parent state, to an insincere, and unnatural foreign alliance."

H h

, But this was not all, general de la Fayette, a young French nobleman then in the American service, and who, has since made so conspicuous and gallant a figure in the Gallic revolution, considering the honour of his sovereign wounded, actually sent a challenge to lord Carlisle, to which his lordship returned the following temperate and dignified answer :

" Sir—I have received your letter, transmitted to me from monsieur Gimot, and I confess I find it difficult to return a serious answer to its contents. The only one can be expected from me as the king's commissioner, and which you ought to have known, is, that I do and ever shall consider myself responsible to my country and to my king, and not to any individual for my public conduct and language. As for any opinion or expressions contained in any publication issued under the commission, in which I have the honour to be named, unless they are retracted in public, you may be assured I shall never, in any change, be disposed to give an account of them, much less recall them in private.

" The injury alluded to in the correspondence of the king's commissioners to the congress, I must remind you, is not of a private nature, and conceive all national disputes will be best decided by the meeting of admiral Byron and count D'Estaing."

On the 18th of June, general Clinton following in-structions received from the parent country, evacuated Philadelphia. It is probable that all idea of negociation was now considered hopeless, as the commissioners ac-companied the army. Their accompanying a retreat from a city, which might be properly called the capital of America, was not very likely to procure for them any terms to which Great Britain could possibly listen; on the contrary, this circumstance only swelled the pride and increased the insolence of the American rulers. The whole British army marched out of the town at three o'clock in the morning, and crossed the Delaware before noon with all its baggage.* General Washington, by some means, was apprized of this movement ; in consequence of which he sent expresses into the Jerseys, to collect troops. The American army then likewise passed the river, and were hourly joined by reinforce- ments , of the regular troops, and of their militia. General Gates, with an army from the northward, was fast advancing. In this situation, general Clinton re- treated across the country towards Sandy Hook, at which place he could with facility effect the passage to New York.

At this juncture, Washington was far from being inactive ; he pursued the retreat of the British, and also sent the marquis de la Fayette, with a strong body of chosen troops, to harrass their rear ; general Lee, (who had been some time exchanged,) followed with a division, to support him, and the commander in chief finally so managed his own movements, that with the main body he covered and sustained the whole.

On the 27th of June, the British army encamped in a strong position in the neighbourhood of Freehold Court House, in the county of Monmouth ; the follow- ing morning the van division of the Americans, under general Lee, commenced the attack. General Clinton had already, with due precaution, directed general Knyphausen to take the baggage of the whole army under his division, which consisted of the 17th light dragoons, the 2d battalion of light infantry, Hessian

* Several of the loyalists of Philadelphia went along with the British army ; some, who remained behind, were treated with great severity by the Americans. Messieurs Roberts and Carlisle, gentlemen of respectable characters of the Quaker persuasion, suffered death for their attachment to the royal cause.

yagers, 1st and 2d brigades, British, Stern's and Loo's brigade of Hessians, Pennsylvania loyalists, West Jersey volunteers, and Maryland loyalists. General Clinton was induced to this order, under the firm persuasion that the baggage only was Washington's object, it having been his constant practice to avoid a general engagement with the British ; the general, therefore, with much wisdom and foresight, placed it in a state of security, and prepared himself to encounter the American Fabius. Under the head of baggage was comprised not only all the wheel carriages, of every denomination, but also the bat horses ; a train, which as the country admitted but of one route for carriages, extended near twelve miles. Sir Henry Clinton had with him the 16th light dragoons, 1st and 2d battalion of British grenadiers, 1st battalion of light infantry, Hessian grenadiers guards, and the third, fourth, and fifth brigades.

The total disagreement between the British and American accounts of this action, is not a little perplexing to the impartial narrator ; both parties claim the advantage, but the Americans, particularly at that time, had their reasons for their misrepresentations—reasons which did not at all influence the reports of the British commanders.

The marquis de la Fayette, who commanded the American cavalry, began the attack. They were instantly charged with great spirit by the light dragoons. The Americans did not wait the shock, but fell back in disorder upon their own infantry. The British then proceeded on their march ; but, on the rearguard descending from the heights above Freehold into a plain near three miles in length, and above one in breadth, several columns of the enemy appeared, and descended into it also. About ten o'clock they began to cannonade the rear of the British. Sir Henry Clinton, as has already been observed, being apprehensive that the baggage was their sole. object, determined on the attack of these divisions, in order to oblige those troops who were at that time on his flanks to return. These divisions were endeavouring to gain his front, that they might attack the baggage, and therefore impede his progress.

The British grenadiers, guards, light infantry and queen's rangers now engaged the enemy with such vigor, that their first line, commanded by general Lee, was completely broken ; their second line withstood the attack with great obstinacy, but was also defeated ; they both rallied, however, and posted themselves with a morass in their front. They were again charged by the British troops, and were with difficulty preserved from total defeat by the junction of their main body, which was supposed to consist of twenty thousand men, under general Washington.

When Washington found the division under general Lee retreating in disorder, he rode up to Lee, and proposed several questions to him, which implied censure. Lee answered with warmth and unsuitable language. Washington then ordered two of his battalions to form on advantageous ground, which he judged suitable for giving a check to the advancing enemy. Lee was then asked, if he would command on that ground, to which he consented, and added to Washington, in a haughty tone, " Your orders shall be obeyed, and I will not be the first to leave the field." Lee continued until the last on the field of battle, and brought off the rear of the retreating troops.

In this action the bravery and discipline of the British forces were gloriously conspicuous. Facts speak for themselves. They forced an enemy, superior in numbers, from two strong positions, and endured excessive fatigue, both from unremitting toil, and the intense heat of day. The British general took up the position from whence the enemy had first been driven, after they had quitted the plain ; and having reposed the troops till ten o'clock at night, to avoid the excessive heat of the day, he took advantage of a fine moon light-night to rejoin general Knyphausen, which he effected near Middleton. On the 30th of June the whole royal army arrived at Sandy Hook, without the loss of either their covering party or baggage ; from whence it passed over to New York without further molestation.

After the evacuation of Philadelphia, much praise was due to admiral lord Howe for the excellent dispositions which he made to cover the troops passing the Delaware. It is pretty evident that Washington was at first deceived by his own caution and dread of being decoyed into a general engagement, and that he then ascribed the slow movements of the British to a design on the part of Sir Henry Clinton, of gaining the strong grounds above him, and so inclosing his army to the river.

The loss of the royal army in killed, wounded, and missing, was three hundred and fifty-eight men, fifty-nine of whom, through excessive heat and fatigue, fell dead without a wound. The honorable lieutenant colonel Monckton, who commanded the 2d battalion of grenadiers, fell in the action. " This gallant officer," says one of the writers on the American war, " who had frequently encountered death in all its forms, had the fortune of being more than once grievously wounded, both in the last war and the present ; and after the hair-breadth escape of a recovery, when left among the dead on the field, was only reserved to be killed on this day, at the head of the second battalion of grenadiers." A braver soldier never expired on the field of battle.

The conduct of Washington on this occasion, (however he might have been self-deceived, relative to some of the movements of Sir Henry Clinton,) was highly creditable to his military skill.

His timely interposition with the main body of the American army, prevented the rest from being entirely cut off; and by his subsequent movements, he succeeded in gaining it such an advantageous position, as entirely secured it from attack.

The loss of the Americans, however, in killed and wounded, was very considerable.* Colonel Bonner and major Dickinson, officers highly esteemed by their country, fell in this engagement. The emotions of mind, added to the fatigue of a remarkably hot day, brought on such a suppression of the vital powers, that numbers of the Americans, as well as the English, were found dead on the field of battle, without any marks of violence on their bodies.

After the engagement the American general drew off his troops to White Plains, near King's Bridge. Taking up a commanding position, he remained there until the latter end of autumn, watching ' the motions of the British, when he retired to Middle .Brook, in Jersey.

In the mean time, the haughty spirit of Lee could not brook the language which general Washington had hastily used when he met his troops retreating before the British, on the 28th. It is probable that Washington intended to take no further notice of Lee's conduct on the day of the action; but, upon the general's receiving from him a letter couched in the most disrespectful terms, and replete with the most violent invective, he was immediately put under an arrest, and a

---

* According to their own accounts it amounted to three hundred and sixty-one men, including thirty-two officers.

court martial, of which lord Sterling was president, was held upon him. His accusation consisted of three principle charges: viz. Disobedience of orders, misbehaviour in action, and disrespect to his commander. He was found guilty upon every charge, and suspended from all his military commands for twelve months.

Immediately on the departure of the British troops from Philadelphia, the congress returned to that city, and gave public audience to monsieur Gerrard, minister plenipotentiary from the court of France.

It may now be necessary to revert to the maritime events of the war. Early in the spring, count D'Estaing had been dispatched from the port of Brest, with twelve ships of the line and six frigates; there were six thousand soldiers on board, for the assistance of the American cause. The whole armament suffered considerably on the voyage, and did not arrive off the coast of America before the beginning of July.

On finding that lord Howe had sailed to New York, count D'Estaing followed him, and in a few days the French fleet appeared off Sandy Hook. The British admiral had only eleven ships, very inferior in magnitude and weight of metal. The French commander seemed fully determined to attack the English fleet, and force his way into the harbour of New York. The British admiral ranged his ships with much nautical skill to receive him. He was powerfully supported by the inhabitants. Upwards of one thousand volunteers, from the trading vessels, then lying at New York, entered on board the British ships of war; the masters and mates of the transport-ships took their situations at the guns, with the common seamen; others put to sea in light vessels, in order to watch the motions of the enemy; and in our army, the officers and privates contended with so much eagerness, to serve on board

the ships of war, as marines, that it became necessary,
to decide the point of honor by lot.

After the French fleet had remained at Sandy Hook for
eleven days, they weighed anchor and put to sea. Lord
Howe's fleet was, at that time, every way for resistance
inferior. Indeed, nothing but the excellent disposition
made by the noble admiral, and the determined activity,
not only of the respective crews, but also of the volunteers, could possibly have saved it, had the count felt
himself inclined to come to action. The tacit compliment that he paid to the skill, the resolution, and the
the character of lord Howe, by not daring to attack him
with so decided a superiority of strength, raised that
nobleman's name to a degree of exaltation which, will
make it live for ever. So freely, however, was the
matter spoken of in America, that, in order to save
the credit of the French admiral, it was reported that
he determined to force the harbour; but the American
pilots on board, declared it impossible for the large ships
of his squadron to pass the bar. On this curious apology,
it is not surely too much for an old subject of the
British empire, (and who has been on the spot,) to
declare his belief, that if admiral Nelson had commanded
D'Estaing's fleet, he would have found water enough
to have brought the largest ships in that squadron
alongside the quay of New York.

The next attempt of D'Estaing was against Rhode
Island, in order to co-operate with general Sullivan,
in an enterprise against Newport. General Sir Robert
Pigot, who commanded on the island, having been reinforced, made every preparation for a vigorous defence.
In the mean time, lord Howe being reinforced by
some ships from England, (part of a squadron commanded by admiral Byron), immediately stood out to
sea, though still inferior in force, in order to give

battle. D'Estaing, finding that he was pursued to Rhode
Island so quickly, (as he only had entered the harbour
of New Port the day before,) determined to hazard an
engagement; accordingly, he put out to sea with his
whole fleet.

But, while the two commanders were busily employed in manœuvring for the weather gage, a tremendous tempest arose, which separated the fleets.
Amidst this conflict of the elements, the Languedoc,
of ninety guns, D'Estaing's own ship, after losing her
masts, fell in with the the Renown, of fifty guns, commanded by captain Dawson; who attacked her with
great fury, when the appearance of six French ships
of the line, compelled him to desist. Captain Raynor,
in the Isis, and commodore Hotham; in the Preston,
each of fifty guns, fought with much gallantry the
Tonnant of eighty guns and the Cæsar of seventy-four
guns; but no ship on either side struck her colours.
Lord Howe, with all possible dispatch, followed D'Estaing
to Boston; and entered the bay, under the hope of a
favorable opportunity of attack but, to his great mortification, he found the French fleet lying in Nantucket
road, so well defended by the forts and batteries on that
island, that it was found to be absolutely impractible

In the mean time, general Sullivan and his army in
Rhode Island, with the people of the northern colonies, complained loudly of the conduct of D'Estaing.
For this they boldly assigned their reasons; which were,
that they had engaged in an expedition of great expense and danger, under prospect of the most effective co-operation of the French fleet; that depending
thereon, they had risqued their lives on an island,
where, without naval protection, they were likely to
be enclosed, like wild beasts, in a toil, and that in this
situation they were first deserted, and then totally
abandoned, at the very time when they stood most in

need of help. It was a fact, at that time pretty generally admitted in America, that it was under these
apprehensions their general was deserted by most of
the militia, (who composed nearly half of his army)
which obliged him to retreat from his lines; and though
he was most vigorously pursued, and repeatedly attacked
in every quarter by the British forces, yet, his measures were so well conducted, that he gained the north
end of the island, from whence he passed his troops
over to the continent without any considerable loss.
Indeed, before he quitted the island, the marquis de la
Fayette, who commanded under him, set off for Boston
by land, to request the speedy return of the French
fleet. To this requisition D'Estaing would not consent.
He had been very roughly handled a few days before
by a British captain, and he knew very well the
great danger his master's fleet would be exposed to,
if he again fell in with the British navy. But he
offered to lead the French troops which he had on
board against Rhode Island, in co-operation with the
American forces.

The most remarkable transactions, during the remainder of this campaign, might, from their nature,
almost be termed naval expeditions, at least they were
intimately connected with maritime warfare.

In October 1778, lord Howe sailed for England, on
account of his health, and the command of the fleet
devolved on admiral Gambier.

There is no doubt but it was part of the insidious
policy of the French cabinet to strike a blow at the
British possessions in the West Indies. How this plan
had been methodized, it is impossible at this period
to ascertain; but its operations became so intimately connected with American affairs, that it is necessary to take
some notice of them.

The projects of D'Estaing being effectually disconcerted at Rhode Island, he sailed in the beginning of No-

vember for the West Indies, in order to second the operations of the Marquis de Bouille, governor of Martinico, who had already captured the island of Dominique. Three days before the French fleet left Boston, the 4th, 5th, 15th, 27th, 28th, 35th, 40th, 46th, 49th, 55th, regiments, and a corps of Hessians, under the command of general Grant, sailed from New York, in order to strengthen the garrisons of the West India Islands.

It may be necessary that the reader may the more clearly understand the sequel of American transactions, to mention the progress of the British arms in the West Indies. Upon the arrival of the troops there, a descent was made on the island of St. Lucia, and by the active exertions of brigadier general Meadows, the advanced posts were carried. While these operations were going on, D'Estaing appeared in view. That commander upon his arrival at Martinico had been joined by a fleet of transports, with nine thousand land forces on board, with which he had hoped to effect the entire reduction of the British islands. Admiral Barrington's squadron, which was greatly inferior to the French fleet, was stationed across the entrance of the Carenage, and was supported by several batteries, erected on the shore. The French admiral bore down with twelve sail of the line; but met with so gallant a reception, that he thought proper in a short time to draw off. In the afternoon he renewed the attack, with his whole squadron, and a furious cannonade, directed chiefly against admiral Barrington's division, was kept up for several hours. This, however, made no impression on the English fleet, and the French admiral was again obliged to desist from the attack. He then landed a body of nine thousand troops, which he formed in two divisions; putting himself at the head of the right, he gave the Marquis de Bouille orders to lead on the left. They advanced rapidly towards the English lines, keeping up a heavy fire as they proceeded The British troops reserved their fire until they saw them mount their trenches; then a tremendous fire was poured upon the assailants, which immediately stopped their progress, and threw them into disorder ; before they could recover, they were charged by the British. The slaughter was dreadful; and it was with difficulty the French reached their ships. The count re-embarked his troops, and left the island to its fate. It soon after surrendered to the British arms.

The American government had, in the begining of the year projected the reduction of West Florida ; and several detachments of their troops had made some successful incursions into that country. This awakened the attention of the British commanders to the southern colonies ; and an expedition against them was resolved on. Georgia was the place of its destination ; and the more effectually to ensure success, colonel Campbell, a brave and prudent officer, with the 71st, and two battalions of Hessians, four battalions of provincials, and a detachment of artillery, embarked at New York; while general Prevost, who commanded in East Florida, was directed to set out with all the force he could spare. The armament from New York, under commodore Sir Hyde Parker, arrived at the mouth of the Savannah, in the month of December ; and though the enemy were very strongly posted in an advantageous situation on the shore, the British troops made good their landing, and the light infantry, under captain Cameron, of the 71st, regiment, formed and advanced. A body of Americans, however, attacked them with great bravery ; but the Highlanders rushed on, and drove the Americans into the woods. Captain Cameron, a spirited and valuable officer, with two Highlanders, were killed, and five were wounded. The British

troops then advanced towards Savannah, the capital of
the province. The day, however, was destined for still
further triumph to the royal cause. They had not
marched far when they attacked and defeated the American troops, who opposed them with great resolution
and bravery. This victory was complete: upwards of
one hundred of the Americans were killed, thirty-
eight officers, four hundred and fifteen privates, forty-
eight pieces of cannon, twenty-three mortars, the fort
with its ammunition and stores, the shipping in the
river, a large quantity of provisions, with the capital
of Georgia, were all, in the space of a few hours,
in the possession of the conquerors. The broken remains of the American army retreated across Savannah river into South Carolina. The different posts upon
that river were secured by the British troops, and the
province of Georgia was entirely at peace in seven
days after the defeat of the American army. General
Prevost now arrived at Savannah, and took the command
of the British troops. The conquest of South Carolina was next projected.

While these operations were carrying on in the
southern province, the captured troops in New
England, as already described,* were ordered to march
to the east parts of Virginia.

This was universally considered by the privates as a
very great hardship, and by the officers as a shameful
violation of the articles of capitulation. The application of general Burgoyne to general Gates on this
subject, has already been mentioned. It should seem
that the origin of the whole delay was ascribable to
the congress; for the members hesitated not to declare,
when pushed hard on the violation of the seventh article of the convention, "that if the troops were
suffered to embark for Great Britain (according to the
spirit of that article,) as soon as they left their

* Page 209.

coasts, they would form a junction with the British garrisons in America." Still further to colour their breach of faith, with an apparent shew of justice, they alleged, that it had been often asserted by the British nation, "that faith was not to be kept with rebels," and that therefore, congress would be deficient in attention to the interests of America, if they suffered the captured troops to depart.

When I saw that the American rulers had no intention of allowing the British troops to return to England, I determined on attempting my escape into New York. The idea immediately suggested itself to me, that it would be much more agreeable, and indeed less dangerous, to have companions in my flight; I therefore resolved to induce as many of my comrades as I could to join me. I soon made myself acquainted with the route which it was necessary that we should take; I found that we were to cross the North River, only sixty or seventy miles above New York. This then appeared to me the most favorable point from which to attempt our escape. Unfortunately, however, for my scheme, our officers (fearful of their regiments being, at their return to Europe, reduced to mere skeletons) had previously issued orders, that if any soldier should absent himself from his regiment only for one day or night, he should be returned as a deserter; and if brought back to his regiment by any of the inhabitants or American soldiers, he should be tried by a court martial; and punished accordingly. I was fully aware, that the intention of this order was to keep the men together, and likewise to deter them from remaining in the country, it being the constant practice of the Americans to induce the captive soldiers to become settlers. These orders prevented many from attempting their escape. But for them, numbers like myself, and

the companions of my journey, would have made good
their escape into New York.

While the Americans protected to the uttermost
those deserters, who left the British army to settle
among them, they who were caught by them in the
attempt to join the king's forces at New York, had
every thing to fear, nor was the least their being
brought back to their respective regiments under
the odium of desertion.

I weighed in my mind all the consequences that
would most probably result, should I be taken by the
natives, and the more I thought of the attempt, the more I
began to feel a degree of enthusiasm, to which I was before
a stranger. I looked forward, not without hope, to the
prospects before me, and I began already to indulge
the exultation of effecting my escape. Indeed I had
wrought myself up to such a pitch of firmness, that
I am persuaded, the most agonizing cruelties which
the Americans could have inflicted on my body, would
have been unable to have effected any alteration in
my resolution.

I communicated my scheme to two of my comrades,
over whom I had most influence, and persuaded them
to join me in the attempt, one of these soldiers understanding the French and German languages, was a
powerful assistant in effecting our escape, as our guards
were chiefly composed of German troops. By his conversing with these men, we obtained permission to go
to a house in order to buy some necessaries which we
wanted. When we got to the house, we took care not
to return to the line of centries again, but moved further
from the guards, by degrees, until we entirely lost
sight of them. We then began to fear, lest the next
inhabitants we met, might pick us up and bring us
back. We therefore thought it best to conceal ourselves. Just at this critical moment, we perceived a

a small hut ón the verge of a wood. On our entering it, we found a poor woman with two children. We entreated her to hide us for a few hours, as we were apprehensive that the American soldiers would soon miss us, follow, and make search for us. As the chief inducement to obtain her assistance, we immediately shewéd her some silver money, which we promised to give her, if she assisted us in making our escape. To this she readily consented, and as a pledge of sincerity left her little child with us. She gave us some provisions, locked us all up in a small apartment, and went out in order to gain information. There was a characteristic shrewdness about this woman which highly fitted her for our purpose. She very acutely observed, before she went, that this would be the best method, for if our pursuers should come to the house, and observe it fastened up, they would not, she believed, break it open, unless they had some previous information of our being concealed there; and as nobody had observed our coming into the hut, she hoped there would be no danger.

In this place we remained until dark, under the unpleasant apprehension of being seized every moment by our pursuers, as we were in the very midst of them; however, fortunately for us, not one of them either knocked at the door or demanded entrance.

The woman returned in the evening. " You see," said she, " that I have been faithful to you. Your comrades have all crossed the North River, with most of their guards, and there are very few of the Americans at this side of the river." It may be naturally supposed that we all felt ourselves much indebted to her for her faithfulness; and, as far as was in our power, we rewarded her. We then informed her, that we intended to make our escape into New York. She observed, that that would

K k

be a very hard task to accomplish, as there were several
American encampments in the Highlands, which lay between us and that city   However she gave us a recommendation to a man living a few miles off, who, she
observed, would assist us in getting forward   Taking
an affectionate leave of our faithful hostess, we directed
our course to the house of her friend , but before we
had proceeded three miles, we were stopped by a deep
and rapid stream   My comrades not knowing how to
swim, I proposed to swim across, taking one of them at
a time with me, if they would faithfully and courage-
ously follow my advice, which was to lay their hands
gently on my loins while in the water, striking out with
their feet at the same time.   This method would have
soon carried us all across, as the river was not very
broad , however they both declined it, as too hazardous
an attempt, and proposed to trace the river upwards,
in order to discover a fording place.   We had not
proceeded up the river two hundred yards, when we
perceived a tree lying across the stream , this served
the inhabitants for a bridge.   Such conveniences for
passing rivers are very common in America   We crossed
the river in safety, and pursuing our journey, arrived at
the house to which we had been directed by our late kind
hostess. It stood alone at the edge of a wood, and being
unconnected with any other human dwelling, seemed
admirably adapted to our purpose. The family were
much alarmed when we rapped them up   We, however, soon made the owner acquainted with our intentions, and informed him, that if he would conduct us to
New York, we would give him twenty dollars, exclusive
of the reward he would receive from the commander
in chief. He listened with attention, and seemed willing to comply ; but his wife, overhearing our discourse,
opposed it immediately, and declared, with tears in her
eyes, that he should not go. The rude reasonings of

this woman appeared so powerful an instance of conjugal feeling, that they made a strong impression on my mind at the time. To the married reader little apology is due for their introduction. " What!" said she, " do you mean to break my heart, by foolishly running into the Jaws of death, depriving me of a husband, and my children of a father ? You know that there are several camps and garrisons between this and New York, that you would not be able to go ten miles before you would be taken up, and then you would be hung up like a dog." This discourse operated with all the power of simple nature, when the whole force of the passions is brought to bear on any given point. The man changed his mind in a moment. " Gentlemen," said he, " this is a very dangerous piece of work ; I know that all my wife has said is true ; I know that the Americans have very strong out-posts all along the North River, as far as King's Bridge, and if I were taken in the act of bringing you into the British lines, I could expect no mercy." All our arguments after this, could not prevail with him, though we promised to give him twelve dollars in advance, and two new English blankets ; however he at last, for a small present, conducted us to another friend, who lived two miles further on our journey ; this person, he observed, might probably go with us.

We set off between one and two o'clock in the morning, and arrived at the poor man's hut, which was situated on the top of a high mountain. When we entered the hut, we found his wife ill of a fever, and the husband, with a woman, attending her. After much persuasion, and a small present, we prevailed with this man to bring us to another friend that lived six miles onwards, and whom there was every probability we might obtain for a guide. We set off immediately,

K k 2

and after making our way for six hours, through a
trackless desert, full of swamps, we found ourselves at
day-break very near the out-posts of an American
encampment. Here our guide, on finding where we
were, being much terrified, fled from us with the greatest
precipitation. As his last act of attention, he pointed
out a path-way which led into the woods, and told
us to pursue that track, and it would bring us to a
friend. We took his advice, and continued on that
track for five or six miles, when we came to a small
hut. The inhabitants were astonished at our appearance, but evidently pleased at our company. We informed the woman that we were very hungry. She
immediately prepared a repast for us, which I need not
add, was at that time highly acceptable, as we had not
eaten any thing for the space of forty-eight hours.

The fatigue we had undergone during our march,
from the extent of country which we had traversed,
rendered sleep highly necessary, and we prepared to lie
down. This measure the woman warmly opposed. She said,
" the American soldiers often straggled from their camp
to her hut, and some of them might probably come
upon us while we slept." Her husband now came in,
and seemed glad to see us. We made him acquainted
with our intention of escaping into New York. He repeated the observations of our other directors, relative to
the number of the American posts, particularly on the
North River ; and added, " that it would be an hundred chances to one, if we were not taken." We told
him that we would reward him liberally, if he would
conduct us. He answered, " There is a young man
who lives several miles off, who will, I believe, undertake
it : if he should, I have no objection to go ; but I
will not go by myself, as I well know the dangers which
we shall be exposed to without a second guide."

We remained at this place two days, encouraging them by every argument which we could suggest to make the attempt. At last we prevailed, by giving them ten dollars and the two new English blankets, which we had with us. We set off with our two guides about six o'clock in the evening, and after travelling through deep swamps, thick woods, and over difficult mountains for ten hours, our young guide stopped, and declared that he would not proceed any further with us, unless we gave him forty dollars in hand. He said, " This is a dangerous, troublesome piece of work. Here," continued he, " is an American encampment within a mile of us ; I have been there a few days ago," and I know where all the centries are posted ; if I should be taken, I shall lose my life." As he uttered this, he seemed to be under great terror and fear, which increased when we said, " We are not afraid of one or two American centinels, only conduct us the best way you can ; and if we unavoidably fall in with any of them, you may leave the matter to us and fly for your life." All we could say had no effect on him, and although we offered him on the spot twelve dollars, he would not advance one step further. We then encouraged our other guide to proceed with us, to which, after much entreaty and promises of reward, he consented.

We expected every moment, as we advanced, to fall in with the line of centries belonging to the Americans ; but, happily for us, as it rained very hard during the whole night, and was very dark, we did not encounter one of them, though we passed very near to a log house, which was full of troops. Taking, however, every possible precaution, we immediately struck off into the woods, and after climbing up precipices, and wading through swamps, about five o'clock in the morning, we arrived at the wished for house. This was situated

only two miles from another encampment   Our guide
being well acquainted with this family, told them who
we were, and also our intention   They received us very
kindly, and gave us refreshment, informing us, at the
same time, that it would be highly dangerous, for us to
remain in the house, as the American soldiery were scattered over almost the whole face of the country   We
held a consultation what was to be done under the then
existing circumstances , and it was unanimously agreed,
that we should hide ourselves in a hay-stack, which was
near the house, until our guide could explore the
country, and find out the safest way for our escape.
We were conducted to the spot on which it stood,
when each of us buried himself up to the chin in the
hay, and waited the event   Our conductor was vigilant
in procuring all the intelligence he could with regard
to the station of the American army. This delayed him
much longer than we at first imagined. Our not hearing
aught from him during the space of thirty hours, made
us very uneasy , we were fearful lest he also had for-
saken us, and left us to shift for ourselves   At last he
came, and bad us prepare to follow him. We were at
that time about forty miles from King's Bridge, the out
post of the British army. Thus circumstanced, we
determined to accomplish the march, if possible, that
night, we therefore set off in high spirits, about six
o'clock in the evening

Previous to the commencement of our journey, we
were informed by our guide of our perilous situation,
while we remained concealed in the hay-stack   The
Americans had determined to remove it to the camp
for forage, which probably would have been done the
day before, only that it rained remarkably hard during
the whole of it. Fortunately for us, the storm continued, with unabated violence, all night, and the
darkness was such, that we were completely shrouded

from all observation. These circumstances tended very much to favor our escape.

After as hard a march as any poor fellows ever experienced for the time, over swamps, rivers, and mountains, we arrived a little before day-light at a small house about one mile from the British outposts at King's Bridge, fifteen miles from New York. We boldly rapped at the door, and demanded entrance. The inhabitants were much terrified, on our approach, and their fears began sensibly to increase, when we ordered them to light a candle.. They assured us, that if a light were seen in their house, at that hour, the habitation would be soon tumbled about their ears, for the British fort would immediately fire into it; we were, therefore, constrained to remain in that situation until day-light had commenced, as it would have been highly dangerous to have proceeded to the fort in the dark. Soon as morning dawned we left the house, and with joyful hearts proceeded to the fort. The out-centry challenged us; we answered, " We are British soldiers, who have made good our escape." We were conducted with joy and wonder to the fort, and received with great kindness by the officers and men. I believe we were the first party belonging to general Burgoyne's army, that effected an escape. It would not be very easy to give the reader an adequate idea, either of my own feelings, or those of my associates on this occasion. The toil and hardships we had sustained, the dangers which we had surmounted; captivity, or death, in its most frightful shapes, every moment presenting horrid images to our minds; in avoiding destruction or recapture from the Americans, encountering the hazard of still greater calamities; sinking into the morass or quagmire; drowning in the rapid torrent; tumbling headlong from the dreadful precipice; not to mention the terrors of the woods, among which, the least was

the encountering the venomous bite of the American
serpents   when delivered from all these, we joined our
countrymen and fellow soldiers in arms —Such a moment
must be imagined , it cannot be described

- We were, of course, immediately conducted forward
to New York, when major Andre, the adjutant general,
received us with great affability and kindness, at the
head quarters. As I was the person who first planned
the means of escape, and conducted the whole plan,
under the guides, I was the object to which every inquiry was directed   Sir Henry Clinton the commander
in chief, was an experienced officer, and a sensible
man   He, doubtless, gave private orders, relative to
my examination, willing to gain information of every
circumstance, however minute, that might by (communi-
cating intelligence of the state of the country,)   add
to the security of the British army.   I am also inclined
to think, that much of the bounty that I and my
comrades received, was the result of Sir Henry's secret
benevolence   Major Andre immediately brought me
into the parlour, inquired very minutely into every
circumstance of the route I had taken with my party,
and the dangers I was exposed to   the number of
the enemy,   the usage which the British soldiers received when prisoners, &c &c. &c   When I had
given him all the information which I could, he expressed much satisfaction, and told me, that if I chose,
I might take my passage to England in the next packet
that sailed ,* but, at the same time, he intimated a
wish that I would continue to serve in America   I
answered, "That I would rather remain, and serve
his majesty in America, than go home to England "   .

---

* As I was at that time a non-commissioned officer, I had
the privilege of being sent home.

The major then, with much feeling and politeness, informed me, that he was authorized by Sir Henry Clinton, to offer me my choice of entering in any regiment, then serving in America. I came to the resolution of serving in the 23d, or Royal Welch Fuzileers, then quartered in New York. I was soon after appointed serjeant by colonel, now general Balfour, to whose kind attention I must ever feel myself much indebted. I was immediately sent to an officer,* who was appointed to pay the men who made their escape from confinement, the usual bounty. The distinction made in cases like mine, by general Burgoyne himself, was highly flattering to the military feelings of the soldier. The general used to term them, " honorable desertions."— This distinction he made, even in the house of commons, between these soldiers, who, through every difficulty, made their way to, and joined his majesty's forces, and those who left their regiments, for the purpose of settling among the Americans.

* Colonel Handfield, the present commissary general of Ireland.

~~~~~~

CHAPTER XIII.

Southern Affairs. General Lincoln appointed to the Southern Command. Victory at Briar's Creek. St. James's, St. John's and Port Royal taken, Northern Affairs. Connecticut Expedition. Stoney Point stormed by the Americans. D'Estaing's Attempt against Savannah. Count Polaskie mortally wounded. Some Account of his Life. Colonel Maitland's Death. His Character. Americans send an Expedition against the Indian Settlements.

IT may now be necessary to pursue the thread of this narrative in a different direction, and to turn the reader's attention to the southern affairs.

The reduction of Georgia by general Prevost and colonel Campbell excited great alarm in the congress; nor were the apprehensions of ruin and discomfiture to American independence less without doors, particularly among the inhabitants of South Carolina. In this critical posture of affairs general Lincoln, who served under Gates in the northward, as already related, was appointed to the command of the southern American army. Being reinforced by a considerable body of troops, he encamped within twenty miles of Savannah. Another strong body of troops was posted at Briar's Creek, farther up the river. Thus the extent of ground for the exercise of the British go_ vernment was likely to be circumscribed within very nar_ row bounds. General Prevost therefore determined to dislodge the party at Briar's Creek. Lieutenant colonel Prevost (the general's brother) with three companies of the 60th regiment, Sir James Baird's light infantry, the second battalion of the 71st regiment, captain Tawe's provincial troop of light dragoons, and some militia, amounting in the whole to nine hundred men, were directed to make a circuit, in order to come upon the rear of the American encampment; whilst major Mac- pherson, with the first battalion of the 71st regiment, and two field pieces, appeared in their front. These two dispositions proceeded in strict obedience to orders. It was on the 30th of March, that the Americans were attacked in front and rear, and totally routed, with the loss of seven pieces of cannon, several stand of colours, almost all their arms, and the whole of their ammunition and baggage. Upwards of four hun- dred men were killed, wounded, or taken prisoners; among the latter was general Elbert, the second in command. This victory entirely broke the American measures in the province; of consequence the communication was again opened between the British posts and South Carolina.

This victory proved of considerable service. General Lincoln was thereby reduced to a state of cautious inactivity, and at last moved off towards Augusta.

Lincoln had no sooner quitted his post than the British general determined on the invasion of Carolina. The time was chosen with the most profound judgment, but many difficulties lay in his way. The river Savannah was so swelled by the excessive rains of the season, that it seemed impassable; the shores were so full of

swamps and marshes, that no army could march over
it without the greatest difficulty; to obstruct the
passage still more, general Moultrie was left with a considerable body of troops, to oppose any attempt that
might be made by the British. In defiance of
every opposition, the constancy and perseverance of
the British forces at last prevailed General Moultrie
was defeated, and obliged to retire towards Charlestown,
while the victorious army, after having waded through
the marshes, at last arrived in an open country, over
which they pursued their march with rapidity, towards
the capital

A general alarm, throughout all Carolina, now took
place. Their capital was in danger. Lincoln, with a
numerous army, took possession of all the avenues
leading to Charlestown, and prepared for a vigorous
defence. But all opposition proved ineffectual, the
Americans were defeated in every encounter, and retreating, continually, at last allowed the British army
to come within cannon shot of Charlestown, on the
12th of May, 1779.

The town was summoned to surrender The inhabitants would gladly have agreed to have observed a
neutrality during the war, and would have engaged for the rest of the province ; but these terms
not being accepted, every preparation was made for
a vigorous defence of the place It was not in the
power of the British commander (without being guilty
of that rashness, the danger of which, could not escape
his enlarged and consummate judgment, as an officer)
at that time to make an attack with any prospect of
success. His artillery was not of sufficient weight, there
were no ships to support his attack, and general Lincoln, advancing rapidly with a superior army, threatened
to enclose him between his own force and the town.
The British commander was too wise not to be aware

of the danger ; if he had failed in the first attempt, cer_
tain destruction would have been the consequence. Ge_
neral Prevost's force was about two thousand four hun_
dred strong, and the garrison three thousand three hun_
dred, including the militia. For these reasons the British
general withdrew his forces from before the town, and
took possession of two islands, called St. James's, and
St. John's, lying to the southward ; where, having
waited some time, his force was augmented by the arrival
of two frigates. With these he determined to make
himself master of Port Royal. This island, from its
excellent harbour, and many other natural advantages,
became an object of no small importance, its situation
commanding all the sea coast from Charlestown to
Savannah river. These measures, however, were not
accomplished without opposition from the 'American
general. Perceiving that the British had occupied an
advantageous post on St. John's Island, preparatory
to their enterprize against Port Royal, he attempted, on
the 20th of June, to dislodge them from it ; but after an
obstinate conflict, the Americans were as usual obliged to
retire with considerable loss.

This disappointment was instantly followed by the
loss of Port Royal, of which general Prevost took
immediate possession. He then proceeded to Savannah, and left the command to lieutenant colonel Maitland.
The troops were put in proper stations, and the whole
waited the arrival of such reinforcements as were necessary for the intended attack on Charlestown.

It would swell this volume far beyond its prescribed
limits, to point out the merits of the British officers
and soldiers, who were engaged in these actions ; but
the singular gallantry of one exploit, performed
by captain Moncrief, of the engineers, in the sight
of both armies, ought not to be omitted : that officer,
with only twenty soldiers, sallied out in the face

of the American army, took an ammunition waggon,
and brought it safe within the lines   This was a most
seasonable supply of what was greatly wanted for
such was the scarcity of ammunition in the garrison,
that the last charge was in the guns when the enemy
gave way

The affairs of the American campaigns were sometimes
of a very complicated nature   clearly to comprehend
several leading events of the history of the war, it is
necessary n many instances, that the reader should
be in possession of the joint movements of the British
armies, acting far distant from each other , but on the
co-operation of which the issue of the contest finally depended   It is hoped that this remark will be received as
a sufficient apology for breaking off rather abruptly
from the ~ affairs, transacting in the Carolinas, and
proceeding to detail those of the north.

, Sir Henry Clinton proceeded up the North River. By
great exertions of valor he carried the two important posts of Stoney Point and Verplanks. These forts
securing the communication between the eastern and
western colonies, had been fortified with much skill and
diligence by the Americans.   After leaving garrisons in them, the fleet, with the rest of the troops,
fell down the river and returned to New York.

The province of Connecticut was the great source
from whence the Americans recruited their armies and ,
supplied them with provisions   It had, from its situation, hitherto sustained little of that rage of war,
which most of the other provinces had endured. The '
British commander, to convince the inhabitants that
their province was not inaccessible, and that it was
to our lenity and forbearance they were indebted,
planned an expedition against it. It formed also part
of the general's plan, to compel Washington to quit

his strong situation on the North River, and descend into the country, for the defence of the sea coast.

As this expedition has been greatly misrepresented, both by Ramsay and Belsham, the Author takes the liberty to transcribe from his Journal the following account of this affair ; as he was himself personally employed on the service. He is happy to state, that many respectable British officers are still living, (particularly general Garth, second in command on the expedition,) who can bear full accord to the truth of the following account. Indeed such refutation becomes the more necessary, as the British army still lies under the odium thrown on it by those virulent party writers, which has never yet, to the Author's knowledge, been answered by any one.

The transports, on board which were troops amounting to two thousand six hundred men, weighed anchor at the entrance into the sound, and sailed towards New Haven, the capital of Connecticut, the 4th of July. Major general Tryon commanded the land forces. Commodore Sir George Collier, in the Camille frigate, with the Scorpion sloop, Halifax brig, and Hussar galley, was appointed to the naval command, and escorted the transports. The first division of the troops, under brigadier general Garth, of the guards, disembarked at some distance below the town of New Haven. He had to pass the head of a creek, and was in consequence compelled to take a march of seven miles, amidst the continued opposition of the inhabitants ; he, nevertheless, forced his way, and succeeded in gaining possession of the town. Meanwhile major general Tryon, with the 2d division, landed on the opposite side of the harbour, and took a fort on the heights, the artillery of which commanded it ; a direct communication was thus established between the two divisions of the army, one of which was in possession of the town. The vessels

in the harbour, artillery, ammunition, public stores, &c.
were taken or destroyed ; but, notwithstanding the
opposition of the inhabitants, and their even firing from
the windows, after the troops were in possession of the
town, such was the British humanity, that, instead of
indiscriminate death, which by the laws of war they
were liable to, the town was saved from damage, and
private houses, as much as possible, exempted from
plunder, by placing sentinels before them, many of
whom, (such was the American gratitude,) were actually
wounded on their posts ! The next day a proclamation
was issued, promising protection and pardon to all who
should return to their allegiance, and threatening
to punish as traitors those who did not ! The fort
was then dismantled, the troops were re-embarked,
and New Haven was left in a far better situation than
many less offending places have experienced in all
countries during war.

The expedition next proceeded to Fairfield After
the landing of the troops, the opposition from the inhabitants was far more desperate than at New Haven.
The lenity already shewn to the offenders, serving
only to make them more outrageous, an example of
severity became indispensible. All the public stores,
and the vessels in the harbour, were therefore either
taken or destroyed, and the town itself was laid in ashes.
This example had not its desired effect As the troops proceeded, the opposition became more determined, and of
a nature which no regular army could patiently endure
no established system of warfare pardon. Norwark and
Greenfield, places taken immediately afterward, therefore underwent a similar fate.

New London, the rendezvous for the American privateers, was the last place, the reduction of which general
Tryon had in view ; but as still more obstinate resistance
was apprehended there, it was judged that a supply of

ammunition, and an augmentation of troops should be obtained before it was attacked, though the loss of the British in the expedition amounted only to twenty killed, ninety-six wounded, and thirty-two missing. The fleet, therefore, returned to Huntington Bay, in Long Island, and the commodore went to Frog's Neck, where a conference was held with the commander in chief of the army, fully to arrange the future plan of attack. The immediate occasion of this conference was the intelligence received by Sir Henry Clinton, that the inhabitants of Connecticut, who certainly had suffered much loss, both public and private, during the nine days of the expedition, were highly dissatisfied both with congress and general Washington; in particular they loudly complained of the latter, in permitting the destruction of so many towns on the sea-coast, and remaining fixed, if not inattentive, in his strong position near the North River; and further, Sir Henry had been secretly and positively informed, that many were hesitating, from these circumstances, about withdrawing their support from congress and making terms with the parent country.

Such is the simple, impartial, and unbiassed narrative of an expedition, which Ramsay, and after him Belsham, have endeavoured, with all the artifice of wilful misrepresentation, so to colour as to render the British name odious to humanity. No doubt, in such excursions many scenes occur, at which the feeling heart must revolt; but in war, all that the brave and the humane can do, is to soften and alleviate its horrors; to prevent them entirely, is altogether beyond the power of man. And that this was done almost in every point, by the commanding officers, the Author can aver from his own personal knowledge. But if persons, whose residence unfortunately becomes the seat of war, will

M m

not govern themselves prudently, whom have they to blame, except themselves, for all the disastrous consequences that may ensue?

Mr. Ramsay makes the strange assertion, that at New Haven " the inhabitants were stripped of their houshold furniture and other moveable property; and the harbour and water-side were covered with feathers, which were discharged from opened beds!" Strange, indeed, that soldiers weighed down with arms, ammunition, and provisions, should carry feather beds so far to destroy them! and as for the houshould furniture what were they to do with it? Such slanderous improbabilities refute themselves I never saw any thing of the kind But further, he has the hardihood to assert, that, " an aged citizen, who laboured under a natural inability of speech, had his tongue cut out by one of the royal army," and that " a sucking infant was plundered of part of its clothing, while a bayonet was presented to the breast of its mother." It is literally impossible for one who has been in America during great part of the war, and who has actually fought in several of the engagements, to read such gross falsehoods without feeling more indignation than he can readily express, and heaving a sigh for the depravity of human nature I am certain, that either of these actions, proved on a British soldier, would have been punished by his officers with the greatest severity.

Mr Belsham, although somewhat more cautious and guarded n his assertions than Ramsay, is equally rancorous, and from the art with which he fabricates his deceptions, is a far more dangerous writer His allusion to the words of the proclamation, that " the existence of a single house on the coast, was a striking monument of British mercy," is highly uncandid This was an act of mercy after their cruel behaviour to the troops And the assertion that " all the buildings and farm houses for two miles in extent round the town, were laid in ashes, I can take upon me to contradict as a gross and malignant falshood. And yet these are the men who assume the pompous name of historians, and who transmit the most wanton misrepresentations of public events, together with the most wicked slander of illustrious individuals, to generations yet unborn!

In the mean time the American general made a diversion in another quarter, which broke all the measures which had been taken, with bravery equal to the wisdom with which they were planned. Such is the fate of war, and such sometimes the result of the best laid schemes of man. In the night of the 15th of July, the fort at Stoney Point was taken by surprise. The Americans having had perfect knowledge of all its works, knew well at what points to attack it, with advantage; it was still an enterprise of much difficulty, and greater danger. General Wayne was much praised for his conduct in the assault. He divided his troops into two columns, which entering the works in opposite quarters met in the centre of them about one in the morning of the 16th. The surprise was not so sudden, but that a brave resistance was made: so that the killed and wounded were nearly equal. There were about six hundred men in the fort, commanded by lieutenant colonel Johnson. They consisted of the 17th, regiment, the grenadier company of the 71st, a company of the regiment of loyal Americans, and a detachment of artillery. One hundred and fifty-two were either killed or wounded; the remainder with their commander were made prisoners. General Wayne's force was supposed to be about one thousand five hundred. It is but just, here to praise the conduct of the American commander; he stopped the carnage, and when the place was entirely calmed, not a man of the garrison was put to the sword.

The bravery of general Wayne commanded the highest praises of all parties. As he passed the last abbatis he was wounded in the head by a musquet ball; in which state, he insisted on being carried forward, declaring, " That if he died he wished it might be in the fort."

To the loss of this important fortress must be added, one which was at the time sensibly felt through the whole army. Captain Tew, a brave and distinguished officer, fell in defending the first barrier. He, with the most rare and undaunted heroism, even refused the quarter that was offered him by the Americans, being determined to make a stand until the rest of the garrison were alarmed, or perish on the spot. The effort proved unavailing; and unfortunately he fell a sacrifice! His name, however, must be always dear to the mind of the brave; nor did there an officer fall, during the whole campaigns, who deserved a more splendid monument.

He was most dangerously (and it was at first thought mortally) wounded when serving under general Amherst, in the French war, at Louisbourg. He was shot five times through the body, once through each arm, and likewise in the thigh. Through one of the apertures made by a bullet, which penetrated the body, a large stripe of linen was passed from the belly out at the back during some months. After the engagement, his wounds were so firmly believed to be mortal, that they were not dressed for three days, the surgeon expecting his death every half hour. At length, however, with great care some hopes were entertained; but his recovery was as tedious as his situation had been dangerous, until, at length he was able to accompany the shattered remains of his regiment to England.

At last, by the assistance of the first surgeons, and a good constitution, his wounds so far healed, as to permit his return to the public duties of his profession, and he served at those hazardous expeditions, both with regard to health and life, the sieges of Martinico and the Havannah. In both places the dangers encountered from the enemy, admitted no comparison what-ever with those which arose with the deadly exhalations and descended with the pestiferous dews of the climate. Notwithstanding all these services, he still remained unpromoted, continuing in the rank of a lieutenant, the same in which he left Europe in 1757.

Some time after the peace, he returned to Great Britain ; and an opportunity soon offering, he purchased the captain lieutenancy of the regiment. When they were reviewed by the king, he was pointed out to his majesty, to whom his singular fate was related. His majesty walked up to him, and after conversing with him very familiarly for some time, put his name down in his memorandum book, in order that he might not forget him when an occasion for promoting him should occur.

In 1771, he was, by his majesty's royal favour pro-moted to a company in the regiment, which was then sent to Scotland, where it continued three years ; but being again reviewed by the king, on their return to London, his majesty instantly recognized Mr. Tew's person, and again most graciously condescended to converse with him, giving him hopes of still further preferment.

In the year, 1776, he again embarked for America, where, becoming eldest captain in the regiment, on the appointment of the then lieutenant-colonel and major to other duties, he was promoted to its command. Many and important were the services rendered by this gallant officer to the royal cause, until, at last, we behold him, like the Spartan, LEONIDAS, nobly falling in defending the pass. I have already mentioned the

affairs of Princetown and Germantown, at both which
places he bravely distinguished himself. Indeed in
those two actions his regiment rendered such essential
service, that they received the public thanks of the
commander in chief. It is such men who are the best
guards of the throne, and on whom a nation may with
safety fix its firmest dependence.

Washington's arrangement for the attack on the
North River, included Fort Fayette with Stoney Point.
They were to have been assaulted at the same time.
The detachment which had the attack of Fort Fayette
in charge, did not arrive in time; it, however, advanced under the command of the American general
How, and, to favor its operations, general Wayne
turned the cannon of Stoney Point against Fort Fayette.
Lieutenant colonel Webster commanded there. The
garrison was formed of the 33d regiment, part of the
regiment of loyal Americans, a detachment from the
71st, and another of royal artillery.

Sir Henry Clinton was not unapprized of the danger,
the expedition against New London was suspended,
the transports and troops were recalled from the sound,
and the army moved on to Dobb's Ferry, on the North
River. Brigadier general Sterling, with a detachment,
sailed up the river, and the commander in chief, with
a superior force, followed, hoping that Washington
might be tempted, for the safety of Stoney Point, to
quit his fortresses, and risque an engagement. The
American general was too prudent, and on the contrary,
gave immediate orders for the evacuation of Stoney
Point, and the demolition of all the works which the
time would permit. Colonel Webster bravely defended
his post at Fort Fayette or Verplank's Neck. He sustained
the cannonade of Stoney Point without returning it, and
bent the whole of his attention to the attack, under general How. This conduct succeeded. Before the Americans

were able to effect any thing against the fort, the arrival of brigadier Sterling put an end to the contest; Stoney Point was re-taken; and on the arrival of Sir Henry Clinton, the works were repaired, and brigadier general Sterling, with a more numerous garrison, took the command. As no manœuvre whatever seemed likely to draw Washington from his hold of security in the Highlands, the transports fell down the river, and the troops returned to their quarters.

The idea of forming a settlement on the bay of Penobscot, had been adopted by the British commander. Six hundred men from the 74th and 82d regiments sailed in transports for that purpose, escorted by three sloops of war. The command of this detachment was given to general Maclean. It was suggested that forming a post in this settlement would not only check the incursions of the Americans into Nova Scotia, but also facilitate the supply of timber for the royal yards at Halifax, &c. that part of the country abounding with forests. The bay of Penobscot is about seven leagues broad at the entrance, and seventeen in length. The river Penobscot empties itself into its head. About nine miles below the mouth of the river, on the east side of the bay is a small, but convenient harbour. The point of land on the peninsula forming one side of the harbour, was the spot general Maclean fixed on for the erection of a fort to protect the settlement.

The Americans lost no time in opposing the measure. A fleet, consisting of nineteen armed ships and brigantines, and twenty-seven transports, with three thousand troops, under the command of general Lovell set sail from Boston harbour, under the protection of commodore Saltonstal, to oppose the undertaking.

His detachment arrived in Penobscot bay on the 25th of July, but could not effect a landing until the 28th; three sloops of war, under the direction of captain Mowat

commanding the mouth of the harbour The fleet
could not enter to land the troops on one side the peninsula, and the other was so steep and rugged that
it was almost inaccessible At last it was accomplished
on the morning of the 28th, before day break various
and ineffectual assaults and skirmishes, took place
until the twelfth of August, (a period of fifteen days,)
when a deserter brought intelligence to general Maclean,
that the day following, a general assault was to be made
on the fort, but the arrival of Sir George Collier
caused them to forego their design, and they hastily
reimbarked, with the greater part of their cannon.
The utmost confusion took place on board, and at
last, not daring to wait the shock of the British
squadron, they sought safety by flight . Two of
the armed ships in endeavouring to get to sea by
passing round Long Island, were lost to them, the
one being taken, and the other was ran ashore, and
blown up by the crew The rest, with the transports,
fled in disorder to the head of the bay, and entered
the mouth of the river, closely pursued by the British.
Here they landed in a wild uncultivated country,
destitute of provisions and every necessary, they had
to explore their way through a trackless desert, more
than an hundred miles before they could reach any
place of safety, or obtain succour. A quarrel ensued
between the seamen and the landsmen, each throwing
the blame on the other It terminated in a battle,
wherein fifty or sixty men were killed, and numbers,
before they reached the cultivated part of the province, perished in the woods.

Such, (with all their vast superiority of numbers, was
the event of the American opposition at Penobscot.
General Maclean was entitled to, and received the
highest praise " In the progress and issue of this
expedition," says Stedman, " we see how much may be

effected by a very inconsiderable force, when British officers act with zeal and unanimity in the service of their king and country."

On the English side, seventy were killed, wounded, and missing ; on board the fleet, fifteen killed and wounded.

The loss of the American soldiery was never ascertained ; but it must, on the whole, have more than exceeded two-thirds of their force. Of their fleets there were—

TAKEN.

Warren, 32 guns,	Defence,	16 guns,
Monmouth, 24 do.	Hazard,	16 do.
Vengeance, 24 do.	Diligence,	14 do.
Putnam, 22 do.	Tyrannicide,	14 do.
Sally, 22 do.	Providence,	14 do.
Hector, 20 do.	Spring Bird,	12 do.
Black Prince, 18 do.	Together with 24 sail
Sky Rocket, 16 do.	of transports.
Active, 16 do.	

BURNT.

Hampden, 20 guns,	Nancy,	16 guns,
Hunter, 18 do.	Rover	10 do.

Once more the reader's attention is solicited to other scenes, and following the operations of the southern armies, let us pursue the narrative of affairs before Savannah.

Count D'Estaing, after taking St. Vincent's and Grenada, sailed for America, and arrived an unexpected visitant on the coast of Georgia. His fleet consisted of twenty sail of the line, two of fifty guns, and eleven frigates, with which he surprised and took the Experiment of fifty guns and three frigates.

As soon as his arrival was known to the Americans, general Lincoln marched for Savannah, and in a short

the time place was invested both by sea and land. The
British were diligent in making every preparation for
its defence. Before the arrival of Lincoln, the count sent
a peremptory summons, demanding the surrender of the
place to the arms of France. To this general Prevost
replied, by inquiring on what terms? The French commander rejoined, " That it was for the besieged to offer
terms." A truce for twenty-four hours was then demanded and granted. During this time colonel Maitland,
after encountering incredible difficulties, arrived from
Beaufort, which place he had been ordered to abandon.
The difficulties he had overcome in his march were
astonishing. His arrival decided the fate of Savannah:
for when some of the officers in council were for
capitulating, the colonel resolutely arose, though almost
worn out with fatigue, and said, " that the word
capitulation was what he abhorred," adding, in a firm
tone, " that if he should survive, and go home to
Britain, he would report to the king the name of
the first officer who should dare to propose a capitulation." Thus encouraged, the garrison determined
on the most vigorous resistance. The works of the
garrison were strengthened by the incessant labour
of the troops and the negroes, under the direction of
that excellent engineer major Moncrief. The siege
commenced with nine mortars, and thirty pieces of
cannon from the land side, and fifteen from the water.
It was at this period that general Prevost solicited
leave to send the women and children out of the
place. This was tauntingly refused on the part of
the Americans. Ramsay says (with his usual *candor*
and *truth*) that they were fearful lest the plunder
of the Carolinas should be thus conveyed away, but I
am almost weary with noticing the mis-representations
of this writer.

The hurricane season, so fatal on that part of the American coast, had now commenced, and the sailors began to murmur at delay. This forced them on the desperate attempt of storming the place, which was commenced at Springhold battery, October 9th, early in the morning, by three thousand five hundred French troops, six hundred continentals, and three hundred and fifty of the inhabitants of Charlestown. These troops, under the command of D'Estaing and Lincoln, resolutely marched up to the lines ; but the tremendous and well directed fire of the batteries, joined to that in a cross direction from the gallies, threw their whole columns into confusion ; not before, however, they had planted two standards on the British redoubts.

There were two feints made by the American militia to draw the attention of the garrison from the real point of attack, to their centre and left. Meanwhile it was intended that count Dillon should secretly pass the edge of the swamps, the redoubts, and batteries, and attack the rear of the British lines. The troops were in motion before day-light, but a heavy fog arising with the morning, they lost their way in the swamp, and were finally exposed to the view of the garrison and the fire of the batteries, which was so hot and tremendous, that they in vain attempted to form, and their whole design was defeated.

Lieutenant Tawes, of the 71st regiment, nobly fell with his sword in the body of the third of the assailants he had killed. It was in defending the gate of the redoubt that he fell. The enemy rushed forward, and two standards (one American and the other French) were fixed on the parapet. They were soon displaced, and the conflict for possession of the redoubt became hot and bloody. At last, when every thing hung in suspense, lieutenant colonel Maitland seized the critical moment, and ordered the grenadiers of the 60th regiment, with the marines, to charge the enemy, who began to give way, being annoyed at once by the slaughter in the redoubt, the heavy fire from the batteries, and the guns of the Germaine armed brig, which played incessantly upon them This judicious movement decided the contest. The enemy were driven out of the redoubt with immense slaughter ; they fled in all directions , six hundred and thirty-seven French and two hundred and sixty-four of the Americans were left upon the spot, either killed or wounded

General Prevost did not order any pursuit, as the enemy, notwithstanding their loss, were three times the number of the garrison However their ranks were still further thinned, during their flight, by the heavy and well directed fire of the British garrison, under the command of captain Charleton. The loss of the besiegers, upon the whole, was upwards of one thousand men, among whom were forty-four officers

Count D'Estaing was wounded in two places, neither of the wounds were mortal, and count Polaskie received a ball, of which he died shortly after the engagement.

The event, in Polaskie's life, which will long render him an object of public curiosity, and also of public execration, was the attempt to assassinate the king of Poland He was, at the time he planned the atrocious enterprise, a general in the army of the confederates. The conspirators who carried it into execution, were about forty in number, and were headed by three chiefs, named Lukawskie, Strawenskie, and Kosinski. These three chiefs had been engaged for that purpose, by Polaskie, who, in the town of Cyetscho, now in Great Poland, obliged them to swear n the most solemn manner, by placing their hands between his, either to deliver the king alive into his hands, or, n case that was impracticable, to put him to death On the 2d of November, 1771, about a month after they had quitted

Cyetscho, they obtained admission into Warsaw, un-suspected, by the following stratagem: they disguised themselves as peasants, who came to sell hay, and con-cealed their saddles and clothes under the loads in the waggons. On Sunday night the 3d of November, 1771, a few of these conspirators remained in the skirts of the town, and the others repaired to the place of ren-dezvous, the streets of the Capuchins, where his majesty was expected to pass by, about his usual hour of returning from visiting to the palace. The king had to visit his uncle prince Zartoriski, grand chancellor of Lithuania, and was on his return from thence to the palace between nine and ten o'clock. He was in a coach, accompanied by at least fifteen or sixteen attendants, be-sides an aid-de-camp in the carriage. Scarcely was he two hundred paces from prince Zartoriski's palace, when he was attacked by the conspirators, who commanded the coachman to stop on pain of instant death. They fired several shots into the carriage, one of which passed through the body of a hey-duc, who endeavoured to defend his master from the violence of the assasins. Almost all the persons who preceded and accompanied his majesty, were dispersed; the aid-de-camp abandoned him, and attempted to conceal himself by flight. Mean-while the king had opened the door of his carriage, with the design of effecting his escape, under shelter of the night, which was extremely dark. He had even alighted, when the assasins seized him by the hair, ex-claiming in Polish, with horrible execrations, "We have thee now; thy hour is come." One of them dis-charged a pistol at him, so very near, that he felt the heat of the flash, while another cut him across the head, with his sabre, which penetrated to the bone. They then laid hold of his majesty by the collar, and mount-ing on horseback, dragged him along the ground between their horses at full gallop, for near five hundred paces, through the streets of Warsaw.

It is astonishing that none of the balls which passed through the carriage should hurt or wound the king, several went through his pellise, or sur great coat " I have seen this," says that celebrated writer, Nathaniel Wraxal, Esq " and the holes made in it by the pistol bullets " It is no less wonderful that the assassins should carry him through such a number of streets' without being stopped A Russian sentinel did hail them, but as they answered in Russian, he allowed them to pass, imagining them to be a patrole of his nation The night besides was exceeding dark, and Warsaw has no lamps All these circumstances contribute to account for the extraordinary event

All was confusion during this time at the palace, where the attendants spread the alarm. The foot guards ran immediately to the spot from whence the king had been conveyed ; but they found only his hat all bloody, and his bag , this increased their apprehensions for his life. The whole city was in an uproar, The assassins profited by the universal confusion, terror, and consternation, to bear away their prize. Finding, however, that he was incapable of following them on foot, and that he had already nearly lost his respiration, they set him on horseback ; and then redoubled their speed for fear of being overtaken When they came to the ditch which surrounds Warsaw, they obliged him to leap his horse over In the attempt the horse fell twice, and at the second fall broke his leg. They then mounted his majesty on another, all covered as he was with dirt.

The conspirators had no sooner crossed the ditch, than they began to riffle the king, tearing off the order of the black eagle of Prussia, which he wore round his neck, and the diamond cross hanging to it

He requested them to leave him his handkerchief, to which they consented; his pocket book escaped their rapacity.

A great number of the assassins retired, after having thus plundered him, probably to notify to their respective leaders the success of their enterprise, and the king's arrival as a prisoner. Only seven remained with him, of whom Kosinski was the chief. The night was exceedingly dark; they were absolutely ignorant of the way; and as the horses could not keep their legs, they obliged his majesty to follow them on foot, with only one shoe; the other being lost in the dirt.

They continued to wander through the open meadows, without following any certain path, and without getting any great distance from Warsaw. They again mounted the king on horseback, two of them holding him on each side by the hand, and a third leading his horse by the bridle. In this manner they were proceeding, when his majesty finding they had taken the road, which led to a village called Burakow, warned them not to enter it, because there were some Russians stationed in that place, who might probably attempt to rescue him.* Finding himself, however, incapable of accompanying the assassins in the painful posture in which they held him, he requested them at least to give him another horse and a boot. This request they complied with; and continuing their progress through almost impassable lands, without any

---

* This intimation may at first sight appear unaccountable; but was really dictated by the greatest address and judgment. He apprehended, with reason, that on the sight of a Russian guard, they would instantly put him to death and fly; whereas, by informing them of the danger they incurred, he in some measure gained their confidence. In effect, this behaviour of the king seemed to soften them a little, and made them believe he did not mean to escape from them.

road, and ignorant of their way, they at length found
themselves in the wood of Bielany, only a league distant
from Warsaw   From the time they had passed the
ditch, they repeatedly demanded of Kosinski, their
chief, " If it was not yet time to put the king to
death ?" and these demands were reiterated in proportion to the difficulties they encountered.

Meanwhile the confusion and consternation increased
at Warsaw. The guards were afraid to pursue the
conspirators, lest terror of being overtaken should
prompt them in the darkness to massacre the king
and on the other hand, by not pursuing, they might
give them time to escape with their prize, beyond the
possibility of assistance   Several of the first nobility
at length mounted on horseback, and following the
track of the assassins arrived at the place where his
majesty had passed the ditch   There they found his
pellise, which he had lost in the precipitation with
which he was hurried away   it was bloody, and pierced
with holes made by the balls or sabres   This caused
them to imagine that he was no more.

The king was still in the hands of the seven remaining assassins, who advanced with him into the wood
of Bielany, when they were suddenly alarmed by a
Russian patrole or detachment   Instantly holding council, four of them disappeared, leaving him with the other
three, who compelled him to walk on   Scarce a quarter
of an hour, after a second Russian guard challenged
them anew   Two of the assassins then fled, and the
king remained alone with Kosinski, the chief, both on
foot   His majesty, exhausted with the fatigue he had
undergone, implored his conductor to stop, and suffer
him to take a moment's repose   Kosinski refused it,
menacing him with his naked sabre, and at the same
time informed him, that beyond the wood they should
find a carriage   They continued their walk until they

came to the door of the convent of Bielany. Kosinski appeared lost in thought, and so much agitated by his reflections, that the king, perceiving his disorder, and observing that he wandered without knowing the road, said to him, " I see you are at a loss which way to proceed. Let me enter the convent of Bielany; and do you provide for your own safety." " No," replied Kosinsksi, " I have sworn."

" They proceeded till they came to Mariemont, a small palace belonging to the house of Saxony, not above half a league from Warsaw. Here Kosinski betrayed some satisfaction at finding where he was, and the king still demanding an instant's repose, he at length consented. They sat down together on the ground, and the king employed these moments in endeavoring to soften his conductor, and induce him to favor or permit his escape. His majesty represented the attrocity of the crime he had committed, in attempting to murder his sovereign, and the invalidity of the oath he had taken to perpetrate so heinous an action. Kosinski lent attention to this discourse, and began to betray some marks of remorse. " But," said he, " if I should consent and reconduct you to Warsaw, what will be the consequence? I shall be taken and executed."

" This reflection plunged him into new uncertainty and embarrassment. " I give you my word," answered his majesty, " that you shall suffer no harm; but if you doubt my promise, escape while there is yet time; I can find my way to some place of security; and I will certainly direct your pursuers to take the contrary road to that which you have chosen." Kosinski could not any longer contain himself, but throwing himself at the king's feet, implored forgiveness for the crime he had committed, and swore to protect him from every enemy; relying totally on his gene-

O o

rosity for pardon and preservation. His majesty reite-
terated his assurances of safety. Judging, however, that
it was prudent to gain some asylum without delay,
and recollecting that there was a mill at some considerable distance, he immediately made towards it
Kosinski knocked, but in vain, no answer was given.
He then broke a pane of glass in the window, and
entreated for shelter, to a nobleman who had been
plundered by robbers. The miller refused, supposing
them to be a banditti, and continued for more than
half an hour, to persist in his denial. At length the
king approached, and speaking through the broken
pane, endeavored to persuade him to admit them
under his roof, adding, " If we were robbers, it would
be easy for us to break the whole window, instead of
one pane of glass." This argument prevailed. they
at length opened the door, and admitted his majesty
He immediately wrote a note to general Coccei, colonel of the foot guards. It was literally as follows:

"By a kind of miracle, I have escaped from the
hands of the assassins. I am now at the mill of Mar-
riemont. Come as soon as possible and take me from
hence. I am wounded, but not dangerously."

" It was with the greatest difficulty that the king could
persuade any one to carry this note to Warsaw, as
the people of the mill, imagining that he was a nobleman who had just been plundered by robbers, were
afraid of falling in with the troop. Kosinski then
offered to restore every thing he had taken, but his
majesty left him all, except the blue ribband of the
White Eagle. When the messenger arrived with the note
at Warsaw, the astonishment and joy was incredible.
Coccei immediately rode to the mill, followed by a detachment of the guards. He met Kosinski at the door with
his sabre drawn; who admitted him, as soon as he knew him.
The king had sunk into a sleep caused by his fatigue,

and was stretched on the ground, covered with the miller's cloak. Coccei immediately threw himself at his majesty's feet, calling him his sovereign and kissing his hand. It is not easy to describe the astonishment of the miller and his family, who instantly imitated Coccei's example, by throwing themselves on their knees. This mill is still standing, rendered memorable by so singular an event. It is a wretched polish hovel, at a distance from any house. The king rewarded the miller to the extent of his wishes, in building him a mill upon the Vistula, and allowing him a small pension. His majesty returned to Warsaw in general Coccei's carriage, and reached the palace by five in the morning. His wound was found not to be dangerous; and he soon recovered the bruises and injuries which he had suffered during this memorable night.

" The king in his speech to the Diet, on the trial of the conspirators, interceded strongly for Kosinski; or John Kutsma, to whom he gratefully expresses himself indebted for these favors, in the following words: " As I was in the hands of the assassins, I heard them repeatedly ask John Kutsma, if they should not assassinate me, but he always prevented them. He was the first who persuaded them to behave to me with greater gentleness; and obliged them to confer on me some services, which I then greatly wanted; namely, one to give me a cap, and another a boot; which at that time were no trifling presents; for the cold air greatly affected the wound in my head; and my foot, which was covered with blood, gave an inexpressible torture, which continued every moment increasing."

Lukawski and Strawenski were both executed. They both suffered without manifesting the least contrition

for their guilt, the latter behaved with that fortitude
which was worthy a better cause "

After the conclusion of these troubles, Polaski escaped from Poland, and repaired to America, where he
raised a regiment of horse, and was appointed by congress a major general of their armies

But although death thus swept away from the American service a most active and dangerous character,
the triumph of the British garrison was alloyed by a
event, on their part of the most distressing nature This
was the loss of that highly esteemed and much beloved
officer, colonel Maitland. The noxious vapours which
rise from the American marshes during the summer
season, proved fatal to his constitution Before he
left Beaufort he was attacked with a billious disorder,
which was increased by his route through the marshes
to Savannah. The anxiety and hardships of the siege
served only to aggravate the complaint, which terminated in the dissolution of an officer whose name will
be dear to Britons, until patriotism ceases to be a virtue,
and loyalty becomes a crime Soon after his death a
character of him appeared in Rivington's New York
Royal Gazette, the elegance, strength, and beautiful
diction of which (I have no other reasons) inclines me
strongly to suspect that, it was written by his friend
major Andre.

"The late colonel Maitland was one of the most
active officers at the commencement, and during the
progress of the American war his zeal and gallantry
were sufficient incitements to lead where danger
dignified, and rendered a post honorable Though he
possessed an easy fortune, had a seat in the house of
commons, and was of an advanced age, yet he never
availed himself of such powerful pretensions, or expressed a desire of returning from the field of honor
Unshaken loyalty, genuine patriotism, undaunted bra-

very, judicious conduct, steady coolness, and unre_
mitting perseverance, constituted his character as an
officer. His benevolence was ever exerted when indi-
gence presented; he not only relieved, but sympathized
with the distressed: to inform him of any person that required charitable exertion, was an ample recommendation.
His disposition was so extremely amiable that to know him
was to admire him. His address was easy and engaging;
his language strong, nervous and persuasive: his affabi_
lity rendered him pleasing to every observer: he was
beloved by his friends, respected by his acquaintances,
and revered by every officer and soldier under his
command. His country will feel the loss of so accomplished a chief; his acquaintance will long lament the
loss of so venerable a friend; the indigent search in
vain for another so eminently benevolent, and the
soldiers, long accustomed to his pleasing command,
lament his death, and revere his memory."

About this time the congress, in order to terrify the
Indians into neutrality, gave orders for an expedition
which should convince them that the inhabitants of
the sea coast were possessed of the means of carrying
devastation into the heart of their territory. It was
imagined that such a measure would deter them from
again invading and ravaging the American settlements.
Five thousand men with artillery and field pieces, under
the command of major general Sullivan, entered the
Indian possessions. The natives fled as they approached, and a general destruction of every thing
commenced; "more," says Stedman, "than one hundred and fifty thousand bushels of corn were destroyed;"
their gardens were laid waste, even the fruit trees were
cut down; and one wide and spreading desolation every
where met the eye." Meantime the Indians invaded the
provincial towns and settlements, and thus mutual destruction commenced. The Indians were enraged, but not

overcome, and the little benefit and great expense of the
measure, rendered it very unpopular—Congress became
dissatisfied—it never had general Washington's approbation—and general Sullivan, on his return, resigned all
his employments and retired. While the northern
Indians were thus suffering under the invasion of general Sullivan, those of the south, were also made to
feel the effects of American retribution Such a system
of warfare is shocking to humanity, and, after all, its
very policy seems to be at best but problematical

CHAPTER XIV

*Sir Henry Clinton, with a large Body of Troops sails
from New York, and arrives, after much Difficulty,
in South Carolina. Charlestown Capitulates to the
British Forces. Memoirs of Captain Grattan, of
the 64th Regiment. . Sir Henry Clinton returns
to New York Lord Cornwallis takes' the' Command
of the Royal Forces in the Southern Provinces.
Battle near Camden. Major Ferguson defeated.*

TOWARDS the latter end of the year 1779, Sir
Henry Clinton entrusted the command of the royal
army in New York, to lieutenant general Knyphausen,
and embarked for the southward, with a formidable
force, provisions, ammunition, &c The whole sailed
from Sandy Hook on the 26th of December, under
convoy of admiral Arbuthnot The passage proved
both tedious and dangerous. Part of the ordnance,
some of the artillery, and most of the cavalry horses
were lost, nor did the fleet arrive at Tybu, in Georgia, until the 31st of January, 1780

In a few days the transports sailed with the army
for North Edisto They landed about thirty miles from
Charlestown (after a short passage) and took possession
of John's Island, Stono ferry, James's Island, and
Wappo-cut. A bridge being thrown over the canal,

part of the forces took post on the banks on Ashley river, opposite Charlestown

The tedious passage from New York, afforded opportunity to the Americans to fortify Charlestown, and from the losses which the expedition had sustained, Sir Henry Clinton deemed it prudent to send orders to New York for a reinforcement of men and stores. He also drew twelve hundred men from the garrison at Savannah. Brigadier general Patterson who commanded this detachment, crossed the river Savannah, and traversing the country, arrived on the banks of Ashley river. The siege was immediately commenced. A depot was formed at Wappo, on James's Island; fortifications were erected there, and on the main land, opposite the southern and western ends of Charlestown. An advanced party crossed the river, and broke ground at eight hundred yards from the American works, and batteries were erected on Charlestown neck. Nor were the Americans idle during this period; they put the town into every possible state of defence.

Charlestown is said to contain about one thousand four hundred houses, and about eight thousand inhabitants, including the blacks, who are by far the more numerous, almost every white man, in this boasted land of liberty, keeping a great number of slaves! The inhabitants are very extravagant in their living, splendid equipages, &c. But the merchants suffered so much "during the war," that it is doubtful if they will ever regain their former wealth. They boast of their town as the most polite place in America, but it is far exceeded by several others, in riches as well as convenience; the waters are frequently putrid, its climate unhealthy, and every necessary of life much dearer than in any other part of America.

But there is one circumstance, which, in the opinion of every wise as well as of every good man, must operate as a drag chain of Almighty vengeance about the neck of any state, practised here to a greater extent than in all the other cities of America, viz. that abominable and notorious traffic, the slave trade. How any people pretending, as the Americans do, to the profession of christianity, can dare to drive on an horrible traffic in the blood of their fellow creatures, their co-heirs in redemption, and thus stab the religion which they profess in one of its most vital parts, is, a dreadful solecism, at which a Pagan may laugh; a Mahometan triumph; a deist exult, and which even a Jew might pity. But the sincere christian must lament the continuance of the deplorable evil, alike ashamed of the practice, as incompetent to its cure. These reflections struck the mind of the Author, when he perused the following paragraph, relative to the inhabitants of Charlestown, in the historical review of North America:

" In the midst of every appearance of festivity and joy, scenes of misery, with the horrors of slavery, momentarily intervene to assault the eye and ear ! The feelings of humanity are shocked, with the hardships of incessant toil ! The very ground is damp with the sweat and tears of the unhappy Africans. The crack of the whip too frequently intercepts the joys of convivial mirth ! Here may be seen every day, and all day long, thousands of our fellow creatures branded, chained, and treated like cattle in every respect, but that of humanity ! They are indeed fed the same, but are harder worked, and more severely abused."

The British troops carried on their parallel from the 3d to the 10th of April. Immediately on the completion

P p

of the first parallel, the town was summoned to surrender, the batteries were opened; and from that time, a constant fire commenced. On the Wando River, at Simpson's Port, and Santic Ferry, posts were established, and works thrown up by the Americans, to guard their reinforcements and secure their retreat

Meanwhile, admiral Arbuthnot passed Fort Moultrie, on Sullivan's Island, though strongly opposed from the American batteries, and anchored under James's Island, with the loss of twenty-seven seamen killed and wounded, some damage to the shipping, and the burning of the Acteus transport, which grounded within gun shot of the island The American commander, with his fleet, fell back to Charlestown.

The Americans, to keep up the communication with the country, formed a camp at Monk's Corner, which was the rendezvous of their militia. This post was surprized by lieutenant colonel Tarleton, which gave the British the command of the country, and enabled them to intercept the supplies of provisions.

Our batteries soon obtained a superiority over those of the enemy, a council of war was held by the Americans, in consequence of which, the town offered to surrender, on condition of " security to the persons and property of the inhabitants, and leave being given for the Americans to withdraw "

These terms were instantly rejected by general Clinton, as soon as they were offered , but the garrison would not alter their conditions, under the hope that succours would soon arrive from the neighbouring states, in consequence of which, the town was closely invested, both by land and water, Fort Moultrie surrendered, and the American cavalry, which had escaped from Monk's Corner were all either killed, captured, or dispersed.

On the 9th of May, the town was again summoned, and Lincoln was inclined to surrender his army pri_ soners of war ; but the inhabitants thought to obtain better terms, and the siege recommenced. The third parallel was opened, shells and carcasses thrown into the town, and the cannon and mortars played on the garrison at less than one hundred yards distance ; the pickets, crossed the ditch by sap, and advanced within twenty-five yards of the American works.

Matters continued in this state till the 11th, when the inhabitants addressed general Lincoln to ca_ pitulate, which was accordingly done, and major ge_ neral Leslie took possession of the town on the 12th. There were in it upwards of four hundred pieces of artillery. The garrison, as prisoners of war, marched out of the town ; their drums were not allowed to beat a British march, nor their colours to be uncased. They laid down their arms in front of the works ;. the militia returned home, on parole ; the inhabitants were considered as prisoners on parole, and like the militia, held their property accordingly ; a vessel was allowed to proceed to Philadelphia, with general Lincoln's dispatches, unopened ; upwards of five thou- sand troops, and near one thousand sailors surren- dered ; all the ships of war, and other vessels were taken.

Among the officers were, two major generals, five brigadier generals, three majors of brigade, sixteen colonels, nine lieutenant colonels, fifteen majors, eighty- four captains, one commodore, eighty-four lieutenants, thirty-two second lieutenants or ensigns. The deputy governor, council, and civil officers were all made

prisoners.   The total loss of the British from their de-
barkation to the surrender, was as follows †

Ensign M'Gregor, 71st, Regiment, killed.
——— Cameron, do   do   do.
1 Serjeant,   do
73 Rank and File,   do
Lieut White, grenadier company, 22d Regiment, wounded
——— Bever,   33d   do   do
——— Grant,   42d   do   do
——— Freeman, light infantry, 64th   do   do
Captain M'Leod,   71st   do   do
Lieutenant Wilson,   do.   do.   do.
2 Serjeants,   do.
176 Rank and File.   do.

Captain Grattan received a severe contusion in the
head, by the bursting of a shell in one of the trenches.
He however recovered, returned to Ireland, and died
during the rebellion in Wexford Of this brave and
amiable officer, the author has received the following
brief account, from authority, which is indisputable

Captain William Grattan, studied surgery under the
celebrated Mr Cleghorn of the city of Dublin When
he had attained a perfect knowledge of his profession,
he was appointed assistant surgeon to his majesty's
64th regiment of foot, at that time commanded by
his friend and patron general Pomeroy The regiment lay n Cashel, in the county of Tipperary, when
they received orders for the theatre of war They
marched to the Cove of Cork, and embarked for the
continent of America.

When they arrived at the place of destination, Mr.
Grattan, who was at that time very young, glowed for
more ardent employment, and possessing the soul of
a soldier, he longed to weild the sword in the field of

---

* * · A few days after the capitulation, a magazine took fire in
Charlestown, and captain Collins, a valuable officer, with several
men of the royal artillery, perished by the explosion.

battle, to espouse his country's cause, and amidst the dreadful terrors of war, to meet the hostile foe. He purchased a commission in his own regiment, and shortly after a lieutenancy. Our young soldier avoiding the follies and extravagancies, of which too many are guilty, applied himself closely to the knowledge of the military science, in all its various departments, which he soon acquired. He was often heard to say, " Gambling and extravagance were the bane of a soldier." What he disapproved in others he never allowed in himself. He lived with economy and frugality, and in the course of a few years, he purchased a company. Captain Grattan possessed a strong understanding, sound judgment, and deep penetration; these, with a perfect knowledge of his profession, made him an invaluable officer. He became the soul of his own regiment, which he never exchanged for another. Merit like his could not be hid. He was honored with the confidence of his commanding officer, consulted on all matters of importance, appointed assistant engineer to Sir Henry Clinton, and was universally beloved by all, as well the privates of his own regiment, as the generals of the army.

" In September 1781, when Count De Grasse, with a powerful French fleet, had the entire possession of the Chesapeak, and general Washington had formed a junction with the French troops, commanded by the marquis De La Fayette, for the purpose of surrounding lord Cornwallis, at Yorktown, Sir Henry Clinton dispatched captain Grattan, with information that eight thousand British troops would immediately march to reinforce him. Captain Grattan encountered most imminent danger on this service; but he arrived safe with his dispatches at Yorktown, the 15th of September, and had the honor of receiving lord Cornwallis's thanks in public orders.

" Captain Grattan was seventeen years absent from
Europe , he served in all the American war, and was
in the West Indies During this period he was not
one day absent from his regiment, unless when
engaged on business of great importance, or in
public employ.

Captain Grattan was in many battles, and displayed
the greatest valor and intrepidity   He served at the
battles of Long Island, Germantown, Monmouth, Danbury, Brandywine, in Pennsylvania, the Eutaw Springs,
in South Carolina, Brooklyn, on Long Island ; Monmouth, at the burning of the enemy's stores on Peek
Hill, at the siege of Charlestown, where he was
wounded , at the affair of Chamblee River, where the
famous colonel Laurens, son to the president of congress,
was killed, and his party defeated by the 64th and a
party of the 17th, besides a most fatiguing duty of two
years in South Carolina, where the regiment lost upwards of four hundred men

On Saturday morning, the 15th of May, 1784, captain
Grattan landed at Portsmouth, with six other commissioned officers, and the remains of his regiment. On
his arrival in England, he wrote to his friends in Ireland , the September following he arrived in Edenderry,
in the King's County, where he was joyfully received
by his aged parents, three brothers, and two sisters, as
one restored from the dead.

In the year 1792 he married miss Giffard, a lady of
amiable qualifications, the daughter of Sir Duke Giffard,
of Castle Jordan, baronet He then retired from the
army, and settled in Rathangan He was magistrate
for the county, and sovereign of Kildare, When the
penetrating mind of captain Grattan foresaw the approaching rebellion, he did not think it his duty to be
an idle spectator ; he applied to government for an

appointment, and was shortly after made deputy general in the commissariat department.

In the year of 1798, while in Dublin, he received orders to join general Needham, and march to the relief of Wexford. He fought at the battle of Arklow. He was also at the taking of Enniscorthy, and Vinegar Hill. On the 20th of June, after the fatigue of the day's action was over, captain Grattan who had been on such arduous duty since he had left Dublin, felt the need of refreshment. Invited by the lovely appearance of the Slaney, flowing under the hill, and attended by a faithful servant, he proceeded to it, to enjoy the refreshment of bathing; as he had not been in the cold bath since he returned to Europe, we may naturally suppose it was the cause of what followed. Sometime after he arrived in Wexford he was confined to his bed. He experienced the greatest kindness and attention from Mrs. Hattan, a lady of fortune, who resides near the town, and colonel Finley, of the county of Dublin Militia. They hardly ever left him. Colonel Finley wrote to Mrs. Grattan, who was at that time in Dublin, and informed her of his illness. His amiable wife, with no other companion but her sister, immediately set out to join him, and faced all the dangers of the counties of Wicklow and Wexford at that perilous time. She arrived safe; but though she did, how afflicting must her anguish have been, when her good and amiable husband expired shortly after her arrival!

The finest perfections enriched his character. He was an obedient and dutiful child to his parents, to the latest moments of their lives—a kind and good brother—an affectionate husband—a sincere friend—an elegant gentleman, and an experienced and valiant soldier. The former are known by his friends, and the latter can be proved by his military zeal in the service of his country, and the following letters of thanks from lord Cornwallis

" Wynnsborough, Nov 21, 1780

" SIR—I have just heard from colonel Balfour, that you are returned from your expedition to general Leslie, where you have succeeded to my most sanguine wishes I beg you will accept of my sincere acknowledgments for your *zeal*, *prudence*, and *good management* n this important business

I am, Sir, your most obedient,
And most humble servant,
" CORNWALLIS."

* To captain Grattan, 64th regiment.*

" Culford, August 19, 1784

" SIR—It gives me great concern to hear of the particular hardships of your situation, in regard to your commission of Quarter Master of the 64th Regiment. I shall, at all times, be ready to bear testimony of your *merit*, and *good services*, when you were under my command , and I shall ever acknowledge my obligations to you, for your *zeal* and *diligence* for the public service, in executing an important commission at my request in 1780.

I am, Sir, your most obedient,
And most humble servant,
" CORNWALLIS "

" To captain Grattan, 64th regiment.

As the besiegers made no sallies or desperate assaults, their loss amounted to only eighty-nine killed, and one hundred and forty wounded This was the first instance in which the Americans had ventured to defend a town The event demonstrated the policy of Washington's system, who never during the whole war, attempted the defence of any town, against the investment of regular troops. In favor of general

Lincoln, it is however but just to remark, that Charles.
town was the only considerable place in the southern
boundary of the confederacy; for its preservation South
Carolina and the neighbouring states seemed willing
to make great exertions: the congress and both states
of the Carolinas promised an army of near ten thousand men to its support. These were actually on
their march; but the British had taken such a position,
that succours could not be thrown into the place,
or any retreat successfully made.

Sir Henry Clinton, with a liberal policy, held forth
every inducement to the inhabitants that was likely
to draw them back to their allegiance, and issued
strong and salutary threats, to those who should continue contumacious. In a few days, in conjunction
with admiral Arbuthnot, as commissioners for restoring
peace, the inhabitants were offered " pardon for their
past treasonable offences, and a reinstatement in the
possession of all their rights and immunities, which
they heretofore had enjoyed, under a free British government; exempt from taxation, except by their
own legislatures."

The next object with general Clinton, was to bring
back to their allegiance the whole southern states.
Garrisons were therefore posted in different parts of
the country, to awe the inhabitants. The troops
marching for the relief of Charlestown were encountered on the borders of North Carolina, by different
bodies sent out for that purpose. One of these
consisting of three hundred Americans, commanded by
colonel Buford, was overtaken at Wacsaws, by lieutenant colonel Tarleton, and completely defeated. Upwards of one hundred officers and men (says colonel
Tarleton, in his own History of the Campaign), were
killed on the spot, three colours, two six-pounders,
and above two hundred prisoners, with a number of

waggons, two royals, quantities of new clothing, other
military stores, and camp equipage were taken " Colonel
Tarleton ascribes much of the " complete success" of
this difficult enterprise, to the blunders and mistakes
of the American commanders

Sir Henry Clinton (leaving between three and four
thousand men for the southern service) embarked early
in June for New York. On his departure the command devolved on earl Cornwallis.

Almost the whole of South Carolina was now restored
to its legal government, but the calm was only temporary the submission was only nominal for when a
levy was attempted to be raised among the young
men who had no families, to form a body to act against
the hostile Americans, the spirit of disaffection broke
out in various ways, and it evidently appeared
that they possessed a hatred to the British government

In the mean time the Americans marched an army
through Jersey and Pennsylvania, which embarking at
the head of the Elk, landed soon after at Petersburgh,
and thence proceeded through the country toward
South Carolina It consisted of Maryland and Delaware troops, commanded by major general Baron de
Kalb, who afterwards resigned to general Gates The
Americans expected much from the popularity of the
latter.

As the American army approached to South Carolina,
our army, which then consisted of seventeen hundred
infantry, and two hundred cavalry was concentrated at
Camden. The army with which Gates advanced, was
by the arrival of the militia, increased nearly to six
thousand men On the night of the 15th we marched
from Camden, intending to attack the Americans in
their camp at Rugeley's Mills In the same night Gates
put his army in motion, with an intention of surpris-

ing our camp, or posting himself on an eligible position near : Camden.   Our .army was ordered to march
at ten o'clock P. M. .The American army was ordered
to) march iat .the ; same) hour. ;The advance guard of
both armies met about two o'clock in the morning.
Some of the American cavalry, being wounded in the
first fire fell back on others, who recoiled so suddenly,
that the first Maryland regiment was broken, and the
whole line of their army was thrown into confusion.
The enemy soon rallied and, both they and we
kept our ground, and a few shots only from the advanced
centries of each army were fired during the night.
A colonel Patterfield, on whose abilities general Gates
particularly depended, was wounded in the early part
of 'this skirmish As soon as day light appeared,
we saw at a few yards distance our enemy drawn up
in very, good order in three lines.   Our little army
was formed in the following plan :

Four companies of light infantry, Royal Welch Fusileers, or
        23d regiment, on the right wing,
     led on by lieutenant colonel Webster.

Volunteers of Ireland, Legion Infantry, two American loyal
  corps, on the left wing, led on by lord Rawdon.

Two six and two three pounders were placed in the centre,
     between the two wings.

71st, the Legion cavalry regiment, with two six pounders,
     formed the reserve.

It happened that the ground on which both armies
stood, was narrowed by swamps on the right and left,
so that the Americans could not avail themselves
of their superior numbers in out flanking us.   We
immediately began the attack with great vigor, and
in a few minutes the action became general along the
whole line ; there was a dead calm with a little hazi-
ness in the air, which prevented the smoke from rising ;
this occasioned such thick darkness, that it was difficult

to see the effect of the fire on either sides   Our army
either kept up a constant fire, or made use of their bayonets
as opportunity offered   After an obstinate resistance
for some time the Americans were thrown into total confusion, and were forced to give way in all quarters
The continental troops behaved well, but some of the
militia were soon broken. In justice to the North Carolina
militia, it should be remarked, that part of the brigade
commanded by general Gregory acquitted themselves
well , they were formed immediately on the left of the
continentals, and kept the field while they had a car-
tridge to fire   Gregory himself was twice wounded by
a bayonet in bringing off his men . several of his
regiment, and many of his brigade who were made prisoners had no wound except from bayonets   About
one thousand prisoners were taken, two hundred and
ninety of which being wounded were carried into
Camden, and more than twice that number killed   The
Americans lost the whole of their artillery, eight brass
field pieces, upward of two hundred waggons, and the
greatest part of their baggage, tents, &c. with a number
of colors   Almost all their officers were separated from
their respective commands. The fugitives who fled on
the common road, were pursued above twenty miles
by colonel Tarleton's cavalry, and the way was covered
with arms, baggage, and waggons   Baron de Kalb,
the second in command, a brave and experienced officer
in the American service, was mortally wounded, having
exhibited great gallantry in the course of the action, and
received eleven wounds , he was taken prisoner, and
died on the next day of his wounds, we buried him
in Camden with all the honors of war

The baron, who was a German by birth, had long
been in the French service. He had travelled through
the British provinces, about the time of the stamp act,
and is said to have reported to his superiors on his

return, " that the colonists were so firmly and uni_
versally attached to Great Britain, that nothing could
shake their loyalty." The congress resolved that a mo_
nument should be erected to his memory in Annapolis,
with a very honorable inscription.

In compiling an eventful history, like the present,
many circumstances must unavoidably be taken on the
authority of others. For these the author is no farther
responsible than in selecting that report which appears
the nearest to truth. Far different, however, are those
matters which come beneath my own personal observations. On those a writer can dwell with precision. What
he thus produces is the evidence of fact. As in this
engagement, I had the honor of carrying one standard
of colours belonging to the 23d regiment, I was of
course, near the centre of the right wing. I had an opportunity of beholding the behaviour both of the officers
and privates ; it was worthy the character of the British
troops. The recollection still dwells deeply in my
memory. Lord Cornwallis's judgment in planning, his
promptitude in executing, and his fortitude and coolness during the time of action, justly attracted universal
applause and admiration. The earl of Moira, (then
lord Rawdon, who was only twenty-five years of age)
bore a very conspicuous part in the contest. Colonel
Webster also ought to be particularly mentioned. His
conduct was completely consistent with his general
character in the army. Cool, determined, vigilant,
and active ; he added to a reputation established by
long service the universal esteem and respect of the
whole army, as an officer, whose experience and observation were equal to his personal bravery, and the
rigid discipline which he maintained among the troops.
Captain (now general) Champaigne, who commanded
the Royal Welch Fuzileers, also evinced the most perfect
intrepidity and valor. Thus far I speak, not from the

report of others, but from my own immediate observation

In all the various engagements, which the safety,
the honor, the interests of the empire have demanded,
the Irish soldier, has seldom, if ever, lagged behind
n the career of glory On the present occasion, lord
Rawdon was so well pleased with the conduct of his
regiment (the volunteers of Ireland) that he ordered a
silver medal to be struck off, and presented to several
of his men who had signalized themselves in the action

The author cannot conclude the account of this day's
victory, without entreating pardon from the reader,
while he remarks that three years (excepting two months
and a day) had elapsed since he was made prisoner
at Saratoga by general Gates ! He had at length, the
satisfaction of seeing the same general to whom his
majesty's forces, under Burgoyne surrendered, sustain
a signal defeat. What were his feelings at that eventful moment ! How did he bless that Providence which
inspired him with the idea of effecting his escape, and
preserved him to be a partaker of that triumph which
the soldier feels, when his sovereign's troops are victorious over his enemies ! More especially when that
victory was obtained in the hard fought field over a
general whose former success at Saratoga, had been
trumpeted from one end of America to the other, and
who had injured the British name, by charging the
officers and privates with depredations that never existed but in his own imagination.

The river Waterce ran near the scene of action,
on the other side of which the famous American
flying general Sumpter was posted. On the news
of the defeat he immediately shifted his situation,
picking up in his retreat a number of the fugitives
from Gates's army Lieutenant colonel Tarleton, whose

exertions in the late action were deserving the highest
praise was detached with some cavalry and light infantry, in the whole about 350, to attack him. With
great exertion and military skill, by forced marches,
he surprised the party at mid-day on fishing Creek,
near Catawba fords. The greater part was destroyed,
or taken, and the small remainder dispersed ; one
hundred and fifty were killed, two pieces of brass cannon, three hundred prisoners and forty-four waggons
were immediately in possession of the British.

The remainder of Gates's army rendezvouzed at
Charlotte, from whence they retreated to Salisbury.
This retreat presented perhaps the most lamentable
spectacle of misery and wretchedness, exhibited during
the war.

In addition to the incursions of Sumpter and Morgan, colonel Clarke made an ineffectual attempt on
the post of Augusta in Georgia. This induced lord
Cornwallis to detach major Ferguson, with some militia, and the small remains of his own corps, without
baggage or artillery, to Tyson County, under the idea
of intercepting Clarke's party. They pursued the
track along the mountains, far distant from the main
army. A select body of the American troops, about
one thousand of their best men, mounted on fleet
horses, attacked the major on the top of King's Mountain, on the confines of the Carolinas. They formed
three parties ; colonel Lacy, of South Carolina, led
on, and attacked the west end. The two others were
commanded by colonels Campbell and Cleveland ; one
of which attacked on the east, and the other in the
centre. Major Ferguson, with great boldness, defended
himself with fixed bayonets, and compelled them successively to retreat. They formed again, and getting
behind trees and rocks renewed their fire in almost
every direction. The American marksmen took deli-

berate aim at our uncovered men, and numbers were found among the slain, shot through the head Ramsey, in his account of the battle acknowledges, that " rifflemen took off rifflemen with such exactness, that they killed each other when taking sight, so instantaneously that their eyes remained, after they were dead, one shut and the other open, in the usual manner of marksmen when levelling at their object "

Major Ferguson shewed all possible bravery, but' his valiant spirit disdained either to flee or surrender After a severe contest, he received a mortal wound, nobly fell, and the submission of the survivors, eight hundred in number, terminated the carnage one hundred and fifty were killed or wounded , and ten of the refugees who surrendered, were inhumanly banged by the conquerors.

The fall of major Ferguson was in itself a great loss to our army He possessed superior abilities as a soldier, and his spirit of enterprise was uncommon. To a distinguished capacity of planning great designs, he also added the practical abilities necessary to carry them into execution. The advantage which the Americans gained over him' and his party in a great degree frustrated a well concerted scheme for strengthening our army, by the co-operation of the well affected inhabitants, whom he had undertaken to discipline and prepare for active service

' The military science possessed by major Ferguson was profound, and his adoption of it to the use of the smaller arms more correct than any other officer who preceded him. His execution in firing was such that it almost exceeded the bounds of credibility , he very nearly brought his aim at any given object to a mathematical certainty On the 1st of June 1776, he made some experiments at Woolwich, before lord' viscount Townshend, lord Amherst, general 'Harvey,

Deragliers, and several other officers, with the riffle gun, on a new construction, which astonished all beholders. The like had never before been done with any other small arms. Notwithstanding a heavy rain and a high wind, he fired, during the space of four or five minutes (after the rate of four shots per minute) at a target two hundred yards distance. He next fired six shots in one minute. He also fired, (while advancing after the rate of four miles per hour) four times in the minute. He then poured a bottle of water into the pan and barrel of the piece when loaded, so as to wet every grain of the powder; and in less than half a minute, he fired with her, as well as ever, without extracting the ball. Lastly, he hit the bull's eye, lying on his back on the ground. Incredible as it may seem, to many, considering the variations of the wind, and the wetness of the weather, he only missed the target three times, during the whole course of the experiment. A patent was afterwards granted him for all his improvements. It passed the great seal on the 4th of December following.

Sumpter, soon after the dispertion of his troops, found means to collect a large body of volunteers, with whom he carried on from time to time, a kind of skirmishing warfare. He took his chief positions about Evorce, Broad and Tyger rivers, and was a sore annoyance to the British. He was at last attacked at Black Stocks, near Tyger River, by lieutenant colonel Tarleton, and defeated; three American colonels were killed, and Sumpter himself dangerously wounded. The enemy lost one hundred and twenty, and the British only fifteen men. Lieutenant Skinner, of the 16th regiment of infantry, who did duty with colonel Tarleton's legion greatly distinguished himself on this occasion. Lieutenants Gibson and Caope, of the 63d, were killed, and lieutenant Money, a most promising young officer, aid de camp to lord Cornwallis, died of his wounds a few days after.

During the remaining part of the year, general Gates was preparing to take the field He collected a large force at Hillsborough, and advanced to Char-lotte. Congress, however, *resolved to suspend him, and ordered a court of inquiry into his conduct. So much for the gratitude of a republican government The people of Virginia, however, did not so soon forget Saratoga, and when he was at Richmond they complimented him with a very handsome address, replete with 'expressions of the deepest confidence

Such was the issue of this campaign The minds of the Americans were totally alienated from the British government, and to keep them under subjection when conquered, was an enormous expense to the parent country The struggle had almost exhausted the resources of America ; but the cause of Great Britain had not in the least point been forwarded.

CHAP. XV.

Northern Campaign. Incursions into the Jersey's.
French Fleet, under Termoy, arrives at Rhode-
Island. Blocked up by Admiral Arbuthnot. Sir
Henry Clinton returns from Charlestown. General
Arnold's defection. Major Andre's capture. His
Trial. Letters between Sir Henry Clinton and
General Washington. Interview between Colonel
Robinson and General Greene. Major Andre's Let-
ters to Washington, General Clinton, &c. Major
Andre's Death. His Character. Epitaph, &c.

THE northern campaigns of 1780, commenced with
unfavorable auspices on the part of America. Their
army was in great want of clothing; and, when with
the co-operation of France, they fondly expected to
strike an important blow by the capture of New York,
admiral Gucher sailed back to Europe, and left their
most favorite schemes in a broken disjointed state.
Their principal force lay in the strong holds of the
Highlands, on the other side of the North River.

During the summer the British troops made frequent
incursions into the Jerseys, and an unsuccessful attempt
was made by general Knyphausen, with seven thousand
men, to surprise the advanced posts of Washington's
army.

On the 11th of July, 1780, a French fleet of seven
ships of the line, and four frigates, besides armed
vessels and transports, commanded by the chevalier de
Termoy, arrived at Rhode-Island,* with five regiments
of troops, and a battalion of artillery, under the count
de Rochambeau

The arrival of the French troops produced a remarkable circumstance in Washington's camp Hitherto
the Americans had worn blue cockades, but their general now ordered them to wear blue and white inter
mixed, to denote the alliance of the French and American nations.

Admiral Arbuthnot now proceeded with the British
fleet from New York to Rhode-Island, and so completely blocked up the French fleet and army, as to
prevent their co-operation with the Americans.

In the mean time Sir Henry Clinton returned with
his victorious army, from Charlestown.

A circumstance now claims attention, which, if it had
been successful on the part of the British, most probably would have decided the American contest for
ever. This was the defection of the celebrated American
commander, general Arnold.

On the high ground of North River Banks, stood
that Gibraltar of America, West Point. It was built
by the Americans after the loss of Fort Montgomery,
for the defence of the North River, and was deemed
the most proper for commanding its navigation. Rocky
ridges rising behind one another, rendered it incapable
of being invested by less than twenty thousand men
This was the strongest post the Americans had ; the
thoroughfare of communication between the Eastern
and southern states; and was the repository of their

* The British troops had sometime before evacuated the
Island

most valuable stores; the loss of it would have been severely felt. Of this important fortress general Arnold had the command. He was a native of Connecticut, a state remarkable for the republican principles of its inhabitants. He was among the first who took up arms against the parent country. "His distinguished military talents," says Ramsay, his mortal enemy, "had procured him many honors from the state; poets and painters had marked him as a suitable subject, for the display of their respective abilities. He possessed an elevated seat in the hearts of his countrymen, and was for some time in the full enjoyment of substantial fame."

Perhaps the real motive in which Arnold's conduct originated, will never be clearly ascertained. If we may credit himself, his conduct was the result of reflection, conviction, principle; if we give credit to Ramsay and the other republican writers, "he betrayed the American cause for a stipulated sum of money." But this assertion has never been fairly proved.

General Arnold's own declarations are tolerably explicit. He says, "that when he first engaged in the contest between Great Britain and her colonies, he conceived the rights of his country to be in danger, and that duty and honor called him to her defence: a redress of grievances was his only aim and object. He however acquiesced in the declaration of independence, although he thought it precipitate. But the reasons that were then offered to justify that measure, no longer could exist, when Great Britain with the open arms of a parent, offered to embrace the Americans as children and to grant the wished for—redress. From the refusal of these proposals, and the ratification of the French alliance all his ideas of the justice and policy of the war were totally changed, and from that time he had become a professed loyalist. In these

principles he had only retained his arms and command,
for an opportunity to surrender them to Great Britain."

On the contrary, the Americans declared that his
country had loaded him with honors and forgiven
him crimes; that though he was brave, yet he was
mercenary, fond of parade and extremely desirous of acquiring money to defray the expenses of it, that when he
entered Philadelphia after the evacuation of the British,
he made governor Penn's, the best house in it, his head
quarters, this he furnished in a very costly manner,
and lived in a stile far beyond his income. That he
continued this extravagant course of living during his
stay in Philadelphia, that the generosity of the states
was not able to keep pace with the extravagance of
their favourite officer. That about July, 1779, he exhibited heavy accounts and demands against the public,
that the commissioners upon examination, rejected about
one half of the amount. That he then appealed to
congress, and a committee was appointed, who were
of opinion, that the commissioners had allowed more
than the general had a right to expect or demand:
that this provoked him to outrageous proceedings.
Disgusted at the treatment he had met with, embarrassed
in his circumstances, and having a growing and expensive
family, he turned his thoughts toward bettering his
fortune by a change of sides, which afforded the only
hope of evading a scrutiny, and at the same time held
out a prospect of replenishing his exhausted coffers.

In what precise manner the negociation was first
opened between Arnold and Sir Henry Clinton has never
been revealed. One thing, however, the author can
report from the most authentic source of information,
that the unfortunate major Andre, who fell the devoted
victim to it, was a *volunteer* in the business. He was
neither commanded nor solicited by Sir Henry Clinton to
undertake it

In the year 1779, major Andre commenced a correspondence with Mrs Arnold, under the pretence of supplying her,' " says Ramsay with millinery," (a strange kind of service for a British officer ') It was asserted and believed by many, that this correspondence was continued and improved by general Arnold without the lady's being at all 'aware of the designs in which he was engaged But this was never satisfactorily proved And after all, for various reasons that might be assigned, it is highly 'probable that the manner in which this negociation 'commenced will for ever remain unknown.

To facilitate the intercourse between general Arnold and the British commander, the Vulture sloop of war had been previously stationed in the North River. It should likewise be mentioned that letters had passed, by several conveyances, between general Arnold and major Andre, under the fictitious signatures of Gustavus and Anderson The negociation was in some state of forwardness when a personal interview was thought 'necessary' For this purpose, a boat was sent by Arnold to the Vulture to fetch colonel Beverley' Robinson, 'who was the person appointed to negociate with him Colonel Robinson was ill in his birth when Mr Smith* arrived with the boat, and major Andre *volunteered* to go in his stead Mr Smith having recently published a narrative of the whole transaction (and his authority being that on which reliance can be placed) this important event may perhaps be best narrated in his own words. " Colonel Robinson pleaded indisposition, and said Mr Anderson (major Andre) could as effectually answer all the purposes by going on shore as himself, there seemed no reluctance on the part of Anderson to supply colonel Robinson's place, and he appeared in a dress equip-

* Brother to the chief justice of New York'

ped for the purpose, wearing boots and a large blue
great coat.

" Mr. Anderson being ready, we left the ship, and
were rowed in a short time to the western shore, to
the place which general Arnold had appointed for the
interview , this was at the foot of a mountain called
the Long Clove, near the low water mark, whither
my servant had conducted general Arnold on horseback, he being still lame from his wounds.

" On my approach to the place of appointment, I
found general Arnold ready to receive me , *he was
hid among firs.* I mentioned to him colonel Beverley
Robinson's reason for not accompanying me, and the
delegation of a young gentleman, a Mr. Anderson,
whom I had brought with me, and who was then
with the watermen on the strand He appeared much
agitated, and expressed chagrin at the disappointment of not seeing colonel Robinson. He desired
me, however, to conduct Mr Anderson to him,
which being done, he requested me to remain with
the hands at the boat I went as directed, but felt
greatly mortified at not being present at the interview,
to which I conceived myself entitled from my rank
in life, and the trouble I had taken to effect the
meeting. At length they continued such a time in
conference, that I deemed it expedient to inform them
of the approaching dawn of day. Shortly afterwards
both came down to the boat, and general Arnold,
with much earnestness, solicited me to return with
Mr. Anderson to the Vulture , but I pointed out
the impracticibility of effecting his wish, from the
great distance, and the fatigue of the hands. He
then applied to the men, who declared themselves unable to gratify his wish, through want of strength to
accomplish it, and the ebb tide being against them
Convinced of the apparent impracticibility of the at-

tempt to reach the ship, and return before day without being discovered from either shores by the inhabitants, whose eyes were constantly watching the movements on the water, not only from the forts, but the
surrounding shores, he relinquished his solicitations,
and desired I would endeavour to return the boat to
the place from whence we first embarked ; this, with
much labour, and taking the circuit of the eddies,
was nearly effected, (as we left the boat at Crane's
Island) when our attention was called to the cannonade from Gallows Point against the Vulture, which
was compelled to fall down the river, and appeared
to be set on fire ; colonel Livingston, however, must
have been totally unacquainted with general Arnold's
designs, or he never would have fired at that time
upon the ship.

" On my return home, I found that general Arnold
and Mr. Anderson had arrived long before, Mr. Anderson having mounted the horse my servant had rode,
when he followed general Arnold to the Long Clove,
the place of Anderson's landing. He appeared vexed
that the ship had been compelled to leave her position. General Arnold and Mr. Anderson were left
alone the far greater part of the day. Toward the
evening Arnold came to my house, and proposed
that I should convey Mr. Anderson back to the Vulture,
which had nearly regained her former situation. With
a fit of the ague upon me, I was unable to gratify
him ; on which he proposed my accompanying him
part of the way on his return to New York by land,
as soon as my health would permit, to which I made
no objection. He soon after returned, and told me
a difficulty had occurred, of which he was not before
apprised ; for that Anderson had come on shore in a
military dress, which he had borrowed, from pride

S 2

or vanity, from an officer of his own acquaintance at
New York, that it would be impossible for him to
travel in that uniform, he requested the loan of one
of my coats   Being nearly of my size, I lent him
a coat: the other part of his dress, he said, did not
require change. General Arnold then proposed returning
to his command at West Point, leaving Mr. Anderson
very disconsolate with me, he cast an anxious look
towards the Vulture, and with a heavy sigh wished
he was on board   I endeavored to console him by the
hope of his being at the White Plains, or New York,
before her. Finding myself better I promised to accompany him on his way   I could not help remarking
to him, that I thought the general might have ordered
a flag of truce from Stony Point, to have returned
him to the Vulture, without the fatigue of his going
to the White Plains, that appearing to me a circuitous route, unless he had business to transact at that
place of a public nature   From this time he seemed
shy, and desirous to avoid much conversation, he
continued to urge preparations for his departure, and
carefully avoided being seen by persons that came to
the house

"General Arnold had prepared a passport for him
to go to the White Plains, and a flag of truce for
me to go thither and return. We reached the ferry
at Stoney Point before it was dark, intending to proceed as far as major De La Van's that night, we rode
on with an increased speed, and had reached it about
five or six when we were challenged by a patrole
party. On advancing, the commanding officer, a captain Bull, demanded a countersign before we should
pass, and drew his corps about us, he inquired who
we were, the reason of our travelling in the night,
and from whence we came? I told him who I was,
and that we had passports from general Arnold, the

commanding officer at West Point, which we had
received from the general that day ; that we were on
public service, on business of the highest import, and
that he would be answerable for our detention one
moment ; he insisted on seeing the passports, and
conducted us to a house in the vicinity where there was
a light, on approaching the house Mr. Anderson
seemed very uneasy ; but I cheered him by saying
our papers would carry us to any part of the country
to which they were directed, and that no person
dare presume to detain us. When we came to the
light, I presented the passports, which satisfied the
captain.

"With no small difficulty we gained admittance into
a house for the night, while such was the caution
and danger of admitting nocturnal inmates, that we
were obliged to take to bed or keep the family up,
who would not retire until they saw us safely lodged.
We slept in the same bed ; and I was often disturbed
with the restless motions, and uneasiness of mind exhibited by my bedfellow, who, on observing the first
approach of day, summoned my servant to prepare
the horses for our departure. He appeared in the
morning as if he had not slept an hour during the
night ; he at first was much dejected, but a pleasing
change took place in his countenance when summoned
to mount his horse.

"We rode very cheerfully towards Pine's Bridge
without interruption, or any event that excited apprehension ; here I proposed to leave my companion ;
but I observed that the nearer we approached the
bridge, the more his countenance brightened into a
cheerful serenity, and he became very affable ; in
short, I now found him highly entertaining ; he was
not only well informed in general history, but well

acquainted with that of America, particularly of New
York, which he termed the residuary legatee of the
British government (for it took all the remaining
lands not granted to the proprietary and chartered
provinces.) He had consulted the muses as well as
Mars, for he conversed freely on the belles lettres,
music, painting, and poetry, seemed to be his delight.
He displayed a judicious taste in the choice of the
authors he had read, possessed great elegance of
sentiments, and a most pleasing manner of conveying
his ideas, by adopting the flowery coloring of poeti-
cal imagery. He lamented the causes which gave
birth to and continued the war, and said if there
was a correspondent temper on the part of the Americans, with the prevailing spirit of the British ministry, peace was an event not far distant, he intimated that measures were then in agitation for the accomplishment of that desirable object, before France
could establish her perfidious designs. He sincerely
wished the fate of the war could alone be determined
in the fair, open, field-contest, between as many
British in number as those under the command of
count Rochambeau at Rhode Island, whose effective
force he seemed clearly to understand ; he descanted
on the richness of the scenery around us, and particularly admired from every eminence, the grandeur
of the Highland mountains, bathing their lofty sum-
mits in the clouds from their seeming watery base
at the north extremity of Haverstraw Bay. The
pleasantry of converse, and mildness of the weather,
so insensibly beguiled the time, that we at length
found ourselves at the bridge before I thought we
had got half the way ; and I now had reason to
think my fellow traveller a different person from the
character I had at first formed of him

This bridge crosses Croton River, a branch of the Hudson; here we halted, and I mentioned my determination to proceed no farther. Having discharged the bill to the woman, in the local money of the country, my companion requested me to lend him some, and I cheerfully supplied him with the half of my pocket amount, although I was afraid it was not current below that place; the bridge being accounted the south boundary of the American lines. He was affected at parting, and offered me a valuable gold watch in remembrance of him, as a keepsake, which I refused."

The passport given the major by general Arnold particularly mentioned "to go 'to lines of White Plains, or lower, if he thought proper, he being on public business." When he had passed the American lines and thought himself out of danger, he was stopped by three of the New York militia, who with others were on a scouting party between the outposts of the two armies. What strange infatuation seized the major, not to produce his pass, defies all conjecture: had he done so, this would have let him pass; or, if they had proved British scouts, they would only have conducted him where he wanted to go, to the royal lines. On the contrary, he imprudently asked the man who stopped him, "Where he belonged to?" The man answered, "To below," meaning to New York. Thinking himself then perfectly safe, and mistaking them, by this equivocal reply for a party of English, he hastily replied, "So do I," declared himself a British officer, and pressed that he might not be detained, as he was on urgent business. He was soon convinced of his mistake, by the party proceeding to search him. Papers, in general Arnold's hand writing, were discovered in his boots, which contained exact returns of the state of the forces,

ordnance, and defences at West Point, with the artillery orders, critical remarks on the works, &c. The
major offered them his purse and gold watch, if they
would let him pass, which they refused, and delivered him a prisoner to lieutenant colonel Jameson,
who commanded the scouting parties.

When major Andre appeared before him it was
under the name of Anderson, which he supported,
choosing to hazard the greatest danger, rather than
let any discovery be made which could involve Arnold, before he had time to provide for his safety.
With a view to the general's escaping, he requested
that a line might be sent to acquaint him of Anderson's detention, which Jameson granted. General
Arnold on the receipt of this letter abandoned every
thing. He immediately seized the messenger's horse and
instantly proceeded down a precipice, almost perpendicular, to the river where boats were always ready
to pass to and from West Point. He sprang into one,
and directed the hands to row him down the river
and make for the Vulture, but he had scarcely
passed Stoney and Verplanks Point, when colonel
Hamilton arrived at the latter, with orders to stop
him, for by the time general Washington had searched
the house, the packet from Jameson arrived.

Colonel Jameson forwarded to general Washington
all the papers found on major Andre, together with
a letter, of which the following is a correct copy.
Here he manfully assumed his character, bursting
with a noble dignity from that false appearance, which
the safety of general Arnold alone had caused him
to assume. This was the only point on which the
board of American officers could at all criminate him
as a spy thus he generously sacrificed his own life
to the preservation of general Arnold's.

" Sir—What I have as yet said concerning myself, was in the justifiable attempt to be extricated ; I am too little accustomed to duplicity to have succeded.

" I beg your excellency to be persuaded, that no alteration in the temper of my mind, or apprehension for my safety, induces me to the step of addressing you, but that it is to secure myself from an imputation of having assumed a mean character for treacherous purposes or self interest ; a conduct incompatible with the principles that actuated me, as well as with my condition in life.

" It is to vindicate my fame I speak, and not to solicit security.

" The person in your possession is major .Andre, adjutant general of the British army.

" The influence of one commander, in the army of his adversary, is an advantage taken in war. A correspondence for this purpose I held as confidential (in the present instance,) with his excellency Sir Henry Clinton.

" To favor it, I agreed to meet, upon ground not within the posts of either army, a person who was to give me intelligence ; I came up in the Vulture sloop of war for this effect, and was fetched by the boat from the ship to the beach ; being there I was told the approach of day would prevent my return, and that I must be concealed until the next night. I was in my regimentals, and had fairly risked my person.

" Against my stipulation, my intentions, and without my knowledge before hand, I was conducted within one of your posts. Your excellency may conceive my sentiments on this occasion, and will imagine how much more I must have been affected by a refusal to reconduct me back the next night as I had been brought ; thus become a prisoner, I had to concert my escape. .I quitted my uniform, and was passed another way in the night, without the American posts, to neutral ground; and being informed I was out of the reach of all armed parties, and left to proceed for New York, I was taken at Fairy Town by some volunteers.

" Thus as I have had to relate, I was betrayed (being adjutant general of the British army) into the vile condition of an enemy within your posts.

" Having avowed myself a British officer, I know nothing to reveal but what relates to myself, which is true on the honor of an officer and a gentleman.

" The request I have to make to your excellency, and I am conscious I address myself well, is, that in any rigor, policy may dictate, a decency of conduct towards me may mark that, though unfortunate, I am branded with nothing dishonorable, as no motive could be mine, but the service of my king, and as I was involuntarily an impostor

" Another request is, that I may be permitted to write an open letter to Sir Henry Clinton, and another to a friend for clothes and linen.

" I take the liberty to mention the condition of some gentlemen in Charlestown, who being either on parole, or under protection, were engaged in a conspiracy against us, though their situation is not similar, they are objects who may be sent in exchange for me, or are persons, whom the treatment I receive, may in some degree affect

" It is no less, Sir, a confidence in the generosity of your mind, than on account of your superior station, that I have chosen to importune you with this letter

I have the honor to be, with the greatest respect,

Sir, your excellency's most obedient,

And most humble servant,

JOHN ANDRE, Adj Gen.

" His Excellency, George Washington, &c. &c."

Major Andre had been removed under a strong escort to Tappan or Orangetown, when general Wash_ington referred his whole case to the examination and decision of fourteen general officers, (of whom were the marquis De La Fayette and baron De Steubin) with the assistance of the judge advocate, general Lawrence. Major Andre disdaining all sub_terfuge and evasion, and studying to place his character in so fair a light, as might prevent its being shaded by the present circumstances, voluntarily confessed every thing that related to himself, while he concealed with the most scrupulous nicety whatever might involve others. Being interrogated by the board with respect to his conception of coming on shore, under the sanc_tion of a flag, he said with a noble frankness of mind, that if he had, he might certainly have returned under it. The board was exceedingly struck with his candor and magnanimity. They did not examine a single witness, but founded their report merely upon his own confession. In this they stated the following facts: "That major Andre came on shore on the night of the 21st of September in a private and secret manner; that he changed his dress within the American lines; that under a feigned name, and a disguised habit, he was taken on his way to New York, and when taken, several papers were found in his possession, which con_tained intelligence for the enemy." - That major Andre, "ought to be considered as a spy, and that agree_able to the laws and usages of nations he ought to suffer death."

It may be naturally imagined that the British officers were indefatigable in their exertions to save major Andre from his impending fate. Sir Henry Clinton and lieutenant general Robertson wrote letters, in which every suggestion and entreaty were used to

T t

general Washington on the subject, but in vain General Arnold went so far as to take the whole guilt of the transaction on himself He urged, that every thing done by major Andre was transacted at his particular request, and at a time when he was acknowledged commanding officer in the department He contended, " that he had a right to transact all those matters, for which, though wrong, major Andre ought not to suffer death "

An interview also took place between general Robertson on the part of the British, and general Greene on the part of the Americans Every thing was urged by the former that ingenuity or humanity could suggest for averting the proposed execution, Greene made a proposal for delivering up Arnold instead of Andre, but found this could not be acceded to by the British, without offending against every principle of honor and policy, general Robertson urged " that Andre went on shore under the sanction of a flag, and that being in Arnold's power, he was not accountable for the subsequent actions, which were said to be compulsory " To this it was replied that " he was employed in the execution of measures very foreign to the object of flags of truce, and such as they were never meant to authorize or to countenance, and that major Andre in the course of his examination had candidly confessed, that it was impossible for him to suppose that he came on shore under the sanction of a flag " As Greene and Robertson differed so widely in both their statements of facts, and the interference they drew from them, the latter proposed to the former that the opinion of disinterested military gentlemen might be taken on the subject, and generals Knyphausen and Rochambeau were mentioned ; general Robertson also urged that Andre possessed a great share of Sir Henry Clinton's esteem, and hinted, as his last resourse that he would be infinitely obliged if he should be spared. He offered that in case Andre should be permitted to return with him, to New York, any person whatever, that might be named, should be set at libery. All these argnments and entreaties having failed, Robertson presented a long letter from Arnold, in which he endeavored to exculpate Andre, by acknowledging himself the author of every part of his conduct, " that he had particularly insisted on his coming from the Vulture under a flag which he had sent for that purpose.' He declared that if, Andre suffered, he should think himself bound to retaliate. He also observed " that forty of the principal inhabitants of South Carolina had justly forfeited their lives, which had hitherto been spared only through the clemency of Sir Henry Clinton, who would no longer extend mercy if major Andre suffered ; an event which would probably open a scene of bloodshed, at which humanity must revolt." He entreated Washington by his own honor, and for the sake of humanity, not to suffer an unjust sentence to touch the life of Andre, but if that warning should be disregarded, and Andre suffer, he called " heaven, and earth to witness that he alone would be justly answerable for the torrents of blood which might be spilt in consequence." ſ

Indeed every exertion was made by our commanders to save. Andre, but without effect ; it was urged, on the contrary, that the general opinion of the American army, was, that his life was forfeited, and that national dignity and sound policy required that the forfeiture should be exacted.

General Greene was originally a Quaker, a stern republican, and such was the rancor displayed throughout the whole transaction, both by him and the marquis De La Fayette that they may almost literally be said to have thirsted for the blood of the unfortunate victim whom fate had put in their power

Here again I am compelled to notice the misrepresentation and detect the falsehood of the account given by Belsham. 'He says the unfortunate Andre " was apprehended in disguise, *and with a false passport.*" True the major was apprehended in disguise, but his passport was *not a false one* It was signed by the commanding officer of the American district from whence he came Was the signature " ARNOLD," a forgery ? It was a true passport on the part of major Andre, and general Arnold who signed it alone was accountable to the American government for it But this is Belsham's constant practice, by coupling a truth with a falshood, (as the Jews vend a damaged article with a sound one) they both pass muster with the great mass of mankind, until a critical examination detects the fraud. The same writer tells us, with an air of triumph, that the major " suffered death in that degrading mode which gives the brave, the keenest' wound, notwithstanding the urgent solicitations and *the impotent, injudicious menaces* of Sir Henry Clinton " What injudicious menace escaped from Sir Henry Clinton during the whole unfortunate negociation ? His letter to general Washington is a master piece of prudence, of humanity, of temperate, energetic remonstrance, conjoined with manly dignity I have not the vanity to suppose myself capable of determining the merits of the great body of historians, but certainly, if I may be permitted to give an opinion on those who have published the American transactions, Mr. Belsham is of all the most artful and dangerous His misrepresentations are of deep design, and his false colorings are laid on with so much adroitness, that it is no easy matter completely to detect him But on some points I think he has been sufficiently unmasked

I introduce here a quotation from Smith, which places Sir Henry Clinton's character in the most amiable point of view.

" The noble humanity in his breast, which at the moment when every agonized feeling must have been wounded to its greatest height, alone prevented him from making that sacrifice which the laws of arms and the manes of the murdered Andre seemed almost imperiously to require at his hands.

" The Greyhound schooner, flag of truce which brought general Robertson's last letter to general Washington, dated on board the schooner on the 2d of October, the day major Andre suffered, carried to New York the melancholy account of that event.

" No language can describe the mingled sensations of horror, grief, sympathy, and revenge, that agitated the whole garrison ; a silent gloom overspread the general countenance ; the whole royal army, and citizens of the first distinction, went into mourning. Sir Henry Clinton (although stung with the deepest sorrow for the loss of so valuable an officer,) who best knew how to appreciate his merits, could not indulge a spirit of resentment, in exercising the dictates of passion or policy, by a retaliation on a number of Carolina prisoners, of the first distinction, who had forfeited their lives agreeable to the usage of war. In almost every instance, where humanity could be exercised, the lenity of Sir Henry Clinton was eminently conspicuous, both in civil and military matters."

It is to be regretted, that, we have benefitted so little by so great a literary genius as major Andre was. The following letters (which are extracted from Smith's Narrative) prove him to have been a young man of very considerable intellect.

' Major André to Sir Henry Clinton, dated Tappan,
September 29th

"Sir—Your excellency is doubtless already apprized
of the manner in which I was taken, and possibly of
the serious light in which my conduct is considered,
and the vigorous determination that is impending

"Under these circumstances, I have obtained general Washington's permission to send you this letter,
the object of which is, to remove from your breast
any suspicion, that I could imagine I was bound by
your excellency's orders to expose myself to what has
happened   The events of coming within an enemy's
posts, and of changing my dress, which led me to
my present situation, were contrary to my own intentions, as they were to your orders, and the circuitous
route which I took to return, was imposed (perhaps
unavoidably) without alternative upon me.

"In addressing myself to your excellency on this
occasion, the force of all my obligations to you,
and of the attachment and gratitude I bear you, re-
curs to me..

"With all the warmth of my heart, I give you
thanks for your excellency's profuse kindness to me:
and I send you the most earnest wishes for your welfare, which a faithful, affectionate, and respectful attention can frame.

"I have a mother and three sisters, to whom the
value of my commission would be an object, as the
loss of Grenada, has much affected their income   It is
needless to be more explicit on this subject, I am
persuaded of your excellency's goodness, &c &c

          I have the honor to be, &c
          JOHN ANDRE, Adj Gen "

On October the 2d, the tragedy was closed   The
major was superior to the terrors of death   but the

disgraceful, mode of dying which the usage of war had annexed to his unhappy situation, was infinitely dreadful to him: he was desirous to be indulged with a death worthy of his profession; and accordingly he wrote the day before, the following letter to general Washington:

" Sir—Buoy'd above the terror of death, by the consciousness of a life devoted to honorable pursuits, and stained with no action that can give me remorse, I trust that the request I make to your excellency at this serious period, and which is to soften my last moments, will not be rejected.

" Sympathy towards a soldier will surely induce your excellency, and a military tribunal, to adopt the mode of my death to the feelings of a man of honor.

" Let me hope, Sir, that if aught in my character impresses you with esteem towards me, if aught in my misfortunes marks me as the victim of policy, and not of resentment, I shall experience the operation of these feelings in your breast, by being informed that I am not to die on a gibbet.

I have the honor to be, &c.

JOHN ANDRE, Adj. Gen."

" General Washington consulted his officers upon the subject. Pity and esteem wrought so powerfully, that they were all for shooting him, till Greene insisted on it that his crime was that of a common spy, that the public good required his being hanged, and that if he was shot the public would think there were favorable circumstances entitling him to notice and lenity. His observations had their desired effect, and they resolved that there would be an impropriety in granting the major's request; but his delicacy was saved from the pain of receiving a negative answer. The guard which attended him in his confinement marched with him to the place of execution. The way, over

which he passed, was crouded on all sides with anxious
spectators, as he went along between two officers of
his guard, his arms being locked in theirs, he bowed
himself familiarly to all those with whom he had been
acquainted in his confinement. A smile of compla-
cency expressed the serene fortitude of his mind
Upon seeing the preparations on the fatal spot, he
asked with some degree of concern, " Must I die in
this manner?" He was told it was unavoidable He
replied, " I am reconciled to my fate, but not to
the mode " Soon after recollecting himself, he added,
" It will be but a momentary pang " He ascended
the cart with a pleasing countenance, performed the
last offices to himself, with a composure which excited the admiration of all the spectators." Being told
the final moment was at hand, and asked if he had
any thing more to say, " nothing but to request
that you will witness to the world *that I die like a brave
man* " He died universally esteemed and regretted.
The sympathy he had excited in the American army
was perhaps unexampled, under any similar circumstances Numbers condemned, very few justified,
but all regretted the fatal sentence which put an end to
his valuable life.

" He was a young officer of great abilities, and of
uncommon merit. Nature had bestowed on him an
elegant taste for literature and the fine arts, which by
industrious cultivation he had greatly improved He
possessed many amiable qualities, and very great ac-
complishments. His fidelity together with his place
and character, eminently fitted him for the negociation with Arnold, but his high ideas of candour, and
his abhorrence of dishonorable conduct, made him
inexpert in practicing those arts of deception which
it required. It may not be improper to add, that our
gracious sovereign, who never suffers any public service

to pass unrewarded, has caused an elegant monument to be erected in Westminster Abbey, which, with the historic page both of England and America will perpetuate the virtue and gallantry of major Andre, through ages yet unknown.

Description of the Monument in Westminster Abbey, for MAJOR JOHN ANDRE, *designed by Robert Adam, Esq. Architect, and executed in siatuary marble, by Mr. P. M. Van Gelder.*

This monument is composed of a sarcophagus, elevated on a pedestal, upon the pannel of which is engraved the following inscription:

SACRED TO THE MEMORY
of
MAJOR JOHN ANDRE,
Who, raised by his Merit, at an early Period
of his Life, to the Rank of
ADJUTANT-GENERAL OF THE BRITISH FORCES
IN AMERICA,
and, employed in an important but hazardous Enterprise,
FELL A SACRIFICE
to his
Zeal for his King and Country,
on the 2d of October, 1780, aged 29,
universally beloved and esteemed by the Army
in which he served, and lamented even
by his Foes.
His gracious Sovereign
KING GEORGE III.
has caused this Monument to be erected.

The following description of the characters on the sarcophagus, and remarks on the lamented catastrophe are copied from Smith's Narrative.

" On the front of the sarcophagus, general Washington is represented in his tent, at the moment

U u

when he had received the report of the court martial
held on major Andre, at the same time a flag of truce
arrived from the British army, with a letter for general
Washington to treat for the major's life But the
fatal sentence being already passed, the flag was sent
back without the hoped-for clemency in his favor

" Major Andre received his condemnation with that
fortitude and resolution which had always marked his
character, and is represented going with unshaken
spirit to meet his doom

" On the top of the sarcophagus, a figure of
Britannia reclined, laments the premature fate of so
gallant an officer The British Lion too, seems in-
stinctively to mourn his untimely death

" Ancient or modern history does not exhibit an
instance, where an officer fell so universally lamented
by adversaries and friends; an irrefragable proof of
unsullied honor, and superior merit

" Eulogy cannot do sufficient justice to the deserts
of this rarely accomplished hero, and it must be
some consolation to his surviving friends, that his
and their foes drop the tear of sympathy, and min-
gle their sorrows at the same shrine, made sacred to
virtue and truth "

It has already been noticed, as matter of regret,
that distinguished as major Andre was by literary
talent, so little of his compositions survived him.
The following Poem however the author is enabled to
lay before the reader, from the authority of a respectable person, a native of America, where it is
generally acknowledged to have been the major's
composition. It was written a few days previous to his
execution. Other testimony of its authenticity it is now
impossible to produce, as no British officer was permitted to attend his last moments, console the heroic
sufferer, or receive the dying injunctions of the

man, who fell a martyr to the interests of his coun_
try. But if such report carries with it full conviction
to the author, it will to the mind of the loyal and un_
prejudiced reader, and as for those who were instrumental in robbing the major of life, or who *can* approve
the deed, it would be a waste of words to attempt
the removal of their doubts. Under these circum_
stances, to have suppressed it altogether would have
been criminal, and on this authority it is inserted,
leaving the reader to his own unbiassed judgment
as to its authenticity.

HAIL sovereign love, which first began,
The scheme, to rescue fallen man !
Hail matchless, free, eternal grace,
Which gave my soul a *Hiding Place!*

Against the God who built the sky.
I fought with hands uplifted high,
Despis'd the mention of his grace,
Too proud to seek a *Hiding Place.*

Enwrapt in thick Egyptian night,
And fond of darkness more than light;
Madly I ran the sinful race,
Secure, without a *Hiding Place.*

But thus the eternal council ran,
" Almighty love, arrest that man !"
I felt the arrows of distress,
And found I had no *Hiding Place.*

Indignant justice stood in view,
To Sinai's fiery mount I flew,
But Justice cry'd with frowning face,
This mountain is no *Hiding Place.*

Ere long a heav'nly voice I heard,
And mercy's angel soon appear'd,
He led me in a placid pace,
To Jesus as my *Hiding Place.*

On him Almighty vengeance fell,
Which must have sunk a world to hell,
He bore it for a sinful race,
And thus became their *Hiding Place.*

Should sevenfold storms of thunder roll,
And shake this globe from pole to pole:
No thunder bolt shall daunt my face,
For Jesus is my *Hiding Place*.

A few more rolling suns at most,
Shall land me on fair Canaan's coast,
Where I shall sing the song of grace,
And see my glorious *Hiding Place*.

Major Andre's remains were interred in an open field, belonging to a Mr. Mabie, in the vicinity where he suffered.

The end of the year 1780 was now arriving; winter set in with great severity. The Americans, in addition to the inclemencies of the season, had many hardships to encounter. The three years, for which period the American troops were originally enlisted, being expired; and enraged at the hardships which they had suffered, a spirit of insurrection manifested itself: at first in the troops of the Pennsylvania line, which soon spread to the New Jersey line. The American governors, well acquainted with the grievances endured by the army, wisely redressed them, and passed a general amnesty. The soldiers which were under the immediate command of general Washington also began to betray the most alarming discontent; but actuated by that wisdom for which he was so conspicuous, he remained in his quarters, and by his presence prevented their murmurs from breaking out into absolute resistance.

Mean time the paper currency of the Americans became every hour more and more depreciated. The financial arrangements of the congress, of course fell into the utmost confusion: a general discredit began to prevail, and it was clearly perceived by the most intelligent members of their government, that nothing could possibly preserve their affairs from utter ruin but a foreign loan, and that to a considerable amount. This they attempted with the Dutch, and by means of French influence, in opposition to the stadtholder and the British interest, it was brought into a state of forwardness under the negociation of a Mr. Lee, (formerly an alderman of London, and brother to the American general Lee,) agent for the congress, and John de Neufville, an Amsterdam merchant. This measure, although resorted to at a moment of the most distressing exigence, had been in contemplation ever since the year 1778, at which time the parties first met at Aix-la-Chapelle. It was sanctioned by Van Berkel, grand pensionary of Amsterdam: Provisionary articles were signed by the parties, and copies transmitted to America and Holland. This was all transacted with that secrecy, so consonant to the insidious policy of the Dutch, who negociated in that crafty manner which left them at liberty, according as the affairs of America prospered or failed, to avow or disavow, the treaty to Great Britain.—A remark here must press on the minds of most readers. How strikingly has Providence placed before the world, an awful lesson on national duplicity, by the present humiliation of that money-loving, cunning people, under the French domination!

To ratify this nefarious bargain, Mr. Henry Laurens, the late president of congress, was dispatched from America. He embarked at Philadelphia for Holland, but in the progress of the voyage the vessel was captured by the British, and Laurens, with all his official documents, sent to England; the box which contained the papers was thrown overboard; but a loyal and determined sailor secured it from sinking. The name of the ship which captured Mr. Laurens was the Vestal, commanded by captain Keppel. He was landed in Devonshire, and arrived at the admiralty on the 7th of October, 1780 · On his examination he disclaimed all allegiance to Great Britain, and boldly avowed himself an agent and a subject of the American government

The administration on this occasion, acted with a becoming spirit The papers of Mr Laurens had put them in full possession of the perfidy of the Dutch A memorial was accordingly presented by the British ambassador at the Hague, requiring the states general to disavow the proceedings of the pensionary Van Berkel and his adherents, and demanding their immediate trial and punishment The Dutch, conscious of their guilt, attempted to delay the business, but the English ambassador was finally recalled, and hostilities commenced between the two nations.

Mr. Laurens was committed to the Tower on a charge of high treason, but from circumstances which afterwards arose, never brought to trial

This extraordinary character was of French descent His ancestors fled to America upon the revocation of the edict of Nantz, under Lewis XIV They settled in South Carolina, in the capital of which his father carried on the business of a sadler, for which employment he intended his son. Mr. Laurens was born in the year 1724, his education was very limited, and for some time he followed the business of his father. But, being of an aspiring turn of mind, and eager for the attainment of wealth, he quitted the business of a sadler, and commenced merchant. Remarkable for a rigid punctuality in all his dealings, he established a high character for integrity and attention to business. It is this which does every thing in America for the man of business he became rich, and by degrees respectable He was appointed a provincial colonel in the war with France, and commanded an expedition against the Indians. At the time of passing the stamp act, he was among the friends of government and supported the authority of the parent country. Charlestown at that time be_came the seat of much civil dissention; to avoid taking a part in which he left America and went over to England. Strange to record! it was there that all his principles of loyalty were shaken, and he returned to America a staunch and sturdy republican.

He immediately took part with the American op_positionists, and professed himself a patriot, ready to make any sacrifice in what he termed the common cause, and to defend that cause in every extremity: this was in the year 1775. The Americans at that time were indefatigable in uniting to their side, men of talent, enterprize and integrity. Mr. Laurens possessed the very requisites which they, desired to con_stitute a leading character, and he was accordingly advanced to be president of the provincial congress of Carolina. From that province he was nominated a delegate to the continental congress. There he be_came a distinguished member, and was eventually appointed president of that assembly. The modera_tion, good sense, and ability which he displayed in that office commanded the respect, even of the first men among those, who neither approved his principles, nor wished success to his cause. The importance to America of the Dutch loan, can best be estimated, by the congress sending such a man to transact the busi_ness: his capture by captain Keppel was a sore blow to their interests.

It may be necessary here to rest a moment, and notice the difference in point of humanity between the British government, and the American partizans. With the bleeding wounds of the untimely, and remorse_less fate of major Andre, still fresh on recollection,

the cabinet of St. James paused before they reta-
liated on America, in the person of the late president
of her senate (the highest officer in time of peace,
and in war second to none but the commander in
chief, Washington.) The shade of the murdered
Andre seemed from the grave to cry for vengeance.—
Yet British magnanimity, in the worth of the individual, ameliorated the punishment of the traitor—
and Mr. Laurens, with his friend Turnbull,* deputy
adjutant general of the American forces, suffered
only a partial confinement, for deeds which would
have doomed them to the gibbet, if not to the torture,
under any other state. Surely the sons of many of
the Americans must blush, for the cruel violence of
their fore-fathers in this unhappy contest.

* Mr. Turnbull, son to the governor of Connecticut, and
deputy adjutant general to the American forces, who left
America for France with a major Tyler, and who from thence
came to England, was also apprehended and his papers seized.
Several letters to and from his father and other persons in
America being produced, and his conferences at Paris with
Dr. Franklin fully established, he was committed to the New
Prison, Clerkenwell, about a month after the commitment of
Mr. Laurens to the Tower.

CHAP. XVI.

Southern Campaign under Lord Cornwallis. General
Greene succeeds Gates in the Command of the American
Southern army. Colonel Tarleton defeated at Cowpens.
Lord Cornwallis crosses the Catawba. The Author's
Narrative of that Transaction. . Colonel Webster
joins Lord Cornwallis. They pursue General Morgan.
Junction of the American Armies. General Greene
driven out of North Carolina. Lord Cornwallis's
Proclamation at Hillsborough. General Greene re-
crosses the Dan, and again enters North Carolina:
Lord Cornwallis retires from Hillsborough. Action
of Guilford Court House. British Army arrives at
Wilmington.

QUITTING the affairs of the north, which were conducted by general Clinton, we shall now revert to
events in the south under lord Cornwallis.

The capture of Charlestown, and the reduction of
almost all the whole of South Carolina, naturally inclined
the British commanders to extend their views to the
conquest of North Carolina. The Americans on their part
saw the necessity of reinforcing the southern army;
and general Greene, at the recommendation of Washington, was appointed to its command, which was trans-
ferred to him at Charlotte by general Gates. A
country thinly inhabited, and abounding with swamps,
afforded every advantage to a partizan warfare over a
large and regular army. This system was acted on by
Greene, and accordingly general Morgan, with a nu-

merous detachment was directed to threaten the British
post at Ninety Six, on the western extremity of South
Carolina, the main body under general Greene at the
same time, moving on to north side of Pedee, opposite
Cheraw-Hill

The British army, at that time, had marched two
hundred miles from the sea-coast, and was preparing
for an invasion of North Carolina In order therefore
to drive Morgan from its rear, and deter the inhabitants
from joining his standard, lieutenant colonel Tarleton
with six hundred men (three hundred of which were
cavalry) proceeded against him. The engagement took
place at Cowpens The British, led on by the colonel
himself, advanced, confident of victory, with a shout,
and poured a tremendous · fire on the enemy The
American line gave way, and fled , the British advanced,
and engaged the second. At that critical moment,
colonels Washington and Howard rallied the flying
troops, and, joined by the militia, led them on to the
support of the second line. The British were thrown
into confusion three hundred were killed and wounded;
the whole of the artillery-men (who worked the guns)
that did not share their fate, were taken, with two
three pounders. Colonel Tarleton, with about fifty of
the cavalry, made a last, desperate, but glorious effort:
he charged and repulsed Washington's horse, retook
the baggage of the corps, cut the detachment who had
it in possession to ˈpieces, destroyed the greater part,
and retired with the rest to Hamilton's Ford *

This defeat (particularly the loss of the light infantry)
was a severe loss to the royal camp. The prisoners
were conveyed by forced marches to Richmond , so

---

* In lord Cornwallis's dispatches to government concerning
this engagement, he says, " In justice to the detachment of
the royal artillery, I must here observe, that no terror could
induce them to abandon their guns, and they were all killed
and wounded in the defence of them "

that all attempts of the main army to re-capture them were unavailing. The army halted during two days collecting provisions, and destroying superfluous bag-gage. We then marched through North Carolina, to the banks of the Dan, on the utmost extremities of the province.

On the 1st day of February, at day light in the morning, we were directed to cross M'Cowan's Ford, in order to dislodge a party of the Americans under the command of General Davison, which were strongly posted on the opposite hills. Lord Cornwallis, accord-ing to his usual manner, dashed first into the river, mounted on a very fine spirited horse, the brigade of guards followed, two three pounders next, the Royal Welch Fuzileers after them. Colonel Webster had been previously directed to move with a strong guard divi-sion to Beattie's Ford, six miles above M'Cowan's in order to divide the attention of the Americans.

The place where we forded was about half a mile over. The enemy stood on the hills of the opposite shore, which were high and steep, hanging over the river, so that they had every advantage over us, to facilitate their firing on those who attempted to cross there. Lord Cornwallis's fine horse was wounded under him, but his lordship escaped unhurt. Amidst these dreadful oppositions, we still urged through this rapid stream, striving with every effort to gain the opposite shore; just in the centre of the river, the bombardier who was employed in steering one of the three pounders, unfortunately let go his hold of the helm of the gun, and being a low man, he was forced off his feet, and immediately carried headlong down the river. At that very instant, I was bringing up the division that covered this gun, and encouraging the men to hold fast by one another, and not to be dismayed at the enemy's fire, or from the rapidity or depth of the water, which was at this place more than four feet deep, and very rocky at the bottom. I knew that if this artillery man was either killed or drowned, his loss would be great indeed, as we had no man at hand that could supply his place in working the gun; this consideration darted through my mind in an instant, and I was determined to save his life or perish in the attempt. I therefore quitted my hold of the right hand man of my division, and threw myself on my belly on the surface of the water, and in nine or ten strong strokes, I overtook him. By this time he was almost exhausted, having been carried down the stream heels over head, upwards of forty yards. I got him on his feet, and led him back in safety to his gun. It was very remarkable, and taken particular notice of by the British troops, that during this transaction not one shot was fired at us by the Americans; indeed they might have easily shot us both in the head, as the current of the river carried us very near to them. After this affair the enemy began again a very heavy fire upon us, nevertheless our divisions waded on, in a cool intrepid manner, to return their fire, being impossible, as our cartouch boxes were all tied at the back of our necks. This urged us on with greater rapidity, till we gained the opposite shore, where we were obliged to scramble up a very high hill under, a heavy fire; several of our men were killed and wounded, before we reached the summit. The American soldiers did all that brave men could do, to oppose our passage across the river, and I believe not one of them moved from his post, till we mounted the hill, and used our bayonets; their general was the first man that received us sword in hand, and suffered himself to be cut to pieces sooner than retreat; after his death, his troops were soon defeated and dispersed.

Let the reader only for a moment consider what a situation the British troops were placed in, while they were wading over this ford, upwards of five hundred yards wide, up to their breast in a rapid stream, their knapsacks on their back, sixty or seventy rounds of powder and ball in each pouch, tied at the pole of their necks, their firelocks with bayonets, fixed on their shoulders, three hundred of their enemies (accounted the best marksmen in the world) placed on a hill as it were over their heads, keeping a continual and very heavy fire upon them.

Yet such was the resolution with which they encountered the danger, and such the determined regularity which was observed, that only one officer, (lieutenant colonel Hall) and three privates were killed, and thirty six wounded. A striking instance of what may be effected in situations, deemed by many as invincible impediments to the progress of an army, by coolness, courage, and resolution. It may be necessary to mention, that lord Cornwallis's horse, though he was shot in the water, did not fall until he reached the shore. General Leslie's horses were carried down the river; and such was the rapidity of the stream, that brigadier general O'Hara's horse rolled with him down the current, for near forty yards.

Lord Cornwallis's division having made good the dangerous passage of the Catawba, landed, and the 23d regiment, with the cavalry under colonel Tarleton, set out in pursuit of the militia. Intelligence being gained that the American militia had rendezvoused at Tarrant's Tavern, ten miles from Beattie's Ford, the 23d regiment halted half way, and the colonel proceeded with the cavalry alone. About five hundred were then prepared to receive him, who were immediately charged, their centre broken through, fifty killed and the rest dispersed. The gallantry of these

actions made such an impression on the inhabitants,
that the troops made their way without molestation
to the Yadkin, notwithstanding the inveterate prejudice which this part of North Carolina bore to the
British name. General Greene's plan of waiting till
Huger and Williams joined him, was thus completely frustrated, the troops at the different fords
were withdrawn, and Morgan began a precipitate
retreat to the Yadkin.

Meantime colonel Webster's division passed Beattie's
Ford, on the Catawba, and joined that of lord
Cornwallis on the road to Salisbury. They immediately began to pursue Morgan, but he reached
the Trading Ford, and passed the Yadkin, with the
loss of his baggage, which the flight of the rifle
men left in possession of the king's troops. A
heavy rain which fell during the night, rendered
the fords impassible, and so swelled the river, that
general Morgan having secured all the boats and flats
on the opposite shore, the pursuit was rendered impossible, except by marching up the western banks of
the Yadkin, and passing by the shallow fords near
its source. This gave time for the junction of the
the American armies. In this situation, it was the
aim of lord Cornwallis to get between the American
army and Virginia, and thereby cut off general
Greene's retreat to that place. His lordship was, by
some means, misled by false information relative to
the lower fords being impassible, and began his
march to the upper fords of the Dan. Of this,
general Greene took advantage, and by a rapid
flight, reached Boyd's and Irwine's Ferries, and passed
the river, but so closely was he pursued by his
lordship, that the last division had scarcely crossed,
when the British reached the opposite banks. The
difficulties and hardships which the troops endured

in this ineffectual pursuit, were sustained with an heroism that was inspired by the idea of terminating the contest in this part by one decisive blow, which certainly would have been done, but for the mistake relative to the fords. General Greene having thus made his escape from North Carolina lord Cornwallis returned to Hillsborough, where he erected the royal standard, and issued a proclamation inviting all the loyal inhabitants to join him.

General Greene receiving intelligence of this, and dreading the consequences, took the daring measure of again crossing the Dan, with the legion of colonel Lee, and returning to North Carolina.

A transaction here forces itself on record, more foul, inhuman and abominable than any thing which took place during the war. The loyalists on the branches of Haw River, having risen in numbers, lieutenant colonel Tarleton was dispatched to forward their organization, and give them succour. Colonel Lee was sent with his legion to counteract the measure. On the 25th of February, the assembled loyalists were proceeding in a body to the standard of Tarleton, when they were met in a narrow lane by his legion. They mistook the American cavalry for Tarleton's dragoons, and were surrounded before they perceived their error. In this situation they immediately begged for quarter; but the relentless American refused it, and in the very act of supplicating mercy, two or three hundred were inhumanly butchered.—When did such a deed as this stain the British arms? Had twenty Americans thus fallen, how would the pages of Ramsay, Belsham, and the other republican historians have foamed with the charges of murder, massacre, blood, and malice!!!! However the historian may weep over the record, this is a specimen of republican mercy, as horrible as it is true.

Such was the scarcity of provisions at Hillsborough,
that it was found impossible to support the army in
that place. They were even obliged to kill some of
their best draft horses They therefore passed the
Haw, and encamped in Allamance Creek. This
movement much dispirited the loyalists, and raised
the drooping hopes of the Americans As the British
retired, Greene advanced, crossed the Haw, and posted
himself between Troublesome Creek and Reedy Fork,
carefully changing his position every night, to avoid an
engagement In this situation, lord Cornwallis gave
orders to beat up the American posts at Reedy Fork,
in order to compel them to a greater distance, or
perhaps allure Greene, who lay in the direction of
Guildford Court-House, to a general engagement Early
in the morning of the 6th of March, the army
passed Allamance Creek, and marched towards Reedy
Fork   The Americans were not unapprised of the
movement, and hastily retreated across the Fork.
General Greene instead of marching to their assistance, abandoned them to their fate. At Wedzell's
Mill, they were overtaken by lieutenant colonel Webster, and numbers fell The supplies and reinforcements which Greene anxiously expected, arrived at
last, under Lawson, Butler, and Eaton, with the
North Carolina militia, from the frontiers, commanded
by Campbell and Preston, making his numbers in
the whole upwards of five thousand men.

Thus reinforced, he determined to offer lord Cornwallis battle He re-passed the Haw, and marched to
Guildford Court-House, but twelve miles from the
British army, at the Quakers' meeting house in the
forks of Deep River

On the 15th of March, about four miles from
Guildford, the engagement began, colonel Tarleton
led on the British advance. The Americans were

commanded ·by general Lee, who behaved with the most undaunted bravery, and maintained himself against ·the most formidable ·opposition, until the 23d regiment advancing to the support of Tarleton, compelled ·him to give way. Greene formed ·his order ·of battle on a commanding scite. It consisted of three lines. Two brigades of the North Carolina militia flanked by a wood, composed the first. That of ·Virginia, commanded by Stephens and Lawson, formed ·the ·second. These were compleatly encompassed in the wood, three hundred yards in the rere of ·the first. Four hundred ·yards behind them, in ·open ground, near the Court House, the third was formed, consisting ·of ·two brigades of continental troops. Two corps ·of observation were placed dn the right and left flanks; ·the one commanded by colonel Washington, the other by colonel Lee. The British advance was formed by a column of ·royal artillery, under the command of lieutenant Macleod; and the disposition of the main attack ·was, as ·follows: the 71st, the ·regiment of Bose, commanded by general Leslie, and the ·1st battalion of guards, colonel Norton, formed the right line; the ·23d and 33d led on by colonel Webster, and supported by brigadier general O'Hara, and the grenadiers and 2d battalion of guards, constituted the left; · corps of observation, light infantry of ·the guards, and yagers, on the left of ·the artillery, and the cavalry ,in column behind on the ·road.

These masterly dispositions preluded one of the most signal battles · ever gained ·by British valour. The ·details are so accurately laid down by Stedman, who had every ·opportunity of ·ascertaining even the minutest circumstance, that it may ·be better to quote , his account of it, than by aiming at originality,

Y y

fall short of the particulars " This disposition being made, the line received orders to advance, and
moved forward with that steady and guarded, but
firm and determined resolution wheth discipline alone
can confer It has been remarked by an eye-wit-
ness,* that " the order and coolness of that part
of Webster's brigade which advanced across the open
ground, exposed to the enemy's fire, could not be
sufficiently extolled " At the distance of one hundred and forty yards they received the enemy's first
fire, but continued to advance unmoved When
arrived at a nearer and more convenient distance,
they delivered their own fire, and rapidly charged
with their bayonets· the enemy did not wait the
shock, but retreated behind their second line In
other parts of the line the British troops behaved
with equal gallantry, and were not less successful
The second line of the enemy made a braver and
stouter resistance than the first Posted n the woods,
and covering themselves with trees, they kept up for
a considerable time a galling fire, which did great
execution At length, however, they were compelled
to retreat, and fall back upon the continentals In
this severe conflict the whole of the British infantry
were engaged General Leslie, from the great extent
of the enemy's front, reaching far beyond his right,
had been very early obliged to bring forward the 1st
battalion of the guards, appointed for his reserve,
and form it into line and lieutenant colonel Webster,
finding the left of the 33d regiment exposed to a
heavy fire from the right wing of the enemy, which
greatly out-flanked him, changed its front to the
left, and the ground become vacant by this movement, was immediately occupied by general O'Hara,

* Lieutenant colonel Tarleton.

with the grenadiers, and 2d battalion of the guards. Webster moving to the left with the 33d regiment, supported by the light infantry of the guards, and the yagers, routed and put to flight-the right wing of the enemy, and in his progress, after two severe struggles, gained the right of the continentals; but the superiority of their numbers, and the weight of their fire obliged him, separated as he was from the British line, to re-cross a ravine, and occupy an advantageous position on the. opposite bank, until he could hear of the progress of the king's troops on the right. The British line being so much extended to the right and left, in order to shew a front equal to the enemy, was unavoidably broken into intervals in the . pursuit of the first and second American lines; some parts of it being more advanced than others, in consequence of the different degrees of resistance that had been met with, or of other impediments arising from the thickness of the woods, and the inequality of the ground. The whole, however, moved forward; and the second battalion of the guards, commanded by the honorable colonel Stuart, was the first that reached the open ground at Guildford Court House. Impatient to signalize themselves, they immediately attacked a body of continentals, greatly superior in numbers, that was seen formed on the left of the road, routed them and took their cannon, being two six-pounders; but pursuing them with too much ardour and impetuosity towards the wood on their rear, were thrown into confusion by a heavy fire received from a body of continentals, who were yet unbroken, and being instantly charged by Washington's dragoons, were driven back with great slaughter, and the loss of the cannon that had been taken. Lieutenant

Macleod, advancing along the road with the royal artillery, had by this time reached the open ground. By a spirited and well-directed cannonade he checked the pursuit of the Americans Fortunately also, the 71st regiment, belonging to general Leslie's division, was seen emerging from the woods on the right, and the 23d not long afterwards, made its appearance on the left   To the right and left of these regiments, general O'Hara, although severely wounded, rallied with much gallantry and great expedition, the remains of the 2d battalion of the guards, and the Americans were quickly repulsed and put to flight, with once more the loss of the two six-pounders: two other six-pounders were also taken, being all the artillery which they had in the field, and two ammunition waggons The 71st pushed forward to an eminence at the Court House, on the left flank of the continentals Lieutenant colonel Webster again advanced across the ravine, defeated the corps that was opposed to him, and connected himself with the centre of the British line. The continentals of the American army being now driven from their ground, as well as the militia, a general retreat took place, but it was conducted with order and regularity The 23d and 71st, with part of the cavalry, were at first sent in pursuit of the enemy, but afterwards received orders to return It is probable that, as the British commander became more acquainted with all circumstances of the action, and the number of the killed and wounded, he found it necessary to countermand his orders, and desist from the pursuit The action being now ended n the centre and left of the British line, a firing was still heard on the right, where general Leslie with the 1st battalion of the guards and the regiment of Bose, had been greatly impeded in advancing, by the ex-

cessive thickness of the woods, which rendered their
bayonets of little use. The broken corps of the
enemy were thereby encouraged to make frequent stands,
and to throw in an irregular fire; so that this part of
the British line was at times warmly engaged in front,
flank, and rear, with some of the enemy that had been
routed in the first attack, and with part of the extremity of their left wing, which, by the closeness of
the woods, had been passed unseen.

. " At one period of the action the first battalion of
the guards was completely broken. It had suffered
greatly in ascending a woody height to attack the
second line of the Americans, strongly posted upon
the top of it, who, availing themselves of the advantages of their situation, retired, as soon. as they had.
discharged their pieces, behind the brow of the hill,
which protected them from the shot of the guards,
and returned as soon as they had loaded, and were
again in readiness to fire. Notwithstanding the dis-
advantage under which the attack was made, the guards
reached the summit of the eminence, and put this part
of the American line to flight: but no sooner was it
done, than another line of the Americans presented
itself to view, extending far beyond the right of the
guards, and inclining towards their flank, so as almost
to encompass them. The ranks of the guards had
been thinned in ascending the height, and a number
of the officers had fallen: captain Maitland, who at
this time received a wound, retired to the rear, and
having had his wound dressed, returned immediately
to join the battalion of guards to which he belonged.
Some of the men, too, from superior exertions, had
reached the summit of the eminence sooner than others;
so that the battalion was not in regular order when
it received the fire of the third American line. The
enemy's fire being repeated and continued, and, from

the great extent of their line, being poured in not
only on the front but flank of the battalion, completed
its confusion and disorder, and notwithstanding every
exertion made by the remaining officers, it was at
last entirely broken   Fortunately, at this time, the
Hessian regiment of Bose, commanded by lieutenant
colonel de Bury, which had hitherto suffered but little,
was advancing in firm and compact order on the left
of the guards, to attack the enemy   Lieutenant colonel
Norton thought the fortunate arrival of the regiment
of Bose presented a favorable opportunity for forming
again his battalion, and requested the Hessian lieutenant-colonel to wheel his regiment to the right,
and cover the guards, whilst their officers endeavoured
to rally them   The request was immediately and most
gallantly complied with , and, under the cover of the
fire of the Hessians, the exertions of lieutenant colonel
Norton, and his few remaining officers, were at last
successful in restoring order   The battalion, being
again formed, instantly moved forward to join the
Hessians   the attack was renewed, and the enemy
were defeated   But here the labours of this part of
the line did not yet cease   No sooner had the guards
and Hessians defeated the enemy in front, than they
found it necessary to return and attack another body
of them that appeared in the rear, and in this manner
_they were obliged to traverse the same ground in
various directions, before the enemy were completely
put to the rout   The firing heard on the right, after
the termination of the action in the centre, and on
the left, induced lord Cornwallis to detach Tarleton,
with part of the cavalry, to gain intelligence of what
was doing in that quarter, and to know whether general
Leslie wanted assistance. But before Tarleton's arrival
on the right, the affair was over, and the British
troops were standing with ordered arms , all resistance

having ceased on the part of the Americans, except from a few hardy rifflemen, who lurking behind trees, occasionally fired their pieces, but at such a distance as to do no mischief. These colonel Tarleton, when requested, readily undertook to disperse with his cavalry, and rushing forward under cover of a general volley of musquetry from the guards and the regiment of Bose, quickly performed what was expected of him. In this affair colonel Tarleton himself received a slight wound, but the rest of his corps returned unhurt.

" In this battle the British troops obtained a victory most honorable and glorious to themselves, but in its consequences, of no real advantage to the cause in which they were engaged. They attacked, and defeated an army of more than three times their number,* not taken by surprise, but formed in regular order of battle, and ready to engage; an army too, that is allowed on all hands to have been strongly and judiciously posted, on ground chosen with care, and most excellently adapted to the nature of the troops that occupied it. The resistance of the enemy was in proportion to the advantages they possessed; nor did they yield, but

---

* By the return of the adjutant of the day, it appears that the British troops engaged in the action, amounted to fourteen hundred forty five. The cavalry are not included in this return, and indeed they were not engaged, except for an instant on the right, after the action in the centre, and on the left, was over. The Americans were generally supposed to amount to seven thousand men, and a letter, found in the pocket of one of their serjeants that was slain, specifies seven thousand to be the number of their army: but Gordon in his history, who appears to have taken their numbers, from official documents, states them to be fourteen hundred and ninety continentals, and two thousand seven hundred and fifty three militia; in all; four thousand two hundred and forty three foot soldiers, and two hundred cavalry. But he seems not to have included the back woods men, under Campbell and Preston; so that their whole number probably exceeded seven thousand men.

with extreme reluctance Even the militia, encouraged
by their position, fought with bravery, and greatly
weakened the British line before it reached the continentals The Virginia militia, who composed the
second American line, did not quit their ground, it is
said until their commander, seeing them no longer able
to withstand the attack of regular troops, and ready
to be overpowered, gave orders for a retreat A victory achieved under such disadvantages of numbers
and ground, was of the most honorable kind, and placed
the bravery and discipline of the troops, beyond all
praise, but the expence at which it was obtained rendered it of no utility.

" Before the provincials finally retreated, more than
one third of all the British troops engaged had fallen
The whole loss, according to the official returns, amounted to five hundred and thirty two of these ninety
three were killed n the action, four hundred and thirteen were wounded, and twenty six missing Amongst
the killed were the honorable lieutenat colonel Stuart
of the guards, lieutenant O'Hara of the royal artillery,
brother of the brigadier, lieutenant Robinson of the
23d regiment, ensign Talbot of the 33d, and ensign
Grant of the 71st; amongst the wounded, were brigadiers general O'Hara, and Howard, lieutenant colonels
Webster, and Tarleton, captains Swanton, Schutz,
Maynard, Goodricke, lord Dunglass, Maitland, Peter,
Wilmousky, and Eichenbrodth, lieutenants Salvin, Win-
yard, Schewener, and Grause, ensigns Stuart, Kelly,
Gore, Hughes, and De Troot; and adjutant Colgubourn;
and Fox '

The loss of the Americans in this action has been
variously estimated, and does not appear to have been
fully ascertained If we are to credit their official
returns, their whole loss n killed and wounded, as
well of militia as continentals, did not exceed two

hundred and fifty men. But, by lord Cornwallis's dispatches, it appears that between two and three hundred of their dead, were found upon the field, after the action; and if we proportion their wounded according to the number of the slain, their whole loss in killed and wounded, must have greatly exceeded that of the British troops. The number of those who were missing, according to their own returns, was confessedly great; but as the British troops took but few prisoners, is is probable that the greatest part of the missing, con-sisted of militia, who, escaping from the action, fled to their own houses, and did not afterwards return.

" The wounded of both armies were collected by the British, as expeditiously as possible after the action: it was, however, a service that required both time and care, as from the nature of the action, they lay dis-persed over a great extent of ground. Every assistance was furnished to them, that in the then circumstances of the army could be afforded; but, unfortunately the army was destitute of tents, nor was there a sufficient number of houses near the field of battle to receive the wounded. The British army had marched several miles on the morning of the day on which they came to action. They had no provisions of any kind whatever on that day, nor until between three and four in the afternoon of the succeeding day, and then but a scanty allowance, not exceeding one quarter of a pound of flower, and the same quantity of very lean beef. The night of the day on which the action happened was remarkable for its darkness, accompanied with rain, which fell in torrents. Near fifty of the wounded, it is said, sinking under their aggravated miseries, expired before morning. The cries of the wounded, and dying who remained on the field of action during the night, exceeded all description. Such a complicated scene of

horror and distress, it is hoped, for the sake of humanity,
rarely occurs, even in a military life.

> What loads of mangled flesh and limbs
> (A dismal carnage!) bath'd in reeking gore,
> Lay welt'ring on the ground, while flitting life,
> Convuls'd, the nerves still shivering, nor had lost
> All taste of pain! Here an old vet'ran lies
> Deform'd with years, and scars, and groans aloud
> Torn with fresh wounds, but inward vitals firm
> Forbid the soul's remove, and chain it down
> By the hard laws of nature, to sustain
> Long torment, his wild eye balls roll, his teeth,
> Gnashing with anguish, chide his ling'ring fate.

"History, perhaps, does not furnish a similar instance of
a battle gained under all the disadvantages with which the
British troops, (assisted by a regiment of Hessians, and
some Yagers,) had to contend against, at Guilford Court
House. Nor is there, perhaps, on the records of his
tory, an instance of a battle fought with more determined perseverance than was shewn by the British
troops on that memorable day. The battles of Cressy,
of Poictiers, and of Agincourt, the glory of our own
country, and the admiration of ages, had in each of
them, either from particular local situation, or other
fortunate and favorable circumstances something in a
degree to counter-balance the disparity of numbers,
here, time, place, and numbers, all united against the
British. The American general had chosen his ground,
which was strong, commanding, and advantageous, he
had time not only to make his disposition, but to send
away his baggage, and every incumbrance. His cannon
and his troops, in numbers far exceeding the British,
were drawn out in readiness to commence the action,
when lord Cornwallis approached to attack him."

General Greene fled to Reedy Fork Creek, where,
when he had passed the river, he halted on the opposite
banks to collect his stragglers. When he had partly
accomplished this, he pushed on to Troublesome Creek,

about twelve miles further. Lord Cornwallis, (from the army being in want of provisions, and its several other distresses,) found it would be inadvisable to pursue the fugitives. It on the other hand became indispensably necessary to move towards some place where supplies might be obtained. Accordingly about seventy wounded were left at the Quaker's meeting house, under protection of a flag of truce, and the army slowly retired to Cross Creek.

It was part of lord Cornwallis's plan for the operation in the north, that colonel Balfour, the commandant at Charlestown, should dispatch a force by water, sufficient to take Wilmington, as a post of communication, and a medium of obtaining supplies. This service was executed by major Craig in the end of January, and put in a proper state of defence. Wilmington lies near the mouth of Cape Fear River; and Cross Creek (a settlement of loyal Highlanders) is on a branch of it, about one hundred miles up the country. From thence it was expected the army would obtain supplies, and it was moreover admirably adapted, from its central situation, as a rallying point for those who were well affected to the royal cause. Lord Cornwallis began his march from Guildford Court House by issuing a proclamation, inviting the loyal to his standard, and offering pardon to those who should return to their allegiance. His lordship then proceeded by slow marches to Cross Creek; general Greene following him as far as Ramsey's Mill, on Deep River. Nothing but slight occasional skirmishes ensued during the march. On his arrival at the Creek, every hope was disappointed. Four days forage could not be had in twenty miles, all communication, with Wilmington from the narrowness of the river, was impracticable, and the scattered inhabitants on its lofty banks were irreconcilably hostile. The troops therefore began their march to Wilmington, at

which place they arrived on the 7th of April During
these toilsome movements, the British army sustained
an almost irreparable loss, by the deaths of colonel
Webster* of the 33d, captains Schutz and Maynard of
the guards, ' and captain Wilmouski and ensign De
Trott of the regiment of Bose   They' all received
their mortal wounds at Guildford Court House   Of
colonel Webster's great military talents and virtues,
mention at large has already been made in this
Journal, but :' the sympathetic manner in which
lord Cornwallis communicated to the Rev Dr Webster,
of Edinburgh, the intelligence of his son's death, is at
once a proof of his lordship's goodness of heart, his tender sensibility, and of the high estimation in which he
held the deceased   The following is a copy of his letter
on that occasion :"

                        Wilmington, April 23, 1781
    " Dear Sir—It gives me great concern to undertake
a task which is not only a bitter renewal of my own grief,
but must be a violent shock to an affectionate parent.

    " You have for your support, the assistance of reli-
gion, good sense, and the experience of the uncertainty
of human happiness. You have for your satisfaction,
that your son fell nobly in the cause of his country,
honored and lamented by all his fellow soldiers , that he
led a life of honor and virtue, which must secure him
everlasting happiness. When the keen sensibility of the
passions begins to subside, these considerations will give
you real comfort

    " That the Almighty may give you fortitude to bear
this severest of trials, is the earnest wish of your companion in affliction, and most faithful servant,

                                " CORNWALLIS "

    * It was reported in the army, that when lord Cornwallis
received the news of colonel Webster's death, his lordship was
struck with such pungent sorrow, that turning himself, he
looked on his sword, and emphatically exclaimed, " I have
lost my scabbard "

As the Author belonged to colonel Webster's brigade, he is enabled, (and the Reader will naturally expect it from him,) to state some circumstances unnoticed by any historian, from his own personal observation. After the brigade formed across the open ground, the colonel rode on to the front, and gave the word, *"Charge."* Instantly the movement was made, in excellent order, in a smart run, with arms charged: when arrived within forty yards of the enemy's line, it was perceived that their whole force had their arms presented, and resting on a rail fence, the common partitions in America. They were taking aim with the nicest precision.

> " Twixt host and host but narrow space was left,
> " A *dreadful* interval, and, front to front,
> " Presented, stood in terrible array."

At this awful period a general pause took place; both parties surveyed each other for the moment with the most anxious suspense. Nothing speaks, *the general* more than seizing on decisive moments: colonel Webster rode forward in the front of the 23d regiment, and said, with more than even his usual commanding voice (which was well known to his Brigade,) *" Come on, my brave Fuzileers."* This operated like an inspiring voice, they rushed forward amidst the enemy's fire; dreadful was the havoc on both sides.

> " Amazing scene!
> What showers of mortal hail! What flaky fires!"

At last the Americans gave way, and the brigade advanced, to the attack of their second line. Here the conflict became still more fierce. Before it was completely routed, where I stood, (it is not from egotism, but to be the better understood, that I here, without breaking the thread of precision, assume the first person) I observed an American officer attempting to fly. I immediately darted after him, but he perceiving my inten-

tion to capture him, fled with the utmost speed. I
pursued, and was gaining on him, when, hearing a confused noise on my left, I observed several, bodies of
Americans drawn up within the distance of a few yards.
Whoever has been in an engagement well knows that,
in such moments all fears of death are over. Seeing one
of the guards among the slain, where I stood, I stopped and replenished my own pouch with the car-
tridges that remained in his; during the time I was
thus employed, several shots were fired at me; but
not one took effect. ' Glancing my eye the other way,
I saw a company of the guards advancing to attack
these parties. The Reader may perhaps be surprised
at the bravery of troops, thus with calm intrepidity
attacking superior numbers, when formed into separate
bodies, and all acting together; but I can assure him
this instance was not peculiar;.it frequently occurred
in the British army, during the American war. It was
impossible to join this company, as several of the American parties lay between me and it. I had no time
for deliberation. How to act I knew not. On the
instant, however, I saw lord Cornwallis riding across the
clear ground. His lordship was mounted on a dragoon's
horse (his own having been shot;) the saddle-bags were
under the creature's belly, which much retarded his
progress, owing to the vast quantity of underwood that
was spread over the ground; his lordship was evidently
unconscious of his danger. I immediately laid hold of
the bridle of his horse, and turned his head. I then
mentioned to him, that if his lordship had pursued the
same direction, he would in a few moments have been
surrounded by the enemy, and, perhaps, cut to pieces
or captured. I continued to run along side of the
horse, keeping the bridle in my hand, until his lordship,
gained the 23d regiment, which was at that time drawn
up in the skirt of the woods. '

CHAP. XVII.

General Greene marches back to South Carolina. Surrender of several British Posts. Camden evacuated. Ninety-Six invested. Surrender of Augusta. Greene repulsed with loss at Ninety-Six. Lord Rawdon forces Greene to retreat. Ninety-Six evacuated. Action at Eutaws.

IT was the intention of lord Cornwallis to have moved on to Camden, to obtain supplies, and messengers were accordingly dispatched to lord Rawdon, but unhappily they never reached his lordship. The intelligence that Greene had marched to attack lord Rawdon, and that probably the fate of Camden was already decided, inclined his lordship to pursue a different direction, and the army set out for Virginia, to join general Arnold.

An able and heroic defence of Camden was made by lord Rawdon, and Greene was compelled, after suffering severely from a sortie made by the garrison, to retreat to Rugeley's mills, about twelve miles distant.

Amidst all this display of British valour, the presence of an American army, although retreating before the king's troops, occasionally harassed them severely, by acting in small parties, and this produced the open avowal of disaffection among the inhabitants. Fo

Watson, a British post on the Santee river, was surrendered to Lee and Marion. Colonel Watson, however, with a detachment of five hundred men, notwithstanding every obstacle, made his way through the country, and reinforced lord Rawdon at Camden.

With this accession of strength, his lordship attempted once more to bring general Greene to an engagement but he fled before him. The universal disaffection of the Americans in this part, determined lord Rawdon to contract the limits of the British posts, by abandoning Camden: the stores not removable, were destroyed, and the army retired to Monk's Corner, for the greater safety of Charlestown. In consequence of this movement, Fort Motte was surrendered to Lee and Marion, Orangeburgh to Sumpter, and Fort Granby to Lee alone.

Flushed with these partial successes, the American commander, began his operations on the western frontiers. Lee and Pickens formed a junction, and the two commanders sat down before Augusta, which was defended by lieutenant colonel Brown, with all his former gallantry when Clarke besieged it. But at length, after a brave defence, it was surrendered to the Americans on the fifth of June.

These disasters to the royal cause were in a great measure ascribable to the British officers, commanding at the different posts, being ignorant of each others operations, by the vigilance of the disaffected inhabitants, who intercepted almost all their letters, dispatches, &c. Thus the orders sent from Charlestown, and also by lord Rawdon, for the evacuation of Ninety-Six, never reached lieutenant colonel Cruger, and he acted, on local circumstances only, and accordingly fortified the place instead of evacuating it. In this situation it was invested by general Greene. During the course of the siege, which was carried on with a fury almost amounting to desperation by the Americans; that in open day they attempted to set fire to the abbatis with lighted combustibles. And colonel Lee had the meanness and inhumanity to march the British prisoners he brought with him from Fort Augusta in full sight of the garrison, accompanied by music, playing Yankee. tunes, and preceded by a British standard reversed.

At length the garrison became much distressed for want of water. Their only supply depended on the negroes, who were sent out at night naked, and whose colour, in darkness, rendered them objects not distinguishable by the Americans.

Thus dreadfully circumstanced, the British commander did not despair. He still depended on relief from lord Rawdon. Nor were his hopes in vain. A brave and determined American loyalist, in mid day rode through the American picquets, notwithstanding their fire, and delivered a verbal message from his lordship, " that he had passed through Orangeburgh, and was in full march to raise the siege." How this operated on a British garrison, need not be recorded. Three Irish regiments had arrived at Charlestown, which placed that capital in a state of security, and left his lordship at liberty to attempt the relief of Ninety-Six. With the flank companies of these regiments and the army from Monk's Corner, he began his march in a direction to get between general Greene and his force on the Congaree. General Greene was not was apprized of this intended relief, and as a last and desperate effort, attempted to take the place by storm. In the morning of the 18th of June, a heavy cannonade was begun from all the American batteries: at noon two parties advanced under cover of the trenches which approached nearest to the works, and made lodgements in the ditch: these were immediately followed by other parties with hooks to draw down the sand bags, and

3 A

tools to reduce the parapet. The rifflemen, in the mean time, posted on their battery, were ready to take aim at every British soldier that appeared; and the Virginia and Maryland brigades, having manned the lines of the third parallel, fired from them by platoons. The right flank of the enemy was exposed to the fire of a three pounder, as well as to that of the block houses in the village; and major Greene, who commanded in the Star, with much honor to himself, and benefit to the service, from the beginning of the siege, had his detachment ready to receive them on the parapet with bayonets and spears. As the main body of the American army didnot advance beyond the third parallel, and was contented with supporting the parties in the ditch, by an incessant fire from the trenches, the garrison determined to put a speedy period to the assault by an effort of gallantry which confounded the enemy. Two parties of thirty men each, one under captain Campbell of the New Jersey volunteers, and the other under captain French of Delancy's, issued from the sally port in the rear of the Star, entered the ditch, and taking opposite directions, charged the Americans who had made the lodgement with such impetuosity, that they drove every thing before them, until they met in the opposite quarter. The bayonet being the only weapon used, the carnage was great: even the American accounts admit, that two thirds of their people who entered the ditch, were either killed or wounded. General Greene, seeing it useless any longer to continue so hopeless an attempt, called off his troops, and in the evening of the following day, finally raised the siege. His baggage having been previously sent off, his army marched with great expedition, and on the 20th crossed the Saluda. The loss of the enemy, during the siege, according to their own accounts amounted to one hundred and sixty six men, including one colonel, three captains, and five lieutenants: but as the loss of the militia, who, it is said, on this occasion bore the proportion of three to one of the troops, in the pay of congress, was not included in their returns, their total loss must have been much greater. That of the garrison amounted to twenty-seven killed, and fifty-eight wounded."[*]

The following day lord Rawdon arrived before the place, and without delay, in the evening, in defiance of heat and fatigue, set out in pursuit of Greene, who fled before him with the utmost precipitancy. The fugitives were pursued to the banks of the Enorce; but at last the American general found safety in the celerity of his movements.

On his lordship's return, preparations were made for the evacuation of Ninety-Six, and the loyal inhabitants, with their effects, were, under the escort of lieutenant-colonel Cruger, removed within the new frontier.

. After the abandonment of Ninety-Six, his lordship proceeded to the Congaree, and from thence to Orange-burgh, where he was joined by lieutenant colonel Stuart, with the 3d regiment, from Charlestown.

The sultry heat of the American climate, now partially suspended the operations of both armies. General Greene retired to the lofty hills of Santee, where he was joined by Lee, Sumpter, and Marion. Lord Rawdon's health was much impaired, and, on leave of absence, his lordship returned to Europe; the command, of course, devolved on lieutenant-colonel Stuart.

It now became the aim of general Greene to attempt the recovery of South Carolina. Accordingly he marched from the Santee Hills, and came up with the British; who had passed by the Congaree, at its junction with Wateree, at Eutaw Springs, about forty miles from.

* Stedman.

the former river. The regulars were drawn up on the
heights, across the road, the right wing of the army
consisted of the flank battalion, under the command
of major Majoribanks, the remainder of the army on
the left, in an oblique direction. A party of infantry,
with two pieces of artillery, defended the pass of the
road. Four battalions of American militia composed
their first line; three brigades of continental troops
their second; Lee's legion covered their right flank,
the South Carolina state troops, under Henderson,
their left. Colonel Washington's cavalry, and the Delaware troops were the body of reserve; two three pounders
were in front of the line, and two six pounders with
the second line. The legion and state troops constituted
the advance guard. The attack began with great impetuosity, some of the new raised troops were giving
way, when the 63d and 64th regiments rushed on the
enemy with bayonets in hand. The contest was severe
on both sides, the artillery was several times taken, and
retaken. At the first fire, colonel Washington was
wounded, and taken prisoner. Often, when the parties
seemed overpowered, the contest was renewed with increased vigour on both sides. The Americans, however, were at last compelled to retire, leaving behind
them two brass six pounders, and upwards of two
hundred killed on the field, and sixty taken prisoners,
besides the wounded which were carried off during
the action. The total loss, according to the return
which was published by congress, was more than seven
hundred, including sixty commissioned officers, of whom
seventeen were killed, and forty-three wounded, among
the latter was lieutenant-colonel Washington. The
British lost six hundred and ninety-three men, eighty-
five killed, three hundred and fifty-one wounded, two
hundred and fifty-seven missing. Of twenty-nine commissioned officers, three were killed, sixteen wounded,

ten missing. It might well be said, in this bloody and hard fought battle, that

" Frowning war
" All gloomy, like a gather'd tempest, stood
" Wav'ring, and doubtful where to bend its fall."

Congress voted a British standard and a gold medal to general Greene *for the victory;* but the British commander *remained on the ground* the night after the action, and during the following day! This was the last battle of any note which took place in South Carolina.

As we hear no more of general Greene during the American war, some readers may perhaps be curious to know what became of him. There is a brief account of the latter part of his life in Smith's Narrative, which may not be altogether improper to quote here:

" Congress effectually remunerated Greene, by giving him a valuable plantation, in the state of Georgia, the meed of his indefatigable services, but which was, ultimately, his bane, and the cause of his premature death; for depending too much upon his hardy constitution, contrary to the advice of his friends, he would, to accomplish the duties, and acquire the simple character of a planter, venture out, and subject himself to the meridian blaze of the sun, in order to superintend his negro labourers: in one of these perambulations he received the *coup de soliel*, or, stroke of the sun, as the French West Indians term the effects which Europeans feel from too great an exertion, while subjected to the solar heat; and fell a victim to his own obstinacy, unrelented by some, and deplored by others: for political attachments bore their preponderance in that unhappy, divided, and distracted country, till the last hour of the unfortunate war; and even now they are far, very far, from extinction. In the minds of some this general still lives, and is considered as the *deputy*-saviour of his country. Hosanna one hour; and crucify the next, was the prevailing principle among the Americans! *Sic transit gloria mundi!*"

CHAP. XVIII.

Death of General Phillips. Lord Cornwallis joins General Arnold. Charlotteville surprised by Colonel Tarleton. Unfavorable State of the American Cause. Lord Cornwallis retires to Portsmouth, and finally to York-town and Gloucester. Arrival of Count Rochambeau. Joins General Washington. French Fleet arrive in the Chesapeak. Block up York River. New London taken by General Arnold. York-town surrenders to the Americans.

A DEEP laid, but ineffectual plan was about this time formed by Washington, for entrapping general Arnold. A reinforcement of two thousand British, under general Phillips, were arrived in the Chesapeak : that officer being superior in rank, took the command from Arnold, and became general of the whole British force there. He finished the works at Portsmouth, left a sufficient force for its defence, and proceeded up James's River in the smaller vessels of the fleet. The army after twice landing, and re-embarking, joined lord Cornwallis at Petersburgh, at which place general Phillips, (equally beloved and respected for his virtues, and his military talents,) died of a fever, a short period before the junction of the royal forces. The command again devolved on general Arnold ; but shortly after, as matter.

of course, the superior direction of both armies became vested in lord Cornwallis.

The marquis de la Fayette, had followed the route of the British army, under general Phillips; but when he learned the junction of the whole under lord Cornwallis, he took a position on the North of James's River, between Richmond and Wiltown. From this place he however, fled on the approach of lord Cornwallis. Meantime colonel Tarleton with a patrole pushed on to Warwick Court-House, fell in with a party of four hundred militia in that neighbourhood, who were routed with great loss to the Americans. Some time after the colonel, and captain Champagne of the 23d regiment, surprised Charlotteville, (at which place the general assembly was sitting) and took seven of their members prisoners. 'Brigadier general Scott, and several officers and men, were killed, wounded, or taken. " The attempt to secure Mr. Jefferson was ineffectual, he discovered the British dragoons from his house; which stands on the point of a mountain, before they could approach him, and he provided for his personal safety, by a precipitate retreat. The gentlemen taken on this expedition, were treated with kindness and liberality."* A great quantity of stores were found in Charlotteville, which were all destroyed. A successful stratagem of colonel Simcoe, also put the British in possession of all the stores under the care of Baron Steuben, at the point of Fork. At this period the American affairs became much deranged from the want of supplies. Their bills of credit suffered a dreadful depreciation: few would take them for any thing wanted by the army, and they were obliged to have recourse to bills of impress, to compel individuals to part with provisions. For want of pay and clothing, the troops were on the verge of mutinying. Even general Wash-

* Colonel Tarleton.

ington confessed this in one of his letters. " From the posts of Saratoga to that of Dobb's Ferry, inclusive, I believe there is not, at this moment on hand, one day's supply of meat for the army." Their marine was, if possible in a worse condition than their army. In short a general bankruptcy seemed to be fast approaching. Washington saw that the only chance of continuing the war, was by some bold and decisive operation, and New York became his object. But to carry this or any other decisive operation into effect, the co-operation of the French fleet and army, were necessary. This had been promised, and congress during the three preceding years had anxiously expected it. At the end of the last year, they laid before the court of Versailles, the desperate situation to which the American cause was reduced, and the inevitable ruin which await- ed 'them, without powerful succour from France. When all was suspense and terror, intelligence arrived at Washington's camp, that M. de Barras was at Rhode Island, and that he brought dispatches for Count de Rochambeau. The general accordingly set out for Connecticut, to meet him. At this con- ference which was held on the 21st of May, it was agreed to attack New York, and on the arrival of Count de Grasse, to strike some important blow. General Washington wrote to congress, requesting the full com- pletion of his own battalions, and the further aid of six hundred and twenty militia, from the New England states. His dispatches were intercepted in the Jerseys, and immediately sent to Sir Henry Clinton. He ac- cordingly wrote to lord Cornwallis, for part of the troops under his lordship's command, to be sent to the succour of New York. Agreeably to general Clinton's request, Lord Cornwallis left Williamsburg, and passed James's River in his way to Portsmouth. Previous to passing the river he encamped on a spot that covered the Ford into the island of James's Town; and in the evening the Queen's rangers made their, way over: the wheel carriages, the bat horses, and baggage, followed. on the 5th and 6th. The marquis de la Fayette pursued by forced marches, hoping to surprise the rear guard, when the main body had passed over. Of this lord Cornwallis gained intelligence, he permitted the picquets to be driven in to deceive the marquis. The attack began about sunset. . The enemy were routed, and the approach of night alone saved the whole from ruin, The 43d, 76th, and 80th regiments, were in the fiercest part of the action, opposed by the Pennsylvania line, and: lieutenant-colonel Dundas, their commander displayed a bravery, and firmness, which obtained the applause of the whole British army,

The British main body quietly passed the river; the troops destined for embarkation moved on to Portsmouth, and his lordship followed with the rest. After these troops were embarked, and just as they were putting out to sea, an express arrived from Sir Henry Clinton to prevent their sailing, and directing lord Cornwallis to regain Williamsburg, as the means of saving a defensive post for the larger ships, either at Point Comfort, or at Hampton Road. Lord Cornwallis, on due examination found these two places untenable, and accordingly ordered part of the army to sail up the York, River in transports, and take possession of York Town. and Gloucester. On the 20th of August, his lordship evacuated Portsmouth, and fixed his head quarters at York and Gloucester.

On the 30th of August, in a fatal moment which may be said to have turned the wavering scale in favor of the Americans, Count de Grasse arrived in the Chesapeak, with twenty-eight ships of the line. An officer from La Fayette's army was waiting his arrival at Cape Henry. He communicated to the Count,

the perilous state of American affairs; and a disposition
was instantly formed for blocking up York River, on
the banks of which lord Cornwallis was posted, and
for conveying the French land force, which the Count
had brought up James's River to reinforce La Fayette
All this was performed by four line of battle ships, the
others remaining in Lynhaven Bay, within the Capes.

The British admiral (Graves) quitted the entrance of
the Delaware, and came within sight of the French
squadron, when a partial engagement took place, but
from the wind, and other circumstances, it was impossible for him to force the French to a general battle,
and it was their object to decline it, for during this
partial contest, while both fleets were at sea, M de
Barras sailed into the Chesapeak, conveying fourteen
transports, laden with heavy artillery and stores

In the mean time the commander in chief at New
York, with a view of making a diversion in Connecticut,
and drawing general Washington's attention that way,
detached brigadier-general Arnold with a considerable
force to make an attempt upon New London The
troops embarked on this expedition, consisted of the
38th, 40th, and 54th regiments, the third battalion of
New Jersey volunteers, the loyal Americans, the American legion, some refugees, a detachment of yagers,
and another of the royal artillery They passed through
the Sound in transports, and landed n the morning
of the sixth of September, about three miles from New
London, in two divisions, one on each side of the harbour That on the Groton side, consisting of the 40th
and 54th regiments, the third battalion of New Jersey
volunteers, with a detachment of yagers and artillery,
was commanded by lieutenant-colonel Eyre, and that
on the New London side, consisting of the rest of the
troops, by brigadier-general Arnold On the New London side no great opposition was made a redoubt,

from which the enemy had begun a cannonade, was abandoned by them upon the approach of general Arnold with part of his division; and soon afterwards. Fort Trumbull, that commanded the harbour, was entered by captain Millet at the head of four companies of the 38th regiment, through a shower of grape-shot, which the enemy discharged from their cannon, but without doing much mischief, only four or five being killed or wounded in the assault. General Arnold lost no time in taking possession of New London: He was opposed by a small body of the enemy with a field-piece; but they were soon so hard pressed as to be obliged to fly, and leave their piece of artillery behind. On the Groton side of the harbour was Fort Griswold, a regular work of considerable strength. It was assaulted on three sides by the 40th and 54th regiments, under lieutenant-colonel Eyre, and defended by the enemy with the most obstinate bravery.

At length the gallant efforts of the assailants were successful; and with fixed bayonets they entered the works through the embrasures, in the face of the enemy, who were armed with long spears to oppose them. A considerable carnage now ensued, until the enemy were driven from the ramparts, and had ceased from all farther resistance. The honor obtained by the British troops in this assault was great, but too dearly purchased. Two officers, and forty-six soldiers, were killed, and eight officers, with one hundred and thirty-five soldiers, wounded. General Arnold, upon his landing, had been informed that the works at Fort Griswold were incomplete, and its garrison inconsiderable: but when he arrived at New London, and from an eminence, had viewed its great strength, he dispatched an officer to countermand his orders for an assault, who unfortunately reached colonel Eyre a few minutes too late. The fort had refused to surrender, and the action was

3 B 2

begun Of the garrison eighty-five were killed, including colonel Ladyard, their commander, sixty were
wounded, most of them mortally, and seventy made
prisoners Ten or twelve of the enemy's ships were
burnt, that contained an immense quantity of European and West India goods Unluckily they also contained some gunpowder, unknown to general Arnold,
by the explosion of which the flames were communicated to the dwelling-houses in the town, and a great
part of it was consumed, notwithstanding every endeavour to stop the progress of the conflagration Upwards of fifty pieces of cannon, and a great quantity
of military stores found 'in the different works, were
also destroyed *

Notwithstanding the heavy loss which the Americans
sustained by the destruction of New London, Washington continued his progress to Virginia, passed
through Philadelphia, and at the head of the Elk River
embarked his troops in transports sent thither by the
French. The whole reached Williamsburg on the
25th of September, general Washington and Count de
Rochambeau went on board the Ville de Paris, and
with Count de Grasse settled the future operations of
the allied armies.

On the 28th the investiture of York Town commenced.
In the evening dispatches arrived from Sir Henry
Clinton, promising the relief of five thousand troops,
and that twenty-three ships of the line, would sail, as
a further support by the fifth of October. the next
day the investment of the town was pursued , in the
night the enemy began to break ground ; the French
made their approach on the right, the Americans on
the left, forming a junction at a morass, which was
opposite the centre of the British works, at the same

---

* Stedman.

time Gloucester Town was blockaded by the duke De Lauzan. The garrison made a brave resistance, annoying the besiegers at every possible point of attack, particularly from two redoubts, which were carried out near three hundred yards in front of the works. These it became necessary for the besiegers to silence in the night of the 14th, the one was carried by the Americans, and the other by the French. A sortie was made by three hundred and fifty men, under the command of lieutenant-colonel Abercrombie, against two of the enemy's batteries; a detachment of the guards, with the 80th grenadiers, under lieutenant-colonel Lake, executed the one, and another of light infantry, under major Armstrong, carried the other; eleven heavy cannon were spiked, one hundred of the French troops were killed and wounded, and the whole party returned, with very little loss, within the British lines. However gallant this enterprize, the garrison was reduced to the last extremity, not a gun remained on that part of the works attacked by the enemy, scarcely a shell was left, and nothing remained to lord Cornwallis but to attempt an escape, with the army, or immediately to surrender the place. " He determined (says Stedman) to attempt the latter." On the Gloucester side of the river, brigadier De Choise now commanded, and lay with a small corps at some distance, in front of the works. It was determined that he should be attacked before break of day by the whole British force; and the success of the attack was not in the least doubted. The horses taken from him, (for he had a considerable corps of cavalry) would in part mount the infantry, and the rest might be supplied by others collected on the road. A no baggage was to be carried, his lordship intended to have proceeded to the upper country by rapid marches, leaving his future route uncertain, until he came opposite to the fords of the great rivers, when he meant to have turned off suddenly to the northward, upon a supposition, that the enemy's measures would be principally directed to prevent his escape to the southward   After turning to the northward, it was his lordship's design to force his way through Maryland, Pennsylvania, and the Jerseys, and join the commander in chief at New York   Undoubtedly the attempt was beyond calculation hazardous, and the issue totally precarious, but if it afforded even a glimpse of hope, it was preferable to an immediate surrender

" In pursuance of this design the light infantry, the greatest part of the guards, and part of the 23d regiment, were embarked in boats, and transported to the Gloucester side of the river before midnight, when a violent storm arose, which not only prevented the boats from returning, but drove them a considerable distance down the river   The passage of the rest of the troops was now become impracticable, and, in the absence of the boats, those that had already crossed, could not possibly return   In this divided state of the British force, the enemy's batteries opened at break of day   fortunately the boats returned soon afterwards, and brought back, in the course of the forenoon, the troops that had been carried over in the night, without much loss, although the passage between York and Gloucester, was greatly exposed to the enemy's fire. In the mean time, by the force of the enemy's cannonade, the British works were tumbling into ruin: not a gun could be fired from them, and only one eight inch, and little more than one hundred cohorn shells remained   They were in many places assailable already, and if the fire continued a few hours longer, it was the opinion of the engineer, and principal officers of the army, that it would be madness to attempt to maintain them with the present garrison, exhausted by the fatigue of constant watching and unremitting duty, and reduced in its numbers by sickness even more than by the enemy's fire. Under such circumstances his lordship, on the 17th of October, unwilling to expose the remains of his gallant army to the danger of an assault, which, from the enemy's numbers, and the ruined state of the works, could not fail to be successful, made proposals for a capitulation. The terms were adjusted in the course of the next day, which, though not altogether agreeable to earl Cornwallis's wishes or proposals, were, nevertheless, such as his desperate situation, obliged him to accept; and on the 19th, the posts of York and Gloucester were surrendered to general Washington as commander in chief of the combined army; and the ships of war, transports, and other vessels, to the Count de Grasse, as commander of the French fleet. By the articles of capitulation, the garrisons of York and Gloucester, including the officers of the navy, and seamen of every denomination, were to surrender as prisoners of war to the conbined army: the land force to remain prisoners to the United States, and the seamen to the most christian king. The garrison was to be allowed the same honors which the garrison of Charlestown had obtained, when it surrendered to Sir Henry Clinton. The officers and soldiers were permitted to retain their private property; and the officers had liberty to proceed upon parole either to Europe, or any maritime post on the continent of America, in the possession of the British troops. Although the article for exempting from punishment such of the natives, or other inhabitants of America, as had joined the British army, and were then at York, was rejected by general Washington, the same thing was in effect obtained in a different form, by the permission granted to earl Cornwallis, to send the Bonetta sloop of war to New York, with his dispatches without being searched,

and with as many soldiers on board as he should think
fit, so that they were accounted for in any future
exchange. By this permission, he was tacitly empowered to send off such of the inhabitants as were obnoxious to punishment, which accordingly was done.

By the surrender of the posts of York and Gloucester,
the Americans became possessed of a large train of
artillery, many of which were of brass, together with
a considerable quantity of arms, ammunition, warlike
stores, and provisions, and to the French were delivered
up, one frigate, two sloops of war of twenty guns,
and a number of transports, and other vessels, The
Charon, of forty-four guns, and another ship of war,
were set on fire by the enemy's shells, and destroyed
during the siege. The combined army consisted of
seven thousand French, and nearly the same number
of continental soldiers, and about five thousand militia.
On the day previous to the surrender, the rank and
file of the garrisons of York and Gloucester, amounted
to five thousand nine hundred and fifty, but so great
was the number of the sick and wounded, that only
four thousand and seventeen were reported fit for duty "
Sir Henry Clinton in this moment of distressful exigence,
embarked seven thousand troops from New York, to
relieve lord Cornwallis. I have already mentioned that
he apprized his lordship that he would send him assistance by the 5th of October, but from intervening
circumstances, they did not sail from Sandy Hook,
until the 19th, the very day on which the surrender
took place. Sir Henry embarked with the expedition,
himself, nor was it until they arrived off the capes
of Virginia, that Sir Henry received the disastrous
intelligence of the capitulation. Such (observes a writer
on the American War, whom I have frequent occasions to quote, and who was like myself an eye
witness to many of the events which he narrates) was

the fate of an army, which, if success were the uniform result of merit, would have undoubtedly shared a different fate: if bravery in the field, and patient, and even cheerful, submission to fatigue, inclement skies, and the want, not only of the comforts, but sometimes even of the necessaries of life, have any claim to esteem and admiration."

It is truly grievous to perceive the stile of exultation, in which the party writers indulge on this capture of lord Cornwallis. One of them, in direct terms, speaks of "the pride of lord Cornwallis."——What pride? The very reverse was his lordship's true character. In this campaign (I declare these facts from my own knowledge) he fared like a common soldier. He assumed, he would admit of no distinction. Every private under his lordship must acknowledge,

"He bare no hardships but his leader bore."

Sometimes we had turnips served out for our food, when we came to a turnip field; or arriving at a field of corn, we converted our canteens into rasps and ground our Indian corn for bread; when we could get no Indian corn, we were compelled to eat liver as a substitute for bread, with our lean beef. In all this his lordship participated, nor did he indulge himself even in the distinction of a tent; but in all things partook our sufferings, and seemed much more to feel for us than for himself. General indignation ought to follow such a tissue of falsehood and calumny. But when a beloved officer is the object of this viperous attack, it must rouse a resentment in the mind of every old soldier still living, who *knew the contrary to be fact*, which it is not very easy for military feeling to bear, or even christian forgiveness to pardon.

Ramsay, too, has a very prettily manufactured tale on this occasion: " The door keeper of congress, an aged man, died suddenly, immediately after hearing

3 C

the, capture of lord Cornwallis's army.   His death was
universally ascribed, to a violent emotion of political
joy !!!"

Mr. Ramsay strongly reminds me of a celebrated republican preacher, in England, who had the impiety to
take for his text, the words of good old Simeon, " Lord
now lettest thou thy servant depart in peace, for mine
eyes have seen thy Salvation,", when he preached a sermon to celebrate the French Revolution !!!

As a testimony of what the enemies of lord Cornwallis, in America, thought and said of him, I subjoin
the following curious extract from a speech delivered
in congress by the famous Dr. Witherspoon ; without,
however, joining him in the severe censure he passes
on one of our admirals:

" It is incumbent on us to thank heaven for the victory
which we have just obtained, and though over a hand-
ful of troops, yet they were flushed with success, and
led on by a general, whose, valour is no less illustrious than his discretion ; by a general not equalled
in courage by the Macedonian madman, or in wise and
solemn deliberation, by the Roman Fabius; nor has his
defeat tarnished his fame; for he was encompassed about
with a mighty host of the picked troops of France and
America, aided by a formidable navy ; and to sum up
his difficulties, he was attacked by famine in his camp.

It would be criminal in me to be silent on this
occasion, which has diffused such joy in every breast.
To procure America freedom and happiness has ever
been my study, ever since I arrived among you ; for
this I have encountered a variety of hardships, and
suffered not a little, in my private fortune and reputation.

" Now, gentlemen, since victory irradiates our arms,
let us snatch this opportunity of securing to ourselves

advantageous terms of peace, so shall we reap a pro-
fitable benefit from the example of all the wise states
so eminent in history.

" Some may think it very censurable, and highly
derogatory to the dignity of this mighty commonwealth
to crouch and offer terms of peace, when we have
been gathering such blooming laurels; but when we
duly weigh all the circumstances of our overrated victory,
the reasonableness of my advice may more fully appear
to every dispassionate man.

Lord Cornwallis's troops, had boldly marched through
the heart of our country, opposed not only by woods,
rivers, and swamps, but also by all the force we could
send against him, which was greatly superior to him
in numbers; his whole army, I would say this foraging
party (for it does not deserve the name of army) did
not exceed four thousand; and small as it was, it had
spread universal dismay; it had struck terror even into
general Washington's camp, and wondrous to relate!
brought that man of valour out of his lurking place,
(which it would seem he had taken a lease of) at the
head of no less than thirteen thousand troops, whom he had
been training to arms, and teaching to storm mock
castles these three years, in a strong impregnable camp,
where no enemy would ever think it worth while to
disturb his slumbers; and so panic struck was the
American hero, that even with the great and formidable
army under his command, would he not dare to attack
an English foraging party; no, he must first be sure
the French were before him with eight thousand of
the gens d'armes, as a breast work, to save his gallant
troops, whose blood has ever been so precious to him.
And to complete his safety, that thirty sail of the line
of battle ships, manned with twenty five thousand seamen
(half of whom might act ashore) were within call of
him. Heavens! Gentlemen, if every victory is to cost

3 C 2

us so dear, if we must send into the field fifty thousand
men before we can capture four thousand fatigued,
half starved English, we must view at a very remote
distance, our so much wished for independency: to
bring this about if we go on as we have, for these
long seven years, we ought to have more than all the
wealth of all Mexico and Peru, and our women must
bring forth four males at one birth. O dauntless spirit
of immortal Cromwell, behold how enervated are thy
descendants? Gentlemen, trivial and contemptible as
our success is, we got it by mere accident; we got
it not by the vigilance of our allies, or the prowess
of our arms; we got it by the neglect or cowardice of
the British admiral, who would not, when he had the
golden opportunity, take possession of the Chesapeak;
and to this gross blunder alone are we to ascribe our
good fortune. But, gentlemen, although one commander
has abandoned his post, and betrayed the best interests
of his country, can we suppose that his guilt will not
meet that severe and exemplary punishment it deserves?
Can we hope that British vengeance will never wake,
that it will always sleep? When that culpable admiral
is put to death, do you foolishly imagine his successor
will not be alarmed for himself, and profit by his fate?
Yes; he will exert himself, he will be master of the
Chesapeak, upon which you know our destiny hangs;
for if that is once shut up, Virginia and Maryland,
the springs of all our resources, the objects which en-
ticed your good and great ally to aid you, are no
more! Then a few British soldiers may harrass our
planters, lay waste their lands; set their tobacco in
flames, destroy their docks, and block up such ships
as they cannot burn or capture. It is a painful task,
gentlemen, for me to set before your eyes a true picture
of your affairs, but it is the duty of a friend. He
who flatters you at this awful period smiles in your

face while he stabs you in the vitals; it is by exhibiting to you such a picture, that you will be convinced you ought to send commissioners to treat with Britain for peace, without a moment's delay. Our enemies, I own, are surrounded with danger; a strong confederacy is in arms against them: yet although they possess but a speck of land, the fortitude of Britons, their exertions and supplies have astonished the wondering world; they are by no means exhausted: they have hitherto asked for no alliance, they have singly and alone kept all their combined foes at hay. Britain has yet in store very tempting offers to hold out to any potentate whom she may court; she is mistress of our seaports; the large and fruitful colony of Canada is her's; her fleets have all arrived from Quebec, the Baltic, the West Indies, and East Indies, without the loss of a ship; her arms in Asia have carried conquest before them; so long as they hold their dominions there, they will have a perennial source of riches. Such is the situation of our foe; but how much more terrible may she become, if she joins to her already resistless marine the fleet of another power!

" Suffer me to use the words of the prophet Jeremiah, and ask you, " If thou hast run with footmen, ' and they have wearied thee, how then canst thou ' contend with horses?' When your enemy has once made such an addition to her strength, she will rise in her terms upon you, and in the paroxysm of her fury insist upon your submission, your unconditional submission! In order that I may not displease some of you, who hold a man a traitor for telling you wholesome truths, I will suppose all I have said to be exaggerated; I will suppose Britain to be in a galloping consumption: then, let me interrogate you. Do you increase in power and wealth? The very reverse is your case. Your maladies, I am sorry to tell you, are incurable. Where

are your numerous fleets of merchant ships, which were
wont to cover old ocean? Have you so much as one to
convoy your cargoes, or save them from capture? Have
you any goods to export? Where are your luxuriant
glebes and smiling meads? Alas! they are now an
uncultivated waste Your commerce is extinct, the
premium of insurance on the very few ships which
dare to peep out, never more to see their natal shore,
so enormous, seamen's wages so high, (for nothing but
death or an English dungeon is before them!) that ruin
and bankruptcy have overwhelmed all descriptions of
men, hardly any possess the conveniencies, none the
luxuries of life but faithless secretaries, avaricious com-
missaries, and griping contractors These, indeed, loll
in their coaches, live in princely palaces, have a numerous train of vermin to attend them, and fare sumptu-
ously every day ' Curse on the wretch who owes his
greatness to his country's ruin!' Would to God I
could here draw a veil over our calamities! but the zeal
I have to serve you will not allow it I must thunder
in your ears, that your trade is annihilated; your fisheries, that fertile nursery of seamen, that fountain of all
we could ever boast, is no more! Our ploughshares
beat into bayonets, our soldiers mutinying for want of
pay; our planters beggared, and our farmers ruined?
You are oppressed with taxes, not to emancipate you
from bondage—No with taxes to support the lazy; to
pamper the proud, to exalt mean, cunning knaves, and
dissipated gamblers, to the first offices of the state, to
pay armies who have the figures of men, but the hearts
of hares, they are, God knows, numerous enough,
but of what use? Why do we call in soup-meagre
soldiers? Are our own cowards? Are they not disci-
plined after so many years dancing a jig to the fife
and drum? Will they not look an enemy in the face

when their religion, their liberty, is at stake ; when their wives and children are butchered before their eyes.

" O America ! America ! thou art now ruined, and past redemption, consigned to destruction ! Curse on this French connexion !* I see thee prostrate on the ground, imploring mercy at the feet of the Gallic monarch. If France conquers Britain, which, for your sakes, I pray God to prevent ! I tremble when I think of the accumulated miseries with which you will be loaded. The French have already cheated you out of Rhode Island, from whence, as from a flaming volcano, will stream fire to burn your ships, and lay your seaports in smoking ruins. Methinks I see already the Canadians rush upon your possessions in the North, and the French and Spaniards overrun your southern colonies ! like an impetuous torrent they sweep all before them ! And even those of your own flesh and blood, whose lands you have confiscated, whose fathers and brother's you have murdered, join to lay you desolate ! I see you turned into a desert, exposed to the ruthless elements, calling upon some hospitable roof to hide you from the storm ! May heaven save you from calamities, and dispose you to sue for peace ! Now is the appointed time ; now is the day of salvation ! "

* It was said that it was the late Queen of France's party which forced on the king the treaty with America; in the view of depressing Great Britain. Louis considered it as an unfair measure, and threw away the pen, when urged to sanction it with his signature. But in an evil hour for himself and his family, he relented, on repeated importunity, he signed the fatal instrument, which involved both hemispheres in the horrors of war, and, in so doing, he remotely signed the warrant for his own execution. What a lesson is this to men of all ranks, to be just and honourable in all their dealings !

SIMPSON's *Plea for Religion.*

IN consequence of this disastrous capitulation, the Author became a second time a prisoner of the Americans. Fortunately for him, he was not recognized as one who had formerly made his escape, but ordered to march with the rest of the British troops to Winchester, situate, in the back parts of Virginia, upwards of two hundred miles distant from York Town. In this part of his Journal (which, in absence of a better phrase, he almost ventures to call an historical episode) as in the narrative of his escape, after being made prisoner at Saratoga, and for the same reasons, he takes the liberty of conveying what befel him to the Reader's attention in the first person.

ESCAPE FROM YORK TOWN.

AFTER the army under lord Cornwallis became prisoners, I was attached to the general hospital. I had frequently officiated as an assistant surgeon, both in the 9th and 23d regiments; and sometimes, when we had not a professional surgeon, I had endeavored to do that duty, to the best of my knowledge. The great fatigue which I underwent during the siege, brought on a severe illness, from which having somewhat recovered, I determined to attempt my escape to New York, (the distance from York Town to New York is upwards of five hundred miles.) I accordingly waited on the surgeon general, and resigned my situation in the general hospital, acquainting him that I intended to follow the troops to Winchester. Having received the balance due to me, I changed my dress, and appeared as a private soldier. The next consideration was, how to elude the French and American sentinels who guarded the prisoners. This I fortunately accomplished while the guards were relieving, and got outside of the two barriers, on the great road which led to Frederick-town in Maryland. I immediately struck into the woods, to avoid the picquet guard, which I knew was posted on it. Night approaching, and finding myself very weak, I made every exertion to extricate myself from the wood. Before it was completely dark, I perceived a few houses, and went into one of them. I entreated the inhabitants to let me remain there all night; this they refused in the most peremptory terms, and immediately turned me out of doors, threatening, that if I did not instantly depart, they would take me back a prisoner to Gloucester Point. I went away with a very sorrowful heart, and after remaining some time in the woods, scarcely able to determine what course to take, the weather being very severe and cold, and finding myself becoming very weak, I made a desperate effort, and went into a house, where there was a woman surrounded by a number of children. I asked her the favor of remaining in her house for the night. She looked at me very sternly, and said, " How can you

3 D

expect such a favor from me, or any of the Americans, seeing you came from England with an intent to destroy our country?" As I stood talking with her, her husband came in. ' He seemed to be a humane man, and said, " It would be very hard indeed to turn you out of my door such a severe evening as this. I will permit you to remain here this night." He then desired his wife to get a little straw, and make me a bed near the fire place. After supper I lay down; and not being disturbed by the roaring of cannon, and the alarm of war, which had been my portion for many months before, I slept soundly, and awaked in the morning greatly. refreshed. I gave the children some trifling presents, with which they and their parents seemed much gratified, and left them with the warmest emotions of thankfulness.

During this day (the 29th of November) I marched very hard on the main road, without encountering any interruption, this arose from its being the route which our troops had taken, the inhabitants thinking that I had not been able to keep up with the party, had lagged behind, and was endeavouring to overtake them. In the evening I came to a large building, when a gentlemen accosted me, observing; " there are a great many of your men in this house, who are determined to remain in the country, they have hired themselves to different gentlemen. You had better join with them: you shall be well used, and in a short time you may become a citizen of America." Upon my entering the house, I found that there were above forty British soldiers, who had. hired themselves to different gentlemen about the country. Early on the next morning, their masters came with horses, &c. and took them away. I was strongly importuned to go with them; but my mind revolted at the thought. When I was preparing to leave the house, the gentleman said to me, " You

had better remain with me. I am told you can write
a good hand, and understand accounts; I will build
a school-house for you, and make you as comfortable as I can." I felt my whole frame agitated at the
proposal, and notwithstanding the weather was stormy
and severe, and that I was very unwell, I immediately
left his house with indignation. This dishonorable
practice of enticing the British soldiers to become settlers, was but too common, during the greater part
of the American war. When a prisoner with them, I
was often strongly solicited, and promised many rewards,
if I would desert, and remain in the country. But I
was determined to die rather than serve any state
hostile to Great Britain: indeed I could not even patiently support the idea of remaining a prisoner among
them. I had not travelled many miles when I overtook
a serjeant of the 71st, and a drummer of the 23d. I
immediately began persuading them to venture with
me in attempting to escape. They both consented.
How entwined about the very heart of man, is the love
of liberty! From that source more than the soundness
of my arguments, or the probability of realizing them,
I prevailed. It is very easy to talk about going through
a tract of land, five or six hundred miles covered with
enemies; but when entangled in the wood, sinking in
the swamp, or fording the rapid torrent, we find it
an enterprize of much difficulty and danger.

However we addressed ourselves to our journey with
confidence; but the next day our drummer complained
that we marched too hard for him, and that it was
impossible for us ever " to make good our escape.
And (said he) for my part, I will stay where I am,
and solace myself after all my hardships.". No arguments which we could urge, appearing sufficient to
cure his despondency, or alter his determination, we
left him, and proceeded on our journey. The next

day we overtook a waggon which was going to Philadelphia By a short conversation, we soon discovered
that the waggoner was a loyalist, and in consequence
informed him, that we were making our escape to
New York He proposed to conceal us in his waggon
as far as Philadelphia at which place his master lived
This was gladly received on our part, and we promised
him an adequate reward , we proceeded with him in
high spirits · but, unfortunately for us, we overtook an
American soldier, who insisted, on his being taken
into the waggon This disconcerted our plan for the
present We were fast approaching Fiederick-town,
through which we could not pass concealed in the
waggon, on account of the presence of the American soldier we therefore thought it far more prudent
to quit the waggon entirely, and boldly march through
the town on foot The faithful waggoner, before he
left us, promised to wait a few miles on the other side
of the town, until we should rejoin him. But how
vain are all human schemes! Soon as the waggon entered the town, the American gave the alarm, and a
party of soldiers was ordered out to apprehend us
We were seized and brought through the town, in
triumph Many British soldiers were prisoners in this
town, and among them the regiment to which my companion belonged We were huddled among them.
Indeed our place of confinement was a most deplorable
situation Forty or fifty British soldiers crowded together
in a small room. It is true we had a large parade
to walk about in the day ; but as the winter was
remarkably cold, very few availed themselves of that
privilege

I examined this place of confinement minutely, and
soon discovered, that it was surrounded by a chain of
American sentinels I likewise gained information, that
small parties of the prisoners (under a strong guard)

were often ordered out to get wood for firing. It immediately occurred to me that the only chance for my escape, lay in getting myself enrolled in one of these wood cutting parties. I soon obtained this favor, and immediately began to take my measures : I strove to persuade as many of the party as I could to ven_ ture an escape with me. All my arguments proved ineffectual, except with one man, and my old com_ panion the serjeant. I waited with anxious suspense for the moment we were to be called out to wood cutting. I emptied my knapsack, and distributed my superfluous necessaries, putting on three shirts, and taking an additional pair of shoes in my pocket. With my blanket wrapped about my shoulders, I sallied out when the call came, bearing my hatchet : the intended companions of my flight were privately directed to keep as near to me as possible. When we had arrived at the wood, about half a mile from the place of confine- ment, we set to the work of cutting. I observed to one of our guards, that I saw a fine large maple tree a' few yards beyond him ; and begged permission for me and my two companions to cut it down. With that rudeness which ever characterizes the low mind when in office, he, in a surly manner, acquiesced in the proposal, little dreaming that we all intended to give him the slip. The better to color our pretence, and to cover our escape, we immediately set about cutting down the tree, keeping our eyes constantly fixed on the guard. At last he turned himself about, to watch the other pri- soners. We seized the opportunity, and darted into the thickest part of the wood. Fear and hope (being pretty nearly balanced in our minds,) were the wings which urged our flight. Our guards must have pos- sessed the feet of deer before they could possibly have overtaken us. We ran ou through the woods, as near as I could conjecture, during two hours, scarcely stopping to take breath. At last we arrived at a deep and rapid river. Fortunately for us, we soon discovered a ferry-boat, and on paying the fare, we crossed, without being examined, and pursued our way through the woods.

It should have been mentioned, that though we had on our regimentals, we disguised ourselves by wrapping our blankets about us, which rather gave us the appearance of Indians than of British soldiers. We had not, however, proceeded far, when we were met by an armed party of Americans, who instantly surrounded us, and brought us back prisoners to the town The serjeant, my companion, was then separated from me, as his regiment were prisoners near the town ; he was turned in along with them, while I was sent a prisoner to their guard-house, where I was used in the most cruel manner. The weather was extremely cold, (the latter end of November,) the guard-house was an open block-house, through which the snow and frost made their way in every direction. I procured, with much trouble, a little straw to lie upon, in one corner. But I soon found that my lodging would be a very hard one ; for when the guard used to discover that I had fallen asleep, they applied a firebrand to the straw, and as it blazed, they set up a yell like the Indians, rejoicing in my distress, and deriding my endeavours to extinguish the flames. When the relief used to be turned out, I sometimes took the liberty of drawing near the fire, to warm my half frozen limbs, but this indulgence was of short duration, for when the sentinels were relieved they came pouring into the guard-house, and, if found near the fire, I was usually buffetted about from one to the other, and perhaps a dozen fixed bayonets at once placed at my breast. When I found that I could obtain no mercy from these savages, and that every day I was worse used than on the preceding ; I wrote a letter to the American commanding officer, informing him of the cruel usage which I daily received, and entreating him to permit me to be confined in the town goal. This re- quest was at last granted ; but my condition was not bettered. by it.   There I was confined in the upper part of the prison, which I had to ascend by a long board, which was almost perpendicular.   In this dreary situa- tion, without any fire-place, were twelve criminals, These men received a very small allowance of pro- visions ; but, as for my part, not a morsel was alloted me.   My poor fellow prisoners took compassion, and shared their pittance with me.   Had it not been for their compassion, I should have been starved todeath.

I remained in this place during twelve days, suffering the bitings of hunger by day, and shivering all night with the cold.   It can scarcely be imagined that aught could possibly have added to my sufferings : yet was the case worse, for we were continually annoyed with the yellings of a black woman, who was confined for the murder of her child at the bottom of the jail.   She used to yell the wholenight long.

The reason of the bad usage which I in particular received, originated, it is most probable, in two dis- tinct causes.   This town had suffered much by the deaths of several young men, who had been killed during the war : the regiment of horse* which was cut to pieces at Long Island was composed almost entirely of the inhabitants of this part of the country.   This was a source of general inveteracy to all British pri- soners.   I had every mischief arising from this cause to support in common with my fellow prisoners.   But what rendered me still further an object of their particular severity was, their firm conviction that I still meditated my escape.   This principally, if not entirely

* See page 124.

arose, I believe, from one of Burgoyne's army, who
had deserted from his regiment, and was then in town.
This man certainly informed the Americans that I had
made my escape from that army into New York, and
that I would do so again if I was not well taken care
of. However, I was determined, if possible to extricate
myself from my present dreadful situation. With that
intent I wrote a letter to major Gordon of the 80th
regiment, who was then prisoner in the town, letting
him know my distressed situation, and entreating his
intercession with the American commander, to obtain
my liberation from jail, and my being placed with the
rest of my comrades, in their confinement near the
town. The major was not unmindful of me; for although
he was at that time laboring under a complication of
disorders, arising from the excessive fatigue he had
undergone during the siege, and the sufferings of his
confinement, he referred my case to captain Coote
of the 33d regiment, (now lieutenant-general Sir Eyre,
Coote) with his desire that application might be made to
the American commanders for the privilege which I
desired: Captain Coote most humanely interceded for
me, and obtained my request.

While the faculties of my nature remain entire, I
never can forget the affecting interview which took place
between the captain and me. A guard was ordered to
conduct me from the jail to his quarters. While
I was relating to him the sufferings which I had undergone since my being captured at York Town, and my
determination and hope still to effect my escape into New
York, the tear of sympathy filled his eyes, he condoled
with me in our common lot, and encouraged me to persevere. He then directed the serjeants of the 33d regiment
to build me a hut upon the ground where they were confined, and to take me into their mess. He gave me a
guinea, and I went off to my companions in triumph.

But my joy was only of short duration. Scarcely was I settled in my hut (in some degree of ease and comfort, in comparison to my former sufferings,) when I was ordered to be moved under a guard to Winchester, where the regiment to which I belonged was confined. The officers and men were all glad to see me: they had heard of the hardships I had endured in attempting my escape, and they condoled with me: part of the British troops remained here until January 1782, when congress ordered us to be marched to Little York, in Pennsylvania. I received information, that as soon as I fell into the ranks to march off, I should be taken and confined in Winchester jail, as the Americans were apprehensive, that when I got near to New York I should again attempt my escape to that place, I was advised by my officers to conceal myself until the troops had marched. I took the hint and hid myself in the hospital among the sick; here I remained until the American guards had been two days on their march with the British prisoners. I then prepared to follow them; but at a cautious distance. The troops arrived at Little York, and were confined in a prison similar to that which I have already described in page 208, only a little more limited. About two hundred yards from this penn, a small village had been built by the remains of general Burgoyne's army, who were allowed very great privileges with respect to their liberty in the country. When some of my former comrades of the 9th regiment, were informed that I was a prisoner in lord Cornwallis's army, and that I was shortly expected at Little York, they immediately applied to the commanding officer of the Americans for a pass in my name, claiming me as one of their regiment. This was immediately granted, and some of them kindly and attentively placed themselves on the watch for my arrival, lest I should

be confined with the rest of lord Cornwallis's army.
When I entered Little York I was most agreeably surprised at meeting my former companions; and more
so when a pass was put into my hands, giving me
the privilege of ten miles of the country round while
I behaved well and orderly. I was then conducted to
a hut, which my poor loving comrades had built for
me in their village before my arrival. Here I remained some time, visiting my former companions from
hut to hut; but I was astonished at the spirit of industry which prevailed among them. Men, women, and
even the children were employed making lace, buckles,
spoons, and exercising other mechanical trades which
they had learned during their captivity. They had very
great liberty from the Americans, and were allowed to
go round the country and sell their goods; while the
soldiers of lord Cornwallis's army were closely confined
in their pen. I perceived that they had lost that animation which ought to possess the breast of the soldier.
I strove, by every argument, to rouse them from their
lethargy. I offered to head any number of them, and
make a noble effort to escape into New York, and
join our comrades in arms; but all my efforts proved
ineffectual. As for my own part, I was determined
to make the attempt. I well knew, from experience,
that a few companions would be highly necessary.
Accordingly I sent word of my intention to seven men
of the 23d regiment who were confined in the penn,
and that I was willing to bring them with me. I believe, in all the British army that these men (three
serjeants and four privates) could not have been excelled
for courage and intrepidity. They rejoiced at the
idea; and by the aid of some of Burgoyne's army,
they were enabled, under cover of a dark night, to
scale their fence and assemble in my hut. I sent word
of my intention to my commanding officer, captain

Saumarez of the 23d,* and likewise the names of the men whom I purposed to bring with me. As my money was almost expended, I begged of him to advance me as much as convenient. He immediately sent me a supply.

It was on the 1st of March, 1782, that I set off with my party. My pass which had been procured from the American commander would only protect us to Susquehannah River which was not further than ten miles: we therefore marched those ten miles free from any dread of being apprehended. But when we arrived at the river, which was about a mile in breadth, we found that it could not be crossed on the ice, as it had thawed all that day. However when the evening drew on it began to freeze again, which encouraged us to remain until morning, under the hope that it would then be hard enough to hear us. At this place I found a man who had deserted from the Royal Welch Fuzileers about two years before. He seemed at first very shy of us; but after a little conversation he began to be more free. He acquainted us that since his desertion he had been roving about the country working very hard for his livelihood, and further, that, finding himself universally despised by the Americans, he had become very uneasy in his mind. Perceiving him well acquainted with the country, and possessing a thorough knowledge of all the loyal inhabitants, I thought in our present situation, he would be a valuable acquisition to us as a guide. In consequence, I held out to him every inducement, which I imagined might persuade him to accompany us.—I urged, that we would as soon as we arrived at New York, intercede with Sir Henry Clinton for his pardon, which we had no doubt what-

* Lately assistant quarter master general, and inspector of militia in the Island of Guernsey.

ever would be immediately granted   He was also made
thoroughly acquainted with the considerable rewards
which he would receive both from the commander in chief,
and from ourselves   After much entreaty, and supplying
him with repeated drams of peach whiskey, he at last
consented to guide us through Pennsylvania and the
Jerseys, with which part of the country, and the temper
of its inhabitants he seemed perfectly acquainted

As it had froze all night, we ventured to cross the
river at day-light the next morning   Though the ice
was exceeding weak, and broken up in many places,
the love of liberty had such a powerful effect, that
we ventured with the firmest resolution, although the
ice cracked under our feet every step we took, while
we marched in Indian file. Having crossed this mighty
river, we held a consultation what was best to be done.
We had exceeded the bounds of my pass, and consequently were liable to be arrested n our progress
by the first party of American soldiers we met, or by
any of the inhabitants who were disaffected ; and even
the loyalists, who might have succoured an individual
or two, would most probably be fearful of giving assistance to such a party   Our guide, the deserter, informed us, that it would be impossible for us to march
a mile further, unless we divided—that nine n number
were too many together, as such a body of British
soldiers would soon spread an alarm through the country
and cause immediate pursuit   He also strongly advised
us to change our regimental clothes for colored ones.
We all saw the propriety of this advice ; with aching
hearts we took leave of each other   I divided the
party , serjeant Collins of the 23d, (a brave soldier, and
a sensible man,) took three men under his care, and I
took the remaining four and our guide   We parted
with great reluctance , but in full expectation of meeting
each other at New York. The party which I commanded

lay all day in the woods: but in the evening our guide brought us to the house of one of the king's friends, (the loyalists were so termed in America) where we changed our regimental clothes for very bad colored ones. There we remained until eleven o'clock, when, favored by the night, we began our march towards Lancaster. We kept in the woods as much as possible, and about the dawn of morning arrived at a small village. We entered into a house under the hope of procuring some refreshment. Almost immediately we perceived a man rising hastily out of bed. He dressed himself, and ran out of the house in great haste. Apprehensive, that he had ran out to alarm the neighbours, (indeed our appearance was very suspicious,) we left the house immediately, and took shelter in the woods; where we remained, almost perishing with hunger and cold until night. We then began our march. About the dawn of the succeeding day, we espied a large barn and a dwelling house contiguous. With one consent, we resolved to repose our weary limbs in this barn. We soon got in, and concealed ourselves under some sheaves of wheat which were in the loft. We had not remained in this place more than half an hour, when a boy came up to remove the corn for thrashing. He was greatly alarmed when he discovered us, and immediately ran down as fast he could. We thought it most prudent to follow him into the house, lest he should alarm the country. We entered the dwelling house almost as soon as him, saluted the farmer, and were desired to sit down. Our host ordered breakfast to be got ready, which consisted of ground Indian corn, boiled like stirabout. No doubt, from the situation in which we had been discovered, and perhaps more from our looks, he perceived that we were hungry, and he was very right in his observation, for none of us had eaten any thing during more than fifty hours! After

we had taken a hearty, I might add voracious breakfast,
he said, "Gentlemen, I perceive who you are, and
what is your intention, but I'll have nothing to do with
you. Depart in peace." We offered him money; but
he would not accept of it. We then thanked him
warmly, and withdrew to our usual hiding place, the
woods; where we remained for several hours. Our guide
informed us, that ten miles further, on the great road
leading to Philadelphia, lived one of the king's friends,
from whom we should certainly receive entertainment,
and who would probably furnish us with a list of persons
disposed, from principle, to assist us for forty miles on
the way. Encouraged with this information, we set off
towards the house in high spirits, which we reached at
dusk in the evening. We sent our guide into the house,
while we remained concealed in the orchard. He soon
returned, and desired us to come in. We were received
most cordially by the old man, who bad us to sit down
at a fine large fire, until refreshment could be got
ready for us. He then, in the most feeling manner
observed, " you know the great hazard I run in receiving you as friends. It is now (continued he) eight
o'clock. I will let you remain under my roof till twelve.
You must then depart." Having said this, a good supper
was set before us, with plenty of cider. The night
proved very stormy, and the rain poured down like a
deluge, which continued increasing every hour. However the hour of twelve arrived, and gratitude to our
kind host, as well as fear for ourselves forbade our stay;
and we resolutely faced the terrors of the midnight storm.
What will not a captive endure to gain his freedom?
The night was very dark : we therefore ventured to
march on the main road to Philadelphia. It should
have been mentioned, that before we departed from
the house, our host kindly gave us a list of the king's
friends who lived in our line of march, the nearest

of whom was seventeen miles from his house: we therefore proceeded, notwithstanding the inclemency of the
weather, with a degree of spirit animated by hope.
The rain still continued to increase, which in a very
short time drenched us, to the skin; and, what rendered
our journey more distressing, in consequence of the
great fall of water, was, that the road was exceeding deep.
Our guide also began to murmur at the hardships which
he endured: his shoes were almost worn out. Indeed
all our shoes were in a wretched condition. They
were so bad, that we could scarcely keep them on our
feet. We used every suggestion that could possibly
encourage him to proceed; but his spirit at last failed,
and he declared, that he was unable to go any further
with us: adding, with a deep sigh, "Perhaps, after
all my hardships, if I should succeed, and get into New
York, I shall not get my pardon." Just as he had
pronounced these words, we espied a small hovel on
the road side, and a house at a very little distance
from it. We therefore, in order to keep him in temper,
agreed to shelter ourselves from the storm under this
hovel; assuring him at the same time that we would
provide him a pair of shoes, and give him the best
clothes we had in exchange for his bad ones. We
drew near to the house, in order to rest our weary
limbs; but, to our great mortification, we were saluted
with the roaring and loud grunting of pigs which were
in it. We soon found it necessary to march off as
fast as we could from our noisy neighbours, lest by their
outcries the inhabitants of the house should be alarmed.
Thus circumstanced, we were compelled to march on.
At last we came within sight of a large barn. Here
we again thought to take shelter, and were again disappointed; for, as we approached nearer, we perceived
a light in it. Our guide began now to lose all his
fortitude, declaring once more that he was utterly un-

able to proceed any further. A large dunghill happened
to be behind this barn, and as the last resource to humour
our guide, we agreed to rest our limbs on it, and cover
ourselves with the loose litter Here we remained about
half an hour, being unable to continue longer, from
the effects of the extreme cold. We all felt severe
pains in our bones, which were occasioned by the damp
of the dung It therefore became the general resolve
to march on and gain our wished for house, which,
from the distance we had already travelled, we judged
could not be far off. We were further confirmed in
this resolution by the morning breaking fast on us At
this place we arrived about the dawn It was a tavern;
but, to our unspeakable disappointment, we found that
several American officers lodged in the house Thus
circumstanced, we were obliged immediately to proceed
to another friend a few miles forward. We now thought
it best to quit the great road, and turn off towards Valley-
Forge In the course of our march we fortunately happened to come to a shoemaker's dwelling, where we got
all our shoes repaired, and having supplied our guide
with a new pair, and given him our best clothes in
exchange for his bad ones, and (above all) having supplied him with plenty of peach-whiskey, wherever we
could procure it, he seemed determined for the present,
to proceed with us to New York In the evening we
gained the house to which we had been directed. The
lady who inhabited it, was a near relation of general Lee.
Both herself and husband were firmly attached to the
royal cause. The house was situate on the banks of the
Schuylkill 'Here we halted for two days, during which
time we were nobly entertained. At twelve o'clock on
the night of the second day the master of the mansion
provided a canoe, and sent his servant to put us across the
river, giving us the name and place of abode of another
friend. We now continued for some days going from

one friend to another, still keeping our course towards New York. Early one morning we came to a river, which was very broad but only about four feet deep. In the middle of this river was a small island. We prepared ourselves to wade over. The morning was exceeding frosty which made the water very cold. Our guide, now lost all his resolution. He declared with tears in his eyes "That his heart was almost broken with hard_ ships; that he was sure he would never survive if he waded that river;" and all his fears about his pardon returned in full force upon him. We proposed to carry him over on our backs, to give him half the money we had, and renewed our former promises of interceding for him, and procuring his pardon; but all in vain. He turned about, under great terror, and fled from us. We afterwards were informed, that this unfortunate man was, in the course of a few days, taken up, and the fact being proved, that he was seen conducting four men, supposed to be British soldiers, into New York, he was condemned, and hanged.

. When we found it impossible to reclaim our guide, we waded across the river ourselves, and were almost deprived of the power of our limbs when we got on the other side. . Our last protector had directed us to another friend, whose house was situate about two miles from this river. We therefore made what haste we could before the day advanced. We gained the hos_ pitable mansion, and were concealed in the barn, and plentifully supplied with provisions. Thus far we had been successful in our enterprize. We were near the Dela_ ware river, about twenty miles above Philadelphia. That river we were to cross in our progress. But in crossing it our protector could give us neither assistance or recommendation. He had no connexion on its shores which he durst trust. Soon however, as day closed we set off, and arrived on the banks of the Delaware about nine o'clock the same evening. We boldly ventured into a house to inquire for the ferry-house. Contrary to expectation we were kindly entertained, and informed that we were two miles from it. We remained at this place all night, and proceeded to the ferry-house early in the morning. A number of boatmen had just entered the house before us; they were employed in carrying wood to Philadelphia, and landed there (the house being a tavern) to refresh themselves. They were eight in number, and seemed, by their looks and conversation, to suspect who we were. As soon as we perceived this we called for some refreshment, and appeared cheerful and undismayed. After some time they withdrew into an inner room, to consult (as we supposed) how they were to attack and take us. We held a consultation, and were determined to part with our liberty at as dear a rate as we could. Just at this crisis, when we were preparing to act on the defensive, one of our party said, " Let us seize the ferry-boat, and make across the river." This proposal was immediately agreed to; and, after discharging our reckoning, we sallied out of the house, jumped into the ferry-boat and insisted on the negro who had the charge of her rowing us across with all expedition, on pain of instant death. This the terrified creature performed with such celerity, that we were half way over the Delaware before the alarm was given. The negro being in the boat with us, prevented their firing on us. We soon pulled to the opposite shore, and ran into the woods, where we were soon secure from all our pursuers, as we had above a mile and a half the start of them. We lay concealed in the thickest part of the wood that day; and at night proceeded in quest of a house to which we had been directed. After much search we found it, and were entertained a few hours, when we proceeded to the abode of another friend.

Such was the benevolent assistance which we received in this part of the country, that an imperative duty forces itself on me, here to notice the malignant assertions of Belsham, who says,* that when the British troops were retiring to Brunswick, through the Jerseys " the licentious ravages of the soldiery, particularly of the German mercenaries, during the time they were in possession of the Jerseys, had excited the utmost resentment and detestation of the inhabitants;' and that " such havoc, spoil, and ruin, were made by the forces under general Howe's personal inspection and command, as were well calculated to obviate the suspicion that any secret partiality to America yet remained in the breast of the English general."

To this charge (with the most awful appeal for the verity of my assertion) I can aver, that in all the different places in America, through which I have marched as a soldier, been carried as a captive, or travelled in regaining my freedom, I never found people more strongly attached to the British government, than in the very place where Belsham says, " such havoc, spoil, and ruin, were made by the British forces." This we now experienced in a very great degree. These very inhabitants ventured their own lives to secure ours, and at the risque of their whole property, and the jeopardy of all their relatives and friends gave us the means of safe conduct into New York. Why Belsham cherished, and on almost every occasion manifested such inveterate malice against our commanders and soldiers in America, is matter of astonishment to me, and I might add, remains matter of mystery to the discerning and loyal part of the public. If the British troops in America had been capable of cooly and deliberately murdering his father, mother, and all

* Memoirs of the Reign of George III. Vol. I. Page 388 and 408.

3 F 2

his relatives, nay if they had actually perpetrated the horrid deed, he could scarcely have been more rancarous. An historian ought to record the *truth*, and the truth only, whether of friend or foe. The officers who served in the American campaigns were gentlemen (some of them noblemen, or noblemen's sons who have since succeeded to their hereditary titles) of the first families in the empire, for wealth as well as honor. Men who had no earthly temptation to such acts,* and whose high spirits independent of that circumstance would have revolted at the bare mention of the attrocities charged on them   However they ultimately failed in accomplishing the re-union of England and America, still it was the grand object of all their toils, both bodily and mental, and they were as far removed from "amassing fortunes by plunder and rapine," (as is asserted) by Ramsay, as Mr. Belsham and Ramsay are from acquiring fame by candor and truth. But to return to my narrative. We now entered into a country, which was full of American troops, and the nearer we proceeded to New York, the more numerous they were   This constrained us to act with great caution and circumspection   we made but short stages among our friends   On the 16th of March, we found ourselves within thirty miles of Staten Island, at which place was the British out-posts   Our American friend, in whose barn we lay concealed, advised us strongly to take a guide, which he said he could procure for us   To this we readily consented, and waited three days for our conductor   The wished for moment arrived, our guide came, the agreement was made, our friend procured us a bottle of strong spirits, and we set off with our

---

* I am bold to assert that one British regiment was possessed of more property in gold, silver watches, &c than was in general Washington's whole army: even the inhabitants were destitute of gold and silver.

conductor about nine o'clock at night, under the expectation of arriving before morning in the vicinity of Amboy; which town lay opposite Staten Island, being divided only by a river. In two hours march we came to a village which our guide told us we might safely march through, as the inhabitants were all in bed, and no American troops were stationed in it. " But lest, said he, I should happen to be seen with you, I will take a circuit and meet you on the great road on the top of the hill, on the other side of the village." We consented to this plan and marched through the village unperceived, and arrived at the place appointed for meeting; there we remained, expecting our guide every moment; but after remaining two hours we gave up all hopes, and saw clearly that he had given us the slip. It snowed all the time very hard accompanied with a piercing north wind. Our clothes and shoes being all torn, made our situation, while we waited, almost insupportable: we at last came to the resolution of proceeding by ourselves, though we were entirely unacquainted upon what point of the compass Amboy lay. But the stars being rather bright we knew we could not be materially wrong if we proceeded due north. We marched very hard over a broken uneven ground, sometimes on the road and sometimes through the woods. At four o'clock in the morning one of our companions dropped down and declared with tears in his eyes, he was not able to proceed any farther: the soles of his shoes had been worn off and his feet were all bruised and cut. Indeed we were all much in the same way. We proposed to carry him by turns till daylight, when we would repose ourselves. " No," said he, " leave me here to die; for I am quite exhausted: if I live till morning, I will strive to creep to the next house; and if I survive, I will endeavour to follow you."—We were greatly affected at parting with him. To me indeed it was peculiarly distressing, as he was' one of the men I had brought in with me to New York from general Burgoyne's army, and was the man whom I have already mentioned, who understood several languages, and who was of so much service in effecting our escape.

We marched on until the morning when we concealed ourselves in the woods, until the night came on. During this time we were without provisions. Soon as the evening set in we prepared as well as we could, for our march. About two o'clock in the morning we perceived a house, on the side of a narrow road, it was unconnected with any other building. Not knowing, where we were, we agreed to stop, and obtain all the information which we could. We rapped at the door, which was quickly opened by an old man, who with his wife were the only persons in the house. Without discovering who we were, we entered into conversation with them both. It came out; during our discourse, that he was a native of Dublin and had left it about thirty years before. Here my being a native of Ireland was of inestimable service to the whole party. As I could mention several places in Dublin, and many of the transactions which had happened in his time, he became highly pleased with my conversation, and with true native hospitality brought out provisions to entertain his countryman. From several of his answers which he gave to some of the questions which I occasionally, and I may say accidentally, put to him, I perceived he was a loyalist; but being unwilling to commit the whole party, I did not discover to him whom we were. Having gained all the information which we wanted, we left his house.

He had informed us where the American guards were stationed along the banks of the river, who could at all interfere with us, which was only the distance of two miles off. We immediately proceeded towards it, care-

fully avoiding the American posts. About an hour
before day-light we arrived on its banks, and as soon
as morning dawned, we saw with pleasure Staten Island.
But a deep and broad river rolled between us and our
place of refuge. We wandered up and down the shore
in hope of finding a canoe or boat; but in vain. After
a fruitless search for near an hour, the broad appearance
of day much alarmed us, as we dreaded lest some of the
American sentinels, who were posted along the coast,
should discover us. In this dangerous situation, we held
a consultation what was best to be done; when it was
unanimously agreed to return to my countryman's house,
discover who we were, and throw ourselves upon his
protection. We returned, and were not disappointed;
we found him to be a staunch loyalist. He observed,
" The coast is full of troops—I will bring you to a
place of concealment." He then conducted us to a thick
part of a wood, while he went to two friends, who owned
a boat, in which we could at night safely cross the river.
There we remained until a late hour in the evening; when
his two friends, with the boatmen, came to us, and having agreed for our passage, we proceeded to the boat.
The river, where we had to cross, was more than three
miles broad.

Our friends informed us, that an English sloop of war
was stationed there, in order to intercept the American
privateers and other craft, and likewise to keep the
coast in alarm. We entered the boat with joy, and
put off from the shore. They had not rowed a quarter
of a mile, when the wind, which had hitherto been fair
for us, changed against us, and blew very fresh. The
boat, being very small, made a great deal of water.
This greatly alarmed the boatmen; and they immediately made for the shore from whence we came.
When we perceived what they were about, we insisted
that they should turn the boat, and endeavour to gain

the sloop, or, failing in that, row us across to Staten Island They were greatly alarmed at our resolution; and declared, that it was impossible for a boat to live in that gale of wind, and that we should be all certainly lost, if we persisted in the attempt But we were resolved to venture, and peremptorily commanded them to proceed After beating against the wind and waves for near two hours, and being almost perished with wet and cold, we espied a square rigged vessel the boatmen were apprehensive at first that she was an American privateer However, as our boat was every moment in danger of sinking, we determined to make towards her. As we approached, we were hailed, and ordered to come along side To our unspeakable joy, we saw British soldiers standing on the deck. Such was the effect of our sufferings, that we had almost lost the power of our limbs and speech for when I was ordered down to the cabin to captain Skinner, to give him an account who we were, I could not articulate a word. Perceiving my situation, he humanely ordered a large glass of rum to be given me. This soon brought me to my speech, and I then briefly recapitulated to him our whole story The ship's company being informed that we were British soldiers who had escaped from the Americans, were eager to express their joy. We were ordered the best refreshments the vessel could afford. In the morning we were put on shore on Staten Island, with a letter to the captain's father, colonel Skinner, who commanded a regiment of loyal Americans, and who was the commanding officer on Staten Island.

I need not tell the Reader what we felt when we were marching across the island, where we considered ourselves perfectly safe within the British lines. We waited on colonel Skinner, who immediately ordered a boat to convey us to New York. We landed at the wharf, and with cheerful steps marched to head quarters. When the inhabitants, and the soldiers in garrison, understood that we were three serjeants of the Royal Welch Fuzileers, they were struck with astonishment. We had had no opportunity of shaving ourselves for more than three weeks; our shoes were worn out; our clothes all in tatters; our looks wan and meagre. In short so wretched was our appearance, that they commiserated our condition, and with kind attention conducted us to the commander in chief. This was on the 23d of March, 1782.

Sir Henry Clinton received us with great kindness. We communicated to his excellency all the information of which we were possessed, which in any manner tended to the good of the service. After this, we were sent to receive the usual bounty, which was given as an encouragement to those soldiers who made good their escape. After the officer who was appointed to pay us had entered my name in the book, he turned his eye to the top of the first page, and said, " Here is the same name of a non-commissioned officer of the 9th regiment, one of the first who had made his escape from general Burgoyne's army, more than four years ago.". I answered, " I am the man." On which he replied, " if you are the man, your colonel (colonel Hill) who was exchanged, and went to England, has left here all your arrears of pay." " But," added he, " you must prove that you are the identical person." This I soon did, as there were officers both of the 9th and 23d regiments, who knew me well at that time in New York. In consequence, I received a very considerable sum, which was due to me. I then wrote out this narrative, and presented it to major Mackenzie,* deputy quarter master general. The major recommended me to brigadier general Birch, the commandant of New York, and I was appointed his first clerk, for

* Now colonel Mackenzie, and secretary to the military college, London.

which I had a good salary. The major's kindness did not stop there; but through his interest I was made adjutant to the Merchants Corps of volunteers, who were then on permanent duty in the town.

At this place, during two months, I enjoyed a comfortable respite from the hard duty to which I had been accustomed: the only repose, I may truly say, which I had during the eight years I was in America.

Colonel Balfour, having arrived in New York from Charlestown, it being evacuated, ordered me to proceed to King's Bridge, the out post of the British army, and take charge of the recruits of the 23d regiment, who were doing duty there; to which place I repaired accordingly.

The Reader will doubtless feel some anxiety for the fate of the party which I left on the banks of the Susquehannah River. These poor fellows, after enduring innumerable hardships, and travelling through the woods for some hundreds of miles, were unfortunately taken prisoners in Pennsylvania, and confined in Philadelphia jail, the foundation of which they undermined, and the whole four came safe into New York, the latter end of April. Much about the same time, my former companion, whom I had left on the road, likewise arrived at New York, conducted by the last guide, who had divided from us in passing through the village. Thus, though by different routes, the whole party which I took with me from Little York, arrived safe at the British head quarters.

When I reflect on the hardships which I endured, the dangers which I escaped from my first setting out from Gloucester, after our army was taken prisoners, in a march of perhaps not less than one thousand miles, through a wilderness interspersed with swamps, I feel (and senseless must I be if I did not feel it) a degree of thankfulness to that Providence, who, not only preserved my life in several hard fought battles, skirmishes, &c. but also guided my footsteps through those desart tracks, and brought me in safety once more among my friends. It is true, I can state the fact in the language of the great heathen poet :

> "From the din of war,
> Safe I returned without one hostile scar ;
> Though balls in leaden tempests rained around,
> , Yet innocent they flew, and guiltless of a wound."

But I must acknowledge, as a Christian, (however I may by some persons be charged with enthusiasm for it) that in all these wonderful events of my past life, I see and adore an higher direction—an arm Omnipotent which has been my safe guard ; and penetrated with the recollection of which I may truly say—" O God the Lord, the strength of my salvation ; Thou hast covered my head in the day of battle."

Spirit of Political Rancor in America. Captain Huddy's Execution. Correspondence between Generals Washington, Clinton, and Carleton, on the Circumstance. Thirteen Captains, Prisoners under the Convention of Lord Cornwallis and General Washington, draw Lots for Death. The Lot falls on Captain Asgill. Application of his Mother to the Court of France on his behalf. Letters between her Ladyship and Count Vergennes. The Minister of France intercedes on his behalf. Procures his Release. General Washington's Letter to Captain Asgill. Lady Asgill's Letter of Thanks to Count Vergennes. Articles of Peace signed. The Author's Return, &c.

FROM the capture of lord Cornwallis, to the period when the independence of America was acknowledged by the British government, and peace between the two countries concluded, little occurred to interest the Reader, except the circumstance of captain Asgill.‡ As I am in possession, of more accurate information on this subject than most who have written on American affairs, I shall take the liberty of detailing on the facts.

The spirit of political rancor in America had at this period risen to an uncommon height. It raged

‡ Now lieutenant-general Sir Charles Asgill, Bart. commanding the Eastern District, in Ireland.

beyond all bounds. Nor was it possible for the British commanders wholly to restrain the exercise of that retaliation by the loyalists who fought under them, which was inspired, by the violence of the opposite party. Smith, who wrote from observation and not mere report, thus characterizes this party violence. " The malignity, virulence, and savage barbarity, that, at the above mentioned time, pervaded all ranks, classes, and denominations, whether in the civil or military line, cannot be delineated in any terms, but such as must agonize the heart of sensibility, and cause a blush on the cheek of civilized humanity; and the baneful effects of which were not eradicated so late as the year 1801; when at a place called Ninety-Six, and at Augusta, in Georgia, in a large company, among the gentry of the country, where, it would be supposed, humanity would prevail, were it only through decency, and with a view to example, I heard them boast of having committed barbarities shocking to human nature. One instance was that of an old, grey-headed justice of the peace, who solemnly declared, he had during the war, shot, at different actions, and in cold blood, ninety-nine tories,* and felt unhappy he had not accomplished the complete hundred."

At New York an association was formed among the American loyalists, for the purpose of warfare on the opposite party: but which was abused into a retaliation on the continentals, for the death and sufferings of the king's friends. A block-house in Monmouth county was taken by a party of these, and captain John Huddy made prisoner. He was conveyed to a prison-ship, lying in the river, near New York, and there kept in close custody fifteen days, and then told " That he was ordered to be hanged." Four days after he was sent out with a

* American Loyalists.

party of refugees, and hanged on the heights of Middleton. The following label was affixed to his breast :

" We the refugees having long with grief beheld the cruel murders of our brethren, and finding nothing but such measures daily carrying into execution; we therefore determine not to suffer without taking vengeance, for the numerous cruelties, and thus begin, and have made use of captain Huddy as the first object to present to your view, and further determine to hang man for man, while there is a refugee existing. Up goes Huddy for Philip White."

Philip White in retaliation for whom Huddy was hanged, had been taken by a party of the Jersey militia, and was killed in attempting to make his escape.*

Sir Henry Clinton as soon as he was informed of the circumstance of Huddy's execution, ordered a court-martial on the captain who commanded at the transaction; but being superseded in command by Sir Guy Carleton, the court broke up without coming to any determination. The American commander flushed with conquest, was not disposed to await or abide by the judgment of an English court martial, but dispatched the following haughty and indignant letter to Sir Henry Clinton.

Head Quarters, April 21st. 1782.

" Sir—The inclosed representation, from the inhabitants of the county of Monmouth, with testimonials to the fact, (which can be corroborated by other unquestionable evidence,) will bring before your excellency the most wanton, cruel, and unprecedented murder that ever disgraced the arms of a civilized people. I shall not, because I conceive it altogether unnecessary, trouble your excellency with any animadversions on this transaction. Candour obliges me to be explicit—to save the innocent I demand the guilty.

* Ramsay.

" Captain Lippencot, therefore, or the officer who commanded at the execution of captain Huddy, must be given up; or if that officer was of inferior rank to him; so many of the perpetrators as will, according to the tariff of exchange, be an equivalent. To do this, will mark the justice of your excellency's character. In failure of it, I shall hold myself justified in the eyes of God and man, for the measures to which I shall resort.

" I beg your excellency to be persuaded, that it cannot be more disagreeable to you to be addressed in this language, than it is to me to offer it; but the subject requires frankness and decision. I have to request your speedy determination, as my resolution is suspended but for your answer.

" I have the honor to be, &c.

GEORGE WASHINGTON."

To which his excellency, general Clinton, returned the following answer:

" SIR—Your letter of the 21st instant, with the enclosed testimonials, respecting captain Huddy's execution, was delivered to me yesterday; and though I am extremely concerned for the cause, I cannot conceal my surprise and displeasure at the very improper language you have made use of, which you could not but be sensible was totally unnecessary.

The mildness of the British government does not admit of acts of cruelty, or persecuting violence; and as they are notoriously contrary to the tenor of my own conduct and disposition, (having never yet stained my hands with innocent blood) I must claim the justice of having it believed, that if such have been committed by any person under my command, they could not have been warranted by my authority, nor can they have ever the sanction of my approbation. My personal feelings, therefore, required no such incitements to urge me to take the proper notice of the barbarous outrage against humanity, which you have represented to me, the moment it came to my knowledge; and accordingly when I heard of captain Huddy's death, (which was only four days before I received your letter) I ordered a strict inquiry to be made into all its circumstances, and shall bring the perpetrators of it to an immediate trial.

" To sacrifice innocence under the notion of preventing guilt, in place of suppressing would be adopting barbarity, and raise it to the greatest height! Whereas, if the violatros of the laws of war are punished by the generals under whose powers they act, the horrors which those laws were formed to prevent, will be avoided, and every degree of humanity war is capable of maintained.

" Could violations of humanity be justified by example, many from the parts where your power prevails, that exceed, and probably gave rise to this in question, could be produced. In hopes the mode I mean to pursue, will be adopted by you, and prevent all future enormities,

" I remain, &c. H. CLINTON."

His Excellency General Washington.

This mild and dignified reply of the British commander, produced no other effect than the immediate selection of one the British officers to be the sacrifice, which was to atone for the death of captain Huddy. Soon, however, as Sir Guy Carleton arrived, and took on him the command, he dispatched the following letter to general Washington :

Head Quarters, New York, 7th May, 1782.

" SIR—Having been appointed by his majesty to the command of the forces of the Atlantic Ocean, and joined with admiral Digby in the commission of peace, I find it proper in this manner to apprize your excellency of my arrival at New York.

" The occasion, Sir, seems to render the communication proper, but the circumstances of the present time, render it also indispensable, as I find it just to transmit here-with to your excellency certain papers, from the perusal of which your excellency will perceive what dispositions prevail in the government and people of England towards those of America, and what further effects are likely to follow; if the like pacific dispositions should prevail in this country, both my inclination and duty will lead me to meet them with the most zealous concurrence. In all events, Sir, it is with me to declare, that, if war must prevail, I shall endeavour to render its miseries as light to the people of this continent as the circumstances of such a condition will possibly permit.

" I am much concerned to find that private and un-authorised persons have on both sides given way to those passions which ought to have received the strongest and most effectual controul, and which have begot acts of retaliation, which without proper preventions, may have an extent equally calamitous and dishonorable to both parties, though, as it should seem, more extensively pernicious to the natives and settlers of this country.

" How much soever, Sir, we may differ in other respects, upon this one point we must perfectly concur, being alike interested to preserve the name of Englishmen from reproach, and individuals from experiencing such un-necessary evils as can have no effect upon a general deci-sion. Every proper measure that may tend to prevent these criminal excesses in individuals, I shall ever be ready to embrace! And as an advance on my part, I have, as the first act of my command, enlarged Mr. Levingston, and have written to his father on the subject of such excesses as have passed in New Jersey, desiring his concurrence in such measures, as, even under the condition of war, the common interests of humanity require.'

3 H

" I am further to acquaint you, Sir, that it was my intention to have sent this day a similar letter of compliment to congress, but am informed it is previously
necessary to obtain a passport from your excellency, which
I therefore hope to receive, if you have no objection,
for the passage of Mr. Morgan to Philadelphia, for the
above purpose.

" I have the honor to be, with great respect, your excellency's most obedient humble servant,

GUY CARLETON."

To this letter Washington returned a cool and evasive
answer, and finally the congress refused the passport
requested.

Perhaps a scene more awful can scarcely be imagined, than a number of military men convened to
determine by lot which shall become the victim of political rancor. Thirteen captains of Lord Cornwallis's
army were, by the command of general Washington
assembled at Lancaster, in Pennsylvania, to draw lots,
one of which contained the mandate of death. Captain
Asgill drew the 12th lot, which was the fatal one. The
word " *Unfortunate*" was written inside it. The captain
that did not draw, who was the owner of the 13th lot, is
now the honourable Sir G. J. Ludlow, K. B. lieutenant
general and lieutenant governor of Berwick. Five minutes were allowed between the drawing of each lot. A
dreadful pause of suspense !

Soon after captain Asgill had drawn the " unfortunate"
lot, his friend, major Gordon of the 80th regiment,
who commanded the British prisoners belonging to
lord Cornwallis's army, wrote to general Washington,
soliciting permission to accompany the captain in
his confinement. This arose from the most generous
of motives, to soothe and comfort him under his
misfortune. The major humanely supposed that he
must want a friend, more especially when he consi-

dered his youth, (as the captain was not at that time seventeen years of age) general Washington answered this letter, by declaring, " that he would not grant the major's request, unless he would submit to all the rigors of confinement and usage, which the captain should receive." To these terms the major acceded, with the most heroic magnanimity, and voluntarily went into confinement with the captain. No writer on American affairs has recorded this circumstance, which is as exalted an instance of the power of friendship, between two British officers, as can be produced from the most boasted stories of antiquity

. It should also have been mentioned, (to the honor of major Gordon's memory) that when lord Cornwallis's army surrendered at York Town, a field officer was appointed to remain with the captured troops; and lieutenant-colonel Lake (afterwards lord Lake) was the officer to whom that service was assigned. Here the major gave another instance of friendship, as rare as it was disinterested. Knowing the situation of the colonel's health, and that he had a family in England, he voluntarily submitted to remain prisoner in his room, and take command of the captives.

Captain Asgill was conveyed under a strong guard to the Jerseys. Indeed it was with general Washington's usual policy (a policy which his advocates ascribed to the purest humanity) that he was sent there. Huddy's friends lived on the spot, and being spectators of the usage captain Asgill received, they might thereby have ceased their clamors, and even felt something for the innocent victim of retribution.

The officer who guarded him, boasted to him on the road, " that he was a very fortunate officer! for he had had the honor of guarding major Andre after he was taken." This must have been very distressing to young

Asgill   Indeed the captain received very bad usage
throughout his confinement , he was constantly fed upon
bread and water   This hard treatment constrained him to
send his faithful servant to New York, to receive and carry
letters for him   This man ran great hazard in passing
over the North River into New York

During captain Asgill's confinement some letters passed
between him and general Washington   The captain
pleaded the 14th article of the capitulation of York Town,
that it would therefore be the highest breach of faith
according to the laws of nations that he should suffer
death   this article, which the captain alluded to, contains the following sentence —" No article of the capitulation shall be violated under pretence of *reprisals*,
and if it should contain any doubtful expression, it shall
be interpreted according to the ordinary sense and tenor
of words "—" Granted."

To this strong plea general Washington replied, that
on several occasions during the war the British commanders had broken many articles of capitulation, he
therefore, would not be bound, by one solitary article."

This was most erroneous reasoning in so great a man
Is recrimination a proof of innocence or integrity ?   It
amounts merely to this   " Others have committed many
wrongs, I have therefore a right to commit one "   This
was justifying evil by the perpetration of evil.

Captain Asgill had frequent opportunities of making
his escape into New York , his whole guard (so greatly
was he beloved by them) offered to come in along with
him, if he would provide for them in England.   Although
these offers must have been very tempting to a prisoner,
under sentence of death !   yet he scorned to comply, as
it would have involved more British Officers in trouble.
He nobly said, " As the lot has fallen upon me, I will
abide by the consequence "

Meantime general Washington wished to hurry on the

execution of captain Asgill; but that wise general, Sir Guy Carleton (afterwards Lord Dorchester) delayed sending the determination of the court martial, which sat on captain Lippencot, to the American general. This he did in order to give time to captain Asgill to send home word to his father and mother, to make speedy application to the king and queen of France and count Vergennes, to use their powerful intercession with Washington for his life. At last general Carleton, after delaying the report of the court martial on captain Lippencot as long as he could, transmitted intelligence to general Washington, that he was acquitted.* The reception of this intelligence decided the doom of young Asgill, and he prepared to die. He wrote to his family " that before they would receive that letter he should be no more." His parents, although they knew that letters from the court of France were sent to America to save their son's life, imagined that they had arrived too late. Concluding that he had suffered, the whole family went into mourning for him. The reader must already know, that during this period, lady Asgill† had applied to count Vergennes. Her letter contains so much of all that is endearing in maternal feeling that I am induced to transcribe it.

* It appeared in the course of this trial that governor Franklin, the president of the Board of Associated Loyalists, gave Lippencot verbal orders for what he did, and that Huddy had been designated as a proper subject for retaliation; having been, as the refugees stated, a persecutor of the loyalists, and particularly as having been instrumental in hanging Stephen Edwards, who had been one of that description. The court having considered the whole matter, gave their opinion, " That, as what Lippencot did was " not the effect of malice or ill-will, but proceeded from a con- " viction that it was his duty to obey the orders of the Board of " Directors of Associated Loyalists, and as he did not doubt " their having full authority to give such orders, he was not " guilty of the murder laid to his charge, and therefore they " acquitted him."—*Ramsay's American Revolution.*
† Lady Asgill is still living; but, as the Reader must imagine, at a very advanced period of life.

" Sir—If the politeness of the French court will permit
the application of a 'stranger, there can : be. no doubt
but one in which all the tender feelings of an individual
can be -interested, will meet with a favorable reception
from a nobleman, whose character does honor, not only
to his own country, but to human. nature. The subject,
Sir, on which I presume to implore your assistance,
is too heart piercing for me to dwell on ; and common
fame has, most probably, informed you of it ; it therefore renders the painful task unnecessary. My son (an,
only son) as dear, as he is brave, amiable as he is
deserving to be so, only seventeen, a prisoner. under.
articles of capitulation at York Town, is now confined,
in America, an object of retaliation. Shall an innocent,
suffer for the guilty ? Represent to yourself, Sir, the
situation of a family under these circumstances : surrounded as I am, by objects of distress ; distracted with
fear and grief; no words can express my feeling, or
paint the scene. My husband given over by his phy-
sicians a few hours before the news arrived, and not
in a state to be informed of the misfortune : my daughter
seized with a fever and delirium, raving about her
brother, and without one interval of reason, save to
hear heart aggravating circumstances. Let your feelings,
Sir, suggest and plead for my inexpressible misery.
A word from you, like a voice from heaven, will save'
us from distraction and wretchedness.

" I am well informed general Washington reveres
your character ; say but to him you wish my son to
be released, and he will restore him to his distracted'
family, and give him back to happiness. My son's virtue
and bravery will justify the deed. His honor, Sir,
carried him to America. He was born to affluence,.
independence, and the happiest prospects. Let me again
supplicate your goodness ; let me respectfully implore

your high influence on behalf of innocence, in the cause of justice, of humanity; that you would, Sir, dispatch a letter, to general Washington, from France, and favor me with a copy of it, to be sent from hence. I am sensible of the liberty I take in making this request; but I am sensible, whether you comply with it or not, you will pity the distress that suggests it: your humanity will drop a tear on the fault, and efface it. I pray that Heaven may grant you may never want the comfort it is in your power to bestow upon, "ASGILL."

The French minister, moved by so pathetic an appeal, interceded with general Washington; however, before his letter arrived, the determination of the British court martial, on captain Lippencot was received, and young Asgill was ordered for execution. In

" The very lucky minute of his fate,"

the letter from the minister of France arrived, (of which the following is a copy) and he was pardoned. Its elegance, as a literary composition, stands almost unrivalled, and its delicate adaption to all the characteristic feelings of the American commander is such, as to speak no common interest in the life of captain Asgill.

" SIR—It is not in quality of a king, the friend and ally of the United States, (though with the knowledge and consent of his majesty) that I now have the honor to write to your excellency. It is as a man of sensibility, and a tender father, who feels all the force of paternal love, that I take the liberty to address to your excellency my earnest solicitations, in favor of a mother and family in tears. Her situation seems the more worthy of notice on our part, as it is to the humanity of a nation, at war with her own, that she has recourse for what she ought to receive from the impartial justice of her own generals.

" I have the honor to inclose to your excellency a copy
of a letter which lady Asgill has just wrote to me   I
am not known to her, nor was I acquainted that her
son was the unhappy victim, destined by lot, to expiate
the odious crime that a formal denial of justice obliges
you to revenge   Your excellency cannot read this letter
without being affected, it had that effect upon the king
and queen to whom I communicated it   The goodness
of their majesties' hearts induces them to desire, that
the inquietudes of an unfortunate mother may be calmed,
and her tenderness re-assumed   I feel, Sir, that there
are cases where humanity itself exacts the most extreme
rigor, perhaps the one now in question may be of
the number   but allowing reprisals to be just, it is
not less horrid to those who are the victims, and the
character of your excellency is too well known, for
me not to be persuaded that you desire nothing more
than to be able to avoid the disagreeable necessity

" There is one consideration, Sir, which, though it is
not decisive, may have an influence on your resolution
Captain Asgill is doubtless your prisoner, but he is
among those whom the arms of the king contributed to
put into your hands at York Town   Although this circumstance does not operate as a safe guard, it however
justifies the interest I permit myself to take in this affair.
If it is in your power, Sir, to consider and have regard to it, you will do what is very agreeable to
their majesties   The danger of young Asgill, the tears,
the despair of his mother, affect them sensibly; and they
will see with pleasure the hope of consolation shine out
for those unfortunate people

" In seeking to deliver captain Asgill from the fate
which threatens him, I am far from engaging you to seek
another victim; the pardon to be perfectly satisfactory,
must be entire   I do not imagine it can be productive of
any bad consequences   If the English general has not

been able to punish the horrible crime you complain of, in so exemplary a manner as he should, there is reason to think he will take the most efficacious measures to prevent the like in future.

"I sincerely wish, Sir, that my intercession may meet success; the sentiment which dictates it, and which you have not ceased to manifest on every occasion, assures me that you will not be indifferent to the prayers, and to the tears of a family which has ʼse to your clemency through me. It is rendering homage to your virtue to implore it. I have the honor to be, with the most perfect consideration, "DE VERGENNES."

The pardon of captain Asgill was sent to him in the following letter from general Washington, enclosing the act of congress by which it was granted.

Copy of an order of congress releasing captain Asgill, by the United States in congress assembled, Nov. 7, 1782.

"On the report of a committee, to whom was referred a letter of the 19th of August, from the commander in chief, a report of a committee thereon, and motion of Mr. Williamson and Mr. Rutledge relative thereto, and also another letter of the 25th of October from the commander in chief, with a copy of a letter from the count de Vergennes, dated the 29th of July last, interceding for captain Asgill.

"Resolved, that the commander in chief be directed, and he is hereby directed, to set captain Asgill at liberty."

Copy of a letter from general Washington to captain Asgill, covering the above resolve.

"*Head Quarters*, *November* 13, 1782.

"Sir—It affords me singular pleasure to have it in my power to transmit you the enclosed copy of an act of congress of the 7th instant, by which you are released from the disagreeable circumstances in which you have so long been. Supposing you would wish to go into New

3 I

York as soon as possible, I also enclose a passport for that purpose.

"Your letter of the 18th of October, came regular to my hands, I beg you to believe, that my not answering it sooner, did not proceed from inattention to you, or a want of feeling for your situation I daily expected a determination of your case, and I thought it better to await that, than to feed you with hopes that might in the end prove fruitless You will attribute my detention of the inclosed letters, which have been in my hands about a fortnight, to the same cause.

"I cannot take leave of you, Sir, without assuring you, that in whatever light my agency in this unpleasing affair may be received, I never was influenced through the whole of it, by sanguinary motives, but by what I conceived a sense of my duty, which loudly called upon me to take measures, however disagreeable, to prevent a repetition of those enormities, which have been the subject of discussion, and that this important end is likely to be answered, without the effusion of the blood of an innocent person, is not a greater relief to you, than it is to, Sir, your most obedient, and humble servant,   " GEORGE WASHINGTON "

In consequence of the passport transmitted to captain Asgill by general Washington, he gained New York, from whence he sailed for England, and arrived but a very few days after his mother received his last letter. He thought it prudent not to go immediately to her ladyship, but sent the captain of the ship, gradually to prepare her for an interview. Lady Asgill was so overwhelmed with grief, at the supposed death of her son, that she would see no stranger. She shut herself up from almost every visitant. The captain of the ship knocked at the door, and requested to see lady Asgill. He was answered, that she saw no

person, (the captain's father was in the country.)
" Tell her," said the captain, " I am just arrived
from New York, and that I have lately seen her son ;
and perhaps things are not so bad as she imagines."
The captain was admitted to see her; his mission
was soon disclosed ; and the mother and son meet
once more—a meeting which I will not attempt to
describe, and which none but those who, to their utmost
extent, have experienced the parental and filial ties
can imagine.

Lady Asgill with her son and family went over to France
personally, to thank the king and queen, and count
Vergennes ; previous to which her ladyship wrote the
following letter to the count,* a translation of which
I subjoin.

" Epuisée par de longues souffrances, suffoquée par
un excès de bonheur inattendu, retenue dan mon lit par
la foiblesse & par la langueur, anéantie enfin, Monsieur,
au dernier degré, il n'y a que mon extrême sensibilité
qui puisse me donner la force de vous écrire. Daignez
accepter, Monsieur, ce foible effort de ma reconnoissance.
Elle a été mise aux pieds du tout-puissant, & croyez-

---

* The following are the reflections of a French writer who
had occasion to publish the letters. They are placed in the work
from whence they are copied, introductory to the letter itself,
and may serve to shew the sentiment which at that time prevailed in France on captain Asgill's situation.
" Do you not think that the unfortunate lady Asgill, in the
agonies arising from so cruel an expectation, had raised her maternal hands to Heaven an hundred times a day. She remained
dumb at the first rumour of her son's deliverance. O my
Readers, you would know the affecting facts ! She was expiring
her heart was dried up, her voice was dying away, the tomb
was half open before her. Her son lives, she knows it, a
consolatory report has resounded in her ears. I ought to be
silent, she is going to speak, she is going to write to that
humane minister, who has restored her son to her: she is going
to soften him again by her gratitude."

moi, elle a été présentée avec la même sincérité, à vous, Monsieur, & à vos illustres souverains; c'est par leur auguste & salutaire entremise, ainsi que par la vôtre, que moyennant la grace de Dieu, j'ai recouvré un fils à la vie, auquel la miènne étoit attachée. J'ai la douce assurance que mes vœux pour mes protecteurs & pour vous, sont entendus du ciel, à qui je les offre. Oui, Monsieur, ils produiront leur effet vis-à-vis du redoutable & dernier tribunal où je me flatte que vous et moi nous paroîtrons ensemble, vous pour recevoir la récompense de vos vertus, moi celle de mes souffrances. J'éleverai ma voix devant ce tribunal imposant. Je réclamerai ces registres saints où l'on aura tenu note de votre humanité. Je demanderai que les bénédictions descendent sur votre tête, sur celui qui, par le plus noble usage du privilége qu'il a reçu de Dieu, (privilége vraiment céleste) a changé la misère en félicité, a retiré le glaive de dessus la tête d'un innocent, & rendu le plus digne fils à la plus tendre & à la plus malheureuse des mères.

"Daignez agréer, Monsieur, ce juste tribut de reconnoisance que je dois à vos sentimens vertuex. Conservez-le, ce tribut, & qu'il passe jusqu'à vos descendans, comme un témoignage de votre bienfaisance sublime & exemplaire envers un étranger dont la nation étoit en guerre avec la vôtre, mais dont la guerre n'avoit point détruit les tendres affections. Que ce tribut atteste encore la reconnoisance longtems aprés que la main qui l'exprime aura été réduite en poussiére, ainsi que le cœur qui dans ce moment-ci, ne respire que pour donner l'explosion à la vivacité de ses sentimens; tant qu'il palpitera, ce sera pour vous offrir tout le respect & toute la reconnoisance dont i est pénetré.

"THERESE ASGILL."

TRANSLATION.

" Exhausted by long sufferings, overcome by an excess of unexpected happiness, detained in my bed by weakness and langor; in short, humbled before God to the last degree, it is only, Sir, my extreme sensibility that can give me strength to write to you. Deign to accept, Sir, this feeble effort of my gratitude. It has been placed at the feet of the Almighty, and believe me, it has been presented with the same sincerity to you, Sir, and to your illustrious sovereigns; it is by their august and salutary interposition, joined to yours, that under the influence of divine grace, I have recovered a son to life, to whom mine was attached. I have the sweet assurance, that my vows for my protectors, and for you, are heard in heaven, by him, to whom I offer them. Yes, Sir, they will produce their effect, before that last and formidable tribunal, where I flatter myself, that you and I shall appear together, you in order to receive the reward of your virtues; I; that of my sufferings. I will raise my voice before that commanding tribunal. I will *sue* for those holy registers, where your humanity shall have been noted down. I will ask, that blessings may descend upon your head, upon him, who by the most noble use 'of' the privilege that he has received from God, (a privilege truly celestial) has changed misery into felicity, has withdrawn the sword from the heart of an innocent person, and restored the most worthy son, to the most tender and agonized of mothers.

" Deign to receive kindly, Sir, this just tribute of gratitude, that I owe to your virtuous sentiments; preserve this tribute, let it pass to your descendants, as a testimonial of 'your exemplary and sublime beneficence towards a stranger, whose nation was at war with yours, but which war had not destroyed the tender affections. May this tribute still attest that gratitude a long time after the hand which expresses it shall

have been-reduced to.dust, as well as the heart which
at this moment breathes only to give vent to the energy
of its sentiments. · So long as, it 'shall palpitate, it will
be in order to offer you· all the gratitude and respect
with which it is penetrated.   ",TERESE ASGILL."

I shall conclude this account of captain Asgill's provi-
dential escape,,with an extract taken. from the Hibernian
Magazine for 1782 ;*   which may serve to shew what was
the prevailing opinion of the day relative to that officer.

" Captain Asgill is only seventeen years of age, a captain
in the first regiment of foot guards, and only son of Sir
Charles Asgill, Bart. possessed of every virtue that can
endear him to his family or acquaintance, and in the last
campaigns in America, has given sufficient earnest of, a
spirit and conduct under the different commands, (which
have devolved on,him by the illness. or absence of his
senior, officers,) that .would render him an honor to his,
profession and country,   .

" General Washington expressed deep concern, when
he was informedthe unhappy lot had fallen on this worthy
young gentleman, so well known to him by his bravery
and humanity in different instances, particularly when.
the command devolving on him by the illness of his,
colonel, he took a post from the Americans, commanded
by colonel Gregory, who being old and wounded, he supported him himself, with an awful and tender respect most
filial, evincing the true greatness of his amiable mind,"

At length in 1782, preliminaries of peace were signed
betwixt Spain, France, America, and Great Britain.—
Thus ended a contest, which dismembered, England of
far more than half her territory ; but how far her.
commerce, or her local interests as a nation, were
affected by it is a point which I presume not to determine. Various and contradictory have been the

* This Article was written when the news arrived here that
captain Asgill was to die.

opinions of the most profound politicians, concerning it. This work being merely a Journal of events (most of which passed under my own immediate observation) during, the war, it may with far more propriety, than the investigation of such a subject, terminate with my own return to my native land.

I sailed from Sandy Hook on the 5th of December 1783, and on the 17th of January, 1784, landed at Portsmouth with the 23d regiment: from that place we marched to Winchester, where I requested my discharge. At that time I had very great privileges allowed me in the army, and was making money fast; but peace being proclaimed through all Europe, I thought it my duty to come home to my friends in Dublin, after an absence of near twelve years, during which time I had served my country to the best of my power. Colonel Balfour, who commanded the regiment (well knowing that I was making money in my situation,) kindly and humanely reasoned with me, in order to prevail on me to remain in the army: but seeing my determination was fixed, he signed my discharge, and I marched up to London with a number of my companions, in order to pass the board. When the board sat I was considered as too young to receive the pension; and likewise that I had not been long enough in the service. It is true, the general officers who composed the board at that time were unacquainted with me; and besides, as nothing was mentioned in my discharge but the time of my servitude, and " that I was discharged," they could not possibly be aware of the nature and extent of my services, or the claims which I possessed on the bounty of my sovereign.

Lieutenant Calvert,* of the 23d being then in London, I communicated my disapointment to him. He was sorry for me; and said, " Any thing that lies in my power I

* Now major general Calvert and adjutant general of the British forces.

will do for you." He advised me to remain in London
until another board would sit ; but I was determined not to
wait. Lieutenant Calvert was well acquainted with me ;
we had served together in America for some years ; I
have frequently had the honor of obeying his command,
and of fighting by his side in many battles and skirmishes. Even twenty-five years after these services, he
was not unmindful of me ; for when I took the liberty of
writing to him in September 1808, he kindly answered
the letter, and renewed his former acts of friendship
by recommending me to the duke of York.

Attachments of persons in the army to each other
terminate but with life, the friendship of the officer con-
tinues with the man who has fought under his command,
to the remotest period of declining years, and the old
soldier venerates his aged officer far more than perhaps
he did in his youthful days : it is like friendship between
school-boys, which encreases in manhood, and ripens in
old age.

I left London on the 15th of March, and landed in
Dublin on the 19th, to the inexpressible joy of an aged
mother, two sisters, and other relations, who had long
given up every hope that I was alive.

Since that period I have been frequently asked by
various friends to whom I related the circumstances of
the battle of Guildford Court House, why I did not apply
to marquis Cornwallis for some situation, when lord lieutenant of Ireland, in the year 1798 ? My answer was, and
is, that at that time I had a young family ; and was moreover tolerably well settled. I knew his excellency would
have recognized me immediately, as I had been employed
by him during the campaign to write the duplicates of his
dispatches. A commission in a marching regiment would
most probably have been my reward ; which I could not
have accepted, from the state of my health as well as the
reasons assigned.

However, to the honor of lord Cornwallis, it should be mentioned, that when in America his lordship did not forget the service which I rendered him. A few days after the battle of Guildford Court House, I was ordered to mount guard over the prisoners which we had taken at that battle. Among them was an American captain who had committed various depredations on the loyal inhabitants of the country.

This man was particularly mentioned to me, by the provost marshal. I was ordered to be very careful that he should not make his escape, for lord Cornwallis was apprehensive he might murder and destroy the inhabitants, whom he knew had assisted us in our march. Unfortunately, he bribed one of my sentries, who permitted him to effect it. When the circumstance was made known to his lordship he was highly displeased, and commanded the serjeant of the guard to be brought before him, in order to be confined. But when I was approaching towards him, his countenance changed into a smile, and he directed his aid-de-camp to tell me to go to my regiment, and to confine the sentinel who had permitted the captain to get out of confinement.

Having thus brought this volume to a conclusion, I have only to solicit the indulgence of the candid, and the protection of the loyal reader. My wish has been to state *facts* as I knew they happened, in opposition to that tissue of falsehood, which but too many writers have produced on the subject. To elegance of composition I prefer no claim ; but I think, on such matters as the revolution of governments, it is the duty of every man to let the present and the future ages know those *truths* with which he is acquainted, and not to lock them up in his own breast, until the grave closes on all communication, and buries them in oblivion for ever.

If any circumstances have been misrepresented, accident and not intention was the cause. Since the fourth

3 K

number of this work was printed, the Author has been informed, that general Matthews, whose murder by Tippoo Saib he relates, (p. 128) was not the general Matthews, who so gallantly assisted in the reduction of Fort Washington. That brave officer was never in the East Indies; but immediately after the termination of the American War, he went to the West Indies, was appointed governor of St. Vincent, and remained in that island many years. He died a full general in the service.

In the account of the battle of Camden, particular mention ought to have been made of the 33d regiment. The services which they rendered on that day, were long the theme of the soldiers and officers present.

Thus, under the assistance of the Almighty, has this account been brought to a period. It has not been unattended by many impedimental circumstances. The heavy duties of a crowded school frequently compelled the Author to break in on the hours of rest, in order to finish the narrative. This produced sickness, an alarming sickness, that at one time seemed to threaten life itself. Providence in mercy spared the Author; but it was to consign a son (a beloved child!) to the grave. Amidst personal and family afflictions, therefore has this journal been finished. Had the Author been more at his ease, it might, in some points, perhaps, have been better executed. But it would be superfluous in him again to press on the Reader's attention, that the flowers of literature are not to be expected from an old soldier, whose only object in the publication was the unfolding of truth in defence of his country's honor, and the humanity of her officers.

Free School, Whitefriar-lane, June 26, 1810.

THE END.

CPSIA information can be obtained
at www.ICGtesting.com
Printed in the USA
BVHW040213031218
534627BV00021B/475/P